John Henry Wigmore

JOHN HENRY WIGMORE IN THE EARLIER PART OF HIS NORTHWESTERN DEAN-
SHIP

William R. Roalfe

John Henry
WIGMORE

Scholar and Reformer

NORTHWESTERN UNIVERSITY PRESS

EVANSTON

1977

Publication of this volume was made possible by contributions from the following alumni of Northwestern University School of Law:

James E. S. Baker '36
Anthony R. Chiara '37
Angelo G. Geocaris '48
Eugene W. Gordon '48
Raymond P. Gordon '74
Milton H. Gray '34
George Hoban '38
Eugene Kart '36
Mr. and Mrs. Melvin S. Schneider '37
Raymond I. Suekoff '33
Howard J. Trienens '49
Jack M. Whitney II '49

In Memory of Helen S. Roalfe

Valiant, colorful, resourceful, courageous, he was a personality first and a scholar afterward. The facets of that personality were so numerous and so varied that the legend of Wigmore must long live in the lore of American law, alongside his great contributions to the science of the law.

MANLEY O. HUDSON

Contents

Foreword

The subject of this biography is one of the most extraordinary figures in the history of Anglo-American law. William R. Roalfe's story of the life and work of John Henry Wigmore will enlighten even those who remember Wigmore well, and there are many who do remember him, including the writer of this Foreword. For those who know him only by reputation as the master of the Law of Evidence, or as the longtime dean of Northwestern's Law School, many interesting surprises are in store.

Wigmore's writings covered a wide range of legal subjects and probably were more voluminous than those of any other known writer in any field in history. Yet his scholarship is only a part of the story of this amazing man, a story which also embraces long leadership in legal education, outstanding public service, numerous contributions to the practicing bar at home and abroad, active community and national citizenship, and a busy, charming home life.

One could be hopelessly humbled by this account, were it not so full of interesting object lessons for professors, lawyers, students, deans, university presidents, trustees, public officials, and educated people generally. For example, Wigmore was a voracious reader. In addition to his scholarly reading, he averaged, according to Mr. Roalfe's accounting, 179 nonlegal books per year, including great works and detective fiction alike, and he kept brief notes on each book read. He was accomplished in a dozen languages and traveled with his wife to most parts of the world. He wrote numerous songs for lawyers and students and played them on the piano at all kinds of professional gatherings. He carried on correspondence with many people, including great figures of the day, such as Oliver Wendell Holmes, Jr., Roscoe Pound, Louis D. Brandeis and Felix Frankfurter, and with many ordinary and little people as well. A brilliant innovator, he was nonetheless known as a conservative, and yet we learn from this book that he voted for Franklin D. Roosevelt.

Wigmore had strong thoughts about people, but the author finds not a trace of religious or racial prejudice. He fought for what he thought was needed in law reform and legal education with every considerable resource at his command, but usually — though not always — he managed to avoid long-standing personal animosities. He was intensely loyal to Northwestern Law School, and as so often happens in cases of great loyalty, there were those who took him too much for granted and there were a few who treated him badly. Yet they are gone and largely forgotten now, while through this book and otherwise he remains a towering figure, the man who led the Law School into the twentieth century and established it firmly among the leaders, and a man whose life was a great monument to the worth of law reform and scholarship.

In approach, this book really has two parts. The first thirteen chapters cover Wigmore's life from boyhood until his death in 1943. Partly chronological, partly subject-oriented, these chapters are a blend of factual information on key facets of his career and of insight into his personality. From this emerges a remarkably good, often intimate, picture of his daily life, working methods, and attitudes and ideas on dozens of matters, as well as an account of professional and scholarly events.

Early in the book, the reader finds Mr. and Mrs. Wigmore living in Japan for three years. Still in his twenties, he is teaching Anglo-American law at Keio University and inaugurating studies of Japanese law and legal history which are, in some cases, still being carried out. Toward the end of these chapters, amidst the triumphs of scholarship and deanship, we encounter aggravating stories of the frustration he met in his efforts to finance his Law School dreams and a poignant picture of the circumstances of his sudden forced retirement as dean because of new University retirement policies.

The last four chapters comprise in effect a second, very valuable, part in which the author goes back and examines in depth: (1) Wigmore's work on the Evidence treatise and in such other areas as Criminal Law and Legal Aid (Chapter 14); (2) his vigorous leadership and participation in the American Bar Association, the American Law Institute, the Commissioners on Uniform State Laws, the development of air law, and other domestic concerns (Chapter 15); and (3) his contributions to International Law and Organization, his support of the League of Nations and the World Court, and his rather strange withdrawal of his name after he had been nominated by prominent groups of lawyers for membership on the World Court (Chapter 16). An Epilogue rounds out the final moments of his fascinating life.

Professor Roalfe's research has been based upon years of thorough study of the massive collection of Wigmore papers lodged in the Northwestern University Law Library. No one could have been better equipped for this undertaking, for the author was Professor of Law at Northwestern and Head Law Librarian from 1946 to his retirement in 1964, after distinguished service in the same capacity at the University of Southern California and at Duke. At Northwestern, he lived with the facts and the legends of Wigmore as closely as any biographer could hope to do. Closeness has not destroyed objectivity, however, for Professor Roalfe is an unusually conscientious, able legal scholar and author in his own right, thoroughly experienced in both the methods and the hazards of legal, biographical research. During his time as Law Librarian at Northwestern, he was held in great esteem by his colleagues and was recognized as one of the leading figures in the law library world, serving as president of both the American

Association of Law Libraries and the International Association of Law Libraries.

In his research, the author went well beyond the Wigmore papers, interviewing and obtaining statements from many contemporaries of Wigmore and from experts in fields of law related to Wigmore's career. One of the most valuable features of the book is the manner in which the account is richly interlaced with excerpts from letters, documents, songs, and memoranda from others, through which Wigmore and his contemporaries tell much of the story in their own words. The author's own abilities as collector and interpreter weave the complex strands and textures of all this material into a readable, reliable record and a scholarly contribution of great worth to us all.

Objectivity does not preclude admiration, and Professor Roalfe is unabashedly an admirer of his subject. Every now and then he does note a weakness or a possibly faulty position when he sees one in this giant of American law. More often, the differences of opinion in the numerous controversies of law and policy in which Wigmore was involved, and sometimes embroiled, are brought out and left to the reader or subsequent scholar for evaluation. The author marks out the issue; others can pass the judgment. The notes preserve a wealth of sources for all who wish to pursue them.

In the end, the book is not only a valuable record, but a tribute both by the author and by many of the famous contemporaries of Wigmore who are quoted in the text. When one sees the story as a whole, one finds it hard to imagine that any biographer with the thoroughness of Professor Roalfe could come away with a radically different appraisal.

James A. Rahl
Dean (1972–77) and Owen L. Coon Professor of Law
Northwestern University School of Law
July 1977

Preface

Although the name "Wigmore" is familiar to every person concerned in any way with Anglo-American law, Wigmore the man is at the same time perhaps the most neglected and the least appreciated major figure in the broad arena to which he made such a lasting contribution. This is because Wigmore is generally identified only with the law of evidence and is regarded as a specialist who, however competent, made a significant contribution to one aspect of the law alone. And yet, if Wigmore had never written the *Treatise on Evidence*, his other writings and his role as a reformer would still entitle him to a high rank among the leaders of the legal profession. His scholarship was substantial in a number of fields, and for fifty years he was prominently and most constructively identified both with legal education, as dean of the Northwestern University Law School, and with the work of the legal profession, through his participation in the activities of a number of groups concerned with the improvement of the law and its administration.

The forthcoming *Bibliography of John Henry Wigmore*, which has been prepared by Kurt Schwerin, will serve as an invaluable companion piece to this volume. The availability of this list of nearly 900 items has made it possible to view Wigmore's writings in this volume solely in terms of their biographical significance. Thus, in some instances, writings of little or no permanent value have been given consideration — to point up an event that attracted Wigmore's special attention, or to illustrate a strongly held conviction, a deep sense of loyalty to some institution, principle, or person. In order to reflect Wigmore's life as he lived it, heavy reliance has been placed upon contemporary appraisals and events. Copious notes to the text have been added throughout because, in order to confine this account to one volume, it has often been necessary to forgo greater elaboration when this would otherwise have been desirable. For the reader who desires further to pursue his inquiry at any point, or the scholar who wishes more fully to investigate Wigmore's role in a particular field, the notes should provide a convenient point of departure for readers who seek materials relating to each of the many fields with which Wigmore was vitally concerned and which deserve further consideration.

Wigmore regarded biography, and particularly a familiarity with the lives of the leaders of the legal profession, as a most important ingredient in any lawyer's equipment, and his own colorful and dynamic career provides a most convincing example of the soundness of his thesis. Had Wigmore been willing to respond affirmatively to urgent requests for an autobiography, a record in his own gifted style would now be available. However, in 1941, when the project was suggested, he was fully preoccupied with the *Kaleidoscope of Justice*, and, in any event, he was probably not predisposed to undertake the assignment. In writing to the publisher who had asked for it he said, ''I shudder at the amount of digging up and searching of old files which would be indispensable; for I have not kept a diary.'' [1] After Wigmore's death, Nathan W. MacChesney encouraged Arthur Train to undertake a biography of Wigmore,[2] but Train's untimely death intervened and ended the prospect of an account by this close friend and admirer.

The primary source of information for the preparation of this biography has, of course, been the substantial collection of materials in the Northwestern University Law School Library where a complete collection of Wigmore's extensive writings in print is supplemented by his vast correspondence, unpublished writings, documents, and other papers. Among these, two items merit special mention. The first is an unpublished manuscript entitled *Recollections of a Great Scholar and Superb Gentleman, a Symposium*, edited by Professor Albert Kocourek. These impressions, recorded by thirty-five of Wigmore's contemporaries at the time of his death, have been an invaluable source of information. Certainly the names of the contributors to the *Recollections* should be made a matter of record: Edwin C. Austin, Stuart S. Ball, Margaret G. Belknap, Agnes F. Bradley, John W. Curran, Lawrence D. Egbert, Charles B. Elder, Frederick D. Fagg, Jr., Robert H. Gault, Mary E. Goodhue, Hugh Green, Jerome Hall, Edward A. Harriman, Manley O. Hudson, Lynn H. Hough, Beatrice Wigmore Hunter, Charles Cheney Hyde, Albert Kocourek (Preface), Elmer M. Leesman, Stephen Love, Nathan W. MacChesney, Helen K. McNamara, Ann George Millar, Robert W. Millar, Sarah B. Morgan, James F. Oates, Francis F. Philbrick, Roscoe Pound, Alexander N. Sack, Murray Seasongood, Charles H. Watson, Louis B. Wehle, Nelson G. Wettling, and Francis Marion Wigmore.

The second item in the library that merits special mention is the extensive collection of the letters of John Henry Wigmore and his wife written from Japan 1889–92. These letters have been an invaluable source of information concerning this important period in Wigmore's career. Examination of these letters was greatly facilitated by the use of a typed transcription prepared by Miss Mabel Brill under the direction of Mrs. Margaret G. Belknap, a lifelong friend of the Wigmores, and their assistance is gratefully acknowledged.

I am indebted to the library staff, both past and present, of the Northwestern University Law School, and welcome this opportunity publicly to express my appreciation for their valuable assistance. Had not these materials been collected, preserved, and conveniently arranged, the preparation of this manuscript would have been impossible. But to one member of the staff, Miss Elaine Teigler, assistant librarian and head of the Reader's Services Department, I am especially indebted. On occasions too numerous to record, her generous, prompt, and effective assistance has identified or confirmed the information needed to push the text forward or complete a footnote, paragraph, subject, or chapter.

It has also been necessary to rely upon the resources of a number of other libraries. Two deserve special mention. To the California Historical Society in San Francisco I am indebted for information about Wigmore's parents and about his childhood and early life in San Francisco. The valuable assistance of Mr. James Abajian, its librarian, made my brief sojourn in the society's library both pleasurable and fruitful. And to Mrs. James H. Chadbourn, curator of manuscripts and archives at the Harvard Law School Library, I am indebted not only for prompt and informed responses to many inquiries for specific information but also for keeping my special interest in mind and sending additional items — a generosity that reflects her valuable role as curator of a rich collection of source materials.

Happily the foregoing sources of information have been supplemented by written statements supplied by a number of persons — sometimes spontaneously and sometimes in answer to the author's inquiries — which concerned some particular phase of Wigmore's career. Leon Green, Wigmore's successor as dean, and Frederick D. Fagg, Jr., for some years a member of the Northwestern University Law School faculty and later vice president and dean of faculties, were especially helpful. Green not only threw light upon his relationship with Wigmore, but filled in other aspects of Wigmore's career as well. Fagg's account concerned his specialty, air law, which became one of Wigmore's major interests during his later years. The very close working relationship that existed between these two men gave Fagg's statement a special significance. I am also indebted to those who furnished helpful statements or lent letters or other materials: Professor Jerome Hall, Lowell Hastings, Robert G. Howlett, John Knox, Professor Paul G. Kuntz, Dean Willard H. Pedrick, Joseph L. Shaw, Mrs. Margaret Shipley, George T. Wigmore, and Mrs. Ida F. Wright.

The contribution of the late Miss Sarah B. Morgan stands alone. As Wigmore's secretary and co-worker for many years, she has been a unique source of information and has generously responded to inquiries too numerous to mention.

For assistance in preparing the manuscript I am indebted to a number of persons. In the early stages, and until the time of my retirement from the faculty of the Northwestern University Law School, Mrs. Ida May Olson gave the typing and related tasks the same skillful attention that she had provided as secretary for a number of years. When time permitted she and her assistant, Mrs. Walter Hohensee, concentrated on the "deciphering" of the letters Wigmore had received from Justice Oliver Wendell Holmes. This tedious but rewarding task converted Holmes's elusive script into a typed record and a timesaver for every one. After my retirement the typing of the manuscript was done primarily by Mrs. Doris Dodge and Miss Christine M. Finn, both members of the Northwestern University Law School staff, and I am grateful to both of them for their valuable assistance. For the role played by my late wife Helen up to the day before her death, no words of appreciation will suffice. She was helpful throughout the undertaking — in research, in editing, and in the arduous task of finally checking data for accuracy. To a very significant extent this is also her book.

Finally, I am indebted to Dean James A. Rahl for his support of this undertaking since he became dean in 1972 and for his writing of the foreword. I welcome this opportunity to express my appreciation to Mrs. Janice J. Feldstein, who has so skillfully seen the manuscript through the press, and to my wife Emma, who has so generously assisted me in my role as author.

W.R.R.

John Henry Wigmore

1

San Francisco—Boyhood

At the age of eight, young Harry, as John Henry was called by his relatives and friends, stood in line on his first day in public school, "the butt of all the smart things boys can think up for a new boy."[1] Eventually he was settled at a desk in the schoolroom. What happened in the interval we do not know, but three days later the superintendent came in and, indicating Harry, said, "Miss Blank, that new boy belongs in another room."[2]

> This was too much to bear and Harry refused to be moved, winding himself around the legs of the desk so that he couldn't be pried loose short of tearing him apart. So the superintendent desisted for the moment. On going home at noon he told his tale of woe to [his] mother, who was very indignant and declared that he should not go back to that school.[3]

Wigmore later attributed this "ignominous outburst" to the fact that he was bashful and did not like strange faces.[4] At any rate, it brought to a head and settled a difference of opinion between his father and his mother. His father favored a public-school education, which he felt was more democratic, whereas his mother strongly leaned toward the Urban School, a private school where he had begun his formal education the year before. In this instance, as in many others, her view prevailed, and he returned to the Urban School with the "privileged class."[5]

However, this was not the first or only occasion when young Harry had given vent to his explosive feelings. His mother, who was punctilious about the accepted etiquette of the time, had often started off proudly with the little preschool boy to make the calls of the day. All would go well until "the first door of the favored victim was reached and opened by the maid, or, as was often the case in San Francisco, the Chinese servant." At this point, "Harry would kick and scream and refuse to go in." As the "little kicking boy was dressed in a Scotch costume, — sash, sporran, kilt and all,"[6] he no doubt made quite a sight.

This energetic, determined, rebellious, and no doubt troubled lad was born at the Wigmore home, 1515 California Street, San Francisco, on March 4, 1863. With the exception of a half-brother, Alphonso, Harry was the oldest of seven children, five boys and two girls, who grew to maturity.[7] The name given to him honored both his father, John, and his mother, Harriet.[8]

Harry's father was born in Youghal, County Cork, Ireland, in 1828 and was educated there. When he was twenty-two years old, he came to Boston, Massachusetts, and there married Miss Emma Hewitt Newby of his native town. At the age of twenty-six he left for the Pacific coast with his wife and their son Alphonso, going by way of the Isthmus of Panama. During the trip the family all contracted Panama fever, and, shortly after they landed in San Francisco in August 1854, his wife died. Eight months later, his funds completely exhausted, he returned to the eastern states by way of Nicaragua. In 1857 he once more made the trip west and settled in San Francisco. John remained a widower until 1862 when he married Harriet Joyner, the mother of John Henry.[9]

Wigmore is an English name, and the town of Wigmore is in Hertford close to the Welsh border. Wigmore Castle, now largely in ruins, is located nearby. The Wigmore family can trace its ancestry back to the time of William the Conqueror.[10]

Harriet was born in Warwickshire, England, in a small town near Stratford on Avon. As a young girl she came to the United States with her family in a sailing vessel called the *Shackamaxon*, and they settled in San Francisco.[11]

Both of Harry's parents were devoted and very active members of the Episcopal church. John Wigmore was described as "a devoted churchman of the Irish Protestant type."[12] From 1857 to 1867, he was a member of the Church of the Advent in San Francisco and a teacher in its Sunday school. He became a charter member of St. Luke's Mission in which he was superintendent of the Sunday school, and, when it became a parish, he served as a vestryman until he left San Francisco and moved to Los Angeles in 1888. Mrs. Wigmore had a deep interest in the work of the church and participated in its activities in many ways. This, then, was the religious atmosphere in which Harry developed as a child and grew to maturity.

Harry's father began his business career in San Francisco as a cabinetmaker. That he was successful is evident from the fact that in 1867 he built a four-story furniture factory on Spear Street which, unfortunately, was destroyed by fire within a year after completion. Thereafter, John confined his business to the importation of cabinet woods and square-edged hardwood lumber, the only dealer on the Pacific coast to sell these articles exclusively. In 1888 a branch was established in Los Angeles "for the convenience of customers in Southern California and the Territories," which, in addition to their regular line of hardwood lumber and timber, carried "a complete stock of Carriage Material and Hardware, Bar Iron, Steel, Blacksmiths' Tools and General Supplies."[13]

That John Wigmore was a competent businessman is evident not only from the way his enterprise expanded but from the purchase made by him and Alphonso of the Rancho de la Puente near Los Alamos in Santa Barbara County, a tract of 4,800 acres. The Wigmores gave this property a great deal of attention, at first through a tenant, and then, from 1889 on, under the direction of Alphonso. During the early years the property was fenced and its water resources developed for irrigation purposes. Under Alphonso's direction it was "stocked with high grade Durham cattle, and a class of carefully selected mares, in view of breeding horses for draft purposes, from Percheron stock."[14] By 1891, Alphonso was experimenting with deciduous fruits "in view of setting out a large acreage, favoring also the English walnut, olives, grapes and figs."[15]

Thus the young Harry grew up in a comfortable setting. After reentering the Urban School, he continued his education there until he was ready for college. The school, which was organized in 1864, had announced its over-all objective in the following words, "The design of the School is to furnish the best education to boys. The school prepares boys for Eastern Colleges or our own University, for Foreign Universities, for Scientific and Technical Schools, or for a life of business."[16]

Perhaps Harry's brief exposure to the public school was rendered more difficult by the fact that the Urban School claimed among its advantages, "thorough discipline, united with kindness and gentlemanly treatment of every pupil" and an insistence upon "uniform courtesy by the older pupils to new ones."[17] The headmaster was a "charming and erudite gentleman of the old school,"[18] and the curriculum included a wide variety of courses but heavily emphasized the fundamentals. Unfortunately, there is no record of just what courses Harry took. However, he undoubtedly received a good basic education and one that, among other things, provided a foundation for his unusual facility with foreign languages. We do know that his appearances in public exercises included recitations of the "Ode to Napoleon," "The Speech of Balial," a discussion on "The Future of America," and a piano solo, "The Brook."[19]

That Harry took full advantage of the opportunities the Urban School provided is evidenced by the impression of his younger brother Francis Marion, always called Marion by his family and friends:

> He [Harry] evidently made a very definite niche for himself in the school's hall of fame, for when younger brother's time had come to enter the school's portals and begin his studies there, it is my very definite impression that brother Harry's reputation for erudition and phenomenal attainments had reached such appalling heights in the school's traditions, that it was very difficult to live up to what was to be expected from a member of the same family. Furthermore, a melancholy remark or deprecatory gesture from an instructor would serve as a cutting reminder of the great talents of the one who had gone before and attained the coveted goal of entering that renowned seat of learning, Harvard University.[20]

At home Harry's mother dominated the scene, and when differences of opinion arose she eventually had her way. An observer described her as a "regular English story matriarch."[21] One manifestation of her highly romantic propensities was the manner in which she dressed the children. Harry, in Scottish costume, is an example, but the style applied to all the children. The boys were dressed "to resemble the English princes in the

Tower with long curls and black velvet suits,''[22] and the girls in ''mob caps aping the French Revolution, or Empress Josephine dresses, or Connemara capes, for an Irish flavor.'' Mrs. Wigmore derived a great deal of pleasure from the admiration of her friends, who referred to her children ''as the best-dressed children in San Francisco.''

But although Harry's mother usually prevailed, his father was a stern disciplinarian, especially where eating was concerned. On this score Alphonso often took issue with his father in defense of his half-brother. Harry, who was very fond of Alphonso, later recalled an incident involving tomatoes, which he greatly disliked. It was Alphonso who prevailed upon his father not to insist that every bit be eaten.[23] On another occasion, Harry saw his father punish one of his brothers by whipping him, and he was so disturbed by the experience that he resolved at that time to control his temper.[24] Harry was very definitely Mrs. Wigmore's favorite child, a fact that was quite generally recognized in the family and apparently did not stimulate any jealousy on the part of the other children. Mrs. Wigmore not only wanted to provide him with the best possible formal education but had ambitions for him musically. Accordingly, Harry always remembered that he ''was early chained to the piano; for ten years more or less [and] made to practice from one to three hours daily.''[25] Many years later he recalled his dismay one day when he heard a neighbor who was a musician play a composition with rapid runs, over which he himself had labored for months, with great brilliance and effortlessness. Harry was aghast at the thought of the torture his mother must have suffered listening to his practicing. But although young Harry Wigmore may have been irked sometimes by the constant practice, music was from the beginning a major interest.

His brother Marion has testified to an early evidence of musicianship.

> One of the oft repeated anecdotes was that of brother Harry's going on the stage as ''super'' in the opera house in San Francisco, during the operatic tour of one of the grand opera companies in that day of idolized singers and great voices, so that he might thus have the opportunity of hearing and seeing the aristocracy of the operatic world, which he could not well afford otherwise. The crux of the story is, as I remember it, that brother Alphonso and his wife Mollie had gone to one or more of these performances arrayed in that mental and sartorial splendor and pride which, I am sure, we have all indulged upon attending a gala performance of grand opera in its hey-day. Now, lo and behold! Brother Harry's physiognomy was recognized (though disguised as a spearman or arquebusier or what not) in the quality of a ''super'' and the chagrin of elder brother Alphonso knew no bounds.[26]

Not all of Harry's boyhood jobs had such an attractive objective. He often watered the lawn of the family home on Pacific Avenue. Naturally, he regarded this as boring, but he later recalled the lovely view of the Bay looking north toward the Golden Gate with the ships coming and going.[27]

When Harry graduated from the Urban School he apparently expected to continue his education in California, for he enrolled at the University of California in Berkeley across the Bay. But, he discovered at once, if he did not suspect it, that his mother "was under the spell of the New England men and women of letters of the time, and nothing would do but that Harry must go to Harvard."[28] Needless to say, she prevailed. But unable to bear the thought of separation from her firstborn, she moved the entire family to Cambridge, and Harry's father, no doubt most unwillingly, left the business in the hands of Alphonso.

2
Harvard

I|||||||||||⊏⊐||||||||||⊏⊐||||||||||⊏⊐||||||||||⊏⊐||||||||||⊏⊐||||||||||⊏⊐||||||||||⊏⊐||||||||||⊏⊐||||||||||⊏⊐||||||||||⊏⊐||||||||||⊏⊐||||||||

It would be interesting to know what Harry's thoughts were when, at the age of sixteen, he stood in the station waiting to board the train that was to cross the continent to Massachusetts and bring him to Harvard University for his further academic training. Did he look forward to this step out into the world as an adventure? Did he think of his Harvard experience as a first step in a career he had already formulated, at least to some extent? Did he have misgivings in the face of such a drastic change? Unfortunately, the record throws no light on these questions and we are left to speculation. However, we do know that something else was the object of his immediate concern. As a typical adolescent, he was decidedly uncomfortable as he stood in the railroad station surrounded by his mother and his four younger brothers — Marion, George Herbert, Hubert Llewelyn, and Cyril. So embarrassed was Harry that he said to his mother, "You and the children get on first . . . I'll come in later." [1]

The family who accompanied him settled first in Charleston but later moved to Cambridge. [2] Uprooted from his business, John Wigmore contented himself with the ordering of lumber in the East, to be shipped to his firm in San Francisco. [3] During the four-year stay in Cambridge the family was augmented by the birth of two daughters, Violet and Beatrice. Harry's home environment as a student was clearly not a quiet one. [4]

Native ability and his preparation at the Urban School apparently served him well, for his record at Harvard College was certainly creditable. At the end of the first year, he ranked 79th in a class of 240. For raising his rank to 23rd by the end of the next year, he was awarded a prize, "For notable diligence in studies," of Mary Codwen Clarke's *Concordance to Shakespeare*. This encouragement, the first received from outside his family, so aroused Harry's ambition and strengthened his self-confidence that he later became a strong advocate of recognition of this kind. [5] Harry was one of four students to win highest honors in classics in the sophomore year, and he completed the four-year course with distinction. Upon graduation, he also merited honorable mention in Greek, Latin, political economy, and English composition, and he was one of the authors of a commencement dissertation. [6]

Harry's interest in music, which was already firmly established before he left San Francisco, continued unabated. He studied harmony "under the original genius John K. Paine — may his memory ever be revered."[7] According to Harry, Paine could write with either hand, and "he could wield a blue pencil skillfully in both hands at once, marking the errors"[8] in his students' compositions. As a student he participated in many musical activities: as part of the chorus dressed in short Grecian skirts in a production of *Oedipus* for which Paine composed the music, as music director for the Harvard University Boat Club benefit in 1881,[9] in a "Programme" of the "Athenaeum of '84" in May of the same year, in which he played a "Piano Overture" and a "Duet."[10] He also served as an accompanist from time to time and remarked that in his college days he "would rather have been the composer of Sir Arthur Sullivan's 'Iolanthe' than anything else ever written."[11] His choice of subject for a commencement essay was "The Satire and Humor of Sir William Gilbert's Librettos."

Other student activities included membership in the Philological Society in which he held the office of secretary.[12] Little is known about his athletic interests but they were nominal at the most — although perhaps he played at several games, the only record is of participation in cricket.[13]

In June 1883 Harry graduated from Harvard and returned to San Francisco with his family. Until December he read and studied in fields that he felt had not been satisfactorily covered in college. In January 1884, he went to work in his father's lumber yard, serving until September in various capacities, including those of bookkeeper, laborer, and stevedore.[14]

But Harry had already developed another important interest. At Harvard he had worked on a plan for civic reform with Franklin K. Lane, later secretary of the interior in the Wilson administration, and several others. One member of this group, called the Municipal Reform League, was Abe Ruef, later a notorious mayor of San Francisco but at the time much disturbed by the cynicism in policies. As the secretary, Ruef corresponded with various groups around the country, including a "political greenhorn" named Theodore Roosevelt.[15] With boss control one of its most important stated purposes, League members were to hold no offices and enjoy no spoils. Each member was to make himself responsible for specific city districts, taking an active part in all caucuses and meetings. The undertaking was no doubt far too ambitious for a small group of newspaper writers and college undergraduates. At any rate the short career of the Municipal Reform League ended when Harry went back to Harvard to study law in the fall of 1884.[16]

Harry's interest in politics naturally led him to writing, thus beginning his career as one of the most, if not the most, prolific writers in the annals of the law. Now San Francisco newspapers were his primary outlet, and his major interest was the tariff question. On four occasions he wrote in favor of free trade, taking the position that such a policy would benefit both workers and manufacturers; twice he discussed local political figures. He also expressed his views on a pending federal statute, a city ordinance, and a program in support of jury service. By the time Harry reached the age of maturity, his interest in public affairs and his strong propensity for expressing his views in writing had crystallized.[17]

With both parents ardent church members it is clear that Harry's home life was imbued with a religious atmosphere, and there is at least one indication that religion may have been a matter of serious concern during his college days. The New Testament[18] that he apparently received in 1881 not only contains numerous marginal notations but has a handwritten key on the flyleaf to eleven symbols used throughout the text to denote the character and significance of particular passages. His notations include "precepts not now observed," "not understood," "hard to believe and reconcile," "quotable," "gives new aspects of some involved questions," "proofs of the wide extent of God's love beyond the mere pale of nominal Christianity," and "important for me."

Both the symbols and the marginal notes show most careful reading and a wide-ranging interest in the text. Although there is no conclusive evidence as to just when Harry gave the New Testament this meticulous study, the notation appearing on the flyleaf in his own handwriting is "(S.F. Cal)," an almost certain indication that this study occurred during his college or his law-school years and before he left San Francisco at the end of the summer of 1886. In addition to the fact that Harry already had wide intellectual interests, the religious affiliation of his parents was certainly being questioned and would in fact soon become a thing of the past. In his effort to achieve an independent orientation to life, this kind of appraisal might very well have been a part of the process. One thing, however, is clear: throughout his life Harry kept the New Testament close at hand and referred to it frequently.

Though his mother had wanted him to become a clergyman, Harry returned to Cambridge alone in the fall of 1884 and entered the Harvard Law School.[19] He remained in Cambridge during the following summer but returned to San Francisco for the summer of 1886. On the train trip west, Harry and a companion pursuaded the engineer to let them ride on the cowcatcher while going through the mountains. He never forgot the thrill of rounding a steep curve at a place called Cape Horn "and feeling as though he were suspended in the air."[20] Many years later when he was asked if he told his mother he replied, "You bet I didn't!"

Throughout the three-year period at the law school, Harry lived in room 16 of Hollis Hall, built in 1763 and used as barracks by colonial troops in 1776.[21] In the first year he made an average grade of 82 for the four courses taken — real property, contracts, torts, and civil procedure — and ranked first in a class of 61 students taking only four courses. In the second year, he took evidence, equity pleading, property, trusts, and bills and notes. His average grade was 81 and he ranked third in his class.[22] In his day, students could take the third-year final examinations without attending classes, and apparently he so elected, for no grades appear in his record for this period.[23] In 1887 he received both the A.M. and LL.B. degrees.

For Harry the law school unquestionably provided a stimulating environment as, "These were the years in the classic era of that great school. That was the time of Ames, Gray, Langdell and Thayer."[24] Harry was a schoolmate of Samuel Williston and a classmate of Joseph E. Beale and Julian W. Mack, who at a later time became his colleague on the faculty of

Northwestern University. Wigmore, Beale, and Mack were members of a small group who founded the *Harvard Law Review* in 1886.[25] Years later Wigmore said that the venture seemed ". . . daring, even rash,"[26] but "McKelvey . . . was the optimist of our self-selected Board; some of the rest of us were for awhile weak in faith; but he was sure of the results; and he ought to receive acclaim for his faith thus vindicated."[27] According to Beale the "Recent Cases" department was Wigmore's invention,[28] and, at any rate, this was his special assignment. He thus established a feature that has been universally followed by other law-school reviews.

The original objective of the *Review* was to serve as a vehicle for the writings of the faculty, though student contributions were expected to provide the variety usual in such a periodical.[29] The *Review* received the hearty support of the faculty and particularly of Professor James Barr Ames, who contributed the opening article. He also gave constant supervision and advice and became chairman of the board of trustees that became necessary with the journal's increasing prosperity.[30] The first issue of the *Review* appeared in April 1887, with John J. McKelvey as editor-in-chief and Wigmore on the Editorial Board. It was hoped that the members of the newly created Harvard Law School Association — with Louis D. Brandeis (later Associate Justice of the Supreme Court) as its secretary — could be counted upon to support the *Review* as subscribers, and this proved to be justified. When the association entered a year's subscription for each of its members, the result was a permanent increase in circulation that put the publication on a sound financial basis.[31]

Except for the *Law Review*, Harry's extracurricular activities connected with the law school seem to have been slight. Though he was a member of the Pow-Wow Club from 1885 to 1887,[32] he did not actively participate — in part perhaps because he had become interested in Miss Emma Hunt Vogl.[33] Evidence that his affection was reciprocated was the calendar she gave him consisting of a page for each day of the year, on which she had placed a quotation in her own handwriting.[34] At about the same time Harry was making a collection of a somewhat different sort — a scrapbook containing hundreds of jokes and funny stories gleaned from newspapers, magazines, and other sources.[35]

During the third year Harry was ill for two months, but Joseph Beale lent him all his lecture notes, and with their aid Harry came through the final examinations successfully. As a token of his gratitude and "after much reflection" he gave Beale a copy of Holmes, *The Common Law*,[36] a book which Harry had read with a thrill not to be forgotten.[37] The care that he no doubt greatly needed during his illness was provided by Emma's mother, who brought him into their home until he had recovered.[38]

During his law-school experience, Harry lived quite economically because funds received from home were inadequate and he had to supplement them in some way.[39] Thus economic necessity now supported his natural inclination and aptitude for writing, and it was during these years that he first demonstrated his capacity to carry on a large volume of work on a continuous basis.

His continuing interest in public affairs was reflected by a short item appearing in 1885 in the *Daily Alta California*,[40] approving the Willis Education Bill which provided for distribution of funds among the states according to their illiteracy rate, and by a long open letter to the *Century Illustrated Monthly Magazine*[41] entitled "Political Work for Young Men" in which he advocated the union of young men for political purposes. But it was 1887, while he was still in law school, that Harry's orientation to the law became clearly evident. Two of his publications, his initial contributions to a legal periodical, appeared in the *American Law Review*. The first, entitled, "The Boycott and Kindred Practices as Ground for Damages,"[42] defined the wrongs involved in boycotts, discussed their place in the law of torts, and developed the relevant principles. The second dealt with "Interference with Social Relations."[43] Acceptance of the first article was no doubt a source of considerable encouragement, for in later years Wigmore referred to it as his "first professional pat on the back."[44] That both manuscripts had merit was promptly corroborated by Oliver Wendell Holmes, at the time Associate Justice of the Supreme Judicial Court of Massachusetts, who, in acknowledging receipt of copies of the articles wrote:

> I have read your articles on Boycotting and Interference with Social Relations with much interest and hope that as soon as I get through sitting with the full court you will give me an opportunity to talk with you about them. I have not time for writing any detailed observations upon them. But I may say at once that while I reserve my opinion over some of your criticisms and generalizations I have no doubt that you have carried the discussion beyond the point at which you found it and your historical examination of actions for loss of service struck me as far as I could judge off hand as a first rate piece of work.
>
> Sincerely yours,
> O. W. Holmes[45]

What Wigmore did not know was that, in writing to Sir Frederick Pollock at the time, Holmes said, "I don't know anybody here who is doing anything to speak of in that way, perhaps because I am too busy to know.* There is what seems an excellent study of the development of actions for loss of service in 22 Am. Law Rev. 765 [*sic*] in the midst of other matters less important."[46]

* On the outside of the envelope which enclosed this letter Holmes wrote: "I should have excepted Ames in what I say within. He is giving some very careful and instructive lectures on the history of laws."

3

Boston

After graduation from the Law School, Wigmore continued to live in Cambridge. Upon admission to the bar in 1887 he first went into the law office of Champlin, Ryther and Wentworth at 209 Washington Street in Boston. In 1888 he joined forces with Seth P. Smith, and in 1889 he became associated with W. V. Kellen.[1] Clients certainly did not rush to his door, and probably most of those he had were members of the bar for whom he did research work or performed some other service. And he did his share of "leg work." For example, on one occasion his task was to secure the signatures of citizens who agreed that the trolley poles of a proposed street railway should be placed at the sides of the street rather than in the center. On another occasion, his "job was to go around, in one of the suburbs, for many a cold January night, and ring the door bells and persuade certain householders to sign a paper saying they did not notice or did not mind the smell of the glue factory nearby."[2] In several instances he acted for lawyers in other states who needed assistance in matters involving the law of Massachusetts or required local representation. Work for lay clients was certainly a minor part of his docket, and appearances in court, if any, were certainly few.[3]

However, Wigmore was soon brought in touch with two men whose influence would be both immediate and lasting. One was Charles Doe, chief justice of the New Hampshire Supreme Court, who, during the latter part of his career, found the trip to Boston to complete his research in the Social Law Library too arduous. When he asked Mr. Vaughan, the librarian, to suggest someone to collect authorities for him, Wigmore was recommended, and Judge Doe engaged him soon after his admission to the bar. According to Wigmore, at least fifteen cases requiring special research were involved.[4] He describes the form in which he reported to Judge Doe in a letter to Robert G. Pike, later president of the New Hampshire Bar Association:

> I cast my results into the form of judicial opinions; and being much flattered by the task given me, I expected to be able to recognize my handiwork in the published opinions. But — I frankly admit that I never could find any resemblance at all between what I sent and what he turned out. Master mind that he was, my stuff was simply raw material to him, and he used it, or cast it out as

he found fit. I had simply been a searcher, to him, and he made his own use of it in his own way.[5]

However, of the quality of Wigmore's work there can be no doubt, as is evident from Judge Doe's expression of appreciation:

Salmon Falls, N.H.
April 13, '88

Bro Wigmore

Your answers and results, on all my questions, rec'd; and they are all exactly what I want. I wanted to know as well what could not as what could be found. It is disagreeable to know that in the present state of legal and historical collections, no one can be sure he has not failed to find something important and existing in the line of his investigation. And so, on the merely negative side, I am greatly helped by your research. Of course there is something you & I have not found; but the probability of a great amount of undiscovered & material law or fact is largely diminished by the search of a second examiner.

Unless, by some strange accident, you happened to be familiar with the subjects, or were aided by somebody who was familiar with them, or have a facility for handling books and finding things beyond what I can conceive of, you must have spent a great deal of time with intense application. How any young man could do what you have done in the time, without special previous knowledge of the subjects, is something I can't understand. And if you were an old or middle-aged man, the marvel would be very great. The only unsatisfactory thing is the evident inadequacy of your charges. What they should be, I cannot well guess. Enclosed is draft for $50. which cannot be enough. For future work, I must insist that you charge what you think your work is worth, remembering that I appreciate the value of all time spent in search that shows what can not be found. You cannot be more annoyed by the fear of charging too much, than I am by the fear of your charging too little. When I get any idea of what the enclosed ought to be, I will make up the deficiency.

Yours truly, C. Doe[6]

Although Wigmore never met Judge Doe, the significance to him of this relationship is reflected in a postscript written many years later to a letter to Robert G. Pike, after Pike, as president of the New Hampshire Bar Association, had spoken of Doe in his annual address:

P.S. You will see from the letters that I never met him personally. But his letters meant so much to me in my professional beginnings, by the encouragement which so warms a young man's heart, and they showed so kindly an interest, that I ever entertained a deep affection, and I took the occasion of my book's appearance* to try to repay the debt publicly. His picture has for twenty years hung over my desk, daily before my eyes. J.H.W.[7]

* The book was the first edition of the *Treatise on Evidence* published in 1904, and the dedication is as follows: "To the Memory of the public services and private friendship of two masters of the law of evidence Charles Doe of New Hampshire Judge and reformer and James Bradley Thayer of Massachusetts historian and teacher."

The other significant association that Wigmore made in his early days in practice (indeed he regarded this as his first genuine retainer[8]) comes to us directly in his own words:

> A few months after I was admitted to the bar, I was going along Washington Street, Boston (I remember almost the very place), one Monday, when I met Louis Brandeis. (He was then known as the "young Choate" of the Boston Bar). He said to me, "Do you want to earn $100?" Suppressing a near-faint, I answered, "Most hungrily I do." He said, "I am counsel for some mills and must argue next week before a legislative Committee against a bill to condemn all public lakes in Massachusetts for municipal water supplies. Before Saturday night, I must know what is the total potential water power available from Massachusetts lakes." "But," I said, "where does it tell what the total is?" He answered, "Nobody knows; that is just the point." "Well," I asked, "tell me how to figure it out, at least." He answered, "*I* don't know how. And I haven't got time to find out. That is why I employ you." "Well," I said, "I would do blinder things than that for $100. Next Saturday night, you said?" "Yes," he ended, "results by next Saturday." You can imagine what I went through, that week. But I *had* to find out, and I *did* find out.[9]

That Wigmore's service was also satisfactory in this case is evident from the fact that when he transmitted payment of $150 rather than the $100 originally agreed upon, Brandeis said it was for "your very valuable services in the great pond question." [10] Wigmore was similarly associated with Brandeis on several other occasions.[11]

From the beginning, Wigmore's practice neither kept him fully occupied nor provided an income adequate to permit his marriage to Miss Emma Hunt Vogl, to whom he was now engaged, and thus his natural inclination to continue his writing was reinforced by the desire to increase his income. In 1888 he actively sought the post of editor for the supplement to the *Public Statutes of Massachusetts*, recently authorized by the state legislature. However, in spite of strong recommendations from Leonard A. Jones, one of the editors of the *American Law Review*, and from James Barr Ames, John C. Gray, and James B. Thayer of the Harvard Law School faculty, he was not successful.[12] But he did secure the appointment as editor for a digest of the decisions of the Board of Railroad Commissioners of Massachusetts,[13] which had also been authorized by the state legislature. In assuming this responsibility he undertook his first assignment in book form by becoming the compiler of the first digest of decisions in this field published in the United States.[14] In acknowledging receipt of a gift copy of the digest from Wigmore, Holmes said, "I think there is little doubt that I shall find it of practical use and I am much obliged to you both for it and for the kind feeling which led you to send it." [15]

Wigmore's initial effort in the field of criminal law and also in the law of evidence, both areas in which he would have a lifelong interest, was an address entitled "Circumstantial Evidence in Poisoning Cases" for which he was awarded the first prize by the Medico-Legal Society. This address was read before the society on December 12, 1888, and published in the

Medico-Legal Journal.[16] To the young Wigmore, who was finding it difficult to make ends meet, the prize money was most welcome. He applied it to the purchase of a sapphire engagement ring to present to Emma Vogl.[17]

Wigmore dealt with the same field in a newspaper article in the *Boston Globe* entitled "Noted Poisoning Trials."[18] Another indication of his broadening interests is an article entitled "Louisiana: The Story of its Jurisprudence," which appeared in the *American Law Review*,[19] and which Sir William S. Holdsworth, the English legal historian, described as "a very able historical study."[20]

While Wigmore was working for Judge Doe, he was approached by A. G. Sedgwick regarding participation in the revision of *Sedgwick on Damages*,[21] a task which at least offered the advantage of providing much-needed income. Quite naturally, he sought Judge Doe's advice and elicited this observation:

> I don't see how a good ed. of Sedgwick can be made if the text is to be preserved. The book might be worth something to a maker of a new book authorized to use the old book as he pleased. But it isn't like Kent Com [James Kent, *Commentaries on American Law*]. It will sell I suppose; but it would be worth more if you could take any liberty you pleased with the text.[22]

After extended consideration of the matter a formal agreement was made with the publisher involving a total consideration for Wigmore of $750, a not inconsiderable amount for a young lawyer in that day.[23] That Wigmore was establishing something of a reputation as a legal writer is evident from the fact that he was also approached by the Central Law Journal Company about the preparation of some texts for them to publish,[24] but the negotiations never went beyond the discussion stage.

Although Wigmore was, by now, both committed to the law and well started on a career as a writer on legal subjects, he had not lost his interest in politics. He shared fully with his friend Franklin K. Lane the zeal for political reform to which they had been committed together in San Francisco. When Wigmore came east he continued his affiliation with the Republican party. He served on the Republican ward and city committee and acted as secretary of the Cambridge Republican League, in which he was regarded as one of its most valuable members. Quite naturally his interest continued to express itself in writing, and newspapers served as an immediate outlet. In "What to do on Election Day,"[25] he discussed the law relating to ballots, ballot boxes, bets, and bribery and offered hints to voters. And it was during this period that he first exhibited in writing his interest in the international scene as well. In a news story in 1888 he discussed at some length the military situation in Europe, giving his view as to how the nations would be aligned in a general war and concluding that Russia, not France, was the present menace to world peace.[26]

However, Wigmore's major political effort was concerned with ballot reform. His book *The Australian Ballot System as Embodied in the Legis-*

lation of Various Countries with an Historical Introduction was published in 1889. This was followed before the end of the year by a second edition containing an appendix of decisions since 1856 in Great Britain, Ireland, Canada, and Australia. A favorable comment on the second edition which appeared in the *Nation* on October 31, 1889, concluded with these words: ". . . Mr. Wigmore has spared no pains to make a complete record of progress, and in so doing has furnished the only weapon needed by the friends of honest suffrage. We owe to him no small share of the extraordinary success in legislation, during the year now expiring." Not only was the book widely used by proponents of ballot reform as the movement spread from state to state, but Wigmore became an authority on the subject and was frequently consulted. Among those in the ranks of the movement was Franklin K. Lane, who was still in California. At the same time Julian Mack, who was traveling in Europe, provided Wigmore with information about the movement in the various countries he visited. To deal more fully with the constitutional issues involved, Wigmore turned to the *American Law Review*, for which he was by now a recognized contributor, and the September-October 1889 issue contained his article, "Ballot Reform: Its Constitutionality."[27]

In the midst of these expanding activities in Boston and while he was in midstream on the revision of *Sedgwick on Damages*, Wigmore was offered the post of chief professor of Anglo-American law at Keio University in Tokyo.[28] A decided advantage in considering the Japanese offer was the fact that the post would provide a reliable income which would make it practicable to bring his engagement to Emma Vogl, begun in 1887, to a successful conclusion. Whether Wigmore had any serious doubt about the advisability of going to Japan or merely sought the best possible information concerning life there and the opportunities that his assignment would afford, is not clear. It is clear that his parents were not the only persons to express negative opinions about his plan.

He also consulted Harry T. Terry, a practitioner in New York City, who wrote, "My own experience is such as to very strongly incline me to believe that you can not use your work in Japan or every success that you may achieve there as a stepping stone to anything on your return to this country."[29] Another person consulted was W. S. Capen, who summed up his conclusion as follows, "My own experience was that an absence of five years in Japan almost completely effaced my acquaintance professionally. I count those years as practically lost in that way. Yet I worked hard, and enjoyed my life there greatly."[30]

The Japanese offer opened up an opportunity in comparative law, for which he felt a strong attraction,[31] even though, as President Charles W. Eliot of Harvard had previously told him, there was no interest in this subject in the United States and therefore no openings for teachers in this field in American law schools.[32] On the other hand, Wigmore was encouraged to undertake the assignment by President Eliot, with whom he now conferred in respect to his responsibilities as a law teacher in Japan, and he finally accepted the offer.[33] Completion of the revision of *Sedgwick on*

Damages was left in the hands of Joseph Beale, his law-school classmate.[34]

It is impossible to determine to what extent, if any, the negative advice received by Wigmore contributed to the fact that, when he finally accepted the appointment, he not only prepared carefully to take full advantage of every opportunity the assignment afforded but definitely planned to keep in touch with his developing circle of acquaintances in the United States.

One of the most helpful letters came from H. B. Adams of Johns Hopkins University. Adams not only made valuable suggestions, which are reflected in part in the following excerpt from his letter, but invited Wigmore to contribute to the proceedings of the American Historical Association and the Johns Hopkins University Studies.

> I think the duty of American Educators in Japan should be to cultivate greater stability of character and judgment in the Japanese youth and to preserve a consciousness of historic continuity in the institutions and culture of the Japanese people. The introduction of the historic method of studying law, politics and religion would be the salvation of that revolutionary and iconoclastic race. I have no sympathy with the idea of Americanizing or Europeanizing Japanese students, and I do all I can here in this University to preserve the peculiar virtues and excellent characteristics of our Japanese students. I believe you could render a substantial service to New Japan by Historical investigations into the social and legal History of Old Japan.[35]

Adams also gave Wigmore the names of several Japanese who had studied at Johns Hopkins and had returned to Japan to live.[36]

But Wigmore was not concerned solely with outlets in scholarly publications; he could count on the *Harvard Law Review* and the *American Law Review* for such help. He definitely contemplated a journalistic role for himself, regardless of whatever other interests he might develop. In this, Franklin K. Lane, who had recently come to New York as the eastern representative of the *San Francisco Chronicle*, was helpful by providing interviews with editors in that city.[37] The most important connection was with the *Nation*, for which he became the regular correspondent in Japan. However, he also obtained authorizations to represent the *New York Evening Post* and the *New York Times* and made preliminary arrangements for an illustrated article for *Scribner's Magazine* and for articles in the *Green Bag*.[38] In this way, and through correspondence, he planned to preserve and, indeed, cultivate his widening circle of acquaintances even while so far away. Wigmore thus responded to the warnings of some of his friends not by declining the appointment but by taking definite steps to make certain that he would not become isolated.

This careful planning was a reflection of the expectations for his three-year assignment which Wigmore expressed in a letter shortly before he left Boston:

> I have just accepted a professorship of law in one of the two Tokyo universities, and am going out there (in September) prepared to give them the best of myself,

and at the same time to interest myself thoroughly in things human and divine in Japan and to digest and assimilate all that I see and hear, and, in addition, to communicate my observations and conclusions to those at home who care to hear them.[39]

Announcement of the wedding and of the appointment at Keio University brought congratulations and best wishes from all sides and fatherly advice from Judge Doe who, in a letter to Wigmore, said:

Your selection for the work in Japan is a strong testimonial of the quality of your work as a writer, probably as a student at the law school in college.

The greatest danger of men of your stamp generally is in overwork, & a violation of the laws of health of which so few have any knowledge. It is not probable that you will reach the age of fifty with a sound constitution, or any vigor or power of endurance capable of accomplishing anything. You will damage your body in some way so as to make life a burden, & probably bring it to an early close. You will be influenced by no caution on the subject. No such man ever heeds any warning but [suffers] actual disability produced by excessive continuous labor, & lack of exercise, sleep & regular hours.

I trust you will be fortunate in your companion. The wives of the present generation of professional men are generally, in one way or another (often in more than one), a heavy burden & incumbrance, — a drain upon the time, the attention, the comfort, & the mental & financial strength of the unhappy victims. I know more than one able man whose success at the bar has been made impossible by domestic distraction, extravagance, folly, & misery. A young woman of education & refinement, content with her lot, & willing & able to be anything but a constant annoyance & inordinate expense to her husband, has become a rare bird. I hope you will both begin right, with sensible notions of expenditure, contentment & harmony, & thus stand some chance of attaining that position of honor & independence to which your talents are entitled . . . My best wishes and highest expectations go with you.[10]

Brandeis responded to the news of the forthcoming wedding as follows:

I was about to write you regarding your Japanese appointment, when your card came to tell me how well armed you will march into the new land.

Let me wish you every success & much happiness. That you were bound to succeed, I have always believed. Your only danger was over-work, & you have guarded yourself excellently against that.[41]

And Julian Mack wrote from Berlin, "I have never had a doubt but that yours would at the end of ten years be the shining name of '87."[42]

John Henry Wigmore and Emma Hunt Vogl were married on September 16, 1889, in Appleton Chapel at Harvard.[43] Emma was the daughter of "a scholarly gentleman who had come to New England from Prague"[44] and his wife, whom it will be recalled had cared for Harry during his illness while still a student. The young couple not only had the congratulations and best wishes of their friends, but the entire Vogl family had long since accepted Wigmore with great cordiality. This was indeed a happy event as far as his bride's relatives were concerned. However, the absence of members of the Wigmore family denoted far more than a geographic obstacle.[45] Parental consent to the affiliation, most reluctantly given, was coupled with the strong expectation, if, indeed, it was not *based* on the assumption, that Wigmore would return to California and preferably enter his father's business. As Wigmore drifted from his parents' church, expressed his great preference for the Boston area, and finally, announced his decision to go to Japan, the estrangement which had been developing became increasingly acute. In a long series of letters his mother alternated between expressions of love for ''her boy'' without whom she could not live and repeated charges of faithlessness, cruelty, loss of morality, and demands for repentance.[46]

Thus his mother's emotional attachment for Harry, who was unquestionably her favorite child, prevented her completely from recognizing the need to let him go his own way as an adult. Neither parent, in fact, had any conception of their son's sterling character and exceptional talents and of the extraordinary life that lay before him.

4

Japan

Three days after the wedding, on September 19, 1889, the young couple boarded the train for the first leg of their journey to Japan, where Wigmore was to serve for the next three years as the first professor of Anglo-American law at Keio University. They were accompanied by the Rev. Arthur May Knapp, who represented the Unitarian church and had officiated at their wedding. Another newly married couple, Mr. and Mrs. Garrett Droppers, were in the group as Mr. Droppers also had a teaching assignment at Keio University.

Faced with the complete refusal of the senior Wigmores to consider Harry's explanations, expressions of points of view, and declarations of affection, the young couple found it extremely difficult to accede to his mother's latest demand that they visit the family, then in Los Angeles, before going on to Japan. However, as a result of the urgent requests of his brothers and sisters, and particularly of Alphonso, his half-brother, with whom he had always felt a warm bond of affection, they did make a brief stop in Los Angeles. From there the entire family accompanied them to San Francisco to see them off. Also present were a number of Harry's friends who were living in the Bay Area and of course Alphonso and his wife who lived in San Francisco.

Alphonso, who had made all of the sailing arrangements, had the stateroom decorated with beautiful flowers, fruits, drinks, preserves, etc. As to Harry's mother, Emma has recorded that she "did herself proud throughout it all . . . controlled her feelings, was kind and good to Harry, and was very sweet to me." [1] It was certainly an auspicious departure as the S.S. *Gaelic* passed out to sea through the Golden Gate.

The social life on shipboard, both with the members of their party and with the other passengers, was delightful, but unfortunately it was an unusually rough passage and Emma was seasick much of the time. [2] But her sense of humor shines through in a letter to her mother, who, as has already been indicated, was very fond of Harry. She describes the deluge that flooded their stateroom when a skylight in the hall near their door was inadvertently left open during rough weather: "Imagine the dear boy of whom you are so careful, wading about ankle deep in the water, trying to rescue our belongings. . . . We have all had great enjoyment today in recounting our experiences to each other." [3]

Wigmore's first impressions of Japan are recorded in his own words:

> . . . the sail up the bay to Yokohoma was like a sail into fairyland. The
> mountains on either hand were like curious bits of stage scenery — fantastic
> shapes and picturesque effect of light and shade. The volcano of Oshima could
> be seen on the left with a crest of smoke, and after the sun had risen, Fujiyama,
> the great snow-crowned mountain, came into sight far more majestic and beauti-
> ful than we had ever imagined. Soon we passed close to the shore, and the little
> coves, green sward, and fairy trees made one and all of us, feel over and over
> again, that it was a journey into fairyland. In the distance the white and yellow
> bluffs showed in the sun, and all the hills came close to the water's edge. About
> us were little fairy boats, like cockleshells or walnut boats. . . . It [Yokohama] is
> the most picturesque looking town I have ever seen . . . [The natives with]
> their shock of black hair, usually carefully parted, with their olive complexions,
> white teeth, and intelligent earnest looks make them very fascinating. The whole
> affair seemed like a play, from the ship to the hotel. There we found European
> life again.[4]

When the party reached Tokyo they were quite overcome by the warmth
of their reception. As Mr. Yukichi Fukuzawa, founder and ex-president of
the university, could not be present because one of his daughters was very
ill with typhoid fever,[5] he had arranged a demonstration by the students,
who were on hand en masse. According to Emma, "the dear boy [Harry]
was of course unconscious as ever of his own self, and thought only of the
mass of youthful faces about him, and set them almost wild by waving his
hat and I don't know but that he joined in their cheering."

For a time the Wigmores lived with the Knapps. Later they took a large
house with about three acres of grounds which they shared jointly with the
William L. Liscombs. The Wigmores later occupied this house alone, and,
after Mrs. Vogl's visit, which was enjoyed by everyone, the Wigmores
were by themselves for the first time since their marriage two years earlier.[6]
But living with the Knapps initially brought them quickly in touch with a
wide circle of persons living in Japan or passing through Tokyo. And since
Wigmore's teaching responsibilities at Keio University did not commence
until January there was time to meet and talk with many persons with
common concerns.[7] Because Wigmore had had a siege with boils before
leaving the United States, Mrs. Wigmore did everything she could to keep
him away from work, and the young couple spent a good deal of time
shopping and sightseeing. In her own words:

> Harry is out making some swell calls on the French and German Ministers and
> the Master of Napier . . . Of course he is not idle, but it is very different from
> doing regular work, and thus far our life in Japan has had much of a holiday
> aspect. Harry is employing this spare time before his college duties begin, in
> getting acquainted with prominent people and in looking into all sorts of sub-
> jects. I predict great success for him here, for he goes at things in such a
> different way from most of the foreigners here. They seem to earn their money
> in as easy a way as possible, doing only just what is required, and taking no
> interest in the people, but Harry is working hard to make himself conversant on
> many subjects — such as local government, railroads, etc. — and he takes

besides such an intense interest in the people, that I am sure it will "tell" with the Japanese, for they are very observant of one's attitude towards them. His book on Ballot Reform is being translated for the private use of the members of the cabinet, and as one of his brightest pupils said — he it was who brought Harry this information — "This is a great compliment to the book, and your name will receive the most honorable mention."[8]

Among the "subjects" Wigmore was looking into was the language itself. According to Mrs. Wigmore "he was looking over a Japanese grammar" shortly after their arrival. Within a month he was "quite fluent," and after four months she reported to her mother "he is a marvel."[9] Wigmore was also steadily gaining proficiency in German, but here the emphasis was on law.[10] But to secure the broad background of information he desired he not only read many books, but he "read every page of the *Japan Daily Mail* from 1870 to 1890 to get the local and international political history" and the "entire Foreign relations (U.S.A.) correspondence since the 1850's."[11] On many occasions Wigmore and Mrs. Wigmore read aloud,[12] and she quite regularly made copies of his various writings.[13] Time at the piano was an essential feature of the usual daily round.[14] He was apparently absorbed in his work and happy in his activities and with his surroundings, for Mrs. Wigmore wrote her mother on various occasions that "he does not mind either bad weather or work," he "never finds fault or grumbles," "and this trip to Japan seems to be bringing out many strong points which we never knew he possessed."[15]

Aside from the many calls that Wigmore made in connection with his research and writing there was a considerable amount of going and coming among a wide circle of acquaintances and frequent meetings, usually weekly, of "the group" or "combination," a designation for their own immediate circle, whose activities included reading from Shakespeare, singing, reciting original contributions in verse, and the pursuit of a wide variety of interests. Their entertaining involved many Japanese as well as other foreigners with whom they came in contact.[16]

Harry and Emma, so well suited to each other, were very happy alone together in the midst of these numerous activities. However, Wigmore's strong inclination to share pleasures with others was already perfectly evident. As he was leaving home one day he said to Mrs. Wigmore that he was buying four tickets for a certain concert and asked her to invite another couple to be their guests. In the time-honored manner of young brides Mrs. Wigmore protested mildly that it would be nicer if they could go by themselves. "Emma," he said, "we are not going to have such pleasures ourselves unless we can share them with others."[17]

Wigmore sometimes gave expression to his propensity for originality by the manner in which he showed his affection for Mrs. Wigmore. For example, "In the dim light of their first Christmas morning in Japan, Mrs. Wigmore woke with a sensation of being pinned down by some fantastic framework! Light arriving, she was amazed to behold "a small 'Eighteenth Century Geisha writing-table' to which she had often made love in one of the old treasure shops. . . . To leave no doubt that it was her Christmas gift, she observed with silent anxiety that each of its slender rose and bronze legs was encased in one of her best trousseau silk stockings then as rare as were the nylons in a later day.''[18]

But Wigmore also showed some interest in sports. Soon after their arrival he attended some fencing matches given by the police and later took lessons himself. As to these Mrs. Wigmore wrote her mother, ''I wish you could see him in his costume — he makes me think of one of the divers in their strange dress — he enjoys it immensely, and I suppose the exercise is good for him.''[19]

Fond of horseback riding, he also found wrestling matches of great interest and bowling not an uncommon mode of recreation. However, baseball seems to have been his favorite sport, and he played a good many times.[20] Shortstop seems to have been his favorite position, and he believed that he played ''on the first baseball team ever organized in Tokyo; and that team must have helped to start the vogue of baseball in Japan.''[21] An attempt to climb Mt. Fujiyama[22] with some of his friends had an unfortunate aftermath. After completing the descent in a rainstorm, just in time to catch a crowded train for Tokyo, Harry contracted a severe case of intercostal neuralgia which recurred painfully from time to time throughout his life and required him to guard against catching cold if possible.[23]

Although teaching law was Wigmore's principal assignment in Japan, he was also employed by the American Unitarian Association for ''literary work connected with the publishing of its journal in Japan and with other secular business in that place,''[24] and gave a number of lectures under its auspices.[25]

Wigmore had, of course, promptly conferred with Keio University authorities upon his arrival and met his prospective students informally for a number of sessions, in order that they might become familiar with spoken English and he might adjust himself to their sometimes peculiar pronunciations. His formal teaching did not begin until January 11. At the time of his first informal meeting he wrote, ''On the whole I am quite satisfied with the first impressions of the students-to-be. There are some among them who, I foresee, will be quite bright and in every way worth working with.''[26]

When Wigmore began teaching he had six students in one class and about thirty-five in another, and he reported that he liked his work very much.[27] His regular academic day was from nine in the morning until noon, a schedule that allowed him to spend much time in his study at home.[28]

Wigmore of course needed American law books both for teaching and for writing on American legal subjects. He pressed with some success for the purchase of books for the university but had to rely also upon his personal library, for which he made a number of purchases through dealers in the United States.[29]

Wigmore offered courses in common law, torts, and equity for first-year students and Roman law and evidence for second-year students.[30] Very little is known about how the classes were conducted or how the students responded, but that all was not easy sailing is evident from the fact that on one occasion Wigmore complained that the students were ''sullen on the question of Japanese translation of Roman law terms''[31] and recorded in his diary that Mr. Yukichi Fukuzawa thought the students were "lazy boys.''[32] But apparently the university authorities were satisfied or at least wanted to make the maximum use of their young American teacher. By the second year, his initial load of ten hours was doubled. When for the third year he was assigned thirty hours, he examined his contract only to find that it did not contain a provision concerning hours of work. However, when he went to the authorities, they accepted his plea for some relief.[34]

Much later Kenzo Takayanagi, who helped frame the Japanese constitution of 1946 and who had graduated from the Northwestern University Law School while Wigmore was dean, summarized Wigmore's contribution to Keio University as follows:

> Wigmore went there to teach Anglo-American law at Keio Gijiku, a private institution, founded by the famous Yukichi Fukuzawa, whom Wigmore characterized as "a Horace Mann, Horace Greeley and Ralph Waldo Emerson combined in one personality." Wigmore was virtually the founder of the law department of the present Keio University. He arranged the curriculum. The courses offered during the three year period were as comprehensive as those offered in American Law Schools.
>
> As the sole full-time professor, the whole burden of teaching fell on Wigmore, although he was assisted by a few Japanese part-time instructors. . . .
>
> As testified by his former students and many others, he was a conscientious teacher and was respected and loved by everybody.[34]

In spite of Mrs. Wigmore's efforts to keep her husband away from work he apparently began immediately to give some attention to subjects that might be suitable for journalistic efforts for, although he did not reach Japan until October 23, his extended comment on a proposed treaty with Japan, just made public, appeared in the *Boston Herald* on November 28, 1889.[35] Wigmore discussed both its domestic and international implications and hailed the treaty as a triumph of American diplomacy. He also took prompt advantage of an arrangement with the *Japan Daily Mail* by submitting his first contribution to that publication on January 6, 1890, a brief communication entitled, "Education as an Aim in Itself."[36] He was no doubt expressing his attitude toward his teaching assignment at Keio University. Subsequently, the *Japan Daily Mail* became an important outlet for Wigmore's journalistic efforts, and during his three-year stay in Japan it accepted altogether fifty-six articles, notes, and communications, covering a wide range of subject matter including law, politics, public affairs, Japanese history, religion, and international relations.[37]

In the United States, Wigmore's principal journalistic outlet was the *Nation*. After a few months devoted to the necessary investigations, his contributions began: altogether, there were seven articles, six notes, and several book reviews.[38] Most of these concerned the evolving political institutions resulting from the promulgation of the new Japanese constitution. Included were articles on the new Parliament, on Japanese political parties and other representative institutions, and on the reaction of the

Japanese people to Western influences. If we are willing to accept the appraisal of Wendell P. Garrison, the editor, it is evident that Wigmore was a success as a journalist, for his articles were described as "very readable and of permanent value." [39] And when Wigmore advised him of his pending return to the United States, Garrison wrote to express his regret and said he was losing his "best special correspondent." [40] Commenting most favorably on one of Wigmore's early articles, his friend W. V. Keller expressed the hope that he would continue to write: "[It] will keep you en rapport with people here and your name in their mouths." [41]

Wigmore's most ambitious journalistic effort while in Japan was the series of articles on the new Parliament for which he had begun to plan before he left Boston. Although he originally intended it for the *Century*, his proposal was not consonant with that publication's policy, and a series of two articles finally appeared in *Scribner's Magazine* in July and August 1891 under the titles, "Starting a Parliament in Japan" and "Parliamentary Days in Japan." [42] Although Wigmore had hoped to include illustrations in both articles, the artist became ill before the second article was published, and it was therefore illustrated only with an attractive headpiece. Here, again, the editor's appraisal was certainly gratifying. Your article "fulfills in every respect the expectations I had formed for it . . . We shall be indebted to you . . . for the best papers upon the whole subject which will be published." [43]

Wigmore's contributions to the *Green Bag* were eagerly sought by the editor, though they were, of course, addressed to members of the legal profession rather than to the general American public. A series of two articles on "The Legal System of Old Japan" appeared in 1892,[44] and in 1893 a second series of two articles on "Legal Education in Modern Japan," [45] illustrated with photographs of the leading figures in the field, was published. It is clear from the former article that he lost little time in commencing his research on early Japanese law; the latter article demonstrates his broader concern with the whole field of legal education in Japan and not merely with his specific assignment at Keio University. Three brief articles under the title "Japanese Causes Célèbres" also appeared in the *Green Bag* in 1892, 1897, and 1898.[46]

But the youthful Wigmore was by no means fully occupied by his teaching and by his journalistic efforts. He kept in touch with the United States by continuing to write articles in the field of Anglo-American law. In the first place, he made good on his promise to the editor to write an article for the *Harvard Law Review* by submitting one entitled "Nemo Tenetur Seipsum Prodere" [47] in which he indicated that the maxim was a misquotation consecrated by age. This, however, was not Wigmore's only contact with Harvard. He represented the Harvard Law School Association in Japan and for this purpose kept in touch with Brandeis, the secretary. He also conducted the admission examinations for Japanese students interested in going to Harvard and corresponded with President Eliot from time to time.

Wigmore actively continued his relationship with the *American Law*

Review. While in Japan he prepared and submitted "Rights in Rem and Rights in Personam," a letter to the editor, and two articles, "A Summary of Quasi-Contracts," and "Scientific Books in Evidence." [48] In the latter, Wigmore opposed the rule forbidding the admission of scientific books in evidence by considering it to be based upon a plausible reason that was no longer valid. In commenting on the manuscript for the article on quasi-contracts Leonard A. Jones, one of the editors, said, "Although it was much longer than we had anticipated, we shall use it as soon as we can find a place for it . . . it is a very valuable contribution to the law of the subject . . . in fact it is really the first scientific statement of the principles of the subject." [49] That Jones was correct in his appraisal of Wigmore's competence in the field of quasi-contracts is confirmed by the fact that Frederic C. Woodward dedicated his 1913 treatise on the subject "To John Henry Wigmore and the memory of Ernest W. Huffcut." [50]

But important as these various activities of Wigmore's were during his stay in Japan, almost no account has as yet been taken of the area that was at the time not only his most absorbing interest but represented his most significant contribution — namely, Japanese legal history. Almost immediately after his arrival, he became a member of the Asiatic Society of Japan, and he was soon elected to its council, in which he played a very active role. [51] He became immersed in the history of Japanese institutions and particularly in the law, and the *Transactions* of the society soon reflected the fruits of his efforts. His first major undertaking was his work on Duane B. Simmons's *Notes on Land Tenure and Local Institutions in Old Japan*, [52] a resumé of the land system which Wigmore edited from the author's posthumous papers.

This undertaking apparently demonstrated Wigmore's capacity to work through a mass of materials and reflect their significance by intelligent organization and lucid presentation. Dr. Arthur May Knapp commented on the project: "When I recall the higglety-piggled mess of the Simmons' papers when they were put into your hands I am simply amazed at the form they have now assumed bearing witness as they do to an enormous industry and genius for system on your part." [53]

And from William Elliott Griffin, Wigmore won this tribute, ". . . it seems to me to be a contribution of the highest value to the explanation of the unique phenomenon of Japan; indeed, I am inclined to think that in real value it equals anything that has thus far been contributed by any one European scholar, while in some respects it surpasses anything within the range of the Asiatic Society contributions." [54]

Wigmore's scholarly effort also culminated in an edition of the original indigenous civil-law sources entitled *Materials for the Study of Private Law in Old Japan*, in eight parts. Parts I, II, III (Section I), and V were published in the *Transactions* of the Asiatic Society of Japan in Tokyo in 1892. [55]

This manuscript was the outgrowth of the work of the society's Committee on Ethnography of which Wigmore was the chairman, [56] which involved the discovery of important documentary materials, their careful examination, and the translation of basic documents into English. In the report of the society's council it is stated that the committee ". . . owes almost everything to the active enthusiasm of Professor Wigmore [for its work which] has already furnished the Society with voluminous matter, to be printed as a Supplement to the current volume. The Volume with its Supplement will contain more matter than the Society has ever yet printed in one year."[57]

The *Japan Weekly Mail* concluded a review of this work as follows:

> Mr. Wigmore has done his work admirably. Only the first portion has yet been published, but as it fills 244 pages of the Proceedings, some idea may be formed of the magnitude of the work. With many of the most interesting facts and important generalizations, our readers have already been made acquainted by the series of articles recently published in these columns under the title of "New Laws and Old Customs," the writer having at the same time traced the analogies between the *Meiji* Codes and the pre-Restoration usages. But the essays, as printed in full in the Asiatic Society's Proceedings, will represent a work of the highest value, not surpassed by anything that has hitherto appeared in the twenty volumes of that Society's repertoire. We venture to congratulate the Society most heartily on its wisdom in assisting at the birth of such a boon to students of law and ethnology, and the able author, Mr. J. H. Wigmore, on his industry, lucidity, and remarkable powers of analysis and synthesis.[58]

Although Wigmore's teaching was concerned exclusively with Anglo-American law, which had no direct relevance to the contemporary situation in Japan, and although his research was in Japanese legal history, his work had a direct application to a burning contemporary issue. A controversy had arisen over whether the proposed Japanese Civil Code, based on European sources, should be immediately adopted and enforced, or whether there should be some postponement until the new code could also reflect national customs. Wigmore was able to refute the necessity for postponement by demonstrating in detail how the institutions, rules, and principles embodied in the proposed Civil Code did, in fact, reflect Japanese national customs. This was a contention that no Japanese jurist could refute, for, at that time, there was such preoccupation with the study of Western law, which they admired, that they had given little time to the study of early Japanese legal history which they regarded as "old musty feudal law which they held in contempt."[59]

But even in this highly specialized field with its local emphasis, Wigmore was not isolated. Copies of his studies soon came into the hands of scholars outside of Japan, including Justice Holmes, whose favorable commentary and encouragement were no doubt a source of satisfaction to Wigmore. To one of Holmes's letters Wigmore replied:

> It gave me great pleasure to hear that the subject attracted your notice, for as yet in our country the science of comparative law arouses no interest except among a very few scholars like yourself; and the worker in that field is glad for every trifle of encouragement. I hope, by the way, that next year some of the

younger men will be able to initiate a project long talked of by a few of us and organize a society which shall encourage legal science and legal reform in all its higher aspects.[60]

There is no doubt about the fact that Holmes was interested, for he later made a special point to inquire about the parts not originally published, indicating that, if they had since appeared, he would like to see them.[61]

In spite of Wigmore's interest in Japan and his obvious success there, there is no evidence that he planned at any time to stay there indefinitely. In fact, long before the completion of his three-year assignment at Keio University, he was making inquiries among his friends in the United States about possible opportunities, and, when the formal offer of a second three-year appointment came from the university, he declined it with thanks.[62] A teaching post in an American law school was his definite preference as well as Brandeis's strong recommendation:

> It would be a pity for you to return to practice. . . . you can be far more effective in the field which you already occupy, and in which so much remains to be done. . . .
>
> I am particularly anxious to have you in Massachusetts, because there is so much to be done in the law — outside of the Law School and I should hope — with you here that we might make an effort to establish some sort of an institute through which progressive work could be done. The Harvard Law Review has now a good circulation and would serve as an organ for any worthy publication. I shall be glad for my own sake to have you back. The demands of practice have drawn me too much from scholarly scientific work and need such a fellow as you are to build us up again to a higher level.[63]

Wigmore was no doubt encouraged by hearing that Law School matters were in a state of ferment, that his name was under consideration, and that if he were on hand, he "could easily secure a good position."[64] In response to an inquiry from Wigmore, Beale wrote:

> There seems to be a brisk demand, just now, for new Deans in western law schools; and new Deans mean also new professors, I suppose. So if you want to go into the west, this is a favorable opportunity for you to get back. . . . If, as I suppose, you will prefer to stay in Boston, I don't know that one season is much better than another to begin.[65]

But Wigmore not only made inquiries about possible opportunities but planned in advance to include in his return trip a visit to "all the prominent law schools, investigate their methods and thus feel that he is something of an authority on the subject."[66] Fortunately, he had saved enough money to make possible a leisurely appraisal of the situation, and he felt no need to accept the first offer.[67]

In view of subsequent events, Emma Wigmore's reaction to a possible offer from the Chicago area is interesting. In writing to her father at the time she said:

I don't quite agree with you in regard to Chicago, however. Chicago is big, and it may sometime be what you predict, but during our lifetime, I think the most sympathetic, invigorating, stimulating field for a man of brains is either New York or Boston. Yet one might have much worse luck than to go to Chicago and certainly the new University* is to have some fine men.[68]

Shortly before the Wigmores' departure the law students gave him a dinner. According to Mrs. Wigmore, "Harry had a fine time, and the students were most enthusiastic and complimentary."[69] Some appreciation of Wigmore's difficulty in teaching Anglo-American law to students whose mastery of English was hardly complete can be gleaned from the short "speeches" made by two students on this occasion, the texts of whose remarks have been preserved. The warm and appreciative attitude of these students toward their professor is embodied in what must have been most laboriously prepared statements. One confessed that his message reflected "the thought which is issuing from the bottom of my brain," and he made a special point of the fact that "outside of school the professor always treated students like his own younger brothers with a kindest and a warmest heart."[70] The other testified that "With all your diligence and all your kind heart, you inspired us about the Noble Science — the law . . . ''

The Wigmores responded to this gesture by giving a reception for students a few days later.[71]

On December 19, 1892, the Wigmores began the long return journey to Cambridge and the Boston area, stopping in San Francisco and Los Angeles for visits with members of his family[72] and making stops on their way east to visit a number of law schools. However eager they may have been to return to the United States, they must have felt a strong sense of satisfaction as they looked back on the three years spent in Japan. Although Wigmore was now only twenty-nine years of age his achievements were significant, and their value had been publicly acknowledged. An editorial note in the *Japan Daily Mail*, appearing several days before their departure, reflected this recognition:

Mr. and Mrs. J. H. Wigmore leave Tokyo on Monday by the 3:35 train from Shimbashi. It is a subject of great regret that Mr. Wigmore has determined to return to America, though we can well understand his desire to pursue the wider career which his abilities cannot fail to open to him in the States. During the three years of his residence in this country, his researches have been remarkably close and extended, and their results have thrown a flood of light on the customs and canons of the Japanese in pre-Restoration days. His last contribution to the Proceedings of the Asiatic Society is in itself a work that might well represent the result of three years labour. Occupying 443** pages of the Proceedings, it

---

*The University referred to was the University of Chicago, which was established in 1890 and was just getting under way. Its Law School was not started until 1902. Northwestern University, with campuses both in Chicago and Evanston, was established in 1851.

**This editorial apparently appeared before publication was complete. The four parts published in the supplement to volume 20 of the *Transactions* came to a total of 879 pages.

traverses almost the whole ground of private law in old Japan, and though Mr. Wigmore calls it by the modest title of "Materials for the Study" of that difficult and hitherto untouched subject, we are strongly disposed to think that the essay will remain a monograph for many a year to come. This, however, represents only a small fraction of Mr. Wigmore's work. His letters to the *Nation*, his articles in these columns, his lectures and his various papers on Japanese financial, parliamentary, and legal problems, indicate a power of research and a capacity of analysis and synthesis of a very high order. Mr. Wigmore's continued presence in this country would have enormously helped to elucidate much which has remained, and must remain, a *terra incognita*, unless some one similarly gifted with industry and acumen undertakes to exploit it. In bidding him farewell, we may be permitted to predict for him a career of high achievement and solid usefulness, and to thank him in the name of all students of Japan in particular and of ethnology in general for the admirable results he has accomplished. Mrs. Wigmore, we regret to learn, has been confined to her room for some days by a severe attack of lacquer poisoning, and has thus been obliged to dispense with many of the farewell visits which her numerous friend-ships, both foreign and Japanese, would otherwise have dictated.[73]

Many years later, discussing Wigmore's work in Japan, Kenzo Takayanagi cited an old Oriental proverb, "Sandal-wood is fragrant from the bud," meaning "Talent shows itself even at an early age."[74]

5
Northwestern University

Late in January 1893, Wigmore received a letter from Henry Wade Rogers, president of Northwestern University, containing the following statement:

> It now appears probable to me that there will be a vacancy in our Law School at the close of this college year, and my thought turns toward you, as being a suitable man for the position so soon to be vacated.
>
> The prospects for building up a great law school in Chicago are flattering, and our school is now doing magnificent work. One of the most active professors is a graduate of Yale; another a graduate of Harvard; another of Princeton; another of Cornell.[1]

Apparently because there was no suitable opening at the time at Harvard or in New York, Wigmore accepted the firm offer from President Rogers that soon followed[2] and committed himself to this assignment in spite of the fact that, as we have seen, Mrs. Wigmore, and probably Wigmore himself, did not regard Chicago as a particularly promising location at that time.[3]

But Wigmore certainly did not mark time in Boston while he was waiting to report to the law school at Northwestern University in September.[4] His steady flow of writings had now become predominantly legal in character. He also renewed and reinforced by direct contact associations that had been kept alive through correspondence. It must have been most gratifying to be welcomed back by Holmes to discuss his work in Japan[5] and other matters in which they were discovering a mutuality of interests. On a day late in February 1893, and shortly after the Wigmores had returned from Japan, Wigmore was Holmes's guest for lunch at Young's Hotel in Boston.[6] They sat at a window table looking out on the alley opposite the Old Court House while Wigmore listened to Holmes's "words of wisdom." Many years later, in writing to Holmes, Wigmore said, "I then thought that it was a *most* benevolent act, to give me those moments; and it helps me now to be patient with the young men who ask my advice. Your condescension long served to cheer me up."[7] And in writing to Holmes in commemoration of his birthday he said, "your words on that day have been like apples of silver to *me*; and on this your anniversary I like to repeat this acknowledgment of your influence upon your admiring disciple." [8]

Wigmore also lost no time in getting in touch with Brandeis to discuss not only matters concerning the Harvard Law School but a variety of subjects in which both of them had an interest. [9] Indeed his activities in Boston were so absorbing that he declined to teach in the summer school at Northwestern although the offered compensation was attractive. [10]

By the time Wigmore reported for duty in September at a basic salary of $2,500, plus an additional $500 on the understanding that he would act as secretary to the faculty, [11] he had received encouragement about his decision from a number of persons. Among them, Nathan Abbott, then on the Northwestern University Law School faculty, gave this appraisal, "It [Chicago] is the most attractive city I ever was in; the people are most charming; the opportunities in the Law School are the best in the country by all odds." [12]

Julian Mack, who, it will be recalled, was a classmate at Harvard, was already in practice in Chicago and was delighted at the prospect of having Wigmore at hand; he broadened the prospect by pointing out that there was more than one potential opportunity. He wrote, "only hope that you will not follow the other Northwestern men by moving to Evanston but will locate in my neighborhood on the South Side — where you will be in contact with the Chicago Univ. people and be ready to jump in when they organize a law school." [13]

And Charles Eliot, president of Harvard, expressed his attitude toward Wigmore's assignment as follows, "I congratulate you on having got into a missionary diocese. On the whole, missionary work is the most interesting part of the teacher's function, and there is a great need of it in the teaching of law." [14]

Although the Northwestern University Law School was located in downtown Chicago, Wigmore did not follow Mack's advice nor that of Abbott, who had also urged him to live in Chicago because the "suburban traffic is the worst possible." [15] The Wigmores settled near the Evanston Campus of Northwestern University, located on Lake Michigan, north of Chicago. He undoubtedly wanted to keep in close touch with faculty members in other departments of the university.

Wigmore and his wife spent the first few years in the home of Mrs. Sarah K. Rogers on Hinman Avenue, where several other couples connected with the university also lived and where at meal times Wigmore sat at the head of the high table. [16] A glimpse of the Wigmores in their domestic life during this early period is provided by Mrs. Agnes S. Bradley, the daughter of Daniel Freeman Smith, who was at the time the rector of St. Luke's Episcopal Church in Evanston:

> I had never before met such a delightful couple. They were absolutely devoted to one another without any narrowing of interest in other people or in the affairs of the world. She was very beautiful and he, extraordinarily distinguished in appearance, as in fact. To look at them was a delight, to enjoy their company

awakened new and broader interests in one's mind and heart. In spite of all they had to do they always had time for people, and they accomplished wonders at Mrs. Rogers' long dinner table of varied personalities in keeping the conversation at a high level, avoiding the discussion of inconvenient subjects and making each meal time a happy experience. Mr. Wigmore had a number of fascinating games ready to introduce and carry through in the evenings when anyone in the house had guests. But if someone persisted in following up a topic which he thought should not have come up, he quietly removed himself from the room, returning when he was sure the skies had cleared.[17]

While the Wigmores were living at Mrs. Rogers's they often sat on the porch alone together or with other guests. Apparently Harry had standards of deportment not only for himself but also for his wife. Helen K. McNamara recounts an anecdote that sets a scene typical of the period. On one occasion Wigmore suggested to his wife that they should take a short walk. Mrs. Wigmore rose, said she was ready, and started down the steps. "'Emma,' said Mr. Wigmore sternly, 'go upstairs and put on your hat. My wife will never appear on the public streets of any town without a hat.'"[18]

The Law School at which Wigmore arrived in September 1893 was located on the seventh floor of the Masonic Temple at Randolph and State streets, its fifth home in the heart of Chicago.[19] In 1859 two important events had combined to create the school "which was to become Northwestern University's School of Law," the first law school in Chicago. In that year Chicago University (not to be confused with the present University of Chicago, which was not in existence at that time) opened a Law Department, and the trustees of Northwestern University, having discussed the organization of a law school ever since the establishment of the university in 1851, finally authorized its own department in the same year. Doubting the need for two law schools in Chicago at that time, Northwestern University postponed its action pending discussion between the two universities, and on June 24, 1873, the Law Department of Chicago University "was declared to be also the Law Department of the Northwestern University."[20] It was to be operated by a joint executive committee as the Union College of Law of the Chicago University and the Northwestern University, and the universities mutually agreed to furnish $2,000 per annum each for its support, with the understanding that if "either party should fail to meet its financial obligations, the exclusive control of the Law Department should be assumed by the party that should have kept and fulfilled this agreement." In 1886, the old Chicago University discontinued its activities because of financial difficulties and Northwestern University assumed complete control of the Law Department. Formal designation of this department as the Northwestern University Law School took effect on July 1, 1891, and, all graduates who were alumni of the Union College of Law (1,000 at that time) were now declared alumni of the Northwestern University Law School.[21]

Although integration of the Law School into the university was an important step forward, the decade that followed was fraught with difficulties.

The most critical was the retirement at 73 of Dean Booth, an outstanding figure in the community, shortly after the university took complete control. For a decade the school was operated under three part-time administrators. Henry W. Blodgett, Booth's successor, was a federal judge who served for only about a year. In 1892 Northwestern University designated its president, Henry Wade Rogers, to serve as acting dean.[22]

As a teacher and secretary to the faculty Wigmore quickly established an excellent working relationship with Rogers who, as a former dean of the University of Michigan Law School, showed a great interest in the Law School and represented it effectively before the Board of Trustees. However, under such circumstances, Rogers was hard pressed with university problems, and Wigmore expected not only to deal with broad administrative responsibilities but to recruit and interview suitable candidates for faculty positions. Rogers soon recognized Wigmore's ability and broad interests and thus relied heavily upon him in Law School matters and matters of concern to the university as a whole.

In fulfilling his assignment Wigmore profited greatly from his association with Harvard University. President Eliot followed his work with interest and was often helpful.[23] At the Law School he kept in touch with Joseph H. Beale, who at one time proposed that they prepare together a casebook on the conflict of laws[24] and with James B. Thayer, with whom he shared a special interest in the law of evidence.[25] However, James Barr Ames, who became dean of the Harvard Law School in 1895, was his most important point of contact. Ames not only suggested graduates who might be considered for teaching positions but kept Wigmore in touch with what was going on in other law schools, offered suggestions, answered questions, and provided encouragement when developments at Northwestern fell below Wigmore's expectations.[26] This relationship reflected Wigmore's great interest in children. He practically never failed to enclose some stamps for Ames's "Little Robert," an act of thoughtfulness that was greatly appreciated.

As would be expected, Wigmore brought to Northwestern great zeal for the case method of instruction developed by Langdell at Harvard, whose influence was very high at the time. He not only used the method himself, relying on case books that were beginning to be available through direct negotiations with the editors,[27] but sought to persuade his colleagues to do so as well and recommended for appointment to the faculty men who taught in this manner. But moments of discouragement apparently came early, for in February 1894 Ames wrote, apparently in response to some statement by Wigmore, "This is doubtless your hardest year — But I have no doubt of your success just as we in Cambridge . . . have met with success in the face of much opposition."[28]

Beale also responded to an obvious expression of misgivings on Wigmore's part:

> I wish you the greatest success in your good work in the west. I don't believe you will find it at all unprofitable to have at least one man with you working in

the old way. We can convince only by comparison of results; that was the course of things here and at Columbia, and I have no doubt it will be equally true at Northwestern.[29]

Nor was resistance to the case method confined to Northwestern. In another letter Ames referred to Yale as follows: "Storey* ought not to give loose rein to his censorious spirit. From the Yale men I did not expect any sympathy. It is with much interest that I am waiting for the first sign of conversion at the Yale Law School."[30]

Not only the faculty were cool. That the students were by no means receptive is indicated by the following statement in a letter written by a student to Wigmore:

> I have just completed a digest of the Partnership cases and tonight several of us will join in a quiz for our own benefit and to allay the terrors of some of the "weak sisters." The course has been very satisfactory and I am more than ever a convert to the "Case" System.

> I think our class would have accepted the case books without criticism from the beginning had we not felt somewhat, the influence of the Seniors, who were, to the most of us the Oracles, deep in the mysteries of legal science. I know now, that every strong man in the class is a thorough convert to the system.[31]

But it is clear that in Wigmore's relationship to Harvard he was by no means only a recipient. In his correspondence he often discussed matters of interest to Harvard, and he sometimes made suggestions. He encouraged outstanding Japanese applicants to seek admission to the Law School and supported their applications.[32] He was the first person to propose that the Harvard Club of Chicago sponsor a Law School scholarship, and he supported it year after year.[33] Loyalty to the class of '83, he felt, involved more than the payment of dues and answers to requests for information: his expressed appreciation of the efforts of the class secretary brought warm acknowledgment: "Your friendly and thoughtful note has given me needed encouragement, and I beg to offer you my cordial appreciation. . . . you are the first one who has been so kindly inspired as to cheer my efforts by any sympathetic commendation."[34]

Attention has already been called to Wigmore's cordial and constructive working relationship with President Rogers. He was on good terms with the other administrative officers at Northwestern as well,[35] and he sought happily and effectively to attract new men to the law faculty and work with them as colleagues. Blewett Lee acknowledged Wigmore's role in attracting him to the faculty in 1893: "I have just telegraphed and written Dr. Rogers accepting the position offered me in your faculty. The fact of being associated closely with yourself as colleague has been a great factor in inducing my acceptance."[36] And after seven years of such association Lee wrote:

*Moorfield Storey, president of the American Bar Association, in 1895–96.

Accept my very warm thanks for your kindness in making up the list of cases for me. I had no idea of putting you to so much trouble, but I am grateful for it. I might as well realize that it has become impossible for you to do anything in a manner which is not thorough.[37]

In 1899, after Charles Cheney Hyde had been under consideration for a long time he wrote:

It gives me great pleasure to say that last night the Executive Committee of the University confirmed the action of the Law School faculty in regard to my lectureship. I wish I might adequately express my honest appreciation of your kindness to me while the appointment has been pending. I thank you sincerely for all that you have done and for the deep interest you have shown in my work along the lines of American diplomacy.[38]

The courses that Wigmore taught during his early years as a faculty member included Torts and Evidence. Torts was a subject to which he had, as we have seen, contributed significant articles; and Evidence was another major interest and the one with which his name was to become universally identified. In respect to the subject of torts, Ames wrote, ''I am glad you are teaching that subject which needs so much clearing up . . . Pollock* in his books seems to me quite in the dark.''[39]

During his first year, Wigmore also taught Common Law Pleading and Conflict of Laws. In the second year he acquired Quasi-Contracts as a continuing responsibility. Other courses taught during the first few years were the Law of Persons; International Law, Public and Private; Domestic Relations; Bailments and Carriers; and Master and Servant.

Wigmore also participated with other faculty members in the Moot Court program (in which the students thought he was not liberal in granting As)[40] and as a debate adviser, making himself available as an intercollegiate judge on a number of occasions. Because of his wide-ranging interests, this diversity of subject matter, inevitable with such a small faculty, could not have posed any serious problems, other than the necessity for special preparation when the responsibility for a new course was assumed.[41]

There is no doubt that Wigmore was highly regarded as a teacher by his colleagues on the faculty. Although evidence of what the students thought of him at the time is meager, we do have records of student evaluations made later and in the perspective of time. Among many is the following description and appraisal of Wigmore's teaching made by Charles B. Elder, who entered the Law School in 1896 and subsequently practiced in Chicago and served as a nonresident faculty member from 1901–38.

We beginners in the first year, entered Professor Wigmore's class in Torts, and saw as our instructor a rather formal, scholarly appearing gentleman, approaching the middle thirties. He was of medium height, had light brown hair

*Sir Frederick Pollock, English author on the law of torts and other legal subjects.

parted evenly above a high symmetrical forehead, gray eyes, a light brown moustache moderately heavy. He invariably wore a standing collar with rounded wings, a black satin four-in-hand tie, loosely tied, and dark clothes. His hands, backed by round cuffs with large gold buttons, moved the papers before him lightly and skillfully, and he spoke with a moderate, but clear baritone voice.

His classroom work consisted largely of lectures from voluminous notes. Then, as always, he possessed a genius for classification, and, on occasion, a predilection for nomenclature. Some of the students were impatient with "irrecusable obligations," "nexus," and "the tripartite division of torts." The more scholarly followed his thought, read his article in the *Harvard Law Review*,[42] and appreciated the brilliant clarity of his intellectual processes, and the sound law underlying his work. In recitation periods, he sometimes became impatient with individuals, but this was impersonal, instantaneous only, and impartial. He seemed to have no favorites, was reserved, and busy, but not unpopular. He must have excited interest in the subject matter, for the memory of *Scott v. Shepard*[43] and other cases abides with some of us even unto this day. In his second-year course on Evidence, a brief syllabus embodying his admirable classification, with reference to Thayer's *Cases*,[44] and occasionally to Greenleaf,[45] furnished an excellent key to the subject and to the classroom discussions. Students in this class could, and for the most part did, obtain a real reasoned understanding and permanent knowledge of the elements of this important subject.

On rare occasions, before classes, he would pass through the corridor to the faculty room accompanied by Mrs. Wigmore and some lady friend, and loitering students would catch glimpses of that social grace and charm characteristic of him.[46]

Some additional insight into Wigmore's teaching methods is provided by General Nathan William MacChesney, who was a student of Wigmore in the early days and later a member of the university Board of Trustees.

One of my earliest recollections of the enthusiasm of Wigmore and the pains he took to have the students understand what they were studying is in connection with a course on "Carriers" he taught in the first year. He had collected baggage checks, bills of lading, tickets, etc., from all over the world and I can see him yet climbing up on chairs and step ladder and tacking them all over the library . . . He had every student on the move, in business, or traveling for pleasure, in the United States and foreign countries.[47]

And from another student, after several years in practice, came the following appreciative words in a letter to Wigmore:

I desire to express to you my keen appreciation of the excellence of the training of which I was fortunate enough to avail myself, at North Western. Especially to yourself and Prof. Harriman do I feel grateful for the wonderfully thorough and satisfactory courses in your departments, and the benefits I derived from them become more and more apparent to me every day. I assure you that as I feel now I should not be willing to trade my one year at N.W. for two at any other law school in the United States.[48]

Wigmore's impact on the Law School was far greater than that derived merely from his role as a teacher. Even after he relinquished his role as secretary to the faculty in 1895,[49] he worked constantly to improve the conditions under which the faculty worked and to raise the standards of performance of the school as a whole. From the beginning, he was interested in developing a library for the Law School's exclusive use,[50] but progress was slow at first, for funds were difficult to secure. Although as we have seen the case method met with some resistance, it became firmly established and was accepted by the students. A law review was started in 1893, but, apparently, the venture was premature for it was discontinued in 1896.[51]

A significant change in this period was the increase in the required period of study for the Bachelor of Laws degree from two to three years. A report of the faculty, in Wigmore's handwriting, as secretary, urged the university to take this step and called attention to the fact that Boston, Columbia, and Harvard had already adopted such a requirement, that Michigan and Yale planned to do so, and that the legislatures of Ohio and Wisconsin had required it for their states. Although such was not the case in Illinois, the faculty strongly recommended the change, and was supported by President Rogers, who, in his report of June 11, 1895, to the Board of Trustees, said that it no longer seemed "in keeping with the dignity of the University"[52] to confer the degree at the end of two years. On the same day, the board voted to adopt the three-year requirement for the LL.B. degree to become effective with the year 1896–97.[53]

An interesting appraisal of Wigmore's early impact on the Law School is provided by Henry M. Bates, who was later dean of the University of Michigan Law School:

> I think I suggested to you once before that my only criticism of you is that you did not occur early enough. You know what a frightfully stodgy or dogmatic legal education, so-called, I received at Northwestern. You came in the year after my graduation and within an astonishingly short time had assembled a brilliant faculty; but the plain truth is my most important and difficult task in relation to myself has been to divest myself, so far as possible, at least, of all general ideas and of the attitude toward law which I acquired in those two years. Fortunately, I knew at the time that it was not the real thing, though what the real thing was I could only surmise.[54]

Although Wigmore's position as a faculty member had a salutory effect on the Law School, and although the situation in fact improved, the funds available at the time were not sufficient to meet its needs as Wigmore conceived them. The decade of the 1890s was a difficult period and the future was by no means assured. That Wigmore was not entirely satisfied with his prospects is evident from the fact that as early as the spring of 1894 he was making inquiries of a friend about a possible vacancy at the Cornell Law School.[55] He also solicited the support of his friends in San Francisco, including Franklin K. Lane, concerning an expected vacancy at the Hastings College of Law.[56] Nothing came of these efforts, and it is extremely doubtful that the posts would have been attractive to Wigmore had he received an offer.

But the frustrations in the Law School and his disappointments concerning opportunities elsewhere were offset by the fact that Wigmore was attracting attention both as a writer and as a teacher, and it was not surprising that in 1899 he was actively considered for the deanship of the Law School at the University of Illinois.[57]

Although, as is perfectly evident, Wigmore threw himself into his work at the Law School both as a teacher and as secretary to the faculty with his usual enthusiasm and vigor, these activities did not diminish his performance as an able and prolific writer. Among the most significant contributions made during this early period at Northwestern was a series of articles in the *Harvard Law Review* during 1894 and 1895 under the titles: "Responsibility for Tortious Acts, Its History";[58] "The Tripartite Division of Torts";[59] and "A General Analysis of Tort Relations."[60] Following the history of torts law, as developed in the first article, Wigmore said in the second article that the time was ripe for a broader analysis as a general foundation for the treatment of all torts, and identified the three basic elements as (1) harm, (2) responsibility, and (3) excuse. In the third article, Wigmore went forward from the three groupings in the "Tripartite Division of Torts" and attempted an analysis of each division. He accepted the theory that the right to freedom from certain harmful results went beyond the mere right to recover compensation.

Upon reading the proofs of the second part of "Responsibility for Tortious Acts," Ames commented on some matters of detail, "It is a very valuable contribution. It does not occur to me to add anything to what you have written. . . . I am glad for your distinctive comments upon Judge Holmes' 'Duplicate' Theory."[61] Frederick Pollock, in responding to a letter from Wigmore in which Wigmore was apparently concerned over the possibility of the appearance of plagiarism, said:

> I have been following your articles with much interest, but had not noticed that particular coincidence. You have done quite enough of your own to be absolved from any possible suspicion.
>
> I agree with your distinction in the March No. of Harv. Law Rev.[62] between analysis of ideas and exposition of rules. There should be, in a given system, only one true analysis — though perhaps capable of expression in forms that seem widely different at first. But several quite different arrangements of the same matter may be equally helpful and appropriate for different purposes. Speculative jurists have been apt to neglect this consideration.[63]

But Wigmore must have been gratified at the approval of Holmes above all — the relationship between junior and senior scholar had become extremely warm. In thanking Holmes for his words of commendation Wigmore wrote, "I am extremely glad that my generalizations commend themselves to you. You see that I drew my inspiration from your chapters."[64]

In another letter to Holmes, in which he dealt at some length with his tripartite approach, he fell back on his experience in Japan:

I beg to salute you and prostrate myself respectfully nine times (as the Japanese say), for I want to say to you, what I have always said to others, that I venture to regard you as our greatest American or English analyst and jurisprudent. I write this now in the ardor of pleasure at finding in the current Law Review 1) that your great support can now be claimed for what has been for two or three years a solid conviction of mine, what I may call the tripartite division of tort questions into Damage (or Injury), Responsibility, and Justification (or Excuse), and 2) that you believe that Motive and Malice are to be discussed under the last head. I have groaned in spirit at the difficulty of persuading the profession to accept this second point especially (the first can be conclusively demonstrated); but now that you have said it, it must "go," and other men will be listened to where you have sanctioned the thesis they are advancing. . . . We have to thank you for a step which will ultimately make the heterodox orthodox. It has at any rate made me very happy.[65]

Holmes continued this exchange by replying, "As far as I see we agree in our views substantially, and your kind expressions give me great pleasure. You have every good wish from me in this career which you have begun with so much promise and success."[66] In March 1895 Holmes closed a letter by saying, "If you ever come this way let me know it, I beg."[67]

It will be recalled that Wigmore's developing interest in criminal law first reflected itself in his "Circumstantial Evidence in Poisoning Cases" for which he was awarded first prize by the Medico-Legal Society.[68] Another case with which he dealt was the Borden case,[69] a notorious Massachusetts double-murder case in which the defendant was a woman. Wigmore's characteristic thoroughness in preparation was illustrated by the fact that he not only secured all relevant information from the prosecuting attorney in the case but submitted his manuscript for criticisms and suggestions, with the understanding, of course, that the prosecuting attorney was to assume no responsibility for the presentation.[70] This article was followed by one on the Durrant case, involving a murder in San Francisco, in which Wigmore discussed the right of editorial comment and reporting during a trial and the privilege of a witness to be protected from irrelevant questions.[71] A fourth article, on the Luetgert case, appeared in 1898.[72] Wigmore apparently could not resist the Dreyfus case, at least for an oral presentation, and it was the subject of his address before the Chicago Law Club on September 30, 1899.[73]

In all of these cases Wigmore not only considered the law of evidence an important factor but put forth the results of his intensive study of the subject which he had become convinced required a thoroughgoing revision. During this same period he dealt directly with four aspects of the law of evidence under the titles "Proof by Comparison of Handwriting; Its History,"[74] "Proof of Character by Personal Knowledge or Opinion: Its History"[75] (in which he examined the now prevailing reputation rule); "Confessions; A Brief History and a Criticism,"[76] (in which he favored the admission of all well-proved confessions), and "A View of the Parole-Evidence Rule."[77]

But the culmination of this initial work in the law of evidence was
Wigmore's revision of Volume I of the sixteenth edition of Simon Greenleaf's *A Treatise on the Law of Evidence* [78] "to bring the text into harmony
with the established results of modern research." [79] In acknowledging receipt of a copy of the volume, after he had examined it, Professor Thayer
said, "How kindly you speak of me and what I have done, and how much
cause you give me for reflection on some topics. . . . I am sure that you
have put the profession under great obligations to you and that you have
done all that can be done to rehabilitate your learned author." [80] And several
months later he also wrote, "am constantly referring my men to your
Greenleaf." [81] Official recognition also came from home. President Rogers
said, ". . . it is an honor to the University to have such work go out to the
profession as having been done by one of our professors." [82]

For an over-all appraisal of the new Greenleaf we can turn to a review by
Joseph P. Colton, Jr., who rightly called attention to the great difficulties
involved in reflecting within the original framework of the book the many
changes in the law that had occurred since the publication of the first edition
in 1842. Commenting on the book as a whole, he wrote:

> The amount of work in Mr. Wigmore's edition is monumental, more, it seems,
> than if he had written an entirely new Treatise. Not only is the law of evidence
> carefully examined and minutely worked out, but, harder still, all this new
> matter he has fitted into the original Greenleaf, and the work is well done. The
> completeness of the lists of authorities brought down to date, care in composi-
> tion, a thorough grasp of principles, and orderly workmanship at once mark the
> work apart from the modern machine-made text-book. [83]

The appraisal of the publisher, Little, Brown and Company, is also
significant because the Greenleaf volume inaugurated a relationship between the company and Wigmore that lasted for forty-four years, until the
time of Wigmore's death. Of the first manuscript of the man who was to
become the company's most prolific author, the company wrote, "As we
now feel that it is unlikely that another edition of the work will ever be
called for we are especially glad that this one promises to be the most
perfect and complete of all the editions issued." [84]

Little, Brown and Company was unquestionably right about the imprac-
ticability of a further edition of Greenleaf, for there was a brisk demand
among publishers for a completely new work, and the company had a
promise from Wigmore that they would be given the first chance at his
"own magnum opus" [85] for which he had already laid the foundation.
Seymour Thompson, one of the editors of the *American Law Review*,
believed not only that there was such a demand but that it would take ten
large volumes to cover this subject matter and that the work would have a
wide sale. [86] Indeed, Thompson, very much opposed to Wigmore's participation in the revision of Greenleaf, had written: "if you expect to take a
position as the author of a work on Evidence, you have made a mistake in
letting yourself down so far as to become the editor of the work of another
author, however eminent." [87]

Although such an appraisal might perhaps apply to a lesser scholar, the volume was quite clearly recognized as the work of Wigmore. In 1902 it won for him the first Ames Prize, a prize established by his Harvard Law School classmate Julian W. Mack and awarded by the Harvard Law School faculty every four years for the most meritorious law book or legal essay in English that had been published not less than one year or more than five years before the award.

But these writings in the field of torts, criminal law, and evidence were by no means all of Wigmore's early legal scholarship. His interest in comparative law, which permeated so much of his work, bore fruit in "The Pledge Idea: A Study in Comparative Legal Ideas," [88] in which he examined the Germanic, Scandinavian, Jewish, Japanese, Chaldean, Slavic, Mohammedan, Hindu, Roman, and French law. This work was described by Ames at the time as a "solid contribution," [89] by Ernest Freund as "extremely instructive," [90] and, many years later, by Pound as "a lasting contribution on which much has since been built." [91] Robert W. Millar, a student of Wigmore and later a colleague on the Law School faculty, characterized it as "that remarkable essay" that "stamped him at once as possessed of a master hand." [92] Somewhat belatedly, Wigmore's "The Administration of Justice in Japan," a paper presented to the Section of Jurisprudence and Law Reform of the World's Congress on Government which met in Chicago in 1893, appeared in the *American Law Register and Review* in 1897. [93]

But Wigmore was not only making a contribution to legal literature upon which practitioners, teachers, and scholars could draw, he was mindful of his special role as an educator as well. His "Legal Education in Modern Japan" (1893),[94] an illustrated article in two installments, was followed by "A Principle of Orthodox Legal Education," [95] initially an address given before the American Bar Association, in which he contended that adequate training in law cannot be gained while pursuing an outside occupation at the same time — a much debated question in his day, and even now, and one with which the better law schools were concerned. Wigmore also prepared syllabuses in Evidence, Quasi-Contracts, and International Law for the use of students in his own classes, a typical activity for that period.

An important aid in the field of legal education illustrated Wigmore's inclination to make useful information available, particularly when no one else was inclined to do so. Collecting examinations from a number of law schools, he compiled them in a book entitled *Examinations in Law, Consisting of Practical Problems and Cases* (1899). The purpose, as expressed in the preface, was to stimulate the use of "concrete hypothetical cases" not only by the law schools but by the official examiners for admission to the bar. But Wigmore's wide-ranging interests were not restricted within the confines of traditional legal boundaries. He was, among other things, an avid reader of fiction. From the numerous works of fiction that he had read, he selected about a hundred of particular significance from a legal point of view for his "List of Legal Novels," published in 1900 and thereafter from time to time in an expanded form.[96] Among those who thought well of the selection was Franklin K. Lane who sent a copy of the list to young Robert Taft, then a young law student. Wigmore's irresistible impulse to put ideas into verse and his irrepressible sense of humor found outlets in "Reversible Cases in Illinois"[97] and "(Sug-) Jestive Cases."[98]

In spite of Wigmore's responsibilities at the Law School and an already impressive record for scholarly work, he apparently gave up more popular journalistic efforts for which he had shown considerable talent while in Japan only reluctantly. His correspondence shows that he endeavored, unsuccessfully, to interest the *Atlantic Monthly*, *The Forum*, *Harper's Weekly*, and *Scribner's* in such manuscripts.[99] In all cases the rejections stated that the subject matter was not suitable for the particular publication. Although this may in some cases have merely been a polite matter of form, one of several submissions to *Harper's Weekly* elicited this response, "[it] is the most interesting and the soundest article on the subject that I have ever read, but unfortunately it does not lend itself in any way to the purposes of *Harper's Weekly*. . . . However, it is a paper which, it seems to me, ought certainly to be printed."[100] And on behalf of the *Atlantic Monthly*, Walter H. Page wrote:

> We thank you for your kindness in submitting your articles, which we are sorry to say do not come within the proper scope of the *Atlantic Monthly*. It is with great regret that we see papers of such intrinsic value and so well presented go out of our hands, and we should be very glad indeed to hear from you whenever you happen to have any subject that comes within the range of the Atlantic.[101]

At the turn of the century Wigmore reached the age of thirty-seven years. He was emerging as a commanding figure in the world of legal education. The high quality of his scholarship had been clearly demonstrated, and the significance of his contributions was recognized and appreciated. As we shall see later, his potentialities as a leader were also already evident. That he should be restless and somewhat dissatisfied is understandable. He needed a more adequate outlet for his indefatigable energy and the exercise of his diverse talents.

6

Dean

||||||||||||||||||||||||||||||||||||||||||||||||||||||||||||||||||||||||||||||||||||||||||||||||||||||||||||||||||||||||||||||||

Upon landing in New York City in August 1901, after a summer spent in Europe, Wigmore received a telegram from Henry S. Towle, chairman of the Law Committee of the Northwestern Board of Trustees, requesting him to come at once to Chicago.[1] Apparently Wigmore had been reluctant to take any step until there was some affirmative evidence that the Board of Trustees was willing to provide the financial support that Wigmore believed the Law School required. On September 11, 1901, in a letter discussing the situation in the Law School in great detail, E. A. Harriman wrote, "I have entire sympathy with your feelings in regard to the management of the school, but I am not inclined to agree with your conclusion that the best thing to do is to remain in Cambridge until the Trustees do something. . . ."[2]

When this letter was shortly followed by a telegram from Blewett Lee, another colleague on the faculty, reading "In your own interests please return to Chicago at once,"[3] the Wigmores abandoned their plan to pay a visit to Mrs. Wigmore's family in Boston and went directly to Chicago, where Wigmore found that the Board of Trustees had decided to offer him the deanship of the Law School.[4] Knowing only too well the chaotic situation in the Law School at the time, for it had been without an effective head for almost a decade, he accepted with some misgivings. In his own words: "The prospects of the School and of the University at that time were not favorable."[5]

Wigmore's appointment was welcomed by his colleagues on the faculty, by graduates of the Law School, and by leaders in legal education, and he received many congratulatory letters. Indicative of his international reputation was a letter from Professor Alfred Nerincx of the Faculty of Law of the University of Louvain, in which he said, "I congratulate the N.W. men who had the sense to keep you and to let you have your own way with the School. I am sure it could not be in better hands."[6]

But the good wishes of Wigmore's colleagues and friends did not obviate the fact that as dean he would be faced with a difficult situation. President Henry Wade Rogers had resigned in 1900, and the university was under the leadership of Dr. Daniel Bonbright as acting president. Judge Peter S. Grosscup, who had nominally been the dean since 1898, had been completely inactive except to hold an occasional meeting in his office at the request of the faculty; in the last year he had even failed to fulfill his commitment to give a lecture course. The young teachers who had been brought into the faculty by Dr. Rogers in 1893 were being drawn away by the attractions of active practice, and the school "seemed to be disintegrating."[7]

There were, however, several encouraging factors. The university had recently purchased the Tremont Building, in the heart of Chicago, and was remodeling it for university purposes. Thus more adequate quarters for the Law School were in prospect. Wigmore himself had secured almost $10,000 from a canvass among friends to create a basic collection for the law library. And the faculty was planning to develop interest among the alumni who had not been solicited at all.[8]

An event of great concern to Wigmore was the decision of the University of Chicago, under the direction of Dr. William Rainey Harper as president, to establish in 1902, a first-class law school on a permanent and endowed basis. Joseph Beale of the Harvard Law School had been selected to organize the faculty and assume the deanship for two years. In Wigmore's words this was a "blow . . . which for a time threatened virtually to annihilate the School; which it was indeed intended to accomplish."[9] This was clearly Dr. Harper's intention. When Ames told Harper that in establishing another law school in Chicago he would have to consider the Law School at Northwestern University, he replied: "Oh, I know that. I have invited four of its best men and that will be the end of that school."[10]

Shortly after the public announcement from President Harper that the new Law School at the University of Chicago would be established, he invited Wigmore to join the new law faculty at a salary considerably in excess of the increased salary which had just been authorized by the Northwestern University Board of Trustees. Some years later, when recording this episode, Wigmore said, "I was extremely tempted; for Dr. Harper was a very plausible persuader. To overcome my hesitation, he told me to name my own salary; he promised me the succession to Joseph Beale at the end of two years; and he offered to let me name any two of my present colleagues[11] to go with [me] to the new School. Considering all the circumstances, I am at a loss now to understand just how I finally decided to resist his temptations."[12]

If Wigmore had accepted the offer and taken two faculty members with him there is no doubt about the result: the Law School at Northwestern would have been closed by the Board of Trustees.[13]

But now his ships were burned behind him, and Wigmore, at thirty-nine, was confronted with the difficult task of building up the Law School without any endowment. The threat posed by developments at the University of Chicago, however, reinforced him in his urgent request for greater financial support from the university. In the words of his colleague, E. A. Harriman, who had recently resigned from the faculty to devote himself to practice, "Even in December, when I was in Chicago, it seemed to me that you were making a heroic stand against great odds. And now comes Dr.

Harper with his 'Ulpen Rockefeller,' and behold, a stream of gold flows forth, and the humble law professor becomes a coy Danae.''[14]

Harriman's statement as to the sudden availability of funds was of course an exaggeration, but the change in the attitude of the Board of Trustees was significant. The goal of more adequate quarters was now in sight, and there was at least a reasonable prospect of attracting and holding a faculty that could meet the needs of the school, a task that became Wigmore's main objective.[15] Wigmore made sure that these changes in attitude and purpose were reflected in the dissemination of information about the Law School. Harriman, who was following developments with great interest, wrote, ''Your new circular is most interesting; it fairly throbs with new life; but what a task you must have had to arrange for so much!''[16]

When completed, the new Law School quarters were commodious and handsomely equipped. They occupied the entire third floor of the Tremont Building, a floor space of 23,000 square feet, more than seven times as large as the previous quarters. Included were, ''two lecture rooms, a court room, an alumni room, a student's assembly room, several private studies for the school law clubs and similar purposes, besides a set of 200 lockers and the usual offices and professors' rooms, as well as a library and reading-room occupying 5,000 square feet of floor space.''[17]

Wigmore worked hard to convert the third floor of an ''unattractive old building'' into an area having an ''atmosphere separate and distinct from the rest of the building and where the traditions and learning and romance of the law seemed at home.''[18] In what were probably Wigmore's own words, ''the removal to the new quarters on September 1, 1902, will be the signal for a great advance in the usefulness of the School in all directions, and will mark a new epoch in its important function as an early pioneer and a modern leader in legal education in the West.''[19]

In order to dramatize the significance of the new quarters, Wigmore planned an impressive dedication, and President Theodore Roosevelt agreed to appear and speak.[20] When illness prevented the president's attendance, the dedication was postponed for two weeks, and Oliver Wendell Holmes, who had also been invited, was secured as the distinguished guest speaker. Holmes was, at the time, chief justice of the Supreme Judicial Court of Massachusetts, but his name was then before the Senate as a nominee for justice of the United States Supreme Court, a position he assumed on December 4, 1902. Although Holmes was somewhat condescending in his acceptance, he apparently enjoyed the experience, for he wrote to Lady Pollock:

> I have just taken 3 or 4 days off with some qualms to go to Chicago . . . for the purpose primarily of pleasing Wigmore, Dean of the North Western University Law School, and giving him a puff. I think him a very deserving and quite superior man in what I have read and seen of him. He generally has pitched into me — the young fellows are apt to try their swords in that way — but his implications are flattering and his work good. The Chicago Bar united in his invitation by offering me a banquet, and so for two days and a half I was in

alternate crowds of College Presidents (there was a new president to be inaugurated) [Edmund J. James] and of Judges and leaders of the bar, so I was a howling swell for a time and they seemed to like it and I did. I got back last night. I made two speeches[21] which were two more than I felt up to, but they also seemed to please. Indeed, as I soaped the Dean I was sure of having one hearer in my favor. But I said no more than I meant. The next pleasantest thing to being intelligently cracked up oneself is to give a boost to a younger man who seems to deserve it, and who has not yet had much public recognition.[22]

One thing is certain: the cordial relationship between Wigmore and Holmes that had existed since 1887 was ripening into the extremely warm personal friendship that lasted until the justice's death. In writing to Wigmore immediately afterward Holmes said,

Of course my greatest pleasure was seeing more of you than I had before (I include Madame under ''you'') — nothing I am sure will stop your continued success except the possibility that you run your machine too hard. That really made me anxious — don't do it — have fixed hours — *don't work at night* — and have distractions of an un- or not too- intellectual sort . . . There was not a single contretemps and I am very glad I came.[23]

Apparently Holmes's solicitude for him suggested to Wigmore that he might not have appeared in complete command of the situation during the dedication ceremonies, for although Wigmore's letter to Holmes is lost to us, Holmes wrote, ''I detected no symptoms of nervousness in you — and my friendly exhortation was based solely on what I knew you were doing and the fear that it must be too much for anyone.''[24]

Rebuilding and enlarging the faculty was Wigmore's major task, and the added financial support from the Board of Trustees allowed it to become a reality. The *Law School Bulletin* of May 1902 summed up the situation:

First, the sum of $10,000 (the income of a quarter of a million of dollars) was added to the annual income of the School. The result of this is to enable the School hereafter to maintain, as the nucleus of its Faculty, a staff of six professors, giving the whole or the substance of their time to the work of research and instruction. With these will be associated as many more experienced members of the bar, in charge of those subject [sic] which directly involve drill and training in methods of practice. Besides these, a number of lecturers will deliver courses upon special topics. While thus increasing the School's facilities and requirements for scholarly and scientific study and research, its work will be greatly strengthened in all that pertains to practical skill in the use of legal knowledge. The variety and value of the training hereafter to be offered in such subjects as conveyancing, pleading and procedure, trial practice, and the like, may be gathered from the outline of courses announced on page 13 in this number of the BULLETIN. It may be said that the School's facilities in this department of work will now be unexcelled.[25]

However, Wigmore knew that such support as he could expect from the university would not be enough, and in addition to securing donations from individuals interested in the school he also turned his attention to the graduates of the Law School who had previously been more or less ignored. Among these was Elbert H. Gary, a graduate of the Union College of Law and chairman of the board of the United States Steel Corporation, who thereafter repeatedly provided funds for the development of the library collection. In the year 1901–2 the Alumni Association undertook to form branches in each judicial district of Illinois outside of Cook County as well as in every state and territory in which there were graduates of the school — fifty-four groups altogether.[26] Thus a broad base of financial support was established and the groundwork laid for the widespread and extraordinary personal relationships that existed between Wigmore and "his boys," as he liked to call them. Countless letters testify to the fact that Wigmore followed many of them throughout their careers — counseling, encouraging, commending, or congratulating as the occasion required. One graduate who was establishing himself as a teacher replied to a letter from Wigmore with appreciation: "Since receiving your very acceptable letter in reply, I have ceased being the creature and instead have become the creator of conditions."[27] Wigmore's interest in "his boys" often extended to their children and and he and his wife were "uncle" and "aunt" to many.

The following letters from one such young friend who lived in Kankakee, Illinois, are typical:

December 17, 1912.

Dean John H. Wigmore
Chicago, Illinois
Dear Dean Wigmore: —
I am in the second grade at school. I am going to College at Northwestern and then to your Law School. I want you for my teacher.
Dean Wigmore, I like you.
Good night,
Willard J. Buntain

June 29, 1915.

Dear Dean Wigmore: —
I love you. I am coming to Chicago to see your Law School some day. How is Auntie Wigmore? Are they selling fire crackers in Chicago?
Good-bye,
Willard Buntain[28]

Communication with Law School graduates was maintained not only through official alumni groups but also through annual banquets and through the *Law School Bulletin*, which was issued on a quarterly basis beginning in 1902. Though the *Bulletin* evidently contained articles from time to time of more than transitory merit, they were not covered by a general index and in effect are lost to us.

But Wigmore was of course not exclusively preoccupied with the graduates of the Law School. His circle of professional and personal friends constantly expanded, thus enhancing the reputation of the Law School and increasing his stature in the legal profession. His loyalty to both the school and the profession made him sensitive to criticisms, particularly if they were unjustified, but he usually responded with an effort to educate his critics rather than to confront them. Hearing that a prominent minister had expressed the view that lawyers are "parasitical and of little or no value to society," for example, he invited him to attend a meeting at the Law School at which a number of alumni were present. "As he [the minister] gazed at the body of substantial gentlemen and listened to the discussion [one could] see his eyes widen with interest and appreciation. From that time on, the law and the Law School had a real place in his view of things."[29]

But in all of his promotional work Wigmore never lost sight of the importance of the faculty. He had a great capacity for discovering promising young men and encouraging and supporting them in their work. The strong influence of the Harvard Law School on Wigmore's personal background as well as on the curriculum and teaching methods he and his associates adopted has already been mentioned. Yet Wigmore made a strong effort to develop a stable faculty by often selecting the Law School's own graduates and encouraging innovations that reflected the interests of his own faculty members or were responses to local needs. Indeed, Wigmore soon recognized what many other law-school teachers took much longer to appreciate: namely, that the "case method" did not meet all the needs of legal education and should not be regarded as the exclusive method of instruction.

One new member of the faculty, Roscoe Pound, was distinctive from the beginning. He had not attended the Harvard Law School and, therefore, did not, in his training, represent the Harvard influence; nor was he a graduate of Northwestern. Pound first came to Wigmore's special attention through his address "The Causes of Popular Dissatisfaction with the Administration of Justice," which he gave at the American Bar Association meeting in 1906[30] when he was dean of the College of Law at the University of Nebraska. In responding to Wigmore's commendatory letter Pound wrote:

> I am indeed obliged to you for your very kind and encouraging note in the matter of my paper read recently before the American Bar Association. Probably I do not need to tell you that the practitioners do not all take the same view.
>
> Neither do you need to be told that the inspiration and a great deal of the actual material of the paper was derived from a somewhat careful reading of your work on Evidence. Our judges ought to be made in some way to read the critical portions of that book.[31]

Although Pound became a member of the faculty in September 1907, he left in September 1909 to join the faculty of the University of Chicago's new Law School — a fierce blow to a dean who was working desperately to develop his faculty and whose own deep commitment to the Northwestern

Law School was a reflection of his exceptional sense of loyalty. Paul Sayre, Pound's biographer, reproduces a telephone conversation between Wigmore and Dean James P. Hall of the University of Chicago Law School, which he acknowledges may not be literally correct. He reports it as follows:

> Wigmore: "Is this Dean Hall?"
> Hall: "Yes."
> Wigmore: "This is Wigmore."
> Hall: "How do you do, Mr. Wigmore."
> Wigmore: "I called to ask if you propose to steal any other members of our faculty here."

Dean Wigmore spoke in a high-pitched voice and in evident anger. Dean Hall, on the contrary, spoke softly and without the slightest apparent emotion. Dean Hall paused a moment and then with a Brahmin-like calm answered:

> "Let me see, Mr. Wigmore, whom else have you there that is worth stealing?"
> Bang, went the telephone, and that was the end of the conversation.[32]

Wigmore's part in this exchange may very well have been accurately reported, but when his anger cooled he was no doubt able to view the situation more objectively. Subsequent events clearly indicated that he harbored no animus toward the University of Chicago, and whatever his feelings toward Pound may have been at the moment, there was no permanent impairment of their friendship. Their many interests in common provided the basis for a close friendship that extended until Wigmore's death in 1943. Of their brief association on the same faculty, Pound said many years later, "I always remember my short time at Northwestern . . . as one of the highwater marks of my career."[33] Indeed, it was Wigmore who had introduced Pound to Holmes as the "most erudite and clear-seeing mind aged 37 now in this country,"[34] a compliment greatly appreciated by Pound.

However, at the time, Wigmore apparently had some reservations about Pound for, shortly thereafter, when Pound was under consideration for an appointment at the Harvard Law School, Wigmore was asked for a statement. In the draft of a letter in his own handwriting, Wigmore recommends Pound highly but indicates that there is one consideration that he would be willing to communicate orally but is not willing to put in writing.[35] Although we can only speculate as to Wigmore's reservation, Pound's transfer to the University of Chicago after only two years at Northwestern must have raised questions in the mind of one with such a strong sense of loyalty. If this supposition is correct Wigmore obviously concluded that it was unwise to apply his own standard of loyalty to another person. That the same is true of Wigmore's disappointment toward Julian Mack, who had "deserted" the Law School in a time of crisis for the University of Chicago, was evidenced by his affirmative response to Frankfurter's request that he write to President Wilson, Attorney General George W. Wicker-sham, and, by now, Secretary of the Interior Franklin K. Lane, in support of the appointment of Mack to the United States Circuit Court of Appeals in 1913.[36]

Charles B. Elder, who was a nonresident faculty member for many years, gives us a glimpse of the atmosphere that characterized faculty meetings during the Wigmore administration.

> Faculty meetings were leisurely and generally harmonious, and the Dean exacted full attendance on the important occasions preceding Commencement when grades were evaluated and determination of those entitled to degrees and honors were made.
>
> There was, I believe, complete academic freedom and this extended not only to the resident faculty, and to men of surpassing reputation, but to all of the part-time members and special lecturers.[37]

Wigmore's appointment as dean seemingly did not diminish his duties as a teacher. Apparently, however, he felt some deficiency as a speaker for he took private lessons from a member of the School of Oratory on the Northwestern University Evanston Campus and continued his speech exercises for many years.

Among the courses that Wigmore continued to teach after his appointment as dean were Evidence and Torts.[38] His correspondence with Ezra R. Thayer, dean of the Harvard Law School and son of James B. Thayer, reflects his systematic perusal of the court reports in quest of cases of interest to him and his desire to share this information with someone with similar concerns.[39]

From time to time Wigmore also taught courses in Quasi-Contracts, Persons and Domestic Relations, Bailments and Carriers, Conflict of Laws, and International Law.[40] Beginning with the year 1907–8 a course entitled Practical Problems in Contemporary Legislation[41] was designed to give his students a keener sense of their future responsibility as members of the bar. The course was a direct response to William Draper Lewis's address entitled "Legal Education and the Failure of the Bar to Perform its Public Duties," given before the Section of Legal Education and Admission to the Bar of the American Bar Association.[42] Wigmore thought so much of the course that he sent a circular describing it to nearly two-hundred law-school teachers.[43] When Felix Frankfurter, who had special concern for this area, was appointed to the faculty of the Harvard Law School in 1914, Wigmore wrote promptly to congratulate him, adding: "Certainly it indicates an open minded and progressive attitude toward present and future demands, that the Harvard University Law School should see the need of such a professorship."[44] He continued by asking Frankfurter to let him know what kind of work he would be taking up with the students and offering to supply information about his own program if Frankfurter desired it.

Frankfurter, who had not as yet left the War Department for his new assignment at Harvard, responded cordially: "I should like you to know how much strength for the new work it means to be welcomed into it by one who is among the deepest sources of professional inspiration, and one of the profoundest leaders in the task of shaping the law to meet the needs of the modern state." [45] After explaining that he would be giving courses on penal administration and legislation and public-service laws, and would be directing an intensive study of the Interstate Commerce Law, reinforced by consideration of the public utilities of the various states; Frankfurter continued, "You will see, therefore, how closely I shall be trailing in your own course on Practical Problems in Contemporary Legislation and I welcome all you can find time to tell me about it." [46]

Gradually Wigmore further diversified his teaching so as to reflect his expanding and innovative views of an adequate legal education. In 1913 he began to use his *Principles of Judicial Proof* in the Evidence courses. In 1917 he offered a one-hour course on the History of the Bench and Bar, reflecting the importance that he placed upon legal history and his conviction that every lawyer would profit by a greater knowledge about the leaders of the legal profession. Wigmore also began to participate with other faculty members in courses on the History of Anglo-American Legal Institutions and on Sources of Anglo-American Legal History. In 1917–18 he offered a course in General Legal Literature, an inevitable consequence of his conviction as to the importance of a broad background of general reading. He himself was an outstanding example of the aims he set forth: "1) to suggest that law is something just a little bigger than decisions and statutes, in its demands on the lawyer's interests and attainments, 2) to pry them loose from the fixed American notion that nothing can be learned as studied or mastered except by taking a course, etc., etc." [47]

The courses offered on Illinois law reflected Wigmore's belief that "such courses on local state law might well be instituted in every state." [48] He had an astonishing capacity, both as scholar and as teacher, to deal with minute matters of detail, such as in the study of Evidence, and at the same time to comprehend and appreciate the broad expanse of the law that was reflected in his conception of legal education.

Fundamental to all of Wigmore's teaching was the assumption of his student's conscientiousness. He seldom used the class hour for the specific purpose of ascertaining whether they were prepared or not, and he made little effort to provide specific answers to the questions raised in the class discussions. [49] "The occasional recitations on the cases were not to be, we found, a substitute for our own study of the case materials. We were to make our own analyses, rather than to expect a predigested exposition given to us in carefully measured doses from the lecture platform." [50]

It was not unusual for Wigmore to engage his students in discussion of a matter in which he was interested at the moment regardless of its relevance to the subject matter of the course. [51] On the other hand, an entire class hour might be devoted to a single case included in the assignment for the day. And student participation would vary greatly. One student recalls how hard he would press on occasion:

Early in the course, he put a certain state of facts before me and inquired whether I thought such facts constituted a battery. I readily answered in the affirmative. Thereupon he inquired as to my basis for the answer. I replied that the definition of a battery was such that the facts which he related would bring the case within the definition. He demanded to know where I procured the definition. I stated that it came from Bouvier's Law Dictionary and that I had looked it up just before coming to the class. He pounced on me with the words that Bouvier might be wrong. I made a determined stand in favor of the lexicographer and contended that the work was well recognized authority and ought to be given proper credit. We parried with each other until I was fearful that I had been discourteous toward him and that he might remember me unfavorably on account of the incident. After the class was over, he met me in the hall but instead of reprimanding me he surprised me by saying: ''That was surely a fine argument that you made in class today.''[52]

However, Wigmore could quickly dispose of a student if he was not prepared or was not coming to grips with the problem in hand. To a student who was ''very suave in his tones but not especially enlightening,'' Wigmore said, ''Mr. ———, your verbosity exceeds your luminosity by preponderance of magnanimity.''[53]

Wigmore was convinced that every lawyer should be able to read law-Latin, and he frequently quizzed his students for the purpose of determining their ability to do so. His *Cases on Torts* contains a number of quotations in medieval Latin and an appendix sets forth their translations. A footnote in the Casebook aptly expresses Wigmore's attitude: ''These translations are not intended to enable competent students to dispose with the reading of the originals. Nor are they provided in the belief that it is anything less than a disgrace for an educated lawyer to be incompetent to read and use law-Latin.''[54]

Through the eyes of his students we are provided with additional glimpses of Wigmore's performance in class. On one occasion when Wigmore entered the classroom the students were unusually slow in coming to order. He waited patiently until he could quietly say, ''When you are ready to proceed, send a committee to wait upon me.'' Wigmore then walked up the steps, along the long side of Lincoln Hall, and out the door. The class sat in ''horrified silence.'' When the students recovered, a committee was appointed, it waited upon the dean, and he was escorted back to class.[55]

In one of the classrooms that Wigmore frequently occupied there was a bust of Blackstone. ''When a student made a particularly inept recitation, the Dean would shake his head, walk over to the bust of Blackstone and turn Blackstone's face to the wall.''[56] Another student gives a somewhat different version: ''In another class when a few questions indicated that a great many students were not prepared and that their interest could not be aroused and after proceeding for fifteen minutes with little result, the Dean became somewhat disgusted, walked to the end of the lecture platform, turned a bust of Blackstone to the wall and said, 'Class is dismissed.' ''[57]

Wigmore's course on the History of the Bench and Bar also reflected his view that a well-rounded legal education involved more than a study of the law. In his view, some familiarity with the general legal literature and a knowledge of the lives of outstanding leaders of the profession were essential. "Every one of them," he believed, "has somewhere a lesson or inspiration which could never be obtained elsewhere."[58] In this course it was Wigmore's practice to assign to each student some outstanding judge or other legal figure on which he was to prepare a brief biography for presentation to the class as a whole. As one part of the assignment the student was expected to locate the picture of his subject in the large collection that hung on the walls of the Law School and produce it in class. One student, after a diligent search, did not locate the picture, although he felt certain that he had seen it. Consequently, when he made his presentation in class he closed by admitting apologetically that he had been unable to locate the picture. As he sat down Wigmore's face broke into a grin, and he produced the picture from behind his desk, admitting that he had taken it from the wall where it belonged.[59] The dean gave no explanation for his conduct, but it is clear that one student at least had made a fairly thorough examination of the Law School's picture collection.

The examination in this course was based on legal biographies including the *Lives of the Lord Chancellors*. Many of the students

resorted to the stratagem of attempting to familiarize themselves with the material by merely studying a "pony" which some enterprising student had prepared and which purported to summarize the important facts in the life and career of each chancellor. Use of the "ponies" became so extensive that Mr. Wigmore found out about this — to him — new approach to study. He said and did nothing. However, in the following Spring, one of his examination questions was, "what chancellor came to an early end by falling off a horse?" The students guessed all over the lot: Eldon, Ellenborough, etc., etc. The following day there appeared on the school bulletin board the following comment by Mr. Wigmore: "While no chancellor came to an early end by falling off a horse, many a student has been unhorsed by depending on a pony."[60]

In his Evidence classes Wigmore often put the students through the paces in order to determine if they could apply what they had learned. For example, in one practical application

. . . the Dean presented the students with a series of points of evidence with one student arguing to get the evidence admitted and the other student seeking to keep it out. Again the Dean sat at the back of the room, and the students appeared at a podium which was in the front of the room. He would call the case always as a case, "Smith v. Jones," and the two "counsel" would come down to the well of the house and announce that they were ready. . . . one day [one of the students] said, "Ready." From the Dean came a booming and obviously (although probably apparently) angry voice, "Mr. Blank!!!" Blank froze. The Dean continued, "Have you no respect for this court?!!!" Blank still froze, not knowing why he had been disrespectful and not knowing what to say. Then the Dean went on, "You say, 'Ready, Your *Honor*'"[61]

Wigmore frequently dramatized the significance of some rule of evidence by abruptly introducing a situation that called for its application. On occasion, a member of the Law School staff would come in and hand a student a note[62] or the dean a telegram[63] which would be read to the class and would then become the subject of the discussion. Only at the end of the session would the dean reveal the fact that the writing was a forgery and express his dismay that no student had questioned its authenticity or asked to see the document. On one occasion a Law School janitor came into the class and announced that the dean was ill and could not meet with them. However, when the students filed out of the classroom, Wigmore, who was standing in the hall, asked why they were leaving the class. Advised of the janitor's message, he replied, "What authority has the janitor to speak for me?" The students were ushered back to class and an appropriate discussion ensued. Sometimes the dean would make his point even more dramatically:

> One day in another class three members of the faculty came hurriedly into his room, each shouting a different and somewhat confused statement. The Dean promptly named six students somewhat at random but nevertheless covering a cross section of the class, and said, "I subpoena you as witnesses to make proof of these disgraceful occurrences. The class will adjourn to the Moot Court-room." On arriving in this room the students found that a jury had already been impaneled and was waiting. The Dean presided. One after another the six [witnesses] were called to testify as to the statements made by the three faculty members a few minutes before. Then the "judge" asked the jury to make a finding as to what had occurred. Only one of the six "witnesses" had approximated in any way the correct statements of the three professors, but the jury did not believe him. He was a shiftless and somewhat irresponsible character and yet he had keen perception and was able under the disturbed conditions momentarily prevailing to clearly get and retain the statements that had been made.[64]

He gave a graphic illustration of the proper course of action for a trial lawyer to pursue if his adversary persisted in an improper line of questioning to which objections had been sustained. After fair warning, he said, "I would take my papers, put them in my file, slam my trial book shut and leave the courtroom." At this point Wigmore "closed his lecture book shut with a resounding whack and majestically stalked from the lecture room."[65]

This Wigmorian dramatization brings to mind Wigmore's great admiration for John C. Reed's *Conduct of Law Suits*,[66] for which he wrote the introduction to the second edition. It is likely that he brought it to the attention of his students, but, if not, we may be certain that at some time and probably more than once he stressed the fact that its contents "must be so firmly appropriated that they become a part of one's own experience and belief, ready at an instant's call."[67]

Occasionally Wigmore would depart from his usual formality in the classroom by taking up his cigarette holder, lighting a cigarette, and saying: "Now we will have an informal discussion so you can light up your cigarettes."[68] Wigmore's classes took many an original and unexpected turn.

> Verve and zest marked a strikingly original classroom technique of the Dean. His comment might include the parallel between the planetary system and the evolution of the law, and also a criticism of Edgar Allan Poe's use of poetic license in supplementing the facts of the trial that was the source of his famous story, "The Mystery of Marie Roget." Still there was an elegance in his disourse and method.[69]

Not all Wigmore's students were in agreement as to his effectiveness as a teacher (and of what teacher can this not be said?), and as usual the ablest and most diligent gained the greatest profit from his classes. However, in retrospect many of them were convinced that they had received an excellent basic training. Robert W. Millar, one of Wigmore's students and later a colleague on the faculty, remembered "the influence of Dean Wigmore's remarkable personality" in the classroom and "the exceptional richness of the materials that he laid before us, by way of syllabus, in the field of international law and the skill with which he caused his hearers to reflect his own consuming interest in that field."[70] And a successful practitioner after forty years recalled how Wigmore "aroused the intellectual interest of all his students and endeared himself to them in a way that has lasted through the years. His was not routine teaching — he tried out new ideas, and while oftentimes he left us hopelessly behind, he stimulated us all to increased effort and interest."[71]

The development of the Law Library provided additional evidence of Wigmore's willingness to cope with matters of great detail. He devoted to this task the meticulous attention required for the development of a useful collection, especially for scholarly purposes, and his efforts bore fruit. The basic collection that was all that university funds could provide was substantially augmented by contributions made by Elbert H. Gary beginning in 1902 and continuing from year to year thereafter.[72] In order to acquire the necessary bibliographic knowledge, Wigmore made an extended European tour in 1905 visiting all principal law libraries — state, university, and bar "from Christiana to Budapest"[73] — an assignment that was followed by another trip to Europe for the same purpose in the spring of 1908.[74] In addition, Wigmore had the library in mind during his many personal visits to Europe, and he was ever on the lookout for appropriate additions. For a number of years he spent every Sunday morning going over book lists in a dozen languages.[75] By 1908 the collection included some 10,000 volumes of modern Continental law, not equaled at that time in any other library in the United States;[76] 2,000 volumes in international law; nearly 3,000 volumes in Roman and civil law; and a collection of volumes in ancient, Oriental, and primitive law. In addition, substantial beginnings had been made in developing the following collections: English historical materials, books on the philosophy of law, and South American law.[77] Wigmore also began very early to develop the Law School picture collection that grew from year to year under his guiding hand. In 1908 and again in 1910, he donated to the library a number of portraits of men eminent in the law of foreign countries. In 1912, it could be said with complete justification that

> The stamp of Mr. Wigmore's ripe scholarship is visible in this great mass of legal materials. There are legal libraries with more books, and excelling, perhaps, in this or that field, but on the scientific side of the law this is the most valuable law collection in this country. The judgment, learning, and effort evident in this undertaking of making a great law library eloquently proclaim the capacities and abilities of the most enlarged type.[78]

It should come as no surprise that Wigmore was concerned about the safety of this valuable collection and ran to the window whenever he heard a fire engine. This was not, as some students thought, a quaint idiosyncrasy. He fully realized what he later put in words when he was making an appeal for funds for a new Law School building.

> Every year, for ten years past, up and down Lake Street, in our vicinity, one or two ancient buildings have been gutted by fire. By good luck we have escaped, so far. A conflagration would destroy all the work of the last twelve years in building up the most unique Law Library in this country, outside of Harvard University and Congress.[79]

But Wigmore did more than merely run nervously to the window. He organized monitors into a first line of defense:

> Dean Wigmore required each monitor to go through fire protection maneuvers. In those days, the Law School being located on Lake and Dearborn Streets was housed in what some might term a "fire trap." The Dean would fill out slips of paper and hand the same to each monitor at odd times. The slip would tell that there was a fire in Hurd Hall or some other room. It was then up to the monitor to repair to the spot of the supposed conflagration, and go through the motions of putting out the fire with the nearest fire extinguisher or employ such methods as were deemed most effective to prevent a catastrophe. The Dean was so deadly earnest about the procedure that he would not, for one instant, tolerate any variation from the routine demanded. It was his theory that if a monitor habitually attended to the imaginary fire, he would automatically do the right thing in case a real fire occurred.[80]

Early in Wigmore's career as dean, the school was confronted with the necessity of deciding whether to offer instruction in the evening in response to an urgent suggestion made by President Edmond James, who was concerned that the University of Chicago might develop such a program first.[81] Although a faculty committee appointed to study the matter concluded that a four-year evening course would be consistent with high educational standards, it recommended against the adoption of such a program, and its position was sustained by the faculty. There were already four evening schools in Chicago, and it was feared that an evening school, which would inevitably be small, would hopelessly divide the efforts of the school's working forces between the two programs.[82]

In February 1906, a faculty committee was appointed to consider the feasibility of publishing a law review[83] to supplement the *Bulletin* which Wigmore now considered an inadequate outlet for scholarship. Deliberation quickly led to action, and in May 1906, the first issue of the *Illinois Law Review*[84] appeared under the editorship of a member of the faculty and supported by a board of editors composed of faculty members, alumni, and students. Its justification and purpose were stated as follows:

— Undoubtedly the field for law reviews of a general character is already overcrowded. Moreover, it must be conceded that such reviews, however excellent, enlist the interest of but a small minority of the practicing lawyers of Illinois. It is believed, however, that there is genuine and widespread need of a live periodical primarily devoted to the discussion and exposition of Illinois law, and of matters of special practical value to the Illinois bar. In that belief, and with the purpose of supplying that need, this Review is launched.[85]

Wigmore had misgivings about the role of a law review devoted to the interests of practitioners within a given state and expressed his views in an article entitled "The Function of a State Law Review."[86] At meetings of the *Law Review* Board, Wigmore came forward with many suggestions for broadening its appeal, and his colleagues would often receive notes in verse calling attention to a particular case that could appropriately be made the subject of a comment or a note.[87] His devotion to the practical improvement of legal institutions nevertheless left room for articles on the curiosities of the law which were probably inevitable outgrowths of his love of legal history.

It was he who instituted the department of the Illinois Law Review entitled "Diversities de la Lay." In this found harborage for a number of years all manner of curious facts and quaint utterances in the field of law which, full of attraction for the reader could find no other accessible abiding place.[88]

Another evidence of Wigmore's attraction for curious historical facts was the attempt (which occupied him for a number of years) to identify the Lanfranc who had such an important role in English political history with Lafranc (Lanfrancus dePavia), an Italian jurist and commentator of the *Digest*. At long last, in 1942, he reported his findings in an article entitled "Lanfranc, The Prime Minister of William the Conqueror: Was He Once an Italian Professor of Law?"[89]

Wigmore's active support of the *Review* continued throughout his life. For the first volume he prepared two articles (one jointly with Henry C. Hall),[90] eleven case comments,[91] and four editorial notes.[92] Although Illinois law continued to receive special attention, the journal was soon broadened so as to "provide a legal journal of interest and value to lawyers throughout the United States."[93]

Wigmore's interest also extended to the *American Law Review*, the oldest legal periodical in the country, and the one in which a number of his early writings had appeared. Rumors that it was about to cease publication disturbed him, and he was interested in various proposals that would enable the journal to continue its publication. A scheme for purchase by the American Bar Association and another to have it taken over by the Law School (a plan that received the approval of the Executive Committee of the Board of Trustees)[94] did not materialize.

Wigmore and his faculty were pioneers in recognizing the need for continuing legal education similar to that already being provided for doctors. Beginning with the year 1907, the school offered a course in "Legal Tactics," the aims of which were described by Wigmore many years later:

> One evening lecture a week for twenty weeks, gratis; on each occasion an eminent local specialist expounded a different subject, e.g. Special Assessments, Personal Injury, Litigation, Mechanics Liens, etc., etc. Always the theme was the "tactics," i.e., the clinical skill as distinguished from the bare rules of law. For seven or eight years these lectures continued (at cost of great administrative effort), and then the audiences gradually thinned out, until the School was chagrined to offer its lecturer no better a reception. *A priori*, practitioners ought to welcome eagerly such a service; practically, they do not.[95]

Twenty-five years would elapse before Wigmore would be able to congratulate the Cleveland Bar Association for its experiment in "adult education" — an institute for the bench and bar of Northern Ohio, which he said "is exactly in keeping with the trend of the times."[96]

In the same year (1907) an honorary society for the recognition of legal scholarship was organized at the Northwestern University Law School. At Wigmore's suggestion it adopted the name "Order of the Coif." In 1912 the society was merged with Theta Kappa Nu, and the new organization adopted the name formerly held by Northwestern. The merger has spawned fifty-seven chapters representing most of the leading law schools.[97]

As the year 1909 approached, a date that would mark the fiftieth anniversary of the founding of the Law School, Wigmore gave careful consideration as to how that occasion might be properly celebrated, and on December 4, 1908, he submitted to the faculty a proposal to call a National Conference on the subject of Criminal Law and Criminology, and it drew enthusiastic approval.[98] Wigmore's plan was not only broadly conceived as to subject matter (a reflection of his firmly established general approach to the law) but depended on widespread participation. "The conference consisted of delegates called, under the auspices and as guests of Northwestern University, by a local organizing committee, including representatives of the contributory sciences of law, sociology, medicine, psychology, penology, police and philanthropy."[99]

Wigmore sought to focus attention on the Law School and to initiate reforms in the criminal law as well. His efforts to seek the support of the legal profession for the improvement of criminal justice led him to enlist Holmes's aid in securing President Taft as the conference's speaker, since he "would arouse the lawyers to feel an interest, more than any other one influence would do."[100] To his great disappointment Taft was not able to attend.

The delegates were selected from nominations by the organizing committee and from governors, chief justices, and federal judges in the several states and territories. Nearly 150 delegates attended and, because of its timeliness and meticulous planning, the conference was a great success. The participation of small groups with divergent and sometimes antagonistic views and the collaboration of individuals with special interests laid a broader foundation for cooperation than had theretofore existed.[101] The delegates voted to organize on a permanent basis as the American Institute of Criminal Law and Criminology, and Wigmore was elected the first president.[102]

An active program was inaugurated at once, and the *Journal of Criminal Law and Criminology* (the first in the field in the English language) began publication in May 1910, as an appropriate outlet for those working in this field. The institute, however, also carried on an active program, with local and regional meetings held in various parts of the country, and plans for regional surveys of criminal justice. Between 1909 and 1915 a bulletin was issued, proceedings of significant meetings were made available,[103] and committee reports on a wide variety of subjects and a draft of a code of criminal procedure were published.[104]

Wigmore attended board meetings of both the institute and the *Journal* regularly and was an active and stimulating participant. At meetings of the board he not only advanced novel ideas himself, but he was receptive to the ideas of others and encouraged the submission of manuscripts that frequently found their way into the pages of the *Journal*. Robert H. Gault, the editor in chief of the *Journal* for many years, spoke of Wigmore's role: "He was its spiritual father and during all the years that followed he was, without interruption, its zealous guardian. . . . He was the last word in promptness. . . . he never kept a manuscript more than a day, even when he was most active in the Law School."[105] The selection of Gault,[106] professor of psychology in the university, reflected not only the breadth of Wigmore's interests but the wide approach that he thought should be applied to the complex problems involved in improving the administration of criminal justice. And in psychology as in everything else he was ever receptive to the humorous side. Gault reports that one day, when Wigmore was going through a psychological periodical, he came upon an article entitled: "The Psychology of Roosting Crows." "This intrigued him," and many a time thereafter in jest he "turned his mental telescope upon it. 'Aren't roosting crows asleep?' He guessed that it must be particularly difficult to find out how a sleeping crow feels and what he thinks and plans and regrets — if anything; for in such a state he isn't saying even 'caw' by way of telling us about it."[107]

Under Wigmore's leadership the problems of crime were approached in both the institute and the *Journal* with a broad perspective and a sympathetic attitude toward the use of scientific methods wherever they appeared applicable. This attitude elicited support from, and encouraged, leaders in psychology, psychiatry, and the other related social sciences at a time when the general attitude of the legal profession was far from receptive to such broader collaboration. Indeed, the legal profession as a whole showed virtually no concern about or sense of responsibility for the problem of crime; indeed, in the words of Dean Pound, "At that time, American criminal law was in an unhappy condition from which it has by no means wholly emerged." [108]

The first issue of the *Journal* listed Wigmore as an associate editor and "contained a forthright comment . . . upon a recent criminal case," [109] thus beginning his long record as a regular contributor. For the most part he utilized the *Journal* as an outlet for the communication of useful information, for case comments, and for editorial notes as he did the *Illinois Law Review*. Nothing more unmistakably denoted Wigmore's interest in the contemporary scene and his desire to bring about improvements in the law than his propensity to turn aside from his more scholarly work long enough to prepare such writings.

Higher admission requirements and a more substantial and exacting curriculum were bringing Northwestern into competition with the law schools of the University of Wisconsin and the University of Chicago. Wigmore was irked by the diploma privilege enjoyed by Wisconsin graduates who were, by state law, automatically admitted to the bar without being required to pass the state bar examination. Wigmore voiced his objections in an exchange of letters with Dean Eugene A. Gilmore of the University of Wisconsin Law School: that the functions of educating the student and deciding his qualification to practice should be separated, and that by staying in the Association of American Law Schools and adhering to the constitution and by-laws, the University of Wisconsin had "made a moral pledge not to oppose the removal of that privilege." [110]

Wigmore also objected to the practice at both Wisconsin and the University of Chicago of reducing the three-year residence requirement through summer-school study. He wrote to Gilmore, "that it encouraged the student to give the shortest kind of measure that will satisfy the rule," and continued: "The system of reducing by summer work to the net minimum of two calendar years and a quarter, is thoroughly vicious. I am extremely shocked to see that you join with the University of Chicago in the specious acceptance of such a skimpy method of education." [111] And in writing to Ezra Thayer at Harvard, Wigmore said, "Don't give up to having summer school. As things go, Northwestern and Harvard will soon be the only remaining bulwarks against the movement which believes that 'the plant' must not remain idle, and that the casual intellectual tramp must be catered to by prepared scraps of lecture lunches. In that respect at any rate N.W. may hope to put itself in the class with Harvard." [112]

The unfavorable reference to the Law School at the University of Chicago should not be taken as a reflection of a general and prevailing attitude. Wigmore had been in touch with Beale by correspondence before Beale accepted the temporary assignment as the first dean, [113] and in December 1902 the Northwestern faculty had entertained the Chicago Law School faculty for dinner at the University club to wish them well in the creation of the new law school. [114] Although collaboration on a formal basis was nominal, individual faculty members kept in touch, and there were occasional exchanges of courtesies between the schools.[115] And in 1916, when Wigmore presented Harry Pratt Judson, president of the University of Chicago, with an honorary degree from Northwestern University, President Judson followed up with a letter in which he said, "Nothing pleased me more than the fact that I was presented for the degree by yourself. The last paragraph in your statement . . . was absolutely correct, and I am confident that the relations between the two institutions will continue for all time to be thoroughly cordial and cooperative."[116]

Wigmore's ability to work with his superiors was notably demonstrated in his relationship to President Rogers. The skill in getting along with others that he demonstrated as secretary to the Law School faculty, and thereafter as the most dynamic faculty member, was not in any way diminished when he became dean and was in a position to exercise greater authority. His relationship with President Edmund J. James was cordial and constructive. This, of course, does not mean that there were no differences of opinion or tense moments. MacChesney, who knew and worked with Wigmore both as a friend and a trustee, summarized the relationship:

> I would not be understood to say that the process of building was always a smooth one for any one who as colleague or trustee had to help shape the policies of this institution. For he had a drive and conviction it was hard to overcome, even if one did not always agree with him. But his eyes were fixed on the road ahead and he was usually right.[117]

Wigmore had James's whole-hearted support in his efforts to improve the Law School, and when James received an offer of the deanship of the Yale Law School, Wigmore reacted with dismay: "I have just heard of the real situation. I want you to know that you will surely take the very life out of our ambition if you go. The only thing that makes us sure of any future for this University is your staying by us. This is said for every one of our faculty straight from the heart."[118]

However, when James did resign to accept an appointment as president of the University of Illinois, Wigmore established a good working relationship with his successor, Abram W. Harris, and he maintained it in spite of differences of opinion and many frustrations. In 1912 President Harris, who had found that it was a well-established custom for the president to take a box for the season for the Music Festival, wrote "I would be delighted to go into partnership with the Wigmores if they want to go into partnership with me."[119] President Lynn Harold Hough, writing to Wigmore in 1919 to congratulate him upon being designated chevalier in the Legion of Honor by the French Government, concluded his letter with these words of praise: "What a world of important things we have to do together. And I am happy to think of the disciplined attainment and compelling personality which you personally bring to all your tasks."[120]

Wigmore's relationship with William A. Dyche, a member of the Board of Trustees and business manager of the university, was apparently also excellent. In 1915, Dyche answered Wigmore's expression of appreciation for Dyche's support:

> The trustees are not in touch with the educational side of our work. If we are to have a well developed University some plan must be found to bring the faculties into close and official relationship with the trustees. Grave conditions now exist in the University due largely to the weakness above referred to. They cannot be cured, in my judgment, under the present administration — I well remember the stormy days of 1902 and rejoice that I had even a small part in saving the Law School — but the inspiration to the trustees came from you. You have done a great work at great personal sacrifice. I hope your fondest dreams may be realised and that we both may live to see the Law School on a firm foundation — financial foundation — then your sailing will be over smooth seas.[121]

The next year, in acknowledging a birthday reminder, Dyche wrote, "If about nine o'clock tonight your ears itch a little, just remember that I am talking to the Alumni of the University in Rockford and that the Law School, its Dean and his wife will not be forgotten. There is no department of the University in which I am more interested than the Law School."[122]

Some insight as to Wigmore's relationship to his staff is provided by the recollections of Mary C. Goodhue, who became his secretary in 1913. She had joined the Law School staff while the Wigmores were on one of their biennial trips to Europe, and some of the awesome tales that she had heard about the dean from his colleagues filled her "with considerable awe and dread of his home coming."[23] On the day

> of his arrival at the office he came into my room and sat on the corner of the table. I soon realized he was nearly as flustered as I. That day started a friendship which grew with the passing of the years, and has been one of the greatest blessings and inspirations of my life. . . . One thing about which I had been forewarned was that he preferred being called "Mister" rather than "Dean" Wigmore. When school opened that 1913 fall he noticed the habit of calling him Dean Wigmore was prevalent among the students. With him to see something he didn't like was to do something about it. In this case he posted a document on the student bulletin board which has become historic. I can't quote the exact words, but they were to the effect that there is no more honorable title than Mister and that there was no more reason to address him as Dean Wigmore than to speak of Street Car Conductor Jones or Blacksmith Brown. . . . To me, who saw him so constantly, and since he met so many different situations, his most vital characteristic was what I would call his "human-ness." He was too great a man to have to put on a pretense of greatness. There was no "brass hat" affectation about him. He could be, and was, absolutely sincere in his relationships with people. Though he counted among his close friends men who stand at the top of the legal and social world, he had time to perform kindly acts for the most humble of those with whom he had associations.[124]

Wigmore's kindness was demonstrated in the affection he showed to a colored janitor who had served the Law School for twenty years. During his last illness Wigmore contributed generously to a fund which he himself promoted, and when the janitor died he made the trip on a "most inclement Sunday" from Evanston to the South Side of Chicago to attend the funeral, and wrote an appreciation of the janitor's long and faithful service and had it posted on the bulletin board.[125]

Wigmore was also sensitive to the conditions under which people around him worked. In an editorial in the *Evanston Daily News*, entitled "Official Cruelty to Our Postmen," Wigmore wrote:

> Reader, go out into the pantry, take two fifty pound bags of flour, fasten one end of a strap to each, sling them over your shoulder, so that one bag hangs in front and the other behind. Then stagger around the house with them for ten minutes, imagining yourself all the while to be doing it for a living. You will then begin to have some notion of what you are letting Uncle Sam exact of his faithful postmen. . . . And all this is carried amidst conditions which aggravate the physical strain. The shoulder is dragged; the chest is constricted; the spine is stiffened. The pavement may be sloppy or slippery. The eye and hand must be working; the mind must be clear. . . . It is mere brutality — official brutality — and useless brutality, too. Four-fifths or more of the weight is in second class-matter — printed stuff, circulars that pestiferous advertisers are sending, weekly newspapers that could just as well be read tomorrow — common freight, in short. All of that class of matter could and should be delivered by wagon, and once a day only. . . . We call for a nationwide movement to stop it. Our boys in the post-office cannot be expected to initiate the movement. They must do their duty. They cannot refuse to obey orders. They are forbidden to form a union. The only redress must come from a public demand. We hope that the press all over the country wherever this abuse exists, will voice that demand.[126]

Nor did he join so many others in complaining about Christmas time postal service. This was his message:

> Dear Mr. Postmaster:
> The million Christmas cards and the hundred thousand gifts show that, in Evanston at any rate, there is no place for Old Man Scrooge at this season. All grouches are forgotten, and everybody is everybody else's friend. And the Post Office staff deserve our thanks for they work hardest of all as everybody's Goodwill agents.[127]

But Wigmore's interest ran far deeper than mere words. When his own mail carrier was seriously injured in an automobile accident and could not work for more than a year, Wigmore induced a lawyer to look after his legal rights and personally solicited funds from those along the route who had been served by him for many years.[128]

Since neither of the Wigmores had inherited any money, they relied entirely on his earnings. Mrs. Wigmore, who kept the accounts, said they "lived" on her husband's salary and "played" on the royalties from his books.[129] However, their "playing" included:

lending a helping hand financially to many people. Many times they paid doctors' or dentists' bills for people, asking the doctor to send the receipted bill to the patient; or they would present money (as an anniversary gift, etc.,) to friends to help defray their children's expenses in college. When Mrs. Wigmore's sister died in the East, and Mrs. Wigmore was forbidden by the doctor to leave her apartment, and Mr. Wigmore had a severe attack of "flu," they telephoned a distant cousin in Cambridge, at a time of the year when they knew he was busiest, and asked him if he would act for them in making funeral arrangements, etc. Later (I think for a birthday gift) Mr. Wigmore sent him a very substantial check and said it was for his wife and himself to spend for a good vacation. The cousin reported they had a wonderful trip, the first in years.[130]

Hugh Green, a library monitor who sometimes relieved the dean's secretary, provides the following rather amusing glimpse into the daily round of the administrative head of the Law School. It reveals not only his availability but also the sense of humor that helped to carry him through. According to Green, the dean gave him the following explicit instructions:

> When any caller inquires for me, please open my door and announce his presence. It may be that he has an appointment. On the other hand, perhaps some one is boring the life out of me and a new face will be a relief. Or, it may be that the one waiting to see me is the undesirable one and I may wish to continue with the person who is already in my office. In any event, I want the presence of the caller announced, no matter what I may be doing. To make the point plain let me say that even if a stray dog comes in and you think the dog is by any chance looking for me, open my door and announce that a stray dog is out there, evidently wanting to see me.[131]

It is said that Wigmore had a real gift for dealing with a visitor who was not too welcome to begin with, or had outstayed his welcome. He would rise from his desk, put his hand on the visitor's shoulders and ease him toward the door in such a manner that his guest would go his way feeling that he had been treated with the utmost courtesy. After a particularly unappealing person had departed, Wigmore might make a cryptic comment to anyone appropriately at hand. On one occasion he said in the presence of his secretary, "I can't recall that fellow's name but the word 'obnoxious' comes to mind." She regarded it as "most appropriate."[132]

Although Wigmore took the interruptions by visitors in stride, he resented the telephone and for a long time would not have one on his desk, preferring to go out to the booth in the general office. Eventually he accepted the phone as a necessity.[133]

This policy of being available to all extended, of course, to students and was important in winning their loyalty not only to himself but to the Law School as well. As dean he made it a special point to establish a personal relationship with each student. After any extended absence on his part he let it be known that he wished to see every student in his office, and those who did not respond voluntarily found their names posted on the bulletin board with a specific day and time assigned. A student waiting in the outer office for his turn often champed at the bit "because the fellow ahead stayed with the Dean too long. But when his own turn came he seemed as loath to terminate the interview himself."[134]

Although there were always some women in the student body, because they were a small minority, they were not always welcome at social events. On one occasion, when Wigmore had accepted an invitation to act as the master of ceremonies at a joint social event being given by law students at Northwestern and the University of Chicago, a woman student told him that she had been advised by a University of Chicago student that she could not go because it was a stag affair. Wigmore's response was immediate and decisive. He said, "If they exclude the women in the class they will have to secure another master of ceremonies."[135]

Mr. Wigmore was assidous in looking after students who were ill, especially those from out of town. He had a hospital committee formed in each class whose business it was to ferret out such cases and woe to the committee that neglected its task! During World War I, one of the Philipino students contracted tuberculosis and was confined to Hines Hospital for many months. Mr. Wigmore made several trips out there during the winter to visit this homesick boy, traveling via elevated and bus, an arduous trip.[136]

But the lighter side was not neglected. Quite frequently Wigmore would go into the smoking room in the old Law School building, and later into Lowden Hall in the new one, to play the piano but primarily to lead the students in singing. He greatly enjoyed this diversion and so did the students. Wigmore was not only the accompanist and a participant in the singing, but frequently the composer and author of music and words. In some instances the words he wrote were sung to popular tunes: "Ex Contractu Ex Delicto" (The Law Students' Twentieth-Century Ballad of Northwestern); the "Counselor's Chorus," sung to the air of "La Spagnuola" — here the fun-loving side of Wigmore's personality joined with his loyalty to the Law School.

Wigmore's more important musical compositions were brought together in *Lyrics of a Lawyer's Leisure*,[137] published in 1914 but only after a long search for the appropriate stock to meet his specifications for the lavender and white Law School colors. He dedicated this publication to Mrs. Wigmore, "In honor of September sixteenth, 1889," their wedding day. The book included a madrigal, eleven ballads, two processional hymns, and three law-student choruses, some of which were of course sung around the Law School on many occasions both formal and informal.

Among the many words of commendation that Wigmore received for his songs, the following note from Franklin K. Lane, written when he was secretary of the interior, is typical:

By the way, you don't know what delight you have given the whole family with your songs. Nancy plays them on her violin. The two that we particularly like are the lullaby "Sleep Little Pigeon" and the processional "Wider and Wider Yet." Both of them are enchanting and we hum them all the time, and I am introducing them to a group of my friends.[138]

Wigmore showed a great interest in acquiring facility in ragtime, synco-pated music, and "barrelhouse," as one group of students called their particular version, but he confessed he was really never successful at it.[139] Although music was usually the chief preoccupation at such student gather-ings, Wigmore would sometimes come in and converse or tell stories; as one graduate recalled with pleasure, he would sit "on top of his table in the old school, debonair, and charming, telling interesting stories connected with the law, while he smoked his cigarette."[140]

Now and then the entertainment at the Law School "smokers" would be provided by the students. On one occasion a number of them put on a mock faculty meeting and Wigmore laughed heartily at all the imitations, includ-ing one of himself, performed by "a perfect mimic." At the end of the evening he was asked to say a few words: ". . . in this life, we do not often have the opportunity to see ourselves as others see us [I] . . . certainly enjoyed the privilege which has been afforded."[141]

> One of the outstanding experiences of each graduating class was the invitation to Mr. Wigmore's home in Evanston. The gathering was always characterized by a charming informality, good though rather mild refreshments, good stories, and perhaps some unusual games specially prepared for the occasion by Mr. or Mrs. Wigmore, the latter a very charming hostess. Mr. Wigmore apparently did not believe in spending time in playing cards at social gatherings, but preferred some game or pastime that had some real point to it . . .[142]

Where honesty was at stake the dean showed no mercy. When a student advised him that a classmate taking an examination in another faculty member's course was cheating, he went immediately to the examination room. Finding the student with a textbook in his lap, copying the answers, Wigmore ordered him to leave the room and the Law School premises and immediately posted a notice on the bulletin board that he had been expelled for cheating. Wigmore apparently recognized no need to consult the faculty member directly concerned or to act through the faculty as a whole.[143]

Although, as the foregoing incident indicates, Wigmore did not believe in the application of the honor system to written examinations, he did believe that student behavior at the Law School should be under the control of the student body and that "police regulations" would be "detrimental to the fraternal relations of a common scholarship which should subsist be-tween teacher and student." As to written examinations, he believed that, at least in the North, students had no common standard of "honor" which would enable them to call their fellows to account. In his view, a failure to act against the occasional offender was tantamount to a licensing of the evil.[144]

In addition to his direct concern for students, Wigmore actively sup-ported the work of the YMCA with Northwestern students. Their apprecia-tion for Wigmore's generosity is reflected in countless letters in the Law School files.

As a formal gesture of appreciation a portrait of Wigmore was presented to the school by the Class of 1911 at a reception on Friday, November 10, 1911. Those in attendance included not only students and faculty but distinguished representatives of the university, the Chicago area, and the state of Illinois as well.[145] In January 1914, while he was secretary of state, William Jennings Bryan, class of '83, was the principal speaker at a gathering at the Law School, followed by a dinner at the University Club in recognition of Wigmore's twenty years of service. Many other distinguished persons were present to extend greetings and felicitations. A copy of the proceedings of the event was bound together with the many testimonial letters received and presented to Wigmore.[146]

Five years later formal recognition from the faculty as a group came through the sponsorship of a book entitled *Celebration Legal Essays by Various Authors to Mark the Twenty-Fifth Year of Service of John Henry Wigmore as Professor of Law in Northwestern University.*[147]

According to Albert Kocourek, one of Wigmore's closest associates on the faculty, Wigmore was such a

> familiar figure about the university in Evanston and Chicago that he was taken for granted as an able scholar, an urbane gentleman and a man of polite accomplishments. He was accepted through long habit as one accepts the air or sunshine. He was a man of elegant manners, tall, blue-eyed, erect, alert and self-contained. Not many saw beyond the externals regularly expected of those who fashion university life.
>
> Few knew the real stature of the modest, well-groomed, fine-featured and intellectual-looking man who in the Evanston days always carried a green cloth bag. They could not know of the depth and breadth of his learning — certainly not from any disclosures on his part.
>
> On principle, Dean Wigmore rarely used the pronoun "I." Even his colleagues at frequent intervals throughout the long train of years first learned from outside sources of this or that new achievement or accomplishment. Dean Wigmore himself seemed to have a *horror naturalis* of speaking of what he had done.[148]

As we have seen, the offer of the deanship at the University of Chicago Law School in 1902, was for Wigmore a most tempting academic offer, but it was by no means the only one. He had been under consideration for the deanship at the University of Iowa in 1901,[149] and he was suggested as an appropriate successor to President James at Northwestern University when James resigned in 1904.[150] And when James Bradley Thayer died in 1902 many faculty members at Harvard Law School, including Beale and Williston, thought of Wigmore as his most appropriate successor. Again in 1915, upon the death of Ezra Ripley Thayer, dean of the Harvard Law School and son of James Bradley Thayer, Wigmore had strong support for appointment as his successor.[151]

Dean George W. Kirchway's persistent efforts to secure Wigmore for the Law School faculty at Columbia first culminated in a formal offer of the Kent Professorship in February 1903,[152] an offer that Wigmore declined.[153] Whether he seriously considered leaving Northwestern under any circumstances is not clear, but the objections he voiced then concerned (1) the beginning salary of $6,000 with possible increases up to $7,500 in three years, (2) the availability of the courses (other than Evidence, of which he was assured) that he would like to teach, and (3) the conviction that living costs were higher in New York than in Chicago, a fact vigorously disputed both by Kirchway and President Nicholas Murray Butler.[154] To Dr. Robert D. Sheppard, treasurer of Northwestern University, Wigmore wrote: "As I expected I have again heard from Columbia, practically asking me to name my price. And I have just written to say that I stay here. So you see what I am willing to do for Northwestern."[155]

So determined was Kirchway to secure Wigmore that, when in 1906 he turned down a second offer, Kirchway wrote: "*Ita fiat!* It is, after all, only the second trial. The third time I will succeed and win you. Your name must yet be linked with that of Columbia, so that in after time men shall not speak the one without thinking of the other, and you shall yet (*deo volente*), in Rabbi Ben Ezra's phrase, 'grow old along with me.' "[156] Kirchway had sought to persuade Wigmore not only by describing the glowing prospects at Columbia but by pointing to Wigmore's unpromising plight at Northwestern:

> . . . how can you reconcile it with your intellectual conscience to abide in that academic limbo. It may be that you see in the Northwestern University virtues and potentialities which are not visible to the eye at this distance, but — may I say it? — it doesn't loom large on the Western horizon. . . . Thanks to you, the Northwestern University has a good law school, but one good school does not make a university, and it does not seem likely that you will ever emerge from the shadow of your formidable rival on the Midway.[157]

Once again in 1916 Wigmore declined an offer from Yale to organize its "newly founded School of Jurisprudence," and to bring with him any two members of the Northwestern faculty "worthy to fit their program."[158] Wigmore preferred, as in prior instances, to use the offer to strengthen his position with the Board of Trustees. On this occasion he again urged higher salaries for the faculty in order to make the school competitive; an increase in the size of the faculty; and the raising of funds to provide for the foregoing and to provide fireproof quarters for the library and adequate facilities for the Law School.[159]

Dean Thomas W. Swan's regret at Wigmore's unwillingness to come to Yale, however, was less lugubrious than the one that had been voiced by Kirchway a little more than a decade before:

> Although it is a cause of deep personal regret to all of us that we cannot have you to direct the graduate work in law here at Yale, the proposed development of your work at Northwestern cannot fail to be a cause of congratulation to everyone interested in legal education. And the fact that our efforts to draw you East may have hastened the determination of your trustees to make possible that development can be only a source of satisfaction to us.
> I am particularly interested in your bold advance to a four year law course. I

believe this is bound, ultimately, to be adopted by all the good schools. Northwestern is to be congratulated on having the courage to act as pioneer.[160]

Wigmore expressed his attitude toward all of these offers in a letter to a friend: "... you will find that nothing at all will or could happen to change my present relations."[161] His deep commitment and loyalty to Northwestern could not be shaken.

That the Wigmores probably intended to stay in the home on Lake Michigan[162] that they had rented from the university soon after Harry's appointment as dean in 1902 is evident from their engagement of Myron Hunt, an architect and friend, to work out some fairly extensive remodeling of the interior. They lived in this home which, in writing to Holmes, Wigmore described as their "shore-acres shanty,"[163] until they moved to the Lake Shore Club in 1934.

Several years after the remodeling, Hunt, who by then lived in California, responded to the Wigmores' continuing expressions of appreciation for his services by writing, "Any one who can be pleased with a house, the exterior of which is as ugly as yours, must certainly have a good interior both for his house and for himself."[164]

Hunt, now an enthusiastic citizen of Southern California, mildly berated Wigmore because of his disinclination to live in that state. "If you are so thoroughly perverted after having been born and brought up here, I shall not try any missionary work. However, some day you go out on the street corner and draw fifty good long breaths before sending for an ambulance."[165] It is unlikely that Myron Hunt knew that Wigmore's antipathy to California was largely due to his extremely difficult relationship with his parents. Nothing Wigmore ever did seemed to make up for his refusal to accept their church affiliation and to return to San Francisco to enter his father's business.

For a further description of the remodeled house and the activities of the Wigmores in their considerably expanded home environment, we are indebted to his brother Francis Marion:

> My brother's home in Evanston . . . was quite unique. Situated within a stone's throw of Lake Michigan it was modest in size with gabled roof and rather quaint in appearance.
>
> Within, a long room on the lake frontage afforded a fine outlook over that great body of water, and opened upon a broad porch of the same length as the room. In summertime, if they were at home this porch supplanted the living room, and meals were served there, books read, and friends entertained.
>
> The living room contained their grand piano, a large fire-place, Japanese bronzes and other artistic decorations as well as two marble *pièces de résistance*, the little Italian putto and the Roman Augustus. Some fine rugs and dark-stained oak settees, bookshelves, leather upholstered sofa and a table on which interesting antiques and curios were placed, as well as comfortable chairs and writing desk, adorned this room — a real living room.
>
> Harry's study was a small room on the second floor, with a large window looking out upon the Lake, which, in wintertime often presented a wild scene of

icy snow buffeted by winds of gale force and blinding snowstorms. In the study were two desks, Harry's being a small flat-topped one where he worked often until midnight or later — writing letters, articles or deep in the pages of law reports, propped up the better to peruse them. A row of book shelves lined one wall on which were numerous grammars, dictionaries, and practice-lesson books of foreign languages, for in the latter he was very proficient.

Emma's desk occupied a large portion of the remaining space of this tiny room, which at a guess, measured twelve by ten feet. The desk was a roll-top affair and as Emma was really the finance manager, she needed room a-plenty. However, Emma not only acted in the aforesaid capacity, but gave many, many hours as coadjutor in proof reading and in other ways. I think her ever-present determination, and perhaps anxiety was to preserve his health and to try to see to it that nothing whatsoever should be allowed to interfere with his life work.[166]

Francis Marion Wigmore also provides some insight into the daily round.

I lived at their home in Evanston, Illinois for several years and thereby had opportunity to join in the daily customs of their life during those years. For example, it was our habit, when the day's work was over to don our dinner suits for the evening meal, and after dinner we would often indulge in the practice of reading aloud some foreign language story or study-book, thus accustoming ourselves to the sound as well as the syntax and vocabulary of the language.

Harry went from Evanston to Chicago, where the law school itself is situated, several days out of the week. As I remember, his usual breakfast consisted of a huge plate of toasted buttered graham bread with coffee and perhaps orange juice. He and Emma had their breakfast taken upstairs to their room and either Emma, from bed, read the morning paper's headlines to him as he sat and ate, or he had the paper propped up before him and at the same time consumed the food before him. Then, a quick get-away, with his lawyer's green bag full of books and papers and a hurried walk to the suburban station, perhaps three-quarters of a mile. Going in on the train his invariable habit was to get out a foreign language book or other study material from his bag and thus utilize his time of travel. He often carried a pocket volume of Shakespeare also. . . .[167]

In personal appearance my brother was very neat and traditionally always kept his shoes well polished. In the cellar he had a shoe shining holder, blacking brush and polishing cloths and took great pride in the precise method of the polishing operation, which he, of course, did himself. He delighted in working out a "system" for everything and, I think, took as much pleasure in his system of polishing his shoes as in the systematic way, in which he went at his marvelous writings on law.

It may cause a smile or even consternation to hear that Emma acted as tonsorial artist and his hair-do was always impeccable. In the matter of clothes she, too, was largely his mentor. His absorption in his undertakings was so intense and his desire to be unostentatious and even economical in dress so strong that I think it was the gentle but firm prodding of his wife which kept him quite up to a high standard in this regard. His suits were almost invariably ready-made and he could thus be well fitted for he was trim and well-formed, about six feet tall or slightly less.[168]

The Wigmores' homelife "was the acme of gracious living"[169] and included not only a great deal of informal entertaining but "numerous elegant parties . . . although the air of gracious simplicity made all guests feel at ease.''[170] Mrs. Wigmore sometimes worked for days in making preparations so as not to interfere with the maid's routine work. On appropriate occasions Wigmore would of course play the piano, but his animated conversation was always interspersed with stories and parlor tricks.

Thanksgiving dinner for the Wigmores was an evening meal, but it was held early for there were usually children present. Mrs. Margaret G. Belknap (not a relative), who was part of their extended family, provides this picture:

> A kiss from Aunt Emma and Uncle Harry in the hall, then wraps were laid off in the big bedroom overlooking Lake Michigan. I can still see the dinner table, with its huge arrangement of fruit centering the wide expanse of snowy damask, the silver gleaming on the buffet, and the brass sconce from Amsterdam glinting on the wall. . . . The delicious dinner was traditionally served on beautiful porcelains brought back from Japan in the 90s. There were always snappers at each place, and everybody wore a paper cap at dessert. If I forgot, Aunt Emma would remind me after dinner to go to the kitchen to compliment the cooks on the feast they had set before us. The sound of the surf was often in the background as coffee was served in the long book-lined library, with the firelight flashing from the great brass log basket, and perhaps shining on Uncle Harry's dress-shirt front as he sat on the floor to play tiddlewinks with the children. . . . And there was always music — Uncle Harry playing gloriously on the enormous grand piano which didn't seem too large in that long, uneven room.[171]

Unusual toys of various kinds were always on hand for the children — perhaps as a way of protecting the treasures the hosts had brought from Japan.[172]

At the request of one of Wigmore's nieces and her husband the Wigmores had agreed to make all decisions concerning the children's education should the parents die prematurely. When the Wigmores called on the niece and her family after the death of their husband and father, ''A neighbor exclaimed at the sight of the dignified dean of the Law School, his tall hat laid aside and his coat-tails flying in the breeze, playing with the children.''[173] In explanation Wigmore said, ''How can I be competent to give advice on their education if I never play with them!''[174]

On one occasion when Wigmore was ice skating he noticed that a boy ''quite rudely'' refused to skate with a small sister. He ''told the boy most emphatically what he thought of his behavior and then said to the astonished little girl, 'I hope you will do me the honor of skating with me,' and swept her off under the eyes of the abashed brother.''[175] Another ice-skating experience had a somewhat less propitious outcome. Wigmore was eager to teach a niece visiting from California how to ice skate and she reluctantly consented. Wigmore ''took a practice turn, promptly spilled, and broke an arm.''[176] Later, in writing to decline an invitation to speak he explained, ''I broke my arm by falling upon a piece of solid glaciality.''[177]

As the Wigmores never owned an automobile, probably because Mrs. Wigmore had witnessed a fatal accident near their home rather than be-a cause of any reluctance on Harry's part as was generally supposed,[178] the dean was especially conscious of the fact that pedestrians had rights and that they were often disregarded by motorists. At one of their traditional Commencement Day parties (before the installation of stoplights in Evanston) the Wigmores' party was proceeding "under the convoy of the Dean," from the Patton Gymnasium to their home. When the party came to a north and south street it was "confronted with an unbroken line of cars coming from the direction of Chicago." The group waited, "hoping for an interval which would permit our passage but all to no purpose; the continuity of the line persisted. Finally losing patience, the Dean stepped out in the street, in the face of the next advancing automobile, and in a magnificent gesture raised his arm. The effect was electrical. So authoritative was the action that the whole line came to an immediate stop and the convoy was enabled to cross in unhurried safety."[179]

Wigmore's strong sense of loyalty included his own community and its activities. One amusing illustration concerns a benefit play for the Evanston Fire Department. Toward the end of the first act "an engine drawn by dashing horses" came on the stage and drove off as the curtain went down. Wigmore, desiring to give the department a boost, rose and yelled, "Three cheers for the Evanston Fire Department. Hurrah! hurrah! hurrah!" As no one responded or joined him he sat down feeling annoyed at the lack of enthusiasm. The next day the local paper reported that the Fire Department's benefit play "had gone off well with no mishaps except that a drunk had tried to start a disturbance at the end of the first act."[180]

The Wigmores made it a practice to go to Europe every alternate summer, often traveling with the Frank B. Dains. This friendship had originated while Dains was an assistant professor of chemistry in the Northwestern University Schools of Medicine and Pharmacy, from 1895 to 1901. Dains had a special interest in the application of chemistry to the legal aspects of toxicology. Even after he had accepted a professorship at Washburn College in Topeka in 1902 and gone on to the University of Kansas in 1911, the trips continued, and in between the couples maintained their friendship through correspondence. However, the Wigmores also frequently included other friends on such trips, particularly those who might not otherwise have been able to enjoy the experience. Sometimes they would stay in a single country taking short trips from a central base where they could locate inexpensively; on other occasions they would travel more widely. In any event Wigmore would study the language, observe the local customs, and regard all points of interest from a legal point of view.

But Wigmore's zest for travel was not always satisfied with these biennial trips. When he "acquired a wanderlust which could not be indulged at the time, he decided to what part of the world he most wanted to go and then sent for time tables, boat schedules and other necessary data for a successful trip. He would pore over them with as much enthusiasm as if he were really going to leave his own fireside."[181] A variation of this highly constructive "indulgence" occurred with his reading: ". . . whenever he read a story with a geographical setting he took from his library shelf a Baedeker and looked up all the names mentioned, and if the scene lay in a city, he followed the story street by street. In fact, when he went to London, or any large city, he was almost as familiar with it as he was with Chicago."[182]

By the time it was becoming clear that World War I would directly involve the United States, Wigmore, now in his early fifties, had emerged as a towering figure in legal education. His stature was due both to his vigorous leadership in the expansion and improvement of his own Law School and to his stimulating and constructive influence in the field as a whole. Had he written only modestly, his career would have been one of distinction and achievement. This, however, was not the case, and it is because his scholarly writing was so distinguished and so massive, that in the next chapter his record as a scholar will be traced from the time of his appointment as dean in 1901 to the interruption of his administration during World War I.

7
Scholar

W igmore's appointment as dean in 1901, as might well be expected, affected neither the quality nor the quantity of his scholarly work. He managed to discharge his duties as dean and as teacher and yet devote a considerable amount of time to research and writing. Wigmore's secretary lets us in on a rather amusing device that he used on at least one occasion when he wanted to push through some particular piece of writing:

> One summer he kept the itinerary of a two-week vacation a profound secret, but he sent me a card each day, starting "from some place on Lake Mich.," and going through several midwest cities. As I knew at the time, they were all written on the big porch of his Evanston home, facing Lake Michigan. The secrecy enabled him to do uninterrupted work on whatever MS. he was writing at the time.[1]

There were of course other "devices" by which Wigmore's extraordinary capacity for production was enhanced. In order to make the most efficient use of his time when working at home, a "small red trunk"[2] full of books from the Gary Library was shipped out from time to time for his use in Evanston, and those that had served their purpose were returned.

Mrs. Wigmore managed all the necessary household details.[3] Their childless home was free of the usual interruptions and distractions. Wigmore's unusual capacity for sustained effort was further extended by keeping a number of scholarly projects underway at the same time; when he became tired of one, he often turned to another instead of to some form of recreation. He asserted emphatically that the change was restful and relaxing,[4] and the wide range of his interests gave him an unusual variety of alternative subjects from which to choose. Furthermore, he was blessed with the capacity to sleep soundly, and according to Mrs. Wigmore, fell asleep as soon as his head touched the pillow.[5] Thus he was able to get up at five o'clock in the morning, read galley proofs, and leave time for other work later on. In spite of the heavy workload that he nearly always carried, he never seemed in a hurry, and he always had time to be attentive and interested in those around him.[6]

For the first three years after his appointment as dean, Wigmore's writing was almost solely preoccupied with the law of evidence. He prepared eight articles[7] in this field at the same time that he was completing the manuscript for the *Treatise on Evidence*, in four volumes (1904–5),[8] the product of fifteen years of "monastic toil"[9] and the achievement for which he is most widely known. His colleagues marked the occasion at an informal dinner at the University Club to "celebrate the completion of your contribution to legal science" which is "a source of gladness to all of us."[10]

The *Treatise* quickly gained recognition. But this does not mean that it was instantly acclaimed by every court high and low. Nathan William MacChesney recalled an experience that showed the acclaim to be less than universal.

> I was arguing a question of evidence before one of our local judges one day and in the course of my argument used the words "autoptic proference" — as a young and glowing disciple of Wigmore. The judge said "What's that?" I explained the meaning, citing Wigmore with pride to justify the use of the term. The judge said "that's all very well but you better cite a book of evidence some of us know something about and which uses words we can understand."[11]

Another young lawyer who early recognized the value of the *Treatise* observed "that he found it excellent as furnishing a background for understanding questions which arose . . . [and] used it for this purpose, [but] did not quote it in court generally because its presentation was too complete, fair, and impartial."[12]

A supplementary volume to the *Treatise*, covering the years 1904–7, was published in 1908,[13] and a second cumulative supplement covering the years 1904–14 followed in 1915.[14] Edwin Borchard described the preface to the latter as a "brilliant essay" and added, "I wish a copy of it could be put into the hands of every law student."[15]

That Wigmore could work intensely in the midst of confusion and probable interruption is demonstrated by the fact that he did much of his earlier work in the Chicago Law Institute Library, which, at the time of the first edition of the *Treatise*, was used by Northwestern University Law School students as well as by practitioners. His presence there was a common sight. He occupied

> A table in the smoking room . . . aided by numerous cigarettes [applying] himself to the work which was to give him imperishable fame. It was not the quietest place in the world, but he was wholly undisturbed by the activity around him. No one could have been more completely absorbed in a task — an absorption which became all the more understandable when there arrived disclosure of the magnificent product of labors. And with this absorption there attended an air of sureness and serenity, as of one who possessed the certainty that what he was doing would be in perfect fulfillment of his design.[16]

Wigmore's achievement in the preparation of the first edition becomes the more remarkable when it is realized that he had no professional assistance and no stenographic help. His sole assistant was Mrs. Wigmore, who loyally aided and supported him in this task and in everything he undertook. The first edition was sent to the printers in Wigmore's own handwriting, but Mrs. Wigmore had made a copy by hand for fear that the original might be lost in transit.[17]

Her share in putting the manuscript in fine form was not even limited by the need to supervise the household operations, for her mother Mrs. Vogl, who was staying with them at the time, took charge of all household supervision and entertained callers. Nevertheless, on one occasion an "elegant woman" who was selling an encyclopedia got past the maid and urged Mrs. Wigmore to buy the books as a help in her work for her husband. When Mrs. Wigmore replied that she helped with only the mechanical part of the book, the saleswoman put the sample volume "back into the pocket of her voluminous skirt," saying she had no book on "mechanics," and "flounced out of the house." Mrs. Wigmore commented that this was the quickest disposition of a saleslady she could recall.[18]

Later, when Mrs. Wigmore read with surprise the special dedication in several presentation copies of the set acknowledging "her skillful and arduous labors,"[19] she said to her husband, "Oh, you didn't have to say arduous." At this, Mrs. Vogl laughed and said, "I notice you did not object to the word 'skillful.'"[20] Wigmore gave recognition to the two scholars to whom he felt the most indebted: "to the Memory of the public services and private friendship of two masters of the law of evidence Charles Doe of New Hampshire Judge and reformer and James Bradley Thayer of Massachusetts historian and teacher."[21]

Notwithstanding Wigmore's high regard for Charles Doe as a judge, John P. Reid, Doe's biographer, believes that Wigmore did not appreciate the fact that Doe also developed for himself, and applied in deciding his cases, a "harmonious construction of general principles."[22]

In any event, personal considerations probably colored Wigmore's appraisal, and he accorded to Doe a higher standing than was justified, for although Pound placed Doe among the ten most important judges in American judicial history,[23] there is more general support for the view expressed by Willard J. Hurst that "Doe belongs in New Hampshire's Hall of Fame, but not in the national shrine in which Dean Pound placed him."[24]

Just as Wigmore's appraisal was affected by his personal relationship to Doe, Holmes's less flattering evaluation struck a cooler note:

> I never quite understood your predilection for Doe. He seemed to me to write longwinded rather second rate discourses and I thought he did rather an unfair thing when I was a young essayist. I sent him proofs of an article in which I spoke of the gradual working out of a line in the law by contact of decisions grouped about the two poles of an undeniable antithesis — e.g., night and day — almost before my article appeared a decision of his used the notion with no credit given — which in those days I felt. Perhaps my memory is wrong as it was long ago — and I would not do injustice to the dead, but I guess I could find it. But at all events, I thought there was not a great deal of brandy in his water.[25]

As has already been indicated, the *Treatise* was promptly recognized as an outstanding publication, and Wigmore quickly rose "from the rank of a promising but somewhat obscure scholar and teacher to the rating of one of the great masters of the law."[26] However, no work — and certainly not one so ambitious in conception — could run the gauntlet of the critics unscathed. It is obviously impossible to deal adequately with the numerous criticisms and suggestions which greeted the appearance of the *Treatise*.

The three principal objections were (1) the very original and extremely elaborate classification of the subject matter; (2) the introduction of certain novel words, some of them of Wigmore's own creation, with which not even the experts in the field would be familiar; and (3) the advocacy of certain principles of law by statements that were neither logical nor supported by the courts.

As to the first criticism, Joseph H. Beale said in his generally laudatory review:

This analysis is careful, original, and thoughtful; but it is new and strange, and probably would not help a lawyer in practice in his attempt to find the authority bearing upon a particular question at hand. The reviewer must speak on this matter with some hesitation, because use alone can be the final test. To lawyers trained as students in this analysis it may be entirely feasible, but to the present generation of lawyers, to whom it is novel, it may be simply repellent.[27]

Beale was even harder on Wigmore's introduction of a novel nomenclature:

Professor Wigmore presents us with such marvels as retrospectant evidence, prophylactic rules, viatorial privilege, integration of legal acts, autoptic proference, and other no less striking inventions. It is safe to say that no man, however great, could introduce into the law three such extravagantly novel terms and Professor Wigmore proposes a dozen.[28]

In writing to Holmes, Wigmore justified the creation of new terms by saying:

In spite of the self esteem of those Countries [France and Germany], especially the Germans, I believe that a juristic discussion can best be conducted in English. Our historical terms are indeed unscientific e.g. "evidence," "tort"; but our language of today better permits deliberate attempts to discriminate. That is why I felt free to invent some scientific terms in my big book.[29]

Regardless of one's attitude toward Wigmore's inventions, the judicial treatment accorded them by one court is good for a chuckle: "while 'autoptic' is a good word, with pride of ancestry, though perhaps without hope of posterity, the word 'proference' is a glossological illegitimate, a neological love-child, of which a great law writer confesses himself to be the father."[30]

Subsequent events soon demonstrated the wisdom of the qualification that Beale attached to the criticism first quoted above, although at the time he was quite generally supported by others in his attitude toward Wigmore's classification and novel terminology. The utility of the *Treatise* to the practitioner did not by any means wholly await the advent of a new generation of lawyers "trained as students in this analysis" or conditioned to the novel terminology. Only four years later, in reviewing the first supplement, Beale declared that the *Treatise* "has already satisfied the profession of the permanent value of Professor Wigmore's work, which has become not merely the best but the only authority in general use in this country and in England."[31] Edward A. Harriman, Wigmore's former colleague on the faculty but now in practice, concurred: "I am in frequent communion with your over-soul by means of the *magnum opus* which offers constant and unfailing satisfaction to anyone engaged in litigation,"[32] and in 1912 Professor Ralph W. Gifford of Columbia "was informed by one of the staff of a great law library in New York that the book was called for by practitioners 'more than all other works on evidence put together.'"[33] Three years later Frankfurter, in an address at the annual meeting of the American Bar Association, called his listeners' attention to the fact that "we are now witnessing the steady, wholesome influence of Dean Wigmore upon the law of evidence throughout the country."[34]

A novel feature in textbooks at the time no doubt contributed to the *Treatise's* popularity among members of the bar. Not only did Wigmore collect numerous cases supporting the propositions in his text, but he indicated in a few words the distinguishing facts in each case so that a lawyer could quickly determine which cases merited examination.

Although the criticism that some of Wigmore's statements were neither logical nor supported by the courts was to some extent justified, there were many points on which Wigmore's critics were not in agreement among themselves, nor by any means did they always take issue with him on the same questions. Consequently, in some instances, the lively discussion which his efforts obviously either initiated or greatly stimulated had a decidedly constructive effect, and, with the passage of time, there was a general acceptance of many of his views. Upon one point the verdict was virtually unanimous. Regardless of the topic discussed or the position taken, Wigmore had made a valuable contribution to whatever the question under consideration.[35]

A by-product of this important and increasingly successful publication — the *Treatise on Evidence* — was the opportunity that it provided the Wigmores to share royalties with others. One recipient was the two-year-old daughter of a deceased friend to whom the Wigmores became "Uncle Harry" and "Aunt Emma," the "almost unknown fairy-godparents . . . from whom, on each birthday and Valentine's Day, came a check from 'the book' which was carefully put in the bank"[36] for her college education.

When the first edition of the *Treatise* was completed, Mrs. Wigmore cherished the hope that "once 'the book' should be finished her husband would have leisure which they might enjoy together, but before it was in print he had thrown himself into other writing and planning. Her dream receded with the passing years and he was still working like ten men at the time of his death."[37] Certainly the *Treatise* alone would establish his reputation as a scholar, and he was already the author or editor of several books and of numerous pamphlets, articles, case comments, notes, and book reviews. However, even the continuing task of the periodic revision and expansion of the *Treatise* was not a sufficient outlet for his extraordinary literary drive, and he immediately plunged into other writings.

Even in the field of evidence alone the proliferation is impressive. In 1910 *A Pocket Code of the Rules of Evidence in Trials at Law*[38] appeared as a convenient handbook to be used by the practitioner, fully keyed to the *Treatise* so as to give immediate access to the larger work when it was needed. The *Pocket Code* was universally acclaimed and criticisms were few.[39] Even in this handbook which, as one reviewer put it, "charms alike in clarity and conciseness of statement,"[40] Wigmore was not content to merely state the law as it was at the time. He also stated the law as he thought it should be, but in brackets or with footnote references, so as clearly to differentiate fact from fantasy. The *Code* provided Wigmore with an opportunity publicly to pay tribute to Holmes in a dedication: "In grateful acknowledgment of lofty ideals voiced and exemplified for our profession and of many tokens of kindness shown to the author." Holmes responded to the dedication by writing, "I can say no more than that I am much touched and moved by the dedication and am proud that you should feel able to use such kind words."[41]

Wigmore recognized that a single *Code* would not fully meet the needs of the practitioner in respect to the state in which he practiced, and he planned to follow the original *Code* with a series of completely annotated local editions.[42] However, he met with success only in Massachusetts, where Charles H. Harris served as editor for a local edition that appeared in 1915.[43] Although this book no doubt served a useful purpose, the disappointing demand did not encourage a similar venture in other states. Wigmore's periodic transmission of Harris's share in their joint royalty elicited good-humored responses from Harris: in 1921 he referred to the book as "our precious gem" but feared the $3.90 semiannual amount would not enable him "to go to Europe," although "it will suffice to fill the tank with gasoline once more";[44] in 1924 he surmised that the income from the book had risen to $11.05 because it had become "quite a general judges' companion";[45] in 1927 the $5.85 brought the response that just as he had been pondering the question of whether their finances would stand the strain of a trip to California "your remittance has settled the question. Now, we are off, health permitting."[46]

The first edition of the *Treatise* was shortly followed in 1906 by Wigmore's *A Selection of Cases on Evidence for the Use of Students of Law*.[47] This contribution to the field of legal education came out in second and third editions in 1913 and 1932 respectively.[48] Although the casebook, which is largely keyed to the *Treatise*, received a mixed reception as a teaching tool — not surprising in that the choice of a teaching tool is such a highly personal matter — it was quite generally acknowledged that Wigmore had made an excellent selection of cases and had arranged them in a very stimulating manner.

Wigmore was by no means wholly preoccupied with these tasks, for he was at the same time creating his masterpiece, the *Principles of Judicial Proof*, published in 1913.[49] In Wigmore's own words, the "book aspires to offer, though in tentative form only, a novum organum for the study of Judicial Evidence."[50] It was concerned with the science of proof rather than with admissibility (the procedural rules prescribed by the law), for he believed that the latter would become less important and the former more important with the passage of time.

At the time of publication, the volume was characterized as "an extraordinarily interesting volume."[51] Another reviewer said, "no description, indeed, can prepare the reader for the varied fascination of the views opened by many windows into fields of psychology, history and literature." Wigmore has "shown the same sure instinct for the illuminating practical illustration, and the same unfailing power of intellectual stimulation, which are to be seen in his other writings, and he has made his selections with a range and richness unattainable by another."[52] "The mere reading of this book shows how illuminating a course might be based on it if conducted by its compiler; whether it could be made a success by another would depend on how far he had caught the same spirit. . . . But no thoughtful student of the law of evidence can fail to find delight and instruction between its covers."[53]

When Charles C. Moore, in reviewing Wigmore's *Principles of Judicial Proof*, referred to its "aristocracy of style," Wigmore thanked him for his cordial review and added, "could you not have given me credit for a democracy of citations? It sometimes seems like too much democratic leveling to cite in the same type[,] decisions of courts of widely different weight and quality."[54]

Altogether, during the two decades ending in 1920, Wigmore produced, in the field of evidence alone, eleven books, one pamphlet, eleven articles, thirty-four case comments, six notes, two introductions, two book reviews, one address, and one translation.[55]

Wigmore's commanding role in the field of evidence has tended to eclipse the substantial character of his part in the development of the law of torts, a subject that he also taught throughout his term of service at the Law School. His series of three articles published in the *Harvard Law Review* in 1894–95[56] were recognized at the time as significant and elicited words of commendation from Ames, Pollock, and Holmes, as has already been noted.[57] Nearly forty years later Sir William S. Holdsworth said of "Responsibility for Tortious Acts: Its History":

> [it] is a complete and careful survey of the whole history of responsibility for tortious acts, from the days of the Anglo-Saxons down to modern times. For several reasons it is a remarkable contribution to Anglo-American legal history. In the first place, it is one of the few essays on a topic of legal history in which the whole course of that history is surveyed. In the second place, it is remarka-

ble for the manner in which, in the earlier period, foreign sources are used to elucidate the primitive ideas of liability which we find in our own early legal history. In the third place, it is remarkable for the mastery of all the sources of English law from the twelfth century down to modern times.[58]

These early contributions by Wigmore on the law of torts were followed by four articles during 1908, 1909, and 1916,[59] by numerous case comments and notes,[60] and by his *Select Cases on the Law of Torts, With Notes and a Summary of Principles*, in two volumes, published in 1911–12. The latter not only represented a fine selection of cases and related materials but Appendix A, A Summary of the Principles of Torts (General Rights), which Wigmore regarded as the most useful thing for a beginning teacher, came in for especially high praise.[61]

Here Wigmore was not satisfied to rely exclusively on cases, as was the practice in his day, but introduced excerpts from the writings of both lawyers and laymen, including novelists, dramatists, and poets, to "help to convince the student of law that he must extend his outlook."[62] In addition, he introduced problems from current news and from examinations and cited all relevant articles published in law reviews during the past twenty years.

Although the book reflected many years of study, Wigmore characteristically gave credit where it was appropriate. In his dedication he said, "To the memory of James Barr Ames who first inspired for so many of us a never-ending interest in this law of torts and enriched his students with the perpetual influence of his incomparable qualities as a teacher, a scientist, and a man."

Wigmore was fully aware of Holmes's important role in this field, for their correspondence frequently dealt with questions of tort law, but he unquestionably reached some of his conclusions quite independently,[63] and he challenged Holmes's statement that "the law of torts as now administered has worked itself into substantial agreement with a general theory," "asserting that there were many fundamental issues to be resolved."[64] Wigmore acknowledged Holmes's influence not only in their personal correspondence but also by including a substantial number of his opinions, and several excerpts from Holmes's *Common Law*, in the Casebook.[65] He also dealt at length with Holmes's contribution in his article "Justice Holmes and the Law of Torts," in the *Harvard Law Review* in 1916.[66] When this article appeared, Holmes, who had known something was pending, wrote:

> My dear old Humbug:
> What you wrote to me sometime ago led me to expect that you contemplated walking into me. And later I inferred you had given up the notion. The Law Review has come — and all that I can say is that your kindness brought tears to my eyes. I never expected such a reward and you have given me unmixed joy.[67]

That praise from Wigmore was especially appreciated is evidenced by the fact that shortly before, in writing to Pollock, Holmes had said, "I admire his [Pound's] learning and his command of it, but as yet have not perceived a very strong personal reaction upon his knowledge — as one does in Wigmore — whom I hope to see here on January 1 . . ." [68]

Several years later Pollock, who was collecting materials for a new edition of his textbook on torts and had Wigmore's Casebook before him, described it as "profitable" and, no doubt because of its originality, "sometimes amusing." [69]

Although Wigmore made no major contribution in the field of torts after the publication of the Casebook, he kept up his interest in the subject and wrote case comments and notes from time to time throughout his life. [70] When, many years later, Wigmore was asked why he did not take the next step and "render to the profession as great a service as he had with Evidence by writing a treatise on this subject, his reply was that the cases in this department of the law presented a fair picture of 'confusion with delirium' and that no one should do the thing I asked without reading all the cases, that he was older and that life was too short." [71] An evaluation of Wigmore's scholarship in this field must, therefore, be based upon work done entirely during this relatively early period in his career.

In 1966, Leon Green, after fifty years of tort-law teaching and writing, made this appraisal of the Casebook:

> It is interesting to note that it was Dean Wigmore in his 1911, two volume, 2,000 page Select Cases on Torts who first laid out the boundaries of the vast domain of tort law. Even so, his comprehensive analysis was in large part only prophetic of what was to follow. At that time in many areas the decisional materials were scant and the areas had to be filled in by excerpts from the literature of many fields. It was his masterful scholarship and courageous projection of the reach of tort principles that first gave the profession a glimpse of the vast area of the tort field, and I might add, that it left the profession, and especially tort teachers, flabbergasted — so much so that few teachers even attempted to use his book. Dean Wigmore thought of torts as general law that ramifies throughout all law, and out of which special areas of tort law are found in most all other courses of the curriculum. [72]

As to Wigmore's over-all contribution to the law of torts Frankfurter said, "he was one of the founders, with Holmes, of the whole changed outlook of our law in what we now call torts." [73] Leon Green succinctly compares the work of Holmes and Wigmore in this field: "Wigmore's research is superb — in my opinion much more reliable than that of Holmes; though the latter's Olympian pronouncements have had greater acceptance, much of his decisional tort law has now been rejected." [74]

For a comparison of Holmes and Wigmore on a broader front we can turn to Pound: "I think Wigmore understands the problem of application of law — the fundamental problem of jurisprudence today — better than anyone in this country unless it is Mr. Justice Holmes. . . . No one is more fertile in good ideas than Wigmore, and really he is worth careful reading and careful reflection after reading, and I guarantee will yield great results when so read and reflected upon." [75]

Another area that challenged Wigmore's lifelong interest was criminal law and criminology, although he never taught a course in the subject. In addition to his earlier work[76] and his intensive consideration of criminal law in connection with his work in evidence, Wigmore wrote, during this initial period as dean, several articles and a considerable number of case comments, notes, and book reviews.[77] In 1909 he prepared *A Preliminary Bibliography of Modern Criminal Law and Criminology*,[78] the first in the English language, for the use of the delegates to the National Conference on Criminal Law and Criminology held at Northwestern University.[79] This was an example of Wigmore's propensity to undertake a task for which no one else had assumed the responsibility, if he believed it was important. This arduous and time-consuming effort was undertaken by Wigmore although he was at the same time involved in planning the conference.

Valuable as were Wigmore's contributions as an author, they were most significantly supplemented by his work as an editor. He made possible, on a far wider scale than ever before, an international approach to the problem of crime through the publication of the Modern Criminal Science Series, in nine volumes in 1911–17, under the auspices of the American Institute of Criminal Law and Criminology. Wigmore was one of a committee of five appointed to select the treatises to be translated and arrange for their publication. Not only was he the originator of the project, but he performed the major part of the labor of the committee.[80]

This ambitious undertaking was intended to further one of the institute's principal aims, namely, to encourage "the study of modern criminal science, as a pressing duty for the legal profession and for the thoughtful community at large."[81] It was Wigmore's view that it was important "to recognize that criminal science is larger than criminal law. The legal profession in particular has a duty to familiarize itself with the principles of that science, as the sole means for intelligent and systematic improvement of the criminal law."[82] He thought that one of the ways to achieve this objective was to make relevant works in the Continental languages available in English, since far more work in this field had been done in Europe than in the United States.

In 1938, Wigmore recalled some of the history of the series: "In 1909 we knew and cared nothing about criminology — the very name was unknown. But from 1910 to 1917 my Committee published the Modern Criminal Science Series; it was eaten up by all groups of persons concerned with crime repression. Its volumes still pay a royalty to some of the European authors . . . and Criminology is now an established field of study all over our country."[83] After Wigmore's death Robert W. Millar commented on Wigmore's role in the field of criminology: "In such wise there came to pass the dream of Wigmore that there should be available to the English-speaking reader the quintessence of authoritative Continental thought regarding a matter of such high social concern."[84]

It was in his work on this series that Wigmore showed his propensity to appreciate the work of colleagues and particularly younger men. To Robert Millar, the translator of Raffaele Garofolo's *Criminology*, he wrote:

I have just brought home my Garofolo copy, and have glanced through it. And I hasten to say that it is the best-reading translation in *any* of the three series. The English is the only English that has throughout sounded as though the author wrote it in English.

I tried to make my two "General Survey" parts sound that way, but none of our colleague-translators have hitherto dared to do it radically. Somebody else can judge whether *I* did; but at any rate I say you did.[85]

Although it is impossible to give specific consideration to Wigmore's many lesser writings in the field of criminal law and criminology, two comments on current cases, written in this period, may be appropriately mentioned because they demonstrated his inclination to turn from his more scholarly work when some contemporary event stirred him deeply. Nor was Wigmore deterred by the prominence of the individual involved if he believed the person's behavior could not be squared with a sound administration of justice or with the ethics of the legal profession. Although Wigmore, of course, recognized that every defendant was entitled to a fair trial, he said, "we know that the regular criminal practitioner fights to free his client guilty or innocent."[86] Condemning Clarence Darrow's position in the celebrated McNamara case in a scathing comment, Wigmore said that, although Darrow knew the defendants were guilty and foresaw the ultimate plea of guilty from the beginning, "he spent one hundred and ninety thousand dollars of laboring men's innocent money to secure at any cost the escape of men whom he knew to be guilty of this coarse, brutal murder . . . ."[87]

Wigmore was equally hard on the press for the exploitation of the case before the trial and on the public for condoning such conduct. With approval, he quoted at length from a Chicago *Herald-Tribune* editorial that exclaimed, "If we are to have civilization we must try cases in the courts, not in public print."[88]

The second case that drew a strong reaction from Wigmore concerned a decision of the Supreme Court of California involving Eugene E. Schmitz, one-time mayor of San Francisco, who was convicted of extortion by the trial court.[89] The Supreme Court sustained the reversal of the district court of appeals on the grounds that the indictment did not declare that Schmitz was the mayor of San Francisco and that the Court therefore could not take judicial notice of this fact. That the Court could not recognize that Schmitz was the notorious mayor of San Francisco and a man named Ruef its notorious political boss was too much for Wigmore, and he entered "the lists with a dissection of the Supreme Court's reasoning which left that honorable bench with scarcely a rag of legal covering."[90] In conclusion, Wigmore said:

Such disputations were the life of scholarship and of the law six hundred years ago. They are out of place today. There are enough rules of law to sustain them, if the court wants to do so. And there are enough rules of law to brush them away, if the court wants to do that. All the rules in the world will not get us substantial justice if the judges have not the correct living moral attitude toward substantial justice.

We do not doubt that there are dozens of other Supreme Justices who would decide, and are today deciding, in obscure cases, just such points in just the same way as the California case. And we do not doubt that there are hundreds of lawyers whose professional habit of mind would make them decide just that way if they were elevated to the bench to-morrow in place of those other anachronistic jurists who are now there. The moral is that our profession must be educated out of such vicious habits of thought. One way to do this is to let the newer ideas be dinned into their professional consciousness by public criticism and private conversation.

The Schmitz-Ruef case will at least have been an ill-wind blowing good to somebody if it helps to achieve that result.[91]

As testimony to the substantial character of Wigmore's written contributions to the field of the criminal law, it is interesting to note that Augustus F. Kuhlman, in *A Guide to Material On Crime and Criminal Justice* (1929), lists (in addition to Wigmore's twenty-six titles exclusively concerned with the subject) the *Treatise on Evidence*; the *Pocket Code of Evidence*; the *Principles of Judicial Proof*; and *Problems of the Law, Its Past, Present and Future*, because of their broad application to the criminal field.

Even if Wigmore had not been so prolific as a writer, his role as an editor alone would have given him a prominent place as a scholar. The discussion of his work in the field of criminal law has already made mention of the nine-volume Modern Criminal Science Series. Wigmore also was chairman-editor of *Select Essays in Anglo-American Legal History* in three volumes (1907–9) (which included Wigmore's article "Responsibility for Tortious Acts" in revised form);[92] the Modern Legal Philosophy Series in ten volumes (1912–22); and the Continental Legal History Series in ten volumes (1912–28).[93] To Wigmore's delight, Holmes agreed to write the Introduction to the first volume of the latter, saying "there is none in the country but yourself, or perhaps my very old friend John Gray [John Chipman Gray of the Harvard Law School faculty] to whom I shouldn't at once decline any addition to my work here."[94] In acknowledging receipt of the manuscript Wigmore wrote, "What has thy servant done that he should receive such a gem in mark of favor! If I had used telepathy, I could not have made you write it any more to my taste."[95]

Although Holmes identified some "frightful blunders of detail"[96] in the translation of Brissaud, he thought highly of the series. He concluded one letter, in which he pointed out some such errors, as follows: "I really started intending to say what a joy to my eyes it was to see the two volumes which I still say — totis vivibus."[97] Of Brissaud, Holmes said to Pollock, "The book itself strikes me as making one feel and realize the evolution of law and correspondence of change to change of circumstances more than any history I ever read."[98]

Wigmore acknowledged Holmes's approval:

> I was verily glad to receive your letter, and to know that you took pleasure in the Series. For actual pleasure of mind, nothing to my taste equals a good book

of history. As I couldn't be like you and dig out truths myself, I resolved to help spread the truths that other men had discovered. I have sneaked off to work on the Series in the way a boy plays truant. Hence I am glad when anyone reports that the work was worth doing.[99]

That he entered into this undertaking with enthusiasm can be seen in his letter to Francis S. Philbrick, who participated in the series as a translator.[100] "I am more and more in love . . . with the Volume I, and I hope that it will be equal to my imagination of it."[101] Of this relationship to Wigmore, Philbrick said, "how ready he always was to discuss the merits of materials to be chosen for translation, how receptive he was to suggestions, with what friendliness he encouraged my labors . . ."[102]

Originally, Wigmore planned to issue the *General Survey* (Volume 1 of the Continental Legal History Series) in a special edition profusely illustrated with selections from his extensive collection of portraits of European jurists. Although this did not materialize, his objective was probably more effectively achieved by scattering the illustrations through the various volumes and later including them in his *Panorama of the World's Legal Systems*.[103]

The Legal History Series was of course but one reflection of Wigmore's lifelong interests. In 1888, at the very beginning of his career, he had written the article "Louisiana: Story of Its Legal System,"[104] and this was shortly followed by the work in Japan discussed in Chapter IV. His article "The Pledge Idea: A Study in Comparative Legal Ideas,"[105] appeared in 1897, and in 1904 he delivered a lecture at the International Congress of Arts and Sciences in St. Louis, entitled "The Problems of Today for the History of the Common Law."[106] Much later Wigmore was invited to give the Barbour-Page Lectures at the University of Virginia, and they appeared in book form in 1920 under the title, *Problems of Law: Its Past, Present and Future*. These three stimulating lectures advanced views with which all would certainly not agree, but they had one characteristic in common, "the brilliance that sparkles through them all."[107] One of Wigmore's suggestions won the strong support of Benjamin Cardozo: that a court faced with an outworn rule that it felt obliged to apply to the case in hand should accompany its judgment with a statement that it would feel free to apply another rule in the future.[108]

In both the fields of torts and evidence the historical component was substantial, and Holdsworth, in his general appraisal of Wigmore as a legal historian, recognized its usefulness: "It would have been impossible for me to have described the origins of the English law of evidence with any sort of completeness without its [the *Treatise*'s] help."[109]

Indeed, much of Wigmore's work reflected careful attention to the history of the subject matter involved, and he urged others to adopt a historical viewpoint as well. He was a lifelong member of the Seldon Society, and in 1923 he supported the founding of the American Legal History Society. Wigmore's over-all role as a legal historian was probably nowhere more appropriately stated than by Holdsworth:

Of the contributions to legal history of these great men [Holmes, Langdell, Bigelow, Ames, Thayer, Gray] Dean Wigmore's contribution ranks very high both in quantity, and, what is far more important, in quality. Moreover, his work has a characteristic, which is not found to anything like the same extent in the writings of the other great American lawyers who have done so much to elucidate the problems of Anglo-American legal history. This characteristic is the large knowledge which he possesses of foreign systems of law, and the skilful use which he makes of this knowledge to elucidate the history of Anglo-American law. His work is a striking proof of Maitland's aphorism that "history involves comparison" [Frederic W. Maitland, *Collected Papers* (1911), 3:453]; and the part which he took, as chairman of the Editorial Committee, in securing the publication of the eleven volumes of the Continental Legal History Series, together with the valuable Introductions which he contributed to some of the volumes in that Series, constitute a service to the cause of legal history, the importance of which will be more and more appreciated with the passage of time. To me that series is very memorable for a personal reason. It was in connection with my Introduction to the translation of Brissaud's History of French Private Law that I first made the acquaintance of Dean Wigmore. His encouragement, which the charm of his personality renders doubly effective, as well as the assistance which I have derived from his writings, have been of the greatest help to my work, as they have been to the work of many others.[110]

In his work on the Modern Legal Philosophy Series, Wigmore consulted Holmes, and a considerable amount of collaboration developed between them. For one of the volumes he again called upon Holmes for an introduction and wrote to him as follows:

There is a passage in your address at Boston, 1897,[111] in which you said, "A body of law is more rational and more civilized when every rule it contains is referred articulately and definitely to an end which it subserves, and when the grounds for desiring that end are stated or are ready to be stated in words." I quoted this as a motto passage on the front page of my Treatise on Evidence.

Now a book is to appear which is nothing but a realization of your text. And we crave and entreat and adjure that you will, therefore, write us a brief note of introduction for it.[112]

The book was *A General Survey of Events, Sources, Persons and Movements in Continental Legal History*, the first volume of the Continental Legal History Series that has already been mentioned, and the "we" referred to in the letter was the editorial committee of the Association of American Law Schools of which Wigmore was the chairman. Holmes accepted reluctantly, adding "I don't know whether I can write anything worth saying,"[113] and, after actually facing the task, he wrote to Lewis Einstein:

Much against my will, until it was done, I have written an introduction[114] to a book that my friend Wigmore is going to publish; a collection of discourses on all sides concerning the foundations of the law, property, contract, discount, marriage. He had asked me for it before I was ill. I said I must see the proof before I could tell. And so at my busiest moment the galleys began to come in, and as soon as I was free from other duties I became a galley slave. I expect my proofs this afternoon, and when they are corrected and sent off, a very short matter, I shall try to improve my mind during the two weeks of adjournment remaining.[115]

In discussing the introduction with Pollock, Holmes wrote, "It says nothing perhaps that I haven't said before, and is my last appearance in public except in the reports."[116] In writing to Harold J. Laski, he referred to "loathed slabs of galley proof that had been accumulating"[117] on his table. In a subsequent letter to Laski, and referring to the introduction for Wigmore, he said, "never again" and added, "the doctor says it is a miracle I have been able to get through my regular work."[118] Wigmore, although he knew Holmes had done him a favor, probably did not fully realize the extent of the effort his ailing friend had made in his behalf. Gratefully, he acknowledged the introduction with delight. "It was most apt for our purpose. In itself it seems to me the most brilliant and most tellingly wise of your unofficial deliverances."[119]

Publication of the final volumes of the series was delayed by the war, and it was in fact 1928 before Wigmore was able to report to the Association of American Law Schools, which had sponsored the Modern Legal Philosophy Series, that, after twenty years of labor, the last volume in the set of twelve[120] had been published and the editorial committee, of which he had been the chairman throughout, could be discharged.[121]

Although Wigmore's role in these various undertakings was primarily organizational and editorial, he did express his own ideas in the various prefaces and introductions which were invariably noteworthy in themselves.[122] One such idea was his observation that "every volume of session laws contains statutes ending with the proviso that this act shall take effect from January first, and shall not be applicable to any contract made, or cause of action accrued prior to that date. Why could not the judicial doctrine of *state decisis* be applied with the same restrictions? It would be an interesting experiment."[123]

An important original article written by Wigmore during this period was "The Terminology of Legal Science (With a Plea for the Science of Nomo-Thetics) (1914),"[124] in which he declared that English and Japanese were the languages best fitted for scientific discussions and proposed (1) "to offer tentatively a terminology for legal science," and (2) "to make a plea for the special study of one part of legal science, i.e., nomo-thetics as that branch of legal science which tests a proposed or actual rule of law by asking whether it ought to be the law by some standard of ethics or economics, etc." In addition Wigmore somehow found time to work on a complete classification of Anglo-American law involving a manuscript, "enough to fill a suit case," which now lies "in a discarded file" because there was no interest in the subject.[125]

Both before and after publication of these series volumes Holmes's valued but pointed criticisms of the texts prompted Wigmore to explain the magnitude of his undertaking. In a long letter written to Holmes in

November 1912, Wigmore discussed in detail his numerous problems, including those that arose from the fact that some of the translators did not live up to expectations. He prefaced his discussion of matters of detail as follows:

I shall now set forth my answer in equity to your notes. I need not tell you that to get the thing going and keep it going was like driving the 24-mule team which the Borax Trust pictures in its advertisement. As you know, the more intelligent your men, the harder to manage them. With twenty authors, two publishers, seven translators, and five committeemen, and twenty introducers(!), for the History Series, and nearly the same number again for the Philosophy Series *and* the Criminal Science Series, you can imagine some of the complications, disappointments, imperfections, which often were irremediable.[126]

In replying, Holmes said in part, "Your letter would wring tears from a brass andiron. You did add light more than I should or would have done in like circumstances. I should have said the translator is responsible."[127] On another occasion Wigmore wrote to Holmes, "Proof reading the proper names in seven languages is a fearsome thing, I find."[128]

That there would be some outright errors in such monumental undertakings was inevitable, and there *were* disagreements in respect to the translation of words and phrases, as Holmes feared. But that these were sometimes exaggerated was illustrated by a book review that justifiably provoked a reply from Wigmore. In a review of Volume 2[129] of the Modern Legal Philosophy Series by Ernest Bruncken in the *American Political Science Review*, it was stated among other things that "First of all, the proof reader was evidently no linguist. The number of typographical errors in the citations from foreign languages is so great that they constitute a very serious blemish. In fact, there is hardly a sentence in Latin, German or French without ridiculous errors, often such as to make the meaning unintelligible."[130]

Wigmore's reply took the form of a statement addressed to the members of the American Political Science Association which he asked the editor to publish in the *Review*. The editor declined to publish the full statement but agreed to accept one hundred to two hundred and fifty words.[131] Apparently Wigmore was not willing to accept this counterproposal, and it is not clear whether his statement was circulated in any other form. At any rate, the substance of his statement merits consideration here.[132]

After acknowledging the reviewer's competence and the value of his criticisms in general, Wigmore said that a "mis-statement of *fact* is a different matter, especially when it reflects discredit alike on proofreader, translator and editorial committee." Proceeding to the facts, Wigmore pointed out that there was not a single French or German sentence in the whole book. The only errors were in foreign book titles, and out of many hundreds there were only fourteen misprints. As to the Latin, Wigmore asserted that out of "(Probably) a thousand Latin passages ranging from one or two words to eight or ten lines each" there were only thirteen misprints, none of which were misleading. For a book of some eight hundred pages

Wigmore certainly believed the condemnation was entirely too severe — and indeed it was. But loyalty to the translator and to all those in the undertaking with him was not satisfied merely by pointing out the facts. For good measure he added:

> Reviewers are kittle cattle. Sometimes they act like the mighty but stupid bull, in the Spanish arena, who is directed by the shaking of a red cloth, and in a futile attempt to impale it with his horns, exposes himself to a fatal thrust. There is something about translated books, I notice, which especially enrages the mighty reviewer like a red cloth, and often as foolishly. This present book, like others, has had that experience. . . .
>
> The reviewer who thus recklessly makes baseless or exaggerated assertions which are calculated to discourage the reading of a worthy book commits a crime against science.
>
> If he cannot himself contribute substantially to the progress of that science, his proper course is at least to refrain from obstructing those who are making some positive effort to leave the world a little better than they found it.[133]

In spite of the magnitude of the task assumed by Wigmore in seeing the three major series (legal history, legal philosophy, and criminal law and criminology) through to a successful conclusion, he carried, jointly with Albert Kocourek, a similar responsibility for the Evolution of Law Series[134] in three volumes (1915–18) which included in Volume 2, Wigmore's article on the Pledge Idea.[135] Upon reading this volume of the series Holmes said, "Without flattery I got more from your own Pledge article than anything else."[136]

In each of these ambitious undertakings Wigmore provided the driving force that carried the projects through to a successful conclusion. It was generally conceded that he did more work with each volume than anyone except the person primarily responsible, and his voluminous correspondence, which involved selecting authors and translators, prodding reluctant or lagging participants, and making arrangements with the publisher are substantial evidence of this fact. Edwin Borchard described the Continental Legal History Series as an ". . . enterprise . . . as masterful in conception as it is in execution . . . a great work . . . whose importance in our legal education will be estimated at its true value and fully appreciated only in the perspective of time."[137] According to Pound, the Modern Legal Philosophy Series, the Continental Legal History Series, and the Evolution of Law Series together "have had much influence upon the development of jurisprudence not only in America but in the world at large."[138]

Wigmore's extensive study of foreign scholars had gradually convinced him that, because of the ease in entering German universities, American scholars were frequently not only pro-German in their inclinations but were largely unaware of the contributions that had been made both by the French and Italians. As early as 1911, he was pressing this point with a not very receptive Holmes.

I hope it isn't a mere fad of mine; but the fetish of German scholarship has so long obscured to us the merits of the other two, that I take every opportunity to restore the balance where possible. I used to think that Brunner was the only God, till I discovered that Brissaud and Pertile were also worthy of worship, and that really there was to be no relative exaltation of either body of scholars.[139]

As usual Wigmore was not content with half measures. In 1916 he prepared and distributed an appeal under the title "A Proposal to Restore the True Status of French Science and Learning in America,"[140] in which he demonstrated the widespread failure to recognize French science and scholarship, due, he felt, to the fact that until fairly recently American degrees had not been recognized as the basis for advanced standing. The reason for this limitation had been that the "diplomas, in theory issued by the Government, admitted the French citizen to the practice of the professions in France and to the official civil service, and every citizen thus admitted was expected to have been trained under French auspices from the beginning."[141] Thus, in effect, American students had been barred from obtaining degrees in French universities. With this barrier now removed, Wigmore proposed that "ten or more graduate fellowships be established for American students in French universities, to be awarded competitively every year for ten years, beginning in October 1917, each fellowship to hold for two years, if desired."[142]

Wigmore's efforts met with success, and the Society for American Fellowships in French Universities was formed. One outcome was the publication in 1917 of *Science and Learning in France*,[143] of which Wigmore was the editor. This book included an appreciation of French science and scholarship in all fields by American scholars and a survey of the opportunities for American students in French universities. Wigmore was a member of the committee that drafted the Section on Law, but the universal character of the book's contents testified to the breadth of Wigmore's scholarly interests, and his frequent preoccupation with the achievement of practical results, albeit on a long-range basis.

How Wigmore managed to carry these massive editorial assignments in addition to his own scholarly writing is difficult to understand, and yet he also found time to comment on current events, including court decisions, if they attracted his special attention. We have already read of his reactions to the McNamara and Schmitz cases.[144] Under these circumstances it would hardly be expected that one with as pronounced views as Wigmore's would indefinitely confine himself to praise of Holmes and his views, or that differences would always be minor in character. Consequently, it is not surprising that in March 1915 Wigmore wrote to Holmes, "By the way, shall you mind it if some time I take a pot-shot at L.E. Waterman Co. v. Modern Pen Co. on general principles?"[145] That Holmes's curiosity was aroused and that he, too, may have had some misgiving is evident, for in his reply he said, "I wish I knew whether you thought the case you wrote about pitching into [Waterman pen] went too far or not far enough. I stand firm however until further notice."[146]

This preliminary exchange was shortly followed by another letter in which Wigmore said:

> Now I must thank you for not being offended with my ungrateful screed, which our Editor in Chief [George P. Costigan, Jr., editor in chief of the *Illinois Law Review*] submitted to you in advance. I realize well enough that it is not a profound utterance, and that it will seem crude to you. Nevertheless the Waterman case came along as a text for a sermon I have long felt moved to preach. And my assault on some *little* Courts' text would not have attracted notice;[147] I felt that the desired occasion had been providentially furnished. That it happened to be your opinion made me feel like a hound. I did try to exhibit some sense of humiliation at this dilemma, however. And besides, the public presumption will be that I am hopelessly wrong, anyhow. So really I have sacrificed myself for a principle, but not, I hope, sacrificed your benevolent "misericordia regis," nor abated in the devotion of
>
> Yours truly
John H. Wigmore.[148]

Wigmore might well have had misgivings about Holmes's reaction, for in an article entitled "Justice, Commercial Morality and the Federal Supreme Court: The Waterman Pen Case,"[149] and in a manner typical of Wigmore when his emotions were aroused, he vigorously attacked the majority opinion written by Holmes.[150] In this case the L. E. Waterman Pen Company sought to enjoin the Modern Pen Company from using the word "Waterman" or "Ideal" in connection with the manufacture and sale of fountain pens. Although it was conceded that the object of the practice was to draw off the plaintiff's business, the defendant claimed the right to use the name "A. A. Waterman" or "Waterman" because it had secured this right by assignment from A. A. Waterman, a former employee of the plaintiff, L. E. Waterman Pen Company.

In his opinion, Holmes affirmed the decision of Learned Hand, the district court judge, which forbade the use of "Ideal" or "Waterman" and of "A. A. Waterman & Company," except when used "in connection with the following phrase or its equivalent, all words to be written in letters of the same size, 'not connected with the original Waterman pens.' "[151]

Needless to say, Wigmore agreed with the plaintiff that, under the circumstances involved, merely requiring a suffix to read "not connected with the L. E. Waterman Co." afforded no protection because "the public who buy fountain pens and want Waterman pens do not care and do not know what the initials of the famous penmaker are."[152] He adopted with approval Justice Pitney's conclusion, in the dissenting opinion, that the practice was "a mere sham and fraudulent device,"[153] and added, "after sixteen years of litigation the parasite-thief is still free to continue to prey upon the established business."[154] And then he concluded ". . . we have no better claim to use our name as a help to stealing, than we have to use our property or our speech or our money."[155]

But Wigmore's concern extended far beyond this case: generally, he felt, the courts had a "lack of appreciation of this great parasitic phenomenon in modern commercial life"[156] and a callous attitude toward the moral element involved in such cases (which they unquestionably personally abhorred). He concluded:

> But these pages are meant rather as a sober danger-query to the entire bench of today, in its relation to the entire subject. The subject happens to be good illustration of a questionable feature of our judicial decisions in these latter times. That feature is a voluntary divorce of the judicial pronouncements from morality and reality. The judge conceives it his part neither to allude to the one nor to seek for the other. He prefers to keep himself retired within the dry logical network of his legal system. He is disinclined to keep obviously and frankly in touch with morality and with reality. Has not the time come for a different attitude?
>
> The law tends always to Desiccation. The safety-point of this has been passed. We venture to believe that it must now permit itself a period of generous Humectation.[157]

Wigmore was vindicated by the courts in their subsequent decisions, although their opinions have emphasized the protection of the plaintiff's established business interests and the prevention of public confusion rather than the underlying ethical and moral factors involved.[158]

In view of Holmes's excessive desire for recognition and his sensitivity to criticism, Wigmore's piece on the Waterman case could hardly have been pleasing to him. However, it is clear that the relationship between the two was not impaired. Holmes's subsequent letters are obviously warm and cordial, and in March 1917 he wrote, ". . . I have to repeat to you what a constant joy your friendship has been to me and with what pleasure I follow each of your achievements. It has made life happier and easier to me to know you and will, while this machine is to run."[159]

Wigmore's wide reading interests, of course, extended far beyond cases and statutes and other legal materials. Within its broad embrace were the contributions of related disciplines which Wigmore was constantly urging the bench and bar to utilize in the elucidation and development of the law. However, he was quick to detect quackery or exaggerated claims by those who overemphasized the role that these related disciplines could play in the solution of legal problems. Perhaps the most dramatic illustration was his vehement reaction to Hugo Münsterberg's book *On the Witness Stand*,[160] in which Münsterberg greatly overstated the contributions that psychology could make at that time and then took the legal profession to task for not using them. Wigmore hoped that some psychologist would question Münsterberg's claims or submit more solid proof of their applicability to the practice of law.[161] When no one came forward he characteristically undertook the assignment himself, and, after an extensive study of the relevant psychological literature, he refuted Münsterberg's excessive claims in an article entitled "Professor Muensterberg and the Psychology of Testimony, Being a Report of the Case of Cokestone v. Muensterberg."[162] However, Wigmore acknowledged that the legal profession in the United States, more than in any other country, was behind in the scientific study of the criminal law.[163] Wigmore's article achieved considerable popularity among professional psychologists at the time because it surveyed an area that had received very little attention.[164]

Wigmore was also particularly disturbed by the attitude of many Americans toward the Japanese whom he had come to know so intimately as a young teacher. In 1914 he was goaded into action by a news story that appeared in the *Chicago Record-Herald*. He wrote the author, Sumner Curtis, in part as follows:

> Your Washington dispatch of January 23rd, in this morning's RECORD-HERALD, was read by me with surprise and repulsion. It is of the kind that recklessly breeds war where no war would have been. . . . It is based on nothing but a colorless and non-commital statement by one of Japan's Ministers of State, and it uses this to stir up a popular feeling which otherwise would have remained healthily ignorant on the subject until the respective governments had finally reached an accord. . . . It gratuitously makes the untrue assertion that "we are hated by Japan." The truth is — and every man of intelligence knows it — that nine hundred and ninety-nine out of a thousand Japanese do not think anything at all about the American people, but go about their daily bread-winning without caring or knowing anything about us, much less hating us. And our people do the same.
>
> If war should ever come . . . the detestable result will be largely chargeable to journalistic utterances like yours, made on both sides of the water.
>
> On such utterances I invoke the curse of nations.
>
> And may you yourself never have peace, — until you have humbly learned that the moralities of your position command you to devise every possible way of leading the popular mind to peace, instead of intoxicating it to the frenzy of needless war.[165]

Wigmore felt so strongly about the matter that he sent a copy of this letter to William Jennings Bryan, who was secretary of state at the time.[166]

This outburst by Wigmore was provoked not only because the article tended to promote hostility between two nations but because of its display of racial prejudice, of which he was totally free. It is perhaps interesting to note that some years earlier and, shortly after he returned from Japan, in an article dealing with the naturalization of the Japanese,[167] he concluded that "in the scientific use of language and in the light of modern anthropology the term 'white' may properly be applied . . . to the Japanese race."[168]

Such spontaneous responses to the flow of printed matter that attracted Wigmore's attention were of course supplemented by numerous book reviews. In his reviews he almost always had constructive suggestions, however meritorious the work, because he had such an extensive range of knowledge to draw upon. But he could also be critical, and, on occasion, he employed the book review not only to appraise the author's work but to question the legitimacy of the special field with which it was concerned. His review of the sixth edition of Melville M. Bigelow on the *Law of Estoppel* (1914) is illustrative. In Wigmore's view

Estoppel is a mere juristically unworthy cloak for three or four doctrines having a legitimate place under their own names, [that it is] a poor name for a genuinely independent doctrine, which has its own separate right to existence, but is so closely related to certain others that it ought to be frankly acknowledged and treated as their close juristic relative. Some day, let us hope, this demonstration will be made, and the family reunion achieved, to the great advantage of all parties.[169]

As to this appraisal Frankfurter wrote, "Thank you for showing up that lazy child Estoppel. It — I suppose it's neuter — is an old nuisance and I suspect nothing will so effectively show up its illegitimacy as gentle scorn. That is a fine shakedown you gave it."[170] In the same letter Frankfurter commended Wigmore for support of the emerging field of public-health service through his introduction to Henry B. Hemenway's *Legal Principles of Public Health Administration* (1914). Frankfurter said, "And while I am at it I also want to say I liked lots your introduction to Hemenway. That book is a significant sign."[171]

Wigmore could also commend excellence. An example of appreciation and constructive criticism is his thorough review of Virgil M. Harris's *Ancient, Curious and Famous Wills* (1911),[172] in which he characterized the book as "a real addition to literature" and a "source of interest and profit to all readers."[173] After suggesting many improvements for a new edition, he concluded, "These are merely suggestions for the enlargement of a feast which is already so rich and varied that the author may regard them as ungrateful. But a book which has so pre-empted the field as this has, and outlawed everything else of the kind in anticipation as well as in retrospect, will in any event remain a permanent repertory of interest, entertainment and usefulness."[174] In acknowledging receipt of a copy of this review Harris said, "I not only appreciate your complimentary words, but I also appreciate your criticism; coming from your hands, it necessarily commands consideration. . . . Out of several hundred reviews, there are none which exhibit greater care and learning than does yours."[175]

Another example of Wigmore's painstaking attention to a book under review is his meticulous handling of William Carey Jones's edition of the *Commentaries on the Laws of England* by Sir William Blackstone.[176] In Wigmore's words, "We welcome this new edition of the great commentaries. It gives them to the student in their full integrity of text, but with a new body of apparatus exactly adapted to the times. . . . At last we have a Blackstone which is of today. At last the footnotes look forward, not backward."[177] After making a number of suggestions indicating details that he would have "preferred to find otherwise," he concluded: "But having vindicated the privileges of the captious reviewer, we close with a resolution of thankfulness that a Blackstone edition has now been produced which is an ornament to American scholarship, a reflection of the best modern thought, and a fitting guide to the earnest beginner in the law."[178] Jones responded to this "handsome" review by saying in part, "it is the kind of a review that I hoped someone would make, and yet I doubted whether anyone would be at the pains to examine the volumes so carefully, or whether, if anyone did, he would catch the spirit in which I did the work and the purpose I had in view. I could not have asked for a better appreciation of the edition, and, of course, there is no one whose approval is more valued than yours."[179]

One of the many books reviewed by Wigmore was Frederic J. Stimson's *My United States*, of which he said, "It offers a moving picture panorama of almost all the great questions, legal and political, of the last forty years. I have read no book, during the past decade or more, that has such living interest nor such entertaining style. I read every word of it — which I rarely do for a book."[180] To Wigmore, the title would certainly not be repellent, and with his avid reading habits the book was bound to come to his attention. However, when he wrote Holmes that it was well worth reading,[181] Holmes replied that for him the word "my" in the title was a deterrent.[182]

It is well to point out that Wigmore was concerned not only with his own book reviews but also with those of others. In a letter to John M. Zane, who, in Wigmore's view, "knows more about the history of the English Bar than any man on either side of the pond,"[183] Wigmore said, "I have had on my desk for a couple of weeks a recent number of the Journal of Comparative Legislation, containing a review of your 'Great Jurists.'[184] I herewith lend it to you, not because the review is flatteringly complementary to yourself, but because an Englishman's attempt to be critical of an American product is as comical as a pig trying to get away from a railroad train."[185]

But Wigmore's comments were by no means confined to books or to the books reviewed. He "was always reading the articles of tyros, and was prompt to praise and encourage — or sometimes rebuke."[186] "Many a young man who had diffidently published his first paper in a law review was encouraged to enter upon a fruitful career of law writing by an appreciative letter from Dean Wigmore. Not only those who were working for a better administration of justice in America, but those who were doing scholarly work in any field of the law have owed much to the stimulus of his encouragement and example."[187]

He was also generous about reading in manuscript the efforts of others, particularly those of younger men. His comments, criticisms, and praise denoted careful reading and provided constructive guidance and encouragement. But occasionally he could be discouragingly critical in his comments. A young instructor on the faculty translated a foreign work and submitted the manuscript to Wigmore, who quite characteristically agreed to examine it. After reading it Wigmore told the translator that he had no objection to the technical correctness of the translation but that it was too heavy in style and should be entirely rewritten. The instructor was taken aback and said that he did not have the time or energy to do this. Wigmore replied "in a kindly voice"[188] that this was unfortunate because if carefully rewritten the book would be something of value.

Stubbornly resisting Wigmore's suggestion, the instructor soon found a publisher, and in a few months a copy of the publisher's announcement came into Wigmore's hands. The author was identified as a member of the Chicago Bar and no mention was made of his affiliation with Northwestern University.

Wigmore had not heard from the translator in the interval so he did not know whether there had been any response to his suggestion. But "boiling with anger"[189] he picked up the telephone and called him, and the following conversation ensued:

SMITH: Yes, Smith Talking.

DEAN WIGMORE: This is Wigmore.

SMITH: Good Afternoon, Dean Wigmore.

DEAN WIGMORE: I want to know what you mean by publishing a law book without giving the University credit!

SMITH (*flabbergasted*): But, Dean Wigmore, I did not have the consent of the University to use its name in this connection.

DEAN WIGMORE (*irritated*): If you thought it necessary you could easily have gotten that consent.

SMITH (*recovering*): I think you have forgotten that I submitted my translation to you and that you told me it would not do. I did not follow your advice, and I could not ask for your consent to connect the name of the University with my own.

Dean Wigmore replied to this sound and irrefragable point by loudly smashing down the telephone on its hook, and the conversation was closed.[190]

The next day Smith found a note of apology from Dean Wigmore in his mail stating that he had regretted what he had said and asking him to forget the incident.[191] Once again, it was Wigmore's strong sense of loyalty — in this case to the Law School — that stirred his emotions, rather than irritation at the translator for not taking his advice. If he remembered the prior discussion at all he apparently did not remember the thrust of his advice, for he reacted at once and without examining the book to see if his advice had or had not been taken.

Obviously, much of Wigmore's scholarly work involved the writing of letters, and he was indeed an inveterate letter writer, carrying on an extensive personal correspondence at home in addition to the voluminous correspondence dictated at the Law School. The outstanding example was, of course, his correspondence with Holmes, to whom all letters were written in his own hand, regardless of subject matter, in deference to Holmes's known aversion to typed letters. One of Wigmore's general lists of "Friendly Letters" shows that he wrote seventy-five letters in his own hand between October 14, 1906, and June 13, 1907.[192]

A habit of long-standing with Dean Wigmore was to get up almost as early as usual on Sunday morning. He spent the morning in his study writing letters (often on postcards which he enclosed in envelopes) to the many friends, relatives and alumni of the Law School, posting them that afternoon, if he took a walk, or taking them to Chicago on Monday morning when he went to the

School. He never heard of a wedding, a birth, a death, or some change of fortune, or read an article written by one whom he knew, but that he wrote a short note about it. He wrote to authors when their books were especially interesting or pleasing to him.[193]

One example is an appreciative letter to Arthur M. Harris, concerning his book *Letters to a Young Lawyer* (1912), in which Wigmore said in part:

I believe that the special thing about them [the letters] which attracted me was not merely their common sense but also the fact that they assumed throughout that it is still possible for a young man to keep his self-respect and conscience and yet succeed at the bar in a worldly way.

Your book and that of John C. Reed on *The Conduct of a Law Suit* are the twin books that I recommend every young man to study verbatim during the hours of the first year when he is waiting for clients.[194]

So far, only incidental consideration has been given to the extraordinarily broad base of Wigmore's reading and his fund of general information. His interests extended far beyond the legal and near-legal areas. He was not only thoroughly familiar with the classics but most generously sampled the lesser writings of the past and the flow of contemporary publications, including detective stories, of which he was an avid reader. He was in fact "a kind of leviathan who devoured libraries."[195] A familiar figure was Wigmore emerging from the Evanston Public Library with four or five detective stories under his arm. But, apparently, even in this reading he had a purpose, for he once said to the librarian, "do not, I beg you, think I take these solely for amusement. I go through them rapidly to see how the law is carried out."[196] "He usually read with a sharp pencil in his hand, and hundreds of books can be found in the Gary Library showing light pencil, marginal comments, and frequently corrections in his own writing."[197]

It was this extremely broad reading interest, supplementing the court reports, statute books, texts, and periodicals that regularly came into the Elbert H. Gary Library, which provided him with the rich nonlegal resources from which to draw in his writing on legal topics, endowing them with his characteristic breadth and depth of approach. His "One Hundred Legal Novels"[198] has already been referred to. In an introductory statement to this list Wigmore makes a strong case for the novel as an indispensable ingredient in the lawyer's preparation, and he himself was a living illustration of how such reading could heighten the lawyer's professional capacity and augment the resources upon which he could draw in meeting his day-to-day problems. It was this list that started his friend Nathan W. MacChesney "on a lifetime fascinating road."[199] Wigmore explains its value:

For the novel — the true work of fiction — is a *catalogue of life's characters*. And the lawyer must know human nature. He must deal understandingly with its types, its motives. These he cannot find — all of them — close around him; life is not long enough, the range is not broad enough for him to learn them by personal experience before he needs to use them. For this learning, then, he must go to fiction, which is the gallery of life's portraits. When Balzac's great design dawned on him, to form a complete series of characters and motives, he conceived his novels as conveying just such learning.[200]

Apparently, even in his leisure reading, Wigmore was somewhat systematic. At least beginning with the year 1912 he kept lists of these nonlegal books as he read them, and the records available to us now go through February 1943,[201] just a month before he died. Altogether they contain 2,150 book titles or an average of 179 per year for the periods represented. Some months ran very high — for instance 67 in January 1920, 58 in both March and September 1921, and 62 in July 1930. During a vacation at Hot Springs, Virginia, from February 23 to March 27, 1929, he read 67 books. About one-half of these were mystery stories, but the lists include many biographies, travel books, short stories, histories, ancient and modern, books on the First World War by columnists, military analysts, and ex-officers, some poems, and some books on science. Abraham Lincoln was a great favorite, and Wigmore not only read every available biography, but every available speech, message to Congress, letter, and state paper of which Lincoln was the author.[202] Although Wigmore frequently did not read a book through word for word, his brief annotations and his extensive use of the subject matter clearly indicate that he must have identified and absorbed the essentials. A few examples of his annotations are as follows:

> Garry Owen, *The Story of A Race Horse*, by H. DeVere Stacpole. One of the best told stories ever written; American heroine; two Irish lovers; book ends with a conundrum as to which she took.
> *Memoirs of John Hay* by Wm. R. Thayer. Too much W. R. T.
> *America and the New World State* by Norman B. Angell. A wise warning to our self-righteousness.
> *Behind the Bolted Door* by Arthur E. McFarlane. Best constructed detective story, but too much slang.
> *Twelve Men* by Theodore Dreiser. Excellent character sketches.
> *The Spinners* by Eden Philpott. Usual Philpott padding of very little to tell.
> *The Tunnel* by Dorothy Richardson. Arnold Bennet flattened and monotonized to the Nth power.
> *And They Thought We Wouldn't Fight* by Floyd Gibbons. Best correspondent's book on the A.E.F. experiences.   '
> *Their Mutual Child* by P. G. Wodehouse. Eugenics — one of W's best hits.
> *Travels in Italy* by J. W. Goethe. A talented self-conscious, hypocritical prig.
> *The Stream of History* by Geoffrey Parsons. Better than Wells.
> *The Redwaynes* by G. E. Locke. Dime Novel Stuff
> *The Rhododendron Man* by Aubry Tyson. Long Island murders; the best written American detective story.

But Wigmore of course had his enduring favorites, and he was always especially eager to expand his facility with foreign languages. "He always carried in his brief case or Green Bag; a pocket edition of one of Shakespeare's plays . . ., of the Old Testament, of the New Testament, and a book containing stories of every-day life in a foreign language that he was studying or reviewing at the time.''[203]

One of the most interesting facets of Wigmore's broad reading habits was his relationship to Arthur Train. An important strand in the very warm bond of friendship between the scholar and the lawyer-turned-fiction-writer was their joint interest in legal plots that could be used for Train's stories. Train also asked Wigmore to be on the lookout for "references to foolish or forgotten laws which result either in injustices or surprises to litigants."[204] A number of Wigmore's suggestions did in fact find their way into Train's stories. In April 1921, Train wrote, "The story which you suggested with regard to the will in which the scheming wife is outwitted by the apparently senile husband was written and accepted by the Post last summer and will doubtless shortly make its appearance."[205]

In the same letter Train reflected his appreciation for words of approval from Wigmore (in this case Wigmore's statement that *The Prisoner at the Bar* could be used as a reference book): "Your subtle appeals to my vanity are never without response and although my intelligence rebels, my heart inevitably beats faster on hearing from you with regard to my wisdom, integrity, learning and charm."[206] Shortly thereafter Train wrote from Paris, during his honeymoon trip, "Do you mind if I dedicate my next book — 'Page Mr. Tutt,' — to you? It contains one of your plots."[207] And later, when sending a copy of this book to Wigmore, he referred to it as "3/4 lb. of literature dedicated to your name," and added, "Anyhow you are the only lawyer who ever gave me a plot, or I might add, a thrill."[208] Mr. Tutt was no doubt often a central figure in their conversations, as well as in their correspondence. Train once wrote, "I am thinking of putting old Tutt in Cambridge, England, and having him raise hell with the ancient city."[209] Late in 1926, Train wrote to Wigmore saying, "I am writing a sort of legal 'Arrowsmith' and would very much like to chin about it with you. My hero is a bug on 'liberty' and I'd like your ideas."[210]

That Train was eager to develop a working relationship with Wigmore and not merely receive suggestions for his plots, is evident from the following letter to which he appends the name of his famous character Ephriam Tutt:

Dear Wigmore:
    I shall not be able to get out to Chicago for the present. One of the things I wanted to talk to you about is this. I am told on good authority that the name "Mr. Tutt" on a handbook of law — a "house-hold book," so to speak — would prove a literal gold mine — "Mr. Tutt's Handbook of Law" or some such title. It would go as well as Emily Post's famous book on etiquette. But it ought to be a *good* book. There are numberless slants on which it might be written. It could be left *general and instructive* or made *practical and forceful*. Much of it, of course, could be merely a popularized digest of CYC, etc. But there is a great chance in the introductory matter to each chapter to put a good many things straight. I believe there is a real chance here. Now, if you've got the time and like the idea I'll furnish the trademark and do the writing, if you'll do the law. You can appear as author or any way you want. We ought to sell

$2,000,000 worth and make $200,000 apiece. Without a doubt we could be certain of a very large return. How does it strike you? With best regards to you both for a Happy New Year.

Affectionately,
Ephraim Tutt[211]

Nothing came of this proposal — not surprising in view of Wigmore's many commitments.

Train's appreciation for Wigmore's collaboration over many years is best summed up in his own words, "You are the most amiable as well as the most erudite of all my friends."[212] "Oh, never failing font of wisdom! Thank you again for invaluable help!"[213] Of Arthur Train's achievement as a writer in general, and in respect to Mr. Tutt in particular, Wigmore had this to say:

> It is now twenty-eight years ago, writing of "legal novels" and telling of lawyers who were also novelists, that I ventured the prediction that "Arthur Train may well turn out to be our modern Fielding, if he broadens his canvas"; which he has done, and has thereby more than fulfilled the prediction. But though "As It Was in the Beginning" and "Ambition" are unrivalled canvases of professional life, yet Mr. Tutt stands out as a creation, independent of any plot or story.[214]

As the foregoing pages have made perfectly evident, recognition as a scholar came to Wigmore early and mounted with the passage of time. Perhaps the most fitting way to close this chapter is with a brief recapitulation reflected in the words of three of his contemporaries — Holmes, Frankfurter, and Henry M. Bates. The latter had graduated from the Northwestern University Law School immediately before Wigmore's arrival on the scene but had come to know him well as a colleague in the field of legal education and as dean of the University of Michigan Law School. As early as 1905, Holmes concluded a letter with "I scribble off this to thank you and let you know that I still live and blow your horn."[215] And in writing to Pollock in December 1911, Holmes said, "The two best men that I know of, of the generation or half-generation after us, in this country, are Wigmore and Roscoe Pound. . . . I was rejoiced that Harvard should have got Pound and wish it had Wigmore as then I should have thought it better equipped than ever."[216] Later he amplified this statement in another letter to Pollock, "Apropos of Pound perhaps I said before that I keep all his essays. I have one volume bound and the stuff for another. I admire his learning and his command of it, but as yet have not perceived a very strong personal reaction upon his knowledge — as one does in Wigmore — whom I hope to see here on January 1."[217] In March 1912, Frankfurter, in writing to Wigmore, said, "I have the good fortune down here of seeing Justice Holmes from time to time, and when talking of our profession and legal thinking in this country you are a never failing subject of our enthusiasm. It was a distinct achievement, for which the profession will be grateful, to have persuaded the Justice to write that essay for you. Ever increasing power and strength to you."[218] Dean Bates thus expressed his appraisal in writing to communicate his regret that he could not attend a dinner in Wigmore's honor in 1914, "Your greatest service to the cause of jurisprudence has been not the splendid work on evidence, brilliant as that is, but rather your leadership in the movement to strike the fetters of intellectual and legal provisionalism from the bar and in pointing out the way to a conservative and scientific reform and progress in our jurisprudence."[219]

Finally, the tributes of the world of legal scholarship found expression through the publication of the *Celebration Legal Essays by Various Authors to Mark the Twenty-fifth Year of Service of John Henry Wigmore as Professor of Law in Northwestern University*, publication of which, because of the exigencies of war, was delayed until 1918. Although space limitations made it necessary to confine the contributors to those concerned with the law, in disregard of Wigmore's much wider interests, it represented authors from Asia, Africa, America, Australia, and Europe[220] — a testament to Wigmore's world-wide circle of colleagues and friends.

8
Leader

By no means was Wigmore solely preoccupied with scholarly pursuits. He had an unshakable commitment to the development of the Law School, first as a young teacher and then as dean. Yet his work as administrator, teacher, and scholar, broad as it was, still did not encompass the wide range of his interests and activities.

It is not often that one who has achieved distinction as a scholar is, at the same time, recognized as an outstanding leader in his chosen field. But where scholarly contributions have embraced such broad and diversified subject matter as was mastered by Wigmore, the intensive and time-consuming labor involved in the process would seem to preclude all possibility of an outstanding public service. This was not true in Wigmore's case. He was uniquely and extraordinarily endowed as leader as well as scholar.

The creative mind, the ability to plan, often meticulously down to every detail,[1] the genius for organization, and the capacity for sustained endeavor that served him so well in grappling with the most complex subject matter and in formulating his ideas in original scholarly writing were applied with equal vigor to his active participation in the life around him. These faculties gave him a thorough grasp of the various components of any problem and enabled him to frame proposals for which, quite characteristically, he would become an ardent advocate. In addition, he had an unquestionable talent for creating the conditions that would bring his proposals to full fruition. The fact that he almost always seemed poised and serene and not particularly busy was undoubtedly the mark of an exceptionally well-adjusted individual — an individual in full command of his faculties. As Albert Kocourek, one of his closest observers, put it, "At work he reminded one of the easy motion of the long driving shaft of a powerful machine resting on oiled bearings."[2]

On the personal side the great capacity for friendship that grew out of his genuine interest in people and his willingness to listen drew others to him. His ability to inspire them to undertake specific assignments, or to carry forward some project of their own, and his active encouragement and support for their undertakings elicited a loyalty that extended to an ever-widening circle of colleagues and friends. It is impossible to estimate the amount of constructive work done by others largely because of Wigmore's inspiration, encouragement, and support. His own deep sense of loyalty to the persons, institutions, and programs with which he was identified obviously further strengthened the bond. Indeed, this generally admirable attribute was so highly developed that it occasionally colored his outlook or blinded him to the shortcomings of those to whom his loyalty was accorded.

Another important factor related to his wide-ranging leadership was Wigmore's penchant for languages and his thoroughness in preparing for any assignment he undertook. Preparation for a visit to a foreign country always included a year or two of the study of the language of that country — not only to improve his capacity as a scholar, but to enable him to communicate directly with those around him. Altogether Wigmore could read or speak a dozen languages, including the most important European languages and Russian, Japanese, and Arabic as well.

These attributes, coupled with his essentially democratic attitude and his obvious charm, provided Wigmore with an extraordinarily large number of active personal associations, which extended all over the world. The warmth and enduring quality of these relationships has perhaps nowhere been more effectively reflected than in the words of Hugh Green, a student whose close association and friendship lasted for many years:

> Dean John Henry Wigmore was an extremely interesting character to even the most casual observer. He aroused my curiosity the very first time I met him. He seemed so different. His suave manner, scholastic appearance, his unfailing enthusiasm, and mental attainments, coupled with other traits too numerous to mention made him a wonderfully attractive person. Doubtless, a very considerable number of his former students would concur in my first impression. Many of them would also agree that curiosity quickly changed to affection for the man — an affection which became stronger with the passing of time. Those who testify that Dean Wigmore was a truly lovable man are legion.[3]

Whenever Wigmore encountered a situation that called for a remedy, he was apparently impelled to work out a solution or at least devise a step toward improvement. Usually, he was not satisfied merely with a written attack on the problem. He went into action, and because of his inherent modesty he seldom, if ever, allowed personal aggrandizement to stand in the way of the goal he envisioned. He identified himself with the cause and not the cause with himself. His gaze was on the objective.

Although a complete appraisal must await the final pages of this book it is full time to take account of the scholar's early role as a leader. His dynamic approach to the development of the Law School, including the creation and support of the American Institute of Criminal Law and Criminology, has already been discussed. In the field of legal education Wigmore did not allow himself to be circumscribed by the case method of study as it was developed at Harvard, important as it was in the early stage of his career. He was not only responsive to local needs but kept in touch with other schools, many of which, it will be recalled, he visited while crossing the Continent after his return from Japan.

Believing as he did that law teachers and practitioners should work together, Wigmore became a member of the American Bar Association in 1893, at the beginning of his academic career in the United States, and began the active participation in its work that continued for fifty years, until the time of his death. It was in 1893 that the first section of the American Bar Association, the Section on Legal Education, was created. That he was closely identified with this early effort is evident from the fact that at the second meeting of the section in 1894, when the "Section presented a program which rivaled that of the Association itself,"[4] he was one of the "eminent lawyers and educators,"[5] including Woodrow Wilson, to give an address. In his "A Principle of Orthodox Legal Education,"[6] he contended that the study of law was a full-time occupation and that outside activities "were incompatible with an adequate training."[7] This was a much-debated question then, as it is even now, and as he said at that time the principle was "honored more in the breach than in the observance."[8]

Wigmore served on a number of ABA committees, including the Executive Committee for the year 1906–7,[9] and participated in discussions both formal and informal. Strongly in favor of making the association more effective, he offered suggestions with that end in view and supported proposals to achieve this purpose.[10] Among the formal papers he submitted was a study based on "A Statistical Comparison of College and High School Education as a Preparation for Legal Scholarship" (with Frederic B. Crossley).[11] In the association, Wigmore actively supported the case method of instruction,[12] revealing in his argument that he himself had initially felt the characteristic resentment of the student when he was first exposed to the method used at Harvard and had later come to believe that its value in relation to the total legal curriculum was often overstated.[13] In 1917 he set forth his views at some length in an article in the *Harvard Law Review*, concluding his discussion as follows:

> To sum up: I invite assent to the following theses:
> That Law is dealt with, in nature and in thought, by six distinct mental activities or processes, — the analytic, the historic, the legislative, the synthetic, the comparative, the operative;
> That these six processes have greater or less importance at different epochs of a community's legal life; and that in our present epoch the second, third, fourth, and fifth have a relative importance which they have not had for a century past;
> That the case-study method, as hitherto practiced, develops mainly the first only; and yet that method represents five-sixths or more of the student's activity under the ordinary curriculum of today; and that this is disproportionate;
> That therefore greater relative place should be given to the others (relegating the analytic process to, say, one half of the course); and that more suitable methods and materials should be provided for their adequate cultivation.[14]

After the creation of the Association of American Law Schools in 1901 there was frequent collaboration between that association and the Section on Legal Education of the American Bar Association. However, each carried on a distinctive program, one oriented around the interests and problems of law-school faculties, and the other concerned, at least in part, with the point of view of the practitioner. In each of these organizations we find Wigmore defending the need for three years of legal study;[15] opposing the automatic admission to the bar without examination of graduates of certain law schools, the so-called diploma privilege;[16] generally supporting the raising of standards for legal preparation and for admission to the bar,[17] including at least two years of prelegal education;[18] the broadening of the contents of the curriculum[19] and its extension to four years.[20] In 1906–7 Wigmore served on the Executive Committee of the Section on Legal Education and Admission to the Bar.[21]

In addition to his work in the ABA Section on Legal Education, Wigmore served on several committees representing the American Bar Association as a whole. Among these was the Council on Legal Education[22] the Committee on Legal Education and Admissions to the Bar,[23] the Committee on Law Reporting,[24] and the Committee on Jurisprudence and Law Reform.[25] He was also frequently a member of the American Bar Association's Local Council for Illinois.[26]

Wigmore repeatedly pointed out the increasing complexity of the problems with which lawyers had to deal, and his firm belief that the legal profession would never regain its position of leadership unless it insisted that its members be adequately prepared. He also pointed out that every state provided a free college education and that no poor boy with ambition and determination need be excluded.[27] Finally, he said:

> The Bar is overcrowded with incompetent, shiftless, ill-fitted lawyers, who degrade the methods of the law and cheapen the quality of services by unlimited competition. The number of lawyers should be reduced by one-half. As a method of elimination for the future, a stricter requirement for preparation is a sensible method . . . for reducing hereafter the spawning mass of promiscuous semi-intelligence which now enters the Bar.[28]

He also advocated improvement in the standards established by the Association of American Law Schools and in the requirements for admission to the bar[29] as well as legislation to protect academic degrees.[30] His active participation included his advocacy of the four-year curriculum.[31] His interest in the study of legal history[32] and jurisprudence[33] and his long and distinguished career as an editor of the works of outstanding scholars in many foreign countries has already been discussed.[34]

But the impact of Wigmore's participation in the meetings of the Association of American Law Schools was greater than the foregoing recital of his formal activities suggests. Manley O. Hudson, a student at the Harvard Law School shortly after publication of the *Treatise on Evidence*, records his first encounter with the legendary author:

> When I later attended for the first time a meeting of the Association of American Law Schools, I heard the opening address by a tall, thin, dandy-like man with a flushed face, urging some such program as the adoption of a new Greek terminology by American lawyers. Undaunted by the apparently hostile

reception of his thesis, on the speaker went as if he were ushering in a new era. So that was the great god in the flesh. I was introduced to him afterward, and he acted as if he had but waited to see me. Conversant with my preoccupations at the University of Missouri Law School, he gave me such warm encouragement that I began to feel myself somebody in the strange environment. Thus began a friendship which waxed through thirty years!

Not merely did he bring to every meeting of the law professors a pabulum of intellectual excitement upon which they feasted, he was also the life of the party at the annual gala dinner. He selected the songs to be sung, he distributed mimeographed copies of the words, and he was the major domo of the chorus.[35]

But even when acting within the framework of professional organizations, Wigmore's interests went beyond the subject of legal education or the work of the legal profession as usually conceived. In 1904 he was appointed as one of a hundred delegates to the Universal Congress of Lawyers and Jurists held in St. Louis, under the auspices of the Universal Congress and the American Bar Association,[36] having already been selected by the congress to read a paper.[37] His paper, referred to in connection with Wigmore's work as a legal historian, was entitled, "The Problems of Today For The History of The Common Law."[38] In 1908 he became active in the Comparative Law Bureau, beginning as one of the managers representing the American Bar Association.[39] He continued this activity until the bureau, designated a section of the American Bar Association in 1919,[40] operated under the title of Section of Comparative Law.[41] Wigmore strongly favored broadening its scope under the title Section of International and Comparative Law,[42] a title that was later adopted.[43]

The convening of the Second Pan-American Scientific Congress in Washington, D.C., in 1915–16 gave Wigmore another opportunity to play a part in this field. He urged radical changes in the Subsection on Jurisprudence, served on a Subcommittee on Jurisprudence,[44] and read a paper at the Second Session of the Subsection on Jurisprudence on January 4, 1916, entitled, "The International Assimilation of Law: Its Needs and Its Possibilities from the American Standpoint."[45]

In 1917, Wigmore accepted an appointment by President Wilson to fill the vacancy in the United States Section of the Inter-American High Commission created by the death of Elbert H. Gary. The purpose of the section was to secure more harmony in the commercial law of the Latin American republics and to bring about uniformity in methods of fiscal administration. Believing that this kind of "world law" should have the support of the American bar, Wigmore described the process going forward at the time in an article entitled "A Glimpse at World-Law in the Making," which appeared in the *Illinois Law Review* in 1920.[46]

These activities again reflected one of Wigmore's major interests, comparative law, and provided an outlet for the special competence that arose not only from his prolific reading, but from his frequent trips abroad, supplemented by a trip to South America in 1915, and his more or less constant study of foreign languages.

Participation in these various activities of the American Bar Association gave Wigmore some first-hand knowledge of the organization's shortcomings. One consequence was a growing conviction that it could and should be made a more effective professional group. Although other members also recognized the need for some fundamental changes, there were many evidences of dissatisfaction, and the innate conservatism of many of the leaders presented an obstacle that had to be overcome.[47] Indeed, proposals submitted to the Executive Committee in 1907 and 1908 had only met with rejection.[48]

Wigmore's initial move was a proposal to have the association publish an official journal,[49] and to that end he submitted a memorandum in 1911 in some detail.[50] After consideration by the Executive Committee[51] the association, at its meeting in Washington in 1914, authorized the Executive Committee to publish "a journal of the announcements and transactions of the Association, which might also include some of the work of various affiliated bodies," and the first number of the *American Bar Association Journal* appeared in January 1915.[52] Thus Wigmore once again became affiliated with the inauguration of a legal periodical, although he made it clear that he was too heavily committed to act as the editor.[53] Unsatisfied with this modest beginning, however, he urged both the Chairman of the Publications Committee and the members of the Executive Committee to purchase the *American Law Review*, then thought to be available, and make it the association's official organ and the "only law review of distinguished prestige . . . not edited from a University Law School."[54] In this move Wigmore was not successful.[55]

In 1913, believing that the situation was urgent and that "the best chauffeur in the world cannot make a broken down machine go fast and comfortably,"[56] Wigmore offered a resolution for the appointment of a special committee to consider "What amendment, if any, to the Constitution and By-Laws of the Association would be desirable with a view of increasing the membership of the Association, improving its order of business and extending its influence in the profession and in the Community at large."[57]

The resolution was referred to the Executive Committee, but in this case it reported favorably and a Committee on Reorganization was appointed with Wigmore as chairman.[58] However, he regarded the committee as inadequate in both size and composition, and he wrote to George Whitelock, the secretary, "What I want to distill into your ear is the suggestion that the dinky little committee in which I am permitted to vermiculate be enlarged to ten, so that some of those important people in other states, who have shown an interest in the subject, can be used."[59]

When the suggestion was presented to the Executive Committee it was rejected unanimously.[60] The following year the committee requested more time for the extensive work that was necessary. The request was granted. However, the "resounding voice of Gen. W. M. Ketcham appeared to express the feelings of the small body of members present, mostly Association leaders, when he said 'And tell him [Chairman Wigmore] to be damned careful.' ''[61] This statement unquestionably expressed the deep entrenchment of the inner circle and their commitment to the status quo.

In spite of this disappointment, Wigmore continued to devote a great deal of time to the work of the committee. He made every effort to obtain the views of the members at large, and, among other things, sent questionnaires to the presidents of state bar associations and to the vice president of the American Bar Association in each state, requesting their views on the various questions under consideration.[62]

Two years later the committee submitted a report pointing out two general weaknesses in the association[63] — its lack of public influence and its inefficiency. Although the answers to the questionnaires presented in the report showed a wide variety of views, the committee itself could agree on only one recommendation — to devote four entire days to the annual meeting instead of three.[64] But even this recommendation was tabled by the Executive Committee.[65] Thus Wigmore's constructive recommendations, many of which have since proven to be sound and practical, never won the necessary submission to the membership at large.[66]

For the time being inertia had won. ''The Association was in an inflexible mold. Most of its leaders looked upon it as an organization open only to superior individuals — a veritable fountain of honors.'' The chairman of a membership committee that had secured more than 2,000 members was regarded as a ''fanatic for growth.''[67]

In such a climate of opinion resistance to changes in structure and differences as to objectives thrived. Certainly Wigmore's path was not eased by his criticism of the bar for not dealing adequately with the legal problems of the poor and for his advocacy of salaried lawyers employed by the state to perform a function that legal-aid groups had only begun to fill.[68]

No doubt it was Roscoe Pound's address at the St. Paul meeting of the American Bar Association in 1906 that in Wigmore's words ''struck the spark that kindled the fire with flame of high endeavor.''[69] But at this time and for some years afterward Wigmore was one of a small minority endeavoring to make the association a really effective instrumentality, a task with which Wigmore would be concerned throughout his life.

The refusal of the Executive Committee even to distribute the committee reports (minority and majority) in the usual manner was too much for Wigmore. On his own initiative, and with the financial support of the American Judicature Society,[70] he prepared and distributed to the ABA membership a substantial document entitled: ''Read Carefully the First Seven Pages: Then Study the Rest at Your Leisure, If you are Interested.''[71] It embodied the record of the committee's activities and its reports and the action taken by the Executive Committee. The document was prefaced by a statement by Wigmore explaining that he had acted because of the attempt ''to deprive'' the members of the power ''of self-government'' by using ''gag rule'' to prevent ''bona fide and moderate proposals from receiving any consideration on the floor of the meeting, and thus to fortify the control of an over-conservative minority.''[72] Although Wigmore certainly had a following,[73] this move did not win any immediate effective support for his proposals as a whole.

In one respect Wigmore's efforts and those of his committee bore fruit under the leadership of Elihu Root, who had been both friendly and appreciative.[74] Invitations were sent to the state and local bar associations to send delegates to meet representatives of the American Bar Association at a conference in Chicago on August 28, 1916, to consider the development of closer relationships between the American Bar Association and other bar associations.[75] At a second conference called in 1917[76] it was resolved that the conference be made a permanent organization,[77] and in 1919 it became a section of the American Bar Association.[78] This was at least one important step toward Wigmore's major objective. Many years later Wigmore acknowledged that his proposals were premature although basically sound,[79] and through the pages of the *American Bar Association Journal* he again made a vigorous appeal for changes in the constitution and by-laws to enable the American Bar Association ''to formulate rationally its convictions as a representative body and to activate its latent national power with a maximum effect.''[80] This was not the end of Wigmore's role in the work of the American Bar Association. At the end of the First World War, when his civilian activities could be resumed after the interruption of his career at mid-point, his work in the association continued.[81]

Although Wigmore never assumed a major responsibility in either the Illinois State Bar Association[82] or the Chicago Bar Association, he kept in close touch with both organizations by serving on committees and performing other specific tasks in both groups. Informally, he was frequently involved in efforts to improve the law at both the state and local levels, and many of his case comments and editorials in the *Illinois Law Review* were concerned with these problems. Wigmore lamented the fact that law professors did not follow his example and make use of the law reviews for their editorial comments on current issues in which the legal factor was important.[83]

Wigmore's energy and initiative received another important outlet in 1908 when the governor of Illinois appointed him a member of the Commission for the Uniformity of Legislation in the United States.[84] This initiated an active identification with the Uniform State Law movement that continued throughout Wigmore's life.

He took an active part in the work of the following committees: Torren's System and Registration of Title to Land,[85] Compensation for Industrial Accidents, Relating to Lynching, Compacts and Agreements Between States, and Depositions and Proof of Statutes of Other States. In 1909 he served as a member of a joint conference with the National Civic Federation, and he was continuously the chairman of a liaison committee on cooperation with the American Institute of Criminal Law and Criminology. Here again Wigmore's participation extended far beyond the war years, and the account of his later work with this commission will be deferred until a later chapter.[86]

Wigmore's great interest in promoting the efficient administration of justice impelled him to become a prime mover in the creation of the American Judicature Society which was founded in 1913 with headquarters in the Northwestern University Law School. To assist in getting its program under way, he devoted every Saturday for a year to the society.[87] Herbert Harley, the original secretary-treasurer and the holder of the principal administrative office for many years, said, in a letter to Wigmore, in which he referred to a brief history of the society that he had just prepared for publication in the *Journal,*

> In writing this cursory history I am reminded very sharply of the fact that to you, more than any other person, the survival of the Society is due. I am impelled to say this now because it did not seem politic to be so precise in my article. I did not distinguish between your services and those of Kales and Olson, all invaluable.
>
> I remember something of Cicero's insistence that the Savior of the Republic was no less than the founder. You saved us over and over. . . . I want you to know that I realize my debt to you, and appreciate your aid to the Society.[88]

Dean Roscoe Pound summarized Wigmore's contribution in these words, "Another monument to his intelligently directed zeal is the American Judicature Society in which he took a leading part from the beginning."[89]

With Wigmore's broad conception of the role of the legal profession, it was inevitable that he would take a keen interest in public affairs, although he never sought or held public office. His friends sometimes wished that he could do otherwise. For example, Franklin K. Lane suggested Wigmore's name to Woodrow Wilson as a nominee for the office of attorney general.[90] It will be recalled that back in Wigmore's San Francisco days he had been one of the organizers of the Municipal Reform League[91] and that in Cambridge he had been actively identified with the Republican party.[92] In 1911 he served on the Republican Committee of One Hundred organized in Chicago. However, for the most part he indicated no party affiliation and voted as an independent, particularly for state and local positions. His friendship for and correspondence with Franklin K. Lane was his way of keeping in touch with the political scene through the eyes of a friend he greatly respected,[93] and he included Lane among several recommendations he made to Woodrow Wilson for a vacancy on the United States Supreme Court. More significant is the fact that he did not recommend William Howard Taft: "Ex-President Taft made a capable and intelligent Judge twenty years ago," he wrote to Wilson. "In my opinion, he is not capable of understanding the true inwardness or depth or breadth, of the big legal problems of to-day."[94]

In another letter to President Wilson, Wigmore not only shows his concern for the quality of the service being performed by a public official but an interest in the individual himself. The letter involved Henry S. Boutell, minister to Switzerland, about whom, although he completely disagreed with "his ultra-conservative attitude," Wigmore wrote that he had "brilliant and attractive qualities in all other respects." Wigmore urged that he be kept at his present post until he completed a history of democracy in Switzerland that would "enoble American scholarship" with "a notable contribution to the bonds of friendship between Switzerland and the United States of America."[95]

As the foregoing incident suggests, Wigmore kept up the interest in foreign affairs that was already evident while he was a student at Harvard, and he eagerly supported Charles Cheney Hyde, his colleague on the Law School faculty, who was to make a name for himself in this field.[96] On the issue of intervention in the affairs of other nations, Wigmore felt very strongly. As early as 1898 in a letter to the *Nation*[97] he opposed such intervention and argued that if it was accepted as proper in one instance it must be conceded in others, pointing out that the United States had resented proposed intervention by England in behalf of the Southerners during the Civil War. In 1914 he addressed a very strong argument in opposition to intervention in Mexico to President Wilson.[98]

As we have seen, Wigmore had already demonstrated his effectiveness as a reformer in the law. His approach to politics and public affairs was more liberal than is generally recognized, as his attitude toward Taft strongly suggests. However, he was not a revolutionist in any sense of the word. He had "no sympathy with the muckraker." He wanted "to see programs attained by sane, solid methods — following the example of time [as Bacon says], 'which indeed innovateth greatly, but quietly, and by degrees scarce to be perceived.'"[99]

His interest in the broader aspects of education and a reflection of the wide reach of his reputation can be seen in his election in 1916 as the second president of the American Association of University Professors[100] of which he became a lifelong member. Twenty-seven years later, upon looking back to this event, he said, "And I was given to believe at the time, by candid friends that the chief, perhaps the only, reason for nominating me for the presidency was that I might act as a sort of a decoy duck, to draw other law professors into the net."[101]

Although this factor may have been given some weight, for there were then only 18 law professors in a membership of 850,[102] his qualifications as a scholar and as a leader were too obvious to be disregarded. Indeed Walter Metzger, the AAUP historian, names Wigmore as one of the celebrities in the organization at the time along with John Dewey, Basil Gildersleeve, and E.R.A. Seligman.[103] In writing to congratulate Wigmore on his election to the council the year before his election as president, Henry Lerew represented Northwestern University:

> May I take this opportunity of telling you also that, at the New York Mtg. of American Professors, — a really remarkable gathering — one dean was voted off the list of nominees for the Council and another dean (from a large eastern institution) was severely criticized, on every hand, for his frequent expression of opinions. But nobody doubted for an instant that your real business was the teaching of law and not merely university administration. Everyone — and

especially the Northwestern representatives — was delighted to have you on the Council of the Association.[104]

Upon taking office as president, Wigmore expressed what he believed to be the spirit of the organization by quoting from Fichte: "It is the vocation of our profession, that of the scholar, to unite itself in one single body, all the parts of which shall be thoroughly known to each other and all possessed of similar intellectual standards."[105] Twenty years later, in an address to the association, he said, "And the other day, as I was taking my daily glance at Emerson's Essays, I came upon this sentence, which fits our labors: 'What is best written or done by genius in the world was no individual's work, but came by social labor, when a thousand wrought like one, sharing the same impulse.'"[106]

But Wigmore's conception involved more than informal collaboration between scholars. He believed the association should deal actively with the problems with which the group should be concerned and "persuaded the Executive Committee, reluctantly on their part, to authorize seventeen committees; and they were alphabetized from A to Q."[107]

At the close of the year he accounted for his stewardship in a forty-three-page report devoted in large part to his conception of the role of the association and of its seventeen committees. As would be expected, he laid before the members an extremely broad program of activities, emphasizing matters of substance but contained many practical suggestions. He closed his remarks as follows:

> I now close this survey of the work of the Association for the past year. In offering these personal views upon its various activities, I have aimed merely to stimulate reflection by our members upon these weighty problems, and to elicit those views, whether concordant or discordant, which will ultimately focus at our Annual Meeting as the decisive professional verdict.
> May that verdict be a finding of truth and a judgment which shall prevail![108]

That some persons gave Wigmore's selection as president an even broader significance is indicated by the following editorial comment:

> The election of a law teacher, *Dean Wigmore* of the Northwestern University Law School, to the presidency of the American Association of University Professors is a fact significant in the development both of the American University and of American law. Though many of our law schools have been connected with universities, the connection has in the main been merely nominal, and teachers of law have been conspiciously absent in university affairs. We cannot recall a single university leader drawn from the ranks of the law professors. The latter have until recently been attracted by the prizes and honors of the legal rather than of the teaching profession. But the American University, a comparatively recent institution, is slowly but surely assimilating the older professional schools, and raising the standard of their teachers to the high level prevailing in European universities. The effect of this must in the end be revolutionary for American law, since it will tend to make us approach the continental system in

which the scientifically trained law professor has a superior authority in the determination of the law over the politically selected judge. To the traditional lawyer this may seem as unbelievable as would have been the prediction a generation ago that we should acquire foreign possessions and be drawn into the game of world politics; nevertheless those who have followed the influence of the books of Professors Gray and Wigmore on the actual law of this country can realize how far we are approaching the continental system. It is very fitting that the honor of the presidency of the American Association of University Professors should be accorded to Dean Wigmore, who is not only one of our most creative scholars, but who, by promoting the translation of foreign works on the history and philosophy of law, has been a leader in the effort to break down the isolation and provincialism of American legal thought.[109]

Because of Wigmore's loyalty to Harvard and his consistent support of the institution it was no doubt inevitable that sooner or later he would take his turn at the helm of the Harvard Club of Chicago. When he was elected president for the year 1914–15,[110] he took hold with his accustomed vigor.[111] Among other things, he participated in the very careful planning for the Fifty-eighth Annual Dinner of the Club which had more than the usual significance. The theme was "the Pan-Pacific Idea," and the meeting was a prelude to the meeting of the Associated Harvard Clubs at the Pan-Pacific Exposition to be held in San Francisco in 1915, which it was intended to promote. As a result of Wigmore's persistent efforts, General George W. Goethals (honorary LL.B., 1912) was the guest of honor "as the most notable embodiment of the Canal idea and the Panama Pacific triumph."[112] In Wigmore's letter of invitation he said in part:

> Do not allow your mind to progress toward our annihilation by a negative decision, until you have heard how plausible and in the destiny of things it is that you should accept this invitation.
> The logic is this. The Associated Harvard Clubs meet at San Francisco, August 13 next, to do their part towards celebrating the triumph of the Panama Canal and the success of the Pan-Pacific Exposition.[113]

With President Lowell present to represent the university and with several distinguished alumni as guest speakers it was quite an occasion.[114]

General Goethals's invitation to Wigmore to visit the Panama Canal was warmly accepted, and the cordial relationship that developed between the two is evident from their correspondence, which dealt to a considerable extent with some of the problems with which Goethals was confronted at the time.

Wigmore responded to other calls from Harvard as well: to serve as vice-president of the Harvard Law School Association in 1916[115] and as a member of the Law School Committee for the year 1916–17, to which he was appointed by the Board of Overseers of Harvard College.[116]

Wigmore continued his interest in Japan, among other ways, through his membership in the Asiatic Society of Japan. In Evanston he was a member of the local University Club. He was a member of the Chicago Law Club and the Chicago Law Institute, and the University Club of Chicago was usually his social headquarters for visitors who came through Chicago.[117] He supported a number of activities other than those concerned with the law. To these he gave at least the support of membership, but active participation often followed as a matter of course.[118] He also responded to appeals for donations to worthy causes, such as the YMCA for its work with university students; the University Settlement, nominally affiliated with Northwestern University; the Central Howard Association in Chicago, concerned with prison reform; the Evanston Sanitarium; the Evanston Women's Club Building Fund; and famine sufferers in Japan. As his income grew, his contributions to these organizations increased.[119]

But Wigmore's concern for the individual was by no means confined to organized philanthropy. He somehow always made time to lend encouragement or to give direct assistance. His letter[120] to the attorney general of the Philippines commending him for his fine official reporting was followed up by an editorial in the *Journal of Criminal Law and Criminology*.[121] His encouragement of the work of others extended beyond the field of the law as narrowly conceived. Dr. William Healy, director of the Juvenile Psychopathic Institute of the Juvenile Court of Cook County, concluded a letter thanking Wigmore for congratulations on the appearance of his *Individual Delinquent*[122] with these words, "I hope some day I may adequately express my appreciation of all that you have done in this field and for the cause for which we are both working."[123] And Wigmore carried this inclination to help wherever he went. For example, during his short visit to Panama, as the guest of General Goethals, Wigmore became acquainted with the American minister to Panama, a young man for whom he developed a high regard. It was only natural for him to write a letter to Secretary of State Robert Lansing commending the young man highly on the assumption that an outside personal appraisal might be of value;[124] to try to ascertain the competency of a doctor who was taking continuous fees from a woman of very limited means under circumstances that indicated no improvement in her health;[125] to assist a widow in securing an appropriate education for her two promising sons.[126]

Nor was Wigmore hesitant about calling attention to conditions that should be rectified whether they concerned police protection in the Evanston parks,[127] better lighting on the street cars and suburban trains,[128] noise from the motor boats in the lake,[129] or burning leaves in the fall.[130] If one keeps in mind the perfectly groomed and dignified Wigmore, the following letter to the superintendent of the transit company cannot but be of special interest:

Sir:—

I write to make a last protest against the abuses of your system of treating Evanston passengers like cattle at the Howard Avenue change station.

On Thursday, May 7th, I arrived on the South Water Street Howard Avenue train at 5:58 P.M. The rain was pouring and we were notified to change. The next train was three or four minutes in coming. The order was given to cut two and leave three cars. There were sixty people on the platform. On entering the new train, some twenty-five were standing without seats. I notified the brakeman; . . . asking that a fourth car be left on the train. He refused and cut off two. I declined to pay any fare without a seat. I was thereupon ejected, by the starter's orders, two brakemen pushing me out, politely but forcibly. . . . When the next train came, and two cars were cut from it, there were in the third car, which I entered with my friend, only eleven passengers, including ourselves. Now this showed that the starter, using proper judgment, could just as well have cut one car from the first train and three cars from the second one; thus giving ample room on the first train.

You sit up there in your office, and do not feel the personal irritation from such treatment. But put yourself in the position of decent people like yourself, who are slammed in and out of cars like cattle, by husky young cubs who act as if they were cattle-drivers, and provoke peaceful people by driving them about with loud, slave-driving orders. You can then imagine something of the feeling of disgust and anger at your company which such conduct evokes.

Now I have for three years past been a missionary for your road. I have quit riding on the steam train. I have talked and written in your favor, against the grumblers. In the confused times which you had last fall, I counseled patience to all, in view of your difficulties. I have tried to be sensible and considerate.

But I have now reached my limit. I shall take this case as testing whether you in authority are genuinely trying to make your people behave decently in the treatment of Evanston passengers. I shall know whether my patience has been misplaced or not. You have your chance to keep a friend or to make a determined opponent.

After due time for verifying my above facts (and I have a witness), I want an express disclaimer of the conduct of the starter, a statement that he has been rebuked for his bad judgment and overbearing conduct, and a statement that it will be safe for Evanston passengers to take your trains in the expectation of being treated with good judgment and decent consideration at the junction point.

Yours truly,[131]

In another instance, his sense of loyalty, in this case loyalty to Chicago, came into play.

April 14th, 1914

N.H.D.,
  c/o Boston Transcript,
   Washington St., Boston

Sir:

In reading your recent review in the Transcript of Garofalo's Criminology, I came across your sneering allusion to the use of the word "rendition" and its appropriateness for Chicago — a town of Lard.

If the reviewers who write in that way could realize the hurt which they cause to laborious, enthusiastic, conscientious and skillful toilers, who, for the sake of science and the public good, have spent themselves on their work, they would possibly withhold such sneers.

I wish to impress upon you the disgust which one person feels for that style of reviewing.

Yours truly,[132]

Wigmore's substantial achievements in the academic world, in scholarship, and as a leader had, by the time he reached his early fifties, won him recognition in all quarters. He had wrought a dramatic change in the Law School; it was now recognized as one of the leading departments of Northwestern University even though he was almost constantly frustrated by the lack of adequate funds. Outside of the university community recognition constantly increased. Even back in 1906, Wigmore's reputation brought him an honorary LL.D. degree from the University of Wisconsin, and Harvard, as we have seen, gave him similar recognition in 1909.

Wigmore also came under consideration for public office. In 1910 Edmond J. James, president of the University of Illinois, asked permission to submit Wigmore's name for appointment on the Supreme Court of the United States. His friends submitted a memorial to the president in his behalf, but he declined to be considered.[133] And in a letter to Wigmore in 1912, Franklin K. Lane, then secretary of the interior said, "If the man in the White House [Woodrow Wilson] had as much sense as I have he would name you for the Supreme Bench without asking, and 'draft' you as Roosevelt says."[134] Shortly thereafter Lane recommended Wigmore to Woodrow Wilson for the post of United States attorney general.[135] But Wigmore declined all such suggestions. Apparently he displayed no real interest in public office, perhaps because he never really cherished such a role, or because such interruptions would have seriously interfered with plans to which he was so deeply committed.

More and more Wigmore was recognized as an extraordinary person possessed of such a combination of gifts that he could function at different levels simultaneously. As one of his contemporaries said:

A man who can read in a half-dozen continental languages on some obscurity in mediaeval legal history until the clock calls him to a director's meeting of the Legal Aid Society; who can write a fugue and then pass to a lecture on Torts; who can preside over a faculty meeting and then bury himself in the Leges Barbarorum; who can plan a budget and then find satisfaction in the Laocoon; who can smooth over a difficulty for a Freshman, and then at once become absorbed in the Seleucidae; who can exhaust a proposition of current law while receiving a dozen callers; who can investigate an Etruscan antiquity after analyzing the Workman's Compensation Act; — we say that a man who does these unusual things by way of daily routine is an uncommon person. Of course, this is only a characterization, but it is accurately typical of Mr. Wigmore's diversified activity and learning.[136]

Perhaps the greatest wellspring of Wigmore's extraordinarily productive record was his "faculty of originating valuable ideas and of creating the conditions to bring them to full realization."[137] "He invented a way of multiplying his accomplishments by taking hold only when an emergency arose, and others were unable, or unwilling, to do what was needed."[138]

9

Colonel

IIIIIIIIIIⅢIIIIIIIIⅢIIIIIIIIⅢIIIIIIIIⅢIIIIIIIⅢIIIIIIIⅢIIIIIIIⅢIIIIIIIⅢIIIIIIIⅢIIIIIIIⅢIIIIIIIⅢIIIIIIⅢIIIIIIII

It was now 1916 — a year of the utmost significance for Wigmore. For the
new course of action on which he embarked was to divide his career into
three distinct parts: the activities and achievements of his early manhood,
his military service during World War I, and the postwar years that would
bring to full fruition the potentialities of this extraordinary man.

General Enoch H. Crowder, judge advocate general of the army, urgently requested Wigmore to apply for a commission in the Officer's
Reserve Corps of the Judge Advocate General's Office.[1] He was commis-
sioned as a major on November 8, 1916, one of the first six to be appointed
during that year. He was subsequently advanced to lieutenant colonel on
February 15, 1918, and to colonel on July 19, 1918. Although Wigmore
was not assigned to active duty until July 9, 1917, when he reported to
General Crowder in person in Washington, D.C., he did work on a revision
of the rules of evidence in the *Manual of Courts-Martial* with Major
Blanton Winship, who came to Chicago during September and October
1916, for that purpose.[2]

Wigmore had nothing but praise for Winship, both as a man and for his
thorough understanding of the rules of evidence and the accurate manner in
which he had handled them. However, Wigmore declined to bear any
responsibility for the strict enforcement of the technical rules in any particular prosecution, "for the reason that after a record goes to Washington
it must expect to encounter the censorious inspection of sundry lawyers in
Congress, who will complain if the technical rules have not been
applied."[3] In writing to Crowder, Wigmore stressed the importance of
avoiding the error of what Roscoe Pound had called "trying the record, not
the case, on appeal," which would be "lowering the practice of Courts
Martial to the standard of backward-looking lawyers." With such limitations, he said, progress would not be possible. "I have always publicly
stood for the repudiation of some of these technicalities, and I cannot put
myself in a position of publicly endorsing them." Wigmore offered to
identify these technicalities if requested.

When in July 1917 the order came for Wigmore to report for service in
Washington, he did not know whether his assignment would be brief or for
the duration of the war, but, in consultation with the faculty, it was agreed

that it was the patriotic duty of those who remained to shoulder the work of those called into service.[4] He received a leave of absence from the university which ultimately extended until May 1919 and paid one-half of his regular salary.[5] In spite of his pressing responsibilities in Washington, he kept in touch with the Law School by correspondence, and, with occasional short leaves of absence from his military duties, he participated in or made all major decisions.[6]

There is no way to know how the students generally reacted to Wigmore's departure from the Law School, but one at least took the trouble to express his feelings in a letter:

> I was indeed saddened to learn that this morning's lecture on Evidence [would] possibly be your last, this year, — all depending upon the duration of the War and other causes. All my class-mates must surely feel likewise.
> Not only do you inspire the student to learn the law in its most humane, ethical, and philosophical phases, but, as one of my friends aptly remarked, "One can acquire a wide education by merely listening to your lectures." Your profound knowledge of the arts and sciences impresses the students greatly. And the use of that knowledge in "driving a point home" fills him with delight.[7]

And a student who had already enlisted wrote from "Somewhere in France on Christmas Day": "The days I spent in your freshman class in Torts have left a vivid impression in my mind and a keen desire to come back some day and finish the law course. When this war is over I may be able to go back to the great study with renewed vigor and effort."[8]

Wigmore brought to his new assignments in Washington not only his exceptionally broad legal training and experience and his enormous capacity for work, but also a rapport with, and a loyalty to, General Crowder. He had first become acquainted with the general in 1913, when he selected the Northwestern University Law School as one of six law schools to which an officer of the regular army could be sent for a complete legal education. This plan (considered highly constructive by Wigmore) was subsequently eliminated by an express provision of the National Defense Act of July 5, 1916.[9]

Unlike many of his contemporaries, Wigmore was fully aware of what the fateful consequences of a German victory would be for the United States at least as far back as September 1914.[10] He embodied his views in an essay:

MY CREED IN THE WORLD WAR

The Prussian militarist aristocracy — born with a strong man's crude instinct for fist-dominion; nurtured in medieval ideals of force by centuries of internecine combat in the isolated and primitive regions of the Northeast; then emerging from the Napoleonic wars as the self-appointed and unloved champion of German patriotism; then harshly suppressing, or expelling to America, those free spirits who stood out for democratic self-government and liberal thought, and making itself universally disliked among the Germans — arrived at last, by main strength, in 1870, at the imperial domination of the whole German people, a people naturally home-keeping, pious, hospitable, genial, liberal-minded and docile.

Prussian militarism then proceeded to intoxicate the German nation with a false, intolerant and ruthless philosophy of war and statecraft. Like a once peaceful Indian tribe made madly drunken with bad whisky, the German nation has been drugged into supporting Prussian militarism in its obstinate, arrogant, unscrupulous and futile ambition to impose itself upon the world. All Europe is now engaged in a ghastly struggle to save itself and the world's future from this repulsive fate.

Germany must be disarmed, then confined until it sleeps off its intoxication and awakes to remorse for the misery it has caused.

The other countries, and our people most of all, must lend all active sympathy, in this struggle, to the cause of self-defence against a common world-danger — a danger both to our bodies and to our ideals.

On such an issue, we may be neutral; but we cannot be neuter.[11]

Wigmore had not initially favored American entry into the war, in spite of his bellicose attitude toward Germany. He had felt so strongly that the controversy should, if possible, be settled by peaceful means that he had submitted a proposal to President Wilson for a "Neutral International Conference and a Peaceful War."[12] Nevertheless, a September 1914 letter to William Jennings Bryan, then secretary of state, strongly opposing any attempt at a peaceful settlement and expressing his hope that Germany "be licked to the finish," shows his ambivalence.[13] He thought that preparations should be made for any eventuality, and he lent his support to any activities that had this end in view. At the same time he was a member of the League to Enforce Peace, of which William Howard Taft was the president. He actively supported the Commission for Belgian Relief and raised funds to supply tobacco to the French soldiers. Although Wigmore still hoped that the United States could avoid entrance into the war, he believed that, instead of remaining neutral, it should take a strong stand in condemning Germany's actions and give all possible aid and support to the Allies. He, somewhat inconsistently, was vehemently opposed to President Wilson's policy of neutrality, which he said exhibited "a great moral failure."[14] To Franklin K. Lane, then secretary of the interior, he wrote, "I am now running with your fire company on faith only, — faith in yourself and the President. My tank of *reasons* is empty."[15] Apparently disagreement with President Wilson as to neutrality did not destroy all faith in him as a leader. To Wigmore, Lane replied, "things are not looking at all nice as to Germany and Austria. I know that the country is not satisfied, at least part of it, with our patience, but I don't see just what else we can do but be patient. Our ships are not needed anywhere, and our soldiers do not exist."[16]

As to this point, Wigmore had for some time been in favor of some form of compulsory military service. Consequently, early in 1917, and before the United States entered the war, he supported a Compulsory Service Bill which provided for six months of service, though he favored an amendment that would permit college students to serve periods of three months in two consecutive years or two months in three consecutive years. Such a plan, he believed, would prevent a serious setback to college and professional education in the United States.[17] Later in 1917, after the United States had entered the war, Wigmore expressed his belief that when "President Wilson formulated the reasons for taking sides against Germany, he should have placed at the head of the list: *'To vindicate the Rule of Reason against the Rule of Force.'* Sadly enough, he was not inspired to do this. The thesis of self-determination was mistakenly substituted."[18]

Wigmore was also concerned about the role that the organized bar would play when the United States became involved. He pointed out the malevolent rule that some lawyers had played during the Civil War and made a strong plea for high professional conduct in the present crisis. He urged bar associations to be prepared to act against corruption if necessary,[19] and he argued that local bar associations, through special committees, should "indemnify the enlisted brothers against their loss" while they were in service.[20]

Given Wigmore's intense feelings about the war, it is not surprising that he was impelled to compose a patriotic song. At his own expense he prepared and distributed "We'll See Them Through!" which he designated as "a marching song for the National Army" and for which John Philip Sousa prepared an orchestration for a full band.[21] The song apparently received a mixed reception. In some camps and in some areas near military installations it was popular. On the other hand one camp-song teacher wrote that, while "the refrain is catchy and the rhythm is good," the words "are a little too much in the heroic vein for the boys to relish singing the song about themselves."[22]

Manley Hudson gives us a graphic description of Wigmore as he reported for duty in July 1917: "Wigmore took a holiday from his scholarly pursuits. No one ever donned a uniform with more gusto or more grace.[23] 'The Colonel' worked as if the outcome of the war depended on him alone. To him it was a time for action, and discussion became taboo. What many others viewed as grey was black to him; he saw white where others rested on their doubts. Yet never did his social relations, so gently and so skillfully managed by Mrs. Wigmore, suffer."[24] Small wonder that he was disappointed in Holmes, who took little interest in the war, saying that "every man must have one war and that he has had his. Rather poor logic isn't it?"[25]

During the course of his military service, Wigmore contributed to many different phases of the war effort. He was immediately assigned both to the Office of the Judge Advocate General and to the Selective Service Administration, which was also under the direction of General Crowder as provost marshal general. Wigmore's duties in this latter office soon occupied most of his time.

His major initial task was to survey the nation's military and industrial manpower, a study essential to the proper administration of the Selective Service Law, which involved not only the raising of armies but the protection and encouraging of industry. Without such data the administration of the draft would have been more or less unable to strike a balance between military and industrial manpower needs. To this task Wigmore, as chief of the Statistical Division, applied his energy and talent for organization. He formulated and put into effect a plan of statistical tables concerning classification, deferment, industry, and agriculture, and directed the preparation of a comprehensive industrial index containing the industrial qualifications of 10,000,000 registrants. To accomplish these tasks Wigmore directed not only the other officers assigned to him but a staff of 200 to 300 clerks working at long tables, who assembled the data.[26] This gathering of instant information in respect to manpower and special skills·was an undertaking without precedent in the United States or elsewhere.

From time to time Wigmore also sought informal collaboration and support from others. Louis B. Wehle described Wigmore in the military role:

> We met first in Washington in 1917. He was in a colonel's uniform; and his pride in it was evidenced by his abrupt correction of anyone addressing him as Dean. He fully radiated the military tradition; and he bore himself as a soldier. He soon drew me informally into working out for the Provost Marshal General's office, army draft regulations with several men who were meeting at the Cosmos Club. There one could see the methodical technique of the man who had done Wigmore on Evidence and had built up along largely original lines, a great American law school. With swift imagination and disciplined precision he led the groups in developing the ramifications of administrative and penal mechanisms for carrying out the principles of the new draft statute. The contagion of his enthusiasm energized all his team.[27]

Wigmore was also put in charge of the publicity drive for the draft registration, and for a time his office was filled with posters of all sizes and descriptions.[28] He was unstinting in his praise of the support he obtained in this effort from George E. Creel, chairman of the Committee on Public Information, and others.[29] As usual, Wigmore took the trouble to communicate with General Crowder, naming the principal individuals involved in the publicity drive so that the general could express his appreciation of their efforts from his higher rank. The response to General Crowder's appreciative letter, written by Carl Byoir, speaking for the committee, was significant:

> may I not take this opportunity of saying to you that it was the representative of your own office who made possible the coordination of all of these forces for your campaign.
> Colonel Wigmore, confronted with problems that I am sure no military man has ever before had to face, separated from the mass of suggestions that were made at the initial meeting, those that in his judgment seemed practicable, and I am convinced that in every case his judgment was sound. In one very important matter of slides in motion picture theatres, everyone thought it could not be done and Colonel Wigmore did it. I am sure that he has been so generous in his praise of others, that he has probably not troubled to bring to your attention his own part and I should feel remiss not to have brought it to your attention.[30]

The results were most gratifying. Although a little less than 13,000,000 were expected to register, the actual returns came to 13,200,000. For Wigmore, this was, in his own words, "a mysterious and patriotic thing . . . there were virtually no hold-backs throughout the country." [31] In later years, he characterized it as "the greatest thrill that I have ever had." [32]

Since the survey of the nation's military and industrial manpower made Wigmore the outstanding expert on military and industrial mobilization, he was later attached to the army general staff as part of its postwar mobilization plans. [33]

Interesting glimpses of Wigmore in Washington are provided by his secretary, Miss Sarah B. Morgan, who, after having taken dictation from him once, asked to be assigned to him permanently as "his dictation was so wonderful." Her success was perhaps facilitated by the fact that some of the other stenographers said that they could not understand what Wigmore was talking about. At any rate, Miss Morgan's tour of service was to continue for a long time — in Washington and back at Northwestern for as long as Wigmore lived. [34] According to Miss Morgan:

> Major [later Colonel] Wigmore's office was in the Old Land Office Building at 7th and F Streets, a large room, but hardly adequate for three or four other men and their desks and with my typewriter desk in one corner. The ringing of the telephone and the clattering of my typewriter (not noiseless) added to the confusion. Cigarette, cigar, and pipe smoke filled the room. Later, as his duties increased, his office was changed to the third floor, with a secretary's room next to his and with three or four other rooms for assistants, typists, and clerks. Colonel Wigmore also did duty at the Judge Advocate General's Office (this part of his work being done from seven o'clock in the morning) as he always arrived at the Provost Marshal General's office at 9:00 A.M. Everybody worked at night. I have overtime slips showing that I worked eight months overtime during the year and a half I was in the Provost Marshal General's Office.
>
> Colonel Wigmore had two idiosyncrasies which I discovered at that time. One was that he could not stand an electric fan or any noise. Many times during that summer of 1918 I took dictation beside his desk with windows closed, and watched the streams of perspiration roll down his face and his uniform get sopping wet. Of course, I melted in silence but an electric fan awaited me in my room next to his. The other idiosyncrasy was that he would not use a buzzer to summon any one. He would come to the door and ask for assistance in a polite and sometimes unusual way, such as "Will you please write some letters for me?," or "May I borrow your nimble fingers for a while?" This was but one example of his consideration for the interests and welfare of others. [35]

One of his first duties in the judge advocate general's office was to participate in the drafting of the Soldier's and Sailor's Civil Relief Act. [36] At Wigmore's suggestion, General Crowder appointed a committee of three, of which Wigmore was a member, to draft a bill. The only precedents were the brief Civil War Acts, and those were not helpful. The committee labored all through the hot Washington August to provide for every conceivable situation, and the bill was submitted to the House and Senate early in September 1917. The House committee commenced hearings promptly, and enactment followed on October 2, but the Senate, in Wigmore's words, "callously allowed five months (!) to pass, while the men in service [there were 2,000,000 of them by January 1] worried over their legal plight."[37] This was but one of many frustrating experiences with the Senate that underlay his highly critical attitude toward that body.

Wigmore was present when President Wilson signed the bill and gave him the pen used on that occasion for Northwestern University Law School.[38]

In order to avoid disaffection among the troops Wigmore advocated that, while the bill was pending in the Senate, there be an immediate widespread distribution of its terms to local draft boards, through the American Bar Association, the Commercial Law League of America, and the Red Cross.[39] As a further move in this direction, he joined the co-draftsmen of the bill in providing an explanatory statement to accompany the publishing of the text in the *Illinois Law Review* in February 1918.[40]

Another assignment was to collaborate with Lt. Col. Edgar King of the Surgeon General's Office, formerly a psychiatrist at the Fort Leavenworth Barracks, on a revision of the *Regulations for Penal Methods* at the Disciplinary Barracks.[41] His observations and conclusions on this assignment were reflected in an article in the *Journal of Criminal Law and Criminology.*[42] In January 1918, Wigmore served on a Board of Efficiency which made a study of the methods of appellate review of court-martial records in the Judge Advocate General's Office.[43] He also served on the Clemency Board which General Crowder thought would be helped by his participation to gain standing with the legal profession.[44] Thereafter, chiefly occupied with various assignments in the provost marshal general's office, Wigmore had no duties of consequence in the Office of the Judge Advocate General until January 1919, except for an occasional request for his informal opinion on some court-martial record.[45]

In a letter written to Albert Kocourek a little more than six months after he reported for duty, Wigmore gives a succinct appraisal of the situation in Washington at that time:

> Legislative mills grind slowly. The war politics ferment does not tend to speed them. There is less efficiency there than in the least efficient branch of the Govt. Outside Congress the trouble is otherwise — too much brains. So many people of ability and official position are duplicating work here; the need at the moment is system. Soon order will emerge; but the congestion of zealous effort is at present amusingly obstructive. If the Russians will only give us time (!!), all will go very well.[46]

One of Wigmore's many special assignments was service on the War Department Committee on Education and Special Training to which he was appointed in April 1918.[47] In spite of his commitment to the war effort, it is significant that in this role he defended the colleges against undue encroachment in connection with the Student Army Training Corps. In a vigorously worded memorandum prepared for the committee when he realized that the trend of its discussions might lead to an undue interference with enrollment and the curriculum, he emphasized the following points:[48]

1. "That no person be admitted to the Students' Army Training Corps. unless he is qualified by the same standard which qualified the institution to receive a unit, viz. the completion of a four-year high school education."[49] He insisted that for the corps to do otherwise would destroy the entrance requirements that it had taken so long to establish;

2. That not less than 10 hours per week of civilian courses should be open to election by the student;

3. That not more than three hours per week of allied courses should be required;

4. That not more than four hours per week of classroom instruction in military subjects should be required; and

5. That the course in war aims not be required as part of the curriculum.[50]

Wigmore acknowledged that his proposals would have to yield to actual military necessity, but he took the position that, under the existing circumstances, the needed manpower would be available under his proposal. All the men would be in cantonments long enough for the required additional military instruction; indeed one of the objects of the SATC was "to prevent unnecessary and wasteful depletion of the colleges."[51] He also argued that if academic standards were not maintained the quality of the officers would be impaired and there would be no point in training on college campuses, rather than in cantonments.

The "war aims course" referred to above, in which Wigmore had a special interest, was needed essentially by the uneducated, he felt, and had no place in higher education. "Every college instructor in this country has already given to his courses in history, political science, economics, etc., a war complexion which gives all that can be needed or expected."[52] And he continued:

> It cannot be too strongly stated that the function of this committee is purely military . . . the establishment of such a course . . . would mean the imposition on our entire educational system of the personal point of view of one or two individuals on the staff of this committee. . . . It has never been tried before. I may say it has never been dared before. The Federal Authority has never had any Constitutional powers in the realm of education.[53]

Wigmore felt so strongly about this matter that he took the position that if he found himself in a minority in the committee he would consider it his duty to present the matter by memorandum to the secretary of war.[54]

Another important function that Wigmore performed was to serve as chairman of an Advisory Committee for the Preparation of a Course in Military Law[55] for law schools having units of the Student Army Training Corps. This committee recommended the preparation of a supplement to the *Manual of Courts-Martial*, and, because of the urgency of the need. Wigmore was delegated to prepare the volume,[56] which was published under the title *A Source-Book of Military and War Time Legislation* (1919). Although demobilization prevented the realization of its immediate objective, it was a valuable book for anyone concerned with the subject, for it brought together more useful information than was conveniently available elsewhere.

As would be expected, there was a good deal of criticism of the SATC, and, no doubt, the general appraisal by the president of Northwestern University was shared by many: "It can scarcely be said that the Students' Army Training Corps was a marked success from the point of view either of the Army or the University. . . . The experiment, however, should not be condemned, as it grew out of a war necessity and was hastily developed."[57]

Wigmore felt that far more could be said in its favor. Although it was hastily developed, and this was unavoidable, it could be regarded as a success from both the military and the civic point of view. In his words:

> (1) From the *military* point of view of preserving the independence of our nation, the S.A.T.C. provided a reservoir of more than 25,000 trained officer-material, necessary to officer the new 2,000,000 army which was to assist in the 1919 spring offensive, and impossible to provide so rapidly in any other way; . . .
>
> (2) From the *civic* point of view, viz. the preservation of the institutions of higher education, the S.A.T.C. saved more than 500 educational institutions from being disorganized by the second draft, which was due to take all men, revenues and expenditures for education for all of the states in the union. . . .[58]

He also pointed out that the program saved nearly a year in the education of about 150,000 young men, providing "a unique experience of discipline in education" and permitting the contrast of military and civic methods side by side."[59]

It was Wigmore's important work on this committee that kept him in Washington after his work in the Provost Marshal General's Office was completed and after he had been urgently requested to return to the university; but in April 1919, he requested his discharge, and it was issued on May 7, 1919.

When peace came, Wigmore was greatly concerned over the plans for demobilization which he regarded as "cold" and "heartless"[60] and destined to be a failure, and he wrote a long memorandum to General Crowder urging that the Selective Service Boards, local and district, be used as the terminal agencies for demobilization. It was his view that they should handle "all pecuniary and contractual relations remaining undetermined between the Government and the soldier after date of discharge, for integrating him into the economic life of the nation, and for keeping local records of his whereabouts with a view to possible military utilization."[61] Samuel Gompers, president of the American Federation of Labor, also took this position,[62] but a determination was made not to use the Selective Service Boards for this purpose and to have the War Department withdraw as rapidly as possible from the control of military personnel.[63]

It should also be kept in mind that Wigmore saw General Crowder almost daily, no doubt because of Crowder's confidence in the capacity and loyalty of his friend. According to Wigmore this was "Owing perhaps to the fact that I was the officer nearest in age to General Crowder, and that I was then (I think) the only Judge Advocate on duty in the Provost Marshal General's Office who had also been on duty in the Judge Advocate General's Office. I frequently received the personal confidences of General Crowder upon the course of events."[64]

General Crowder's biographer, David A. Lockmiller, summed up the relationship as follows, "The distinguished lawyer and educator . . . worked in various divisions . . . and assumed the role of unofficial advisor and father confessor to the Provost Marshal General."[65] But the scope and significance of Wigmore's part can be best described by General Crowder himself: "there was very little of general policy or procedure emanating from the Provost Marshal General's Office which was not in part the fruit of his counsel and sound judgment."[66]

Wigmore also responded to many calls from Secretary of War Newton D. Baker, whom he knew as a fellow member of the bar and with whom he had a warm friendship. These assignments included consultation on a variety of matters, the occasional review of records involving difficult personnel decisions, and substituting in assignments that Baker was unable to fulfill.

One record referred to Wigmore for review involved the charge by an officer that he was the victim of malice or prejudice by one or more of his superior officers. Wigmore's report to Baker, after a review of the record and a personal interview with the complaining officer and his father, brought forth this response: "I do not know whether my gratitude for the service you have rendered in the Martin case or my admiration for the thoroughness with which you have done it is the greater. Both of them are great emotions with me as I conclude the reading of your careful and painstaking review of the record."[67]

That Wigmore conducted the interview with courtesy, tact, and fairness is evident from what the father wrote to Wigmore immediately thereafter.

> You, I have no doubt, regard your services in the matter as all in the days work. We, however, cannot look at them in that way, but feel that you rendered us a kindness quite beyond our power to compensate; and at the same time put us at our ease in a trying time by a charming courtesy as delightful as it is rare. Whatever the outcome of my son's matter may be, he and I will not cease to recall with pleasure and gratitude your relation to it.[68]

When Wigmore wrote to Baker to commend him personally and for his service as secretary of war, Baker responded as follows: "I regard myself and my profession immeasurably in your debt for the contributions you have made to the literature of the law, but I would now like to add an expression of the distinction I feel in being honored with a fresh evidence of your friendly regard.

"The war has added much to my experience and added many enrichments to my memory and I shall surely always remember with pleasure that we were 'fellow servants' in it.''[69]

Wigmore also took advantage of this personal relationship to communicate his views on matters that he regarded of great importance. An outstanding example was a memorandum to Baker[70] stressing the necessity of maintaining a close relationship between the army and modern science as represented by the universities and scientific organizations. He pointed out that, although scientists had been the salvation of the army in meeting the German thrust, it was unlikely that representatives of the regular army would initiate or maintain measures to achieve such a relationship of their own volition. And upon leaving the service, Wigmore addressed a communication to Baker supporting his strongly held conviction that the basic cause of discontent in the army was the social system that prevailed and not the court-martial system.[71]

Among other things, Wigmore's duties brought him into contact with officials in nearly every department in Washington and in a large number of the bureaus within. However, Wigmore's usefulness extended also to the friends or acquaintances who sought his advice. An example is his collaboration from time to time with Louis B. Wehle on the creation of machinery for the adjustment of labor disputes in the construction of cantonments, the procurement of labor for the shipyards, etc. Of Wigmore's role on these occasions Wehle said:

> Anyone acquainted with the lambent quality of Wigmore's thinking would understand how helpful he was in these matters, even as a casual advisor. But the contribution he could make to the handling of a situation did not depend upon its being in a field of his own activity, for he was a close and patient listener and his mind moved directly to the heart of it.[72]

But in spite of all of these responsibilities Wigmore never forgot the Northwestern men in service. The *Newsletter* he inaugurated and supported, which Mary Goodhue, his secretary at the Law School, edited, was not the only means of communication between Wigmore and the students; he often wrote directly in his own handwriting and did not count his day finished until he had written ''two post cards to two members of the Armed Services.''[73] Not surprisingly these elicited many responses. One Northwestern man wrote, ''I'll bet its the only case on record of a Colonel sending a message, in his own hand, to a buck private.''[74] Of the *Newsletter* one serviceman said, ''Your little news letters are as welcome as a pardon on the scaffold or a good cigarette in France. It certainly puts 'pep' into us to know that you are backing us up.''[75] Another replied that he was studying military law while in service and needed reading matter. In response he received the library's duplicate copy of the *Manual of Courts-Martial*.

In all of Wigmore's efforts he had Mrs. Wigmore's interest and support, and no matter how late he worked at night, she would sit up and wait for him, and then prepare a cup of hot chocolate or have some wine and cookies ready for him. Frequently, he would bring General Crowder with him, and Mrs. Wigmore would serve a certain wine and fruit cake for which he had a special fondness. If possible, the Wigmores took advantage of whatever plays and operas came to Washington.[76]

Although, as we have already seen, Wigmore gave most of his time to the Provost Marshal General's Department, he became increasingly concerned over the mounting court-martial workload in the Office of the Judge Advocate General. As usual, his concern was merely a prelude to action. In February 1918, he asked General Crowder's approval of a suggestion that "A study be made of the courts-martial records of the last four or six months, with a view to obtaining firm ground for proposing such specific measures of improved procedure as may be shown by this study to be necessary."[77] In submitting this suggestion, Wigmore pointed out that the machinery organized for an army of 100,000 led by career officers suddenly had to cope with an army of 1,000,000 men, and that the number of men administering the machinery had been increased tenfold by men brought in from civilian life. He concluded, "The fact is simply that, in my respect and devotion to the great system which I have now had an opportunity to observe from the inside for some months, I have a 'hunch' that at this particular point there is something not working well, and that inquiry may show that it ought to be and can be improved, before it works still less well."[78]

After some hesitation, General Crowder, who did not at first see any need for changes, gave his consent for the study, and Wigmore promptly reported that, after consultations in the Office of the Judge Advocate General, there was a general consensus (a) that proceedings in a "large number of cases show the faults which are dangerous in their possibilities" and (b) that these shortcomings "are chiefly due to the sudden and enormous expansion of the military forces in numbers."[79]

It was Wigmore's conclusion that, on the basis of these facts, what were required were merely "a few simple measures, mainly affecting the organization and the trial procedures."[80] He urged "that these few and simple measures be agreed upon and put into effect immediately, before the evil becomes so considerable as to attract public and congressional attention."[81]

Although there had been some public criticism while these adjustments and improvements were being considered and put into effect, matters came to a head on December 30, 1918, when Senator George W. Chamberlain, in a formal speech, severely criticized the administration of military justice during the war.[82] One consequence of Senator Chamberlain's address was the adoption of a resolution by the Executive Committee of the American Bar Association, in which it referred to its program committee the question of military justice, ". . . with the accompanying pronouncement that in the opinion of the Executive Committee our military law and system of administering military justice is a subject requiring consideration and probable reformation."[83]

Although it was common knowledge in the Office of the Judge Advocate

General that General Samuel T. Ansell, a protégé and trusted colleague of General Crowder, had become disaffected and in fact disloyal, the unscrupulous lengths to which he would go became evident only when it became clear that he was the source of Senator Chamberlain's information[84] and was also carrying on a campaign against General Crowder to the public, beginning with an address before the Chicago Bar Association on January 18, 1919.[85]

On the following day the New York *World* carried an article characterizing military justice as oppressive and arbitrary, which Senator Isaac Siegel read into the *Congressional Record* in connection with a speech complaining about military justice.[86]

On February 13, Newton D. Baker, as secretary of war, transmitted to Senator Chamberlain a letter received from the judge advocate general setting forth the facts concerning the topics about which Chamberlain had complained: "No doubt you will be glad to bring the situation to the attention of the country," Baker said, "in order that the interest which has been aroused on this subject will have before it all the facts which ought to be considered before any judgment is formed."[87] However, Senator Chamberlain never read this letter into the *Record*, and indeed he probably did not even show it to his colleagues on the committee.[88]

Obviously, the discussions in Congress, in the press, and by the public were based almost entirely upon the distortions, misrepresentations, and suppressions emanating from General Ansell.[89] What made his conduct the more reprehensible was the fact that, during most of the period involved, he had been actually in charge of the day-to-day operation of the office, and thus as General Crowder's second in command had the authority to put into effect most, if not all, of the reforms he advocated so loudly. Indeed, he was actively supported and encouraged by General Crowder in effecting reforms. General Ansell was in fact thwarted in only one important particular — namely, in his desire to supplant General Crowder as judge advocate general when his term expired. When Ansell raised this question with Crowder, reasoning that Crowder gave most of his time to the Office of Provost Marshal General and really was not interested in another term as judge advocate general, Crowder referred him to the secretary of war. Ansell, however, by-passed the secretary of war and went directly to the acting chief of staff, who, acting on the assumption that the appointment was satisfactory to all, signed the order. The order, however, was promptly revoked by Secretary Baker, who not only had confidence in General Crowder but preferred to rely on his extended and constructive service as judge advocate general.[90]

It is difficult to explain the complete change in Ansell's behavior except in terms of an overwhelming ambition that blinded him to all other considerations.[91] General Crowder had not only "discovered" him but he had treated him almost like a son and had done a great deal to further his career.

It was inevitable that such a situation would bring into full play one of Wigmore's outstanding characteristics — his exceptional sense of loyalty. In respect to the government it heightened his sense of patriotism. In respect to the Judge Advocate General's Office, it extended to the men he knew had, on the whole, done outstanding work in the face of enormous difficulties. In respect to General Crowder, it was directed toward a friend of unquestioned ability and integrity. Furthermore, Wigmore knew, as many did not, how much Crowder had done to improve the administration of military justice not only during the war but long before.

It should also be kept in mind that Wigmore had gained familiarity with the system of military justice and had developed a real respect for it. He was convinced that, in some particulars, it was superior to the administration of the criminal law in most, if not all, American civil jurisdictions. In view of this general background and Wigmore's close relationship to General Crowder, it is not surprising that he was assigned the task of assembling a reply to the charges against the Judge Advocate General's Office and General Crowder. In consequence, and in response to the secretary of war's request for a "concise survey of the entire field and to furnish the main facts in a form which will permit ready perusal by the intelligent men and women who are so deeply interested in this subject,"[92] Wigmore prepared the statement that took the form of an extended printed letter addressed to the secretary of war, over the signature of the judge advocate general.

The letter was a carefully prepared printed document of sixty-four pages. It briefly reviewed prior efforts to revise the Articles of War; discussed the responsibility of the Judge Advocate General's Office during the war, disclosing the vast increase of cases that had to be handled, often with inexperienced officers; dealt with a number of the cases that had been the subject of controversy; considered the principles and methods of military justice; and concluded with a number of recommendations.[93] As to the latter there was of course no difference of opinion as to the need for improvement. It was entirely a matter of degree. General Ansell called for a complete overhaul of the system. The position of the judge advocate general was that the system as a whole was sound and that the needed reforms were largely procedural. As to the controversial cases, it is significant to note that, in every one, the facts recited by General Ansell and discussed in the congressional debates and in the newspapers differed, usually substantially, from those in the record. In most instances there was also a discrepancy between the allegations made by the critics and the actual dispositions of the cases.

For example, in a case which was criticized as showing the "control which the military commander exercises over the administration of civil justice,"[94] the facts were as follows: A soldier charged with burglary claimed that he had entered the shop in question in search of the burglars. The first finding was not guilty, but at the commanding officer's request the case was reconsidered and, as the defendant's story was not believed, he was found guilty. On review, no legal error could be found in the record, and the evidence appeared to be sufficient to sustain the finding. Nevertheless, the National Office officer concluded that the evidence did not show his guilt beyond a reasonable doubt and recommended reconsideration by the reviewing authority, although, with few exceptions, no Supreme Court would under such circumstances upset the verdict of a jury. Upon reconsideration, the reviewing authority sustained the verdict. On the basis of an elaborate opinion disagreeing with the National Office, the commanding general followed the opinion of his law officer. The case, therefore, illustrated not control by the military commander, but the opposite.

Another case referred to on the floor of Congress was that of a conscientious objector who had not been given an opportunity for noncombatant duty and who disobeyed an order to drill. The sentence was death. Although the charge in Congress was that the prisoner was discharged at the disapproval of the president, the record demonstrated the exact opposite, for "it was not the President's *clemency* that discharged the prisoner; it was the effective *operation of that very system of military law* which the critic supposes not to exist. What happened was that the Judge Advocate General's Office recommended disapproval of the sentence on the strictly legal grounds that the order to drill was . . . not a lawful command [and the] sentence was therefore disapproved and the prisoner discharged . . ."[95]

A third case referred to in a newspaper article and read into the *Congressional Record*[96] involved two death sentences imposed in France for sleeping on post in a frontline trench. In dealing with these cases General Crowder pointed out in his letter that "There are really three distinct questions involved in those cases — first, whether a sentence of death in all cases of this offense should be the inexorable policy; secondly, whether, if not, these particular cases showed sufficient extenuating circumstances; and, thirdly, whether the cases were fairly and fully tried to get at the facts."[97]

As to the first question General Pershing urged adherence to the fixed traditions of military law for the protection of the army in a most dangerous situation, and in this he was supported by his chief legal officer. Nevertheless, when the matter came before General Crowder he included, after reflection, "a recommendation . . . pointing in the direction of clemency"[98] in the record that went to the secretary of war.

As to the second question General Crowder's letter pointed out that "The task laid upon these soldiers was no greater in its exactions than was laid upon hundreds of others at the very same moment in the allied forces doing duty in the trenches."

Obviously the situation was critical because the Allies were face to face with a most dangerous foe. Under these circumstances strict obedience to orders was essential, and sleeping on watch was "an absolute menace not only to that portion of the line held by the American troops, but to the French troops in the adjacent sectors."[99]

In justifying his decision to recommend clemency, General Crowder contended that any fair-minded reader of the record in these cases would recognize it as a disturbing example of the "inevitable mental conflict that arises between the stern necessities of war discipline and the natural human sympathy for men who have incurred the death penalty — a conflict which equally agitates every civil judge and every civil executive when such a case is presented for action. It is unconscionable that this situation should be cited as a peculiarity of the military system.''[100] Whether or not Wigmore personally favored the death penalty in such cases is not clear, but he did favor its application to deserters.[101]

As to the question whether the case was fairly and fully tried, it was admitted that this could have been more thoroughly done. However, after review by several of the most competent judge advocates as well as by General Crowder, no reversible error was found and the facts were substantiated. The only issue was the severity of the sentence.[102]

It should be added that many of the cases under public discussion were so inaccurately described that it was impossible to identify them. As far as they could be identified, they were included in an Appendix[103] to the letter to the secretary of war with explanations based on the records.[104]

In view of the wide publicity that had been given to the distortions and exaggerations expressed by General Ansell and Senator Chamberlain's disinclination to give the government the opportunity to submit its side of the case, it was difficult to decide how to get the judge advocate general's side before the public. If a government agency was ever entitled to take its case affirmatively to the public, this was certainly such an occasion, and Wigmore was apparently the prime mover in persuading the judge advocate general and the secretary of war to take such a step. He proposed, and the proposal was adopted, that a copy of the letter (a sixty-four-page document) be sent to every lawyer in the United States.[105] Furthermore, he obtained consent, somewhat reluctantly given by General Crowder[106] but authorized by the secretary of war,[107] to accompany this letter with a personal letter of his own, appealing to his fellow lawyers to take the time to hear both sides before reaching a decision. Altogether about 100,000 letters were mailed.[108]

Almost immediately, Senator Chamberlain, who had apparently received copies from a recipient, addressed a letter to the attorney general of the United States, enclosing copies of these letters together with an official envelope used by Wigmore bearing the ''Official Business'' frank of the War Industries Board. Senator Chamberlain declared the mailing to be ''A purely private communication addressed by one lawyer to his professional brethern upon a purely professional subject.''[109]

His letter concluded with the following statement:

> But my principal purpose in calling the matter to your attention is to be found in the obvious fact that the transmission of this personal communication through the mails of the United States as official business at public expense is in flagrant violation of the penal laws of the United States prohibiting free transmission of private matter. . . . I have the honor to request that you cause this matter to be investigated, with a view to applying the law to any such as may be found to have violated it.

Senator Chamberlain's letter to the attorney general appeared in its entirety in an extended news story in the *Philadelphia Public Ledger* on April 9, 1919, in which Wigmore was described as the ''ready letter writer'' of the War Department who "knows nothing about the Court Martial system in any respect," but who was directed to prepare a letter "reassuring the people of the beneficence of the existing Court Martial System and to impugn those who would dare question it, and in which he had the distinguished Secretary say that the existing system was one which gave almost perfect justice."

On the question of the use of the franking privilege, both Wigmore and the War Department were promptly cleared by a letter opinion from Attorney General A. Mitchell Palmer addressed to Senator Chamberlain and dated April 26, 1919. In his letter the attorney general said of Wigmore, ". . . it clearly appears that the printing and distribution of these two letters was at the direction of the Secretary of War and can in no sense be said to be the personal or self-asserted act of Colonel Wigmore. He cannot be charged with the alleged unlawful mailing of these letters or either of them."[110]

As to the responsibility of the secretary of war the letter continued:

> I find that somewhat similar situations to the one under consideration have received the attention of former Attorneys General, and while not exactly the same situation, yet somewhat similar ones have received the attention of the courts. It seems well established that a very wide discretion is lodged with the hands of the various executive departments in their determining what they may regard as "official business." . . . If, in his [the Secretary's] judgment, he believed it necessary to direct the printing and distribution of the letters here involved to the end that what he regarded as the truth might be available to the public, his action cannot be called in question by the courts.

There remains, of course the question of propriety. Although Secretary of War Baker may have had some doubts, he gave Wigmore his unqualified support. But these doubts were not shared by Wigmore. In a letter to the secretary he said:

> As to the *propriety* of it, for you, I have also no doubt. There are ample precedents. As to its propriety for me, I have no compunctions. My sole motive was to help in saving others from unmerited disparagement. The form of my help may seem immodest, and it did indeed offend my own sense of modesty and military propriety; I have, I think, consistently suppressed my individuality for the past two years, and have tried to play the military game and be merely an anonymous unit acting under the collective chief. But when General Crowder put me on the Clemency Board he said that he thought my name would help to give it confidence with the legal profession; and from that remark of his I inferred that I could really help in this other opportunity. Moreover, my act of sending it out made it seem less as though the General was attempting to argue his own cause with the public; and this approached the reality, for he was actually diffident and over-scrupulous about defending himself.[111]

But Wigmore did not let the matter rest with the distribution of the letter. When he appeared before the annual meeting of the Maryland Bar Association in June 1919, at which Colonel Edmund Morgan defended the views of General Ansell, Wigmore took advantage of the occasion to state the case for military justice affirmatively in a paper entitled "Some Lessons for Civil Justice to be Learned from Federal Military Justice."[112] Wigmore said, "It is civilian justice that is upon the defensive. It has been on the defensive for an entire generation. It has done very little in that generation to take up that defensive. It is doing very little now." He stressed the principal advantages of military justice over the usual practice in the criminal courts: (1) centralized supervision, (2) verbatim records, (3) automatic appellate review, (4) minimum indeterminate sentences, and (5) psychiatric examination. With his extensive background in criminal law he knew how faulty the practice in most states was in respect to these criteria. His eventual audience lay beyond those who were present, for his remarks were not only printed in the proceedings of the association but were reproduced in whole or in part in a number of legal periodicals.[113] Wigmore also took advantage of an appearance before the New York County Lawyers' Association on March 9, 1919, as the personal representative of Secretary of War Baker to develop the same topic.[114]

But all of these efforts were addressed solely to members of the bar. Realizing the importance of reaching the general public, Wigmore sought the aid of his friend the popular author, Arthur Train, who had been a judge advocate during the war. To him he wrote about "the possibility of your taking up your pen to show the other and good side of this military justice affair which is being so much exaggerated in the newspapers. . . . We have some very convincing dope on the subject."[115]

Train's response was enthusiastic but he expressed his doubts: ". . . it may be somewhat difficult to satisfy General Crowder. I do not know when I met a man who aroused so much of instant respect and admiration."[116]

With the information supplied by Wigmore he prepared a draft of an article, and the collaborative effort eventually evolved into final form. The *Saturday Evening Post*, the regular outlet for Train's popular stories involving the work of the legal profession, declined to participate, not wishing "to fall in at the tail end of this military justice affair."[117] However, *Collier's* accepted the manuscript, an article written in popular style for the general reader.[118] A striking illustration headed the article, showing a number of angry men identified by a placard reading "The Knockers Club," swinging hammers and bearing down on the goddess of justice with accusations against military injustice. The caption read: "Portia Columbia — I can assure you that the quality of mercy is still unstrained." The first subheading for the text at once brought home the fact that "Not a Single United States Soldier has been executed for a Military Offense since the War began" — a fact that no doubt came as a surprise to many readers after the lurid accounts that had been appearing in the newspapers and magazines. Although the article was of course a statement of the case for the army, it was full of indisputable facts that had certainly not been made available by the critics.

Upon receipt of a copy Wigmore wrote Train, "It sounds exactly as I expected it would sound. I rejoice in the reflection that one million copies are being distributed. I trust that you are enjoying the pleasure of a good conscience and of being on the right side.''[119]

The editor of the *Central Law Journal* thought that the article was of such permanent value for its readers that it reproduced it in substantial part for their benefit.[120]

The forum in which this debate was to linger the longest was the American Bar Association, which, as has already been indicated, took the question under consideration after Senator Chamberlain's speech in the Senate[121] gave the discussion nationwide publicity. Of unquestioned significance in the initial stage of the association's inquiry was an exchange of letters between Wigmore and George F. Page, then president of the association, which arose out of a discussion of a case involving a private, Clark E. Turner, who was allegedly involved in an assault with intent to rob.[122] At this time Wigmore was directed by General Crowder to study the case and give Page an opinion on the aspects of special interest to him. Wigmore "carefully read through the record, sitting up until one o'clock to do so, the next night"[123] and embodied his conclusion in a carefully drawn two-page letter reviewing the evidence, pointing out that some of the facts assumed by Page were not correct and concluding that, on the evidence, the defendant was guilty. In Wigmore's view the only question was the suitability of a ten-year sentence for "one of those stupid mischievous things which young men will do to each other when in liquor. However, the necessity of preserving discipline among the soldiers during their visits to the town of Houston may have seemed important.''

Page's acknowledgment was far from appreciative.[124] He said that what he wanted was the "evidence," if it could be found, to sustain the charge and support Wigmore's opinion. He also disagreed with some of Wigmore's interpretations, especially with his apparent acceptance of a sentence which he admitted was excessive.

Although Wigmore replied to this letter at length,[125] dealing with a number of the questions raised by Page and, in addition, enlarging on the favorable aspects of military justice, he did not quote the supporting evidence at length in his reply. He apparently justified his failure to do so as follows:

> As I presumed, and still presume, that you were good enough to value my opinion as that of a humane man, and civilian, not bred to the military career, and an expert student of evidence and proof, I form my opinion in that aspect of the case and shall continue so to form it. It is neither my duty nor my right, under the circumstances, to attempt to treat it as a revisory officer on the Judge Advocate General's staff.

In consequence, and regardless of the merits in the particular case, the president of the association aligned himself firmly with the critics of military justice. As Wigmore saw it, "at the bottom" their differences in this case were (a) "one or two fundamental differences of attitude toward criminal justice" and (b) "one or two important misconceptions of fact . . .

as to what actually goes on in the Judge Advocate General's Office."[126] Although Wigmore was probably correct in his appraisal and further information would most likely not have altered Page's position, it is not easy to justify Wigmore's refusal to supply the exact information requested.

The special committee of the American Bar Association consisted of five able lawyers with Stephen S. Gregory as chairman. Many witnesses both military and civilian were heard, including Wigmore and Ansell. In its report, the committee divided three to two, the majority submitting recommendations generally in favor of the system of military justice then in effect. Gregory, the chairman, prepared the minority report, which in fact reflected more agreement with the majority than the vote alone would indicate.[127]

The majority approved Crowder's suggestions for improvements in courts-martial as outlined in his letter of March 10, 1919, to the secretary of war, with only slight modifications, and agreed with Ansell that the private soldier should have more instruction in the Articles of War. As to the system in general it said:

> We by no means share in the prevalent opinion that the present Articles of War and the practice and procedure which is provided for and advised in the Manual of Courts-Martial is medieval, or cruel or arbitrary, but rather are of the opinion that if the letter and the spirit of these articles and of this manual were lived up to and thoroughly appreciated, there would be little ground for complaint.[128]

Ansell sent a letter to President Page criticizing both the majority and minority reports and the qualifications of the committee members. The letter was referred to Chairman Gregory, who made the following comments on Ansell:

> He is a man with a grievance. He feels that he has been unjustly treated by the military authorities . . . I do say however that it seems to me to be rather inconsistent with efficiency either in the Army or elsewhere to keep a man at the head of an important department who was continually railing at everybody in that department. . . . General Ansell seems to have understood that this committee was constituted to try the great case of Ansell v. Crowder; that as plaintiff he was entitled to take charge of his side of the case. . . . the committee to act as a court. This was not the understanding of the committee. We did not propose to have General Ansell take charge of our inquiry and run it, but we proposed to run it ourselves, in our own way, giving him every opportunity to be heard and to have people he thought should be heard brought before the committee, or their views presented as they saw fit.[129]

In spite of the fact that Ansell and others continued to attack the Judge Advocate General's Department, the American Bar Association refused to set aside the majority report of the committee and disposed of the matter by voting to return both reports to the Executive Committee without instructions. In June 1920, the question was finally closed when Congress enacted the National Defense Act and related bills confirming Crowder's position.[130]

A broader review of the whole controversy, made in the perspective of time, led David A. Lockmiller, Crowder's biographer, to the following conclusion:

> Whatever his motives may have been, and granted that many of the changes he advocated were desirable, one reading the record thirty-five years afterwards must conclude that the methods used were not condusive to success and that the entire episode was unfortunate for the country as well as the chief participants. The changes necessary could have been, and would in all probability have been, adopted without so much public agitation and exaggeration.[131]

That Wigmore's part in the war effort was substantial is beyond question. In summary form it is probably best stated in General Crowder's recommendation that Wigmore receive a distinguished service medal. After identifying Wigmore's outstanding contribution in the administration of the Selective Service Law, Crowder continued,

> To the performance of these duties Colonel Wigmore applied himself with the most unselfish sacrifice and devotion, with tireless and indefatigable zeal and energy. His sound counsel, his breadth of vision, and his remarkable ability for analysis were assets which contributed substantially to the operation of the Provost Marshal General's Office and the success of the Selective Service Organization.[132]

In winding up his tour of duty Wigmore managed to prepare an eighty-seven-page manuscript, "The Conduct of the War in Washington, a Critique of Men and Methods,"[133] for publication after his retirement from service. To a prospective publisher he said, "It has occurred to me that a judicial and impartial critique would be of considerable public interest at this time, when so many extreme criticisms are heard founded more or less upon a fragmentary observation only and upon journalistic hearsay."[134] Of the several magazines approached only the *Forum* expressed an interest, but when the editor insisted on using subheadings that emphasized Wigmore's more caustic comments, he withdrew it saying they would destroy the impartiality that he desired to reflect.[135]

It is an interesting document and one to which Wigmore must have given a great deal of thought and effort, and it would no doubt have stirred up a lively discussion if it had been published. Here a few of Wigmore's observations must suffice, but they will reflect the general spirit of his critique. Of the attitude of the regular army officers toward the reserve officers, he had nothing but commendation. Even in the frankest discussions, where the reserve officers sometimes knew more about the subject than the regular army officers, or vice versa, he had never seen a moment of embarrassment on this score. "Complete harmony of spirit and endeavor prevailed. That this should have been the case, is a matter of no less wonder than gratification."[136] There was, of course, the occasional snob on either side but they were recognized for what they were. Although he had also found a certain amount of Brahmanism in the general staff and particularly in the War College, it was directed against the regular and not the reserve officers.

In respect to the leadership in Washington, Wigmore had very definite ideas. Because President Wilson consulted so seldom and then with only a few people, he felt he was a "conundrum" and that only the perspective of history could give an effective appraisal. Although he acknowledged that Wilson was no doubt responsible for many wise acts for which he deserved credit, Wigmore recognized three terrible blunders:

> The first is the failure to ask Congress for a declaration of war on the day after the sinking of the Lusitania in 1915.
> The second is the failure to retain General Goethals as the chief and active dictator of our shipping plans.
> The third is the assent to open those negotiations with Germany, in October, 1918, which led to an armistice instead of to a surrender.[137]

As to Newton D. Baker, his position as secretary of war required a perfection of attainment that was impossible to fulfill because "perfection would require the possession of the most opposite and incongruous talents."[138] Direction of the military establishment demanded the "quick decision" and the "smiting drive of a steam-hammer." For handling "the political situation not only in Congress but also among industrial, financial and other interests in the Nation at large, there was indispensable a general persuasiveness which would conciliate and amalgamate the conflicting forces, and a cheery and optimistic endurance which would patiently persist and await the proper opportunity for the successful action." In Wigmore's view Baker had the latter qualities "in the highest degree," but he was deficient in drive and "was not notable for his quick finality of decision." There was no doubt, however, about the fact that Baker gave his full support to the chief of staff.[139]

Wigmore said of General March that, when he became chief of staff in the spring of 1918

> The transformation was felt instantly all along down the line. General March had put drive and spirit into the whole process. Everyone within the Department felt that something had happened, without realizing at that time what was the source of the new motive power.[140]
> The American people and the Allies owe him an unending debt of gratitude for those lightning decisions and sledge-hammer orders which from early spring onwards made possible America's decisive share in the combat.[141]

However, Wigmore thought that the very qualities that had made March a success in wartime disqualified him for the task of maintaining a peacetime army. It was Wigmore's view that "The sooner he is succeeded by a Chief of Staff who understands the elements of domestic, commercial and industrial human nature, the better for our future military policy."[142]

As for Congress, it will be recalled that Wigmore's experience with that body began with the Senate's callous disregard of the interests of the men in uniform by not promptly enacting the Soldier's and Sailor's Civil Relief Act. He was disturbed by the same lack of a sense of urgency in respect to most wartime problems and was outraged by the way bureau chiefs were treated when they appeared in support of appropriations for the operations for which they were responsible.[143] "The cross-examination at hearings is regularly marked by innuendos and assertions of official incompetency; and the public debate is interspersed with accusations equally rude and unfounded."[144] As to the inefficiency of Congress and other government agencies, Wigmore said, "Be it remembered then, that wherever there may have been any record of inefficiency during the War administration, a large percentage of the cause must be attributed to the inefficiency of Congress."[145]

Wigmore felt that in general the over-all effort in Washington was upright, honest, faithful, industrious, and successful, and that compared with the Civil War and Spanish-American War experiences the actual achievements were "all the more notable."[146] He concluded, "the grand fact remains that these shortcomings concern relatively minor subjects of criticism, in contrast with the enormous proportion of the virtually impossible which was actually achieved."[147]

Systematic as he was, Wigmore made a list of persons upon whom he wished to make farewell calls. In addition to Holmes and Brandeis, sixty-seven individuals, more than half of them in departments and agencies other than the War Department, were included.[148]

Wigmore was discharged from active duty in May 1919. Now fifty-six years of age, he was free to return to the Law School to resume his duties as dean and to continue his role as a scholar and leader for nearly a quarter of a century, with undiminished vigor.

Times would come when Wigmore would be making brief returns to Washington, for in September 1920 he was appointed a colonel in the Judge Advocate General's Section of the Reserve Officers Corps. In July of that year he had been appointed a consultant to the Advisory Board, Education and Recreation Branch of the War Plans Division of the General Staff, and shortly thereafter he spent several weeks in Washington working on a revision of the *Manual of Courts-Martial*. In 1922 he was appointed a specialist attached to the Advisory Board, Operations and Training Division, and attended a meeting in Washington on personnel methods and a conference of general staff officers and officers in civilian life at the State Department to formulate a plan to be put into use in the event of future wars.

Wigmore again became involved in the revision of the *Manual of Courts-Martial* in 1925, when in response to a request from Major General J. A. Hull he said:

> Your letter of May 5 requesting me to undertake something in connection with the pending revision of the Manual of Courts Martial is very considerately

worded, but amounts to a command, for any one in the military service of the United States. It will therefore be obeyed. Otherwise I should have thought that I was too over-loaded to undertake any fragment of new work.

Moreover, I will have my contribution ready for you sometime in July and will not wait until September 1st.[149]

In 1927, upon reaching the military retirement age of sixty-four, Wigmore was transferred to the unassigned reserve. He continued to regard his status as a reserve officer highly and took all attendant responsibilities seriously. His lifelong devotion to his country was dramatically shown in his response at the age of seventy-nine to an inquiry coming twenty-four years after the end of World War I, when the shadows of World War II were falling upon this country. The substance of the significant questions and his responses were as follows:

Q: *Availability*

A. Having survived a heart collapse in 1938 and a near fatal case of pneumonia in 1939–40, I am by medical advice forbidden to travel or to be subjected to severe strain. . . . Can do library and desk work. Have just completed a Guide to War Law for American Bar Association.

Q: *How much time will you require to arrange your personal affairs before reporting for duty. . . . ?*

A. None.

10

Patriot

Before resuming the account of Wigmore's career as dean, scholar, and leader, it is important to consider some of the lasting effects of his wartime experience on the highly productive and significant twenty-four-year, post-World War I, era of his life. For many years he determined not to travel in Germany again and his interest in the German language cooled. However, he helped many German refugees to come to the United States and assisted them in becoming established.[1] His heightened sense of patriotism and loyalty impelled him to take part in the organization of the Evanston Post of the American Legion and to support it actively. For some years he donned his uniform every May 30 and marched with his comrades in the post, and later he sat in the reviewing stand, and he apparently prepared himself appropriately to grace such occasions. At any rate, in 1928 he wrote to the Chicago Military Stores, "I am sending by messenger one military blouse, to be made over into the new style, which you state will be $12.50."[2] Wigmore regarded such events as matters of importance. On one occasion he wrote to President Scott strongly objecting to the scheduling of the ROTC examinations at a time which would have prevented the men from joining the Memorial Day parade.[3] At home the American flag hung from his window. As the years went by, Wigmore was often called on by the post for advice, perhaps more or less in the role of an elder statesman.[4]

As always, he made significant donations, and perhaps one of the most important concerned the two French war orphans whom he had adopted and for whom he persuaded the post to assume what he felt was its rightful responsibility. He was the prime mover in the raising of the funds, keeping in touch with both orphans by correspondence, and visiting both of them in France, not only to register personal interest but also, by the purchase of clothing and other gifts, to supplement the financial assistance they were receiving from the post.[5]

In both instances the support of the orphans was merited and appreciated. As for the girl, Paulette Chomprenault, a resolution of the Evanston post drafted by Wigmore expressed "our gratification that the little girl whom we accepted in 1921 has now grown to be a beautiful young woman and our pride that we had a share in her education."[6]

The boy, at twenty-five a skilled mechanic in the aircraft factory at Albert, spoke for himself in the following letter:

November 1, 1939

Dear Godfather, I am sorry to have delayed so long in answering your last letter. As you expected in that letter, I am now obliged to put myself at the disposition of the army in defence of our country. But I do so full of courage, inspired by the memory of my father, who gave up his life in the terrible destruction of 1914. Never should such a necessity have arisen again. But we shall do our part as soldiers who have no reason to blame themselves; for our government has done everything that could be done to avoid war.

I am now back in the same camp where I did my military service. But we are now constructing hangars and landing-places, for we believe that this war will be in the air and in the sea; although we do not think that it will last as long as the war of 1914–18.

My mother, who was ill last year, is now quite well again, and asks me to send her regards to you and ask you to express to the Legion Post her sincere thanks for all that they so kindly did for me.

I will now tell you something that may not surprise you. It is that if the war had not come, I was going to be married to a nice girl, whose photograph I will soon send to you. In present circumstances, of course, I cannot tell when the ceremony will take place.

My mother and I speak often of your visit to our home in 1923, but that visit now seems long ago.

Please accept the best wishes of the godson of Evanston Post 42.

Marcel Sevel, 107th Battalion, at St. Andre de l'Eure, Eure, France.[7]

Organizationally, Wigmore's military interests were not confined to the American Legion. Shortly after the Wigmores moved to Chicago he joined the Army Navy Club of Chicago and retained his membership until his death in 1943. In December 1925, he was asked to serve on a committee to organize the reserve judge advocates in the Sixth Corps area[8] with the hope that this unit would serve as nucleus of a national organization.[9] Responding affirmatively, he addressed the organizational meeting held in Chicago in March 1928, along with General Crowder. He also took an active part in the work of the North-Shore-Cook County Chapter of the Reserve Officer's Association of the United States by serving on the executive committee and by working to increase the membership.[10]

Wigmore's reading now included most of the books published about the war, and he regarded James G. Harbord's *The American Army in France 1917–1919* (1936) so highly that he wrote to the author identifying the strong points and closing with a few suggestions for the second edition that he believed was sure to come.[11] In his military reading Wigmore was also on the alert for unjustified criticisms of military personnel. One occasion occurred when an editorial in *Adventure* criticized the War Department because when the United States entered the war it did not grant commissions to Americans who had had flying experience with the Allies in Europe. Wigmore not only pointed out that foreign experience was excluded by the language of the National Defense Act of June 3, 1916, for which Congress, and not the War Department, was responsible, but added:

> I am a devoted admirer and regular reader of *Adventure*: I eat it up. But I have too frequently had a grouch at reading your editorial grouch against the War Department. I too was one of the many scores of "petty," "jealous," "bureaucratic," "unpatriotic," fellows at Washington whom you are frequently sneering at and blaming for errors of personnel and policy. Knowing that I myself had seen none of these bad qualities in my vicinity, I have often suspected that your sneers were baseless. This time I have nailed your error from my own personal knowledge. Hence, I infer that your general grouch is responsible for your former assertions. The officers on duty at Washington were just as highminded and patriotic and impartial as you were. The Campfire columns do a disservice to patriotism and an injustice to fellow-soldiers when they disseminate distrust, groundlessly, of the officers on duty in Washington.
> I wish that you could soft pedal your grouch occasionally, by recalling that the average number of _____ fools is not likely to be any greater in the War Department than it is in editorial offices.[12]

The ingredients in Wigmore's patriotism (his secretary describes him as "fiercely patriotic") not only included his hatred of communism but his intolerance of pacifism in any form, and he was even opposed to the public discussion of the subject under any circumstances. When the pastor of the First Methodist Church in Evanston accepted the vote of a group of students favoring a discussion led by Brent D. Allinson, who had obtained some notoriety as a pacifist, Wigmore responded with a vigorous letter of protest addressed to the pastor. Wigmore pointed out that Allinson's appointment to the Foreign Service had been cancelled by the State Department because it found him "not suitable"[13] and that he was subsequently convicted of desertion and sentenced to imprisonment at hard labor for fifteen years, a sentence later commuted to four years. But Wigmore was not satisfied to let matters rest with the letter, although it was read at a meeting in the church. He also addressed an open letter to the *Evanston News-Index*, setting forth Allinson's record in full as substantiated by the State and War Departments.[14]

This event not only attracted nationwide attention but, because some Northwestern University students were involved, it became identified with the university and aroused the protest of many alumni members. At the same time the "slacker pledge" was being widely circulated by several organizations in various parts of the country. At the request of the president of the Law Alumni Association, a mass meeting of the students was called at the Law School on April 7, 1924, without announcing the purpose. Wigmore was among several speakers.[15] In substance he said that all persons were pacifists in a sense, that freedom of discussion was essential to the development of sound views but did not include disobedience to law. He pointed out that a loyalty-pledge card that had been prepared for distribution at this meeting merely set out the Federal Statute which made "all able-bodied male citizens . . . liable to perform military duty in the Service of the United States.'' This quotation was followed solely by the statement: ''It is my resolution to obey this law.''[16] Wigmore continued by stating that, although they had no doubt about the loyalty of the students, the world outside and the alumni begged for confirmation. ''And especially on June 12, the day of the annual Alumni banquet, I want to be able to tell them by the figures that we can guarantee a *hundred percent roster* of law-abiding lawyers.''[17]

Not only did every student present sign the pledge but as a result of a careful follow-up by Wigmore all the other students responded affirmatively. In reporting to President Scott, Wigmore said, ''Thus it can now be stated that in the Law School there is one hundred percent repudiation of the Slacker oath, and of expression of a resolution to be law-abiding citizens, regardless of varied opinions and with preservation of entire freedom of speech.''[18] President Scott was far from sure about the propriety of the action taken by the Law School, and he was no doubt disturbed by criticisms directed against the university. In writing to Wigmore about the matter he said:

> The universities of America are criticising us very severely. Our treatment of conscientious objectors is interpreted as a limitation upon freedom of speech and of conscience. A false report has gotten out that we are practically compelling our students to sign a pledge which any conscientious objector (unless a coward) would refuse to sign. Does the social pressure that you bring to bear apply also to the Chinese and other foreign students?[19]

There undoubtedly was some justification for the misgivings entertained by President Scott and the criticisms emanating from other universities. Although Wigmore was essentially only asking the students to sign a pledge to obey the law, his position on the matter left little room for the conscientious objector. Furthermore, an urgent meeting called with no subject announced in advance and addressed by the dean in a manner that left no doubt about what the response of the students should be created an extremely difficult atmosphere for dissent. In addition, every student from whom a pledge card was not received, probably because of absence from the meeting, received a notice to see the dean without fail.[20] In view of Wigmore's determination to secure a one-hundred-percent approval, it is obvious that a reluctant student would find himself in a most difficult position. Let the question of loyalty squarely present itself and Wigmore found it hard if not impossible to display a spirit of tolerance.

And this attitude lingered. As late as 1927 Wigmore was so disturbed by the appearance of the names of Robert M. Lovett, Zona Gale, and Clarence Darrow in a lecture series offered under the auspices of the university that he wrote to President Scott:

> These are bad names to be put out to the public under the auspices of Northwestern. Lovett is a devoted exponent of Bolshevism and destruction in this country. Zona Gale is a member of many of the undermining associations.

Clarence is an immoral influence of the highest order, and yet he is put down as lecturing on "Education for Life." I should like to know the names of members of our faculty who have acted as the Committee of selection for these people.[21]

Wigmore was also impressed by the teamwork that could be achieved under military discipline when the individual subordinated his own interests to achieve the immediate end of the group as a whole, and, among matters of detail, he thought the numbering of paragraphs in memoranda and other documents such an excellent idea that he carried it over into his own work. The interest in marching that was a carryover from his military experience had some amusing applications. For example, on one occasion while the Law School was still housed in Tremont House along with other departments of the university, some remodeling in the area occupied by the Dental School created so much noise that Wigmore could not conduct his classes.

Wigmore stood it just so long and then leading his students like a captain at the head of his company, he marched them through the corridors, up the stairs, picked up pieces of scantling as they went, and paraded through the halls and class rooms of the Dental School, banging the scantling like cymbals. The students had a wonderful time. Dean Black of the Dental School was flabbergasted and protested, but there was less interference thereafter with the Law School work below. I believe Wigmore called it "self-help or justifiable homicide."[22]

Wigmore adapted so readily to the military atmosphere and carried over such a respect for and loyalty to the service that the question arises as to whether the desire to lead troops in combat may not have been one of his unsatisfied ambitions. Many years later James F. Oates, one of Wigmore's students, expressed his appraisal of Wigmore in this respect as follows:

Frequently he reverted to being a Colonel and became one of the Nation's greatest legal scholars playing soldier. He loved to be referred to by his military title. It seems strange, if not silly, but it was terrifically human. No boy ever lived and escaped the temptation to play soldier. He was a great man but still at heart such a boy and could never resist the temptation. The students could not help but like it, even though they smiled.[23]

More important, however, was his attitude in dealing with the difficult problems that arose when the rights of the individual and the extent of the authority of the government came into conflict. His intolerance of pacifists affected his approach to all situations involving freedom of speech.

It was this motivation and the deep convictions that sprang from it that impelled him for the second time to take public issue with one of Holmes's opinions, in this instance the dissenting opinion in the Abrams case.[24] And as Brandeis concurred in Holmes's dissent it also brought Wigmore in conflict with the views of Brandeis for whom he had such great respect. It will be recalled that in the Abrams case the majority upheld the conviction of the defendants (all Russians) for the distribution of circulars which, although ultimately intended to prevent interference with the Russian Revolution, advocated a course of action that could impede the effort of the United States to defeat Germany.

Stated briefly, it was Holmes's position that the primary objective of the defendants in issuing the circulars was to prevent interference with the Russian Revolution and that, accordingly, violation of the act was not their "proximate motive" and they did not act with the "intent by such curtailment [of the war effort] to cripple or hinder the United States in the prosecution of the war"[25] against Germany. In short, Holmes held that to constitute the crime as charged there had to be specific and not merely inferred intent and that specific intent had not been proved. Moreover, to Holmes, the danger was not imminent. On this point he said, "Now nobody can suppose that the surreptitious publishing of a silly leaflet by an unknown man, without more proof, would present any immediate danger that its opinions would hinder the success of the government arms or have any appreciable tendency to do so."[26]

In contrast to Holmes, who was almost completely detached from the war, Wigmore had been an active participator, specifically concerned with the manpower problem and gravely conscious of the shortage of munitions and its inhibiting effect on the military effort. To him the situation appeared very different. To advocate strikes against the munitions plants which, among other things, "would keep the Army busy at home," posed an immediate danger, and, in his view, if it was lawful for what Holmes called "an unknown man" to so act it would be "lawful for a thousand others."[27]

Wigmore undoubtedly identified one of the important reasons for the differences of opinion in the case when he said, "The opposite interpretations of the majority and the minority were due, not to genuine ambiguities in the language, but to differences of temperment and attitude towards the issues involved. A pre-existing attitude of the minority disinclined them to interpret the facts as the majority did."[28]

Before pursuing this matter further as it applies to Wigmore, it may be well to take note of how Holmes and others reacted to his article. In writing to Pollock, Holmes said, "Wigmore in the *Ill. Law Rev.* goes for me *ex cathedra* as to my dissent in the *Abrams case*. You didn't agree with it but Wigmore's explosion struck me, (I only glanced at it), as sentiment rather than reasoning — and in short I thought it bosh. He has grown rather dogmatic in tone, with success . . ."[29]

Although Pollock, as indicated above, did not originally agree with Holmes,[30] upon a more extended consideration of the case, he concluded that Holmes was correct.[31] In respect to Wigmore's article he said, "By the way I was sorry to see Wigmore carried away by the panic mongers. His reasons amounted to saying that it is wrong to criticise an indictment for murder because homicide is a very dangerous offense and many murderers are very wicked men."[32]

Not only approval but fulsome praise came to Holmes from Harold J.

Laski and from Pound. In a letter to Holmes Laski said, "My dear Justice: In the midst of a feverish week, I want just to say in so many words that amongst the many opinions of yours I have read, none seems to me to be superior either in nobility or outlook, in dignity or phrasing, and in that quality the French call *justesse*, as this dissent in the Espionage case. It is a fine and moving document for which I am deeply and happily grateful."[33] And in a letter written about two weeks later Laski added, "I must not forget to tell you that Pound spoke to me with emotion about your dissent. He was certain that it would become a classic in the same sense as your *Lochner* case."[34]

Wigmore did not even get support in the *Illinois Law Review*. A case comment in the same number of the *Law Review* in which Wigmore's article appeared identified the Holmes opinion as one "destined to become a classic."[35]

Finally, in an extended treatment of the case as a whole that relates it to the political situation at the time ("the systematic arrest of civilians by soldiers on the streets of New York City . . . and the evidence of brutality at Police Headquarters," etc.), Zachariah Chafee concludes with the following statement:

> The whole proceeding, from start to finish, has been a disgrace to our law, and none the less a disgrace because our highest court felt powerless to wipe it out. The responsibility is simply shifted to the pardoning authorities, who except for the release of the unlucky Rosansky have as yet done nothing to remedy the injustice, and to Congress which can change or abolish the Sedition Act of 1918, so that in future wars such a trial and such sentences for the intemperate criticism of questionable official action shall never again occur in these United States.[36]

But this does not mean that Wigmore stood alone. Not only a majority of the Court were with him but many public leaders as well. Among these was Newton D. Baker who wrote that he read Wigmore's discussions with "infinite delight and complete sympathy." Baker believed that the struggle had been won and that the country was "suffering very much more from overindulgence" than "suppression." In his opinion Holmes had in this case "shut himself up in the covers of a book containing but one sentence [the first amendment to the Constitution], and while he nestled comfortably there with that doctrine he forgot the existence of the world outside."[37]

This sharp attack on Holmes's position in the Abrams case did not impair (except perhaps temporarily) the warm and cordial relationship that had developed between Wigmore and Holmes.[38]

To Wigmore the menace of communism was not only imminent but a far greater threat than it appeared to many others. This is clearly indicated in his review of Kate Holladay's book *The Immigrant's Day in Court*, in which Wigmore showed sympathy for the immigrant, although he took issue with the author's criticism of government policy under Attorney General J. Mitchell Palmer. He concluded the review with the following statement:

The "Little Red Book" used in this country pledged all union members (as candidly quoted by the author) to "a forcible social revolution," "a strike to abolish government," "a quicker liberation of Russia and enslaved humanity in all countries." Any government of vigorous, self-respecting humans, like ours, would have to strike at such a flagrant conspiracy to ruin us. Deportation was the most humane expedient. Prompt measures were vital; ordinary, long-drawn-out judicial proceedings would have been suicidal. Individual mistakes, of course were made; but the individual is nothing when a nation's life is at stake. If some of the deportees were victims of their own ignorance or of subordinate officials' harshness — well, every soldier knows that such things will happen in war; and this was really a war against an enemy. Mr. Palmer saved the country, in my opinion.[39]

That Wigmore's feelings in this respect did not abate is evident from the fact that he became involved in 1927 in a controversy with Felix Frankfurter (then on the Harvard Law School faculty) over the Sacco-Vanzetti case[40] in which the issue of communism played such an important part. It will be recalled that this case concerned the robbery and murder of a paymaster and his guard at a shoe factory in Braintree, Massachusetts, in which the defendants were convicted. Wigmore was convinced that the defendants had a fair trial, and he vehemently attacked Frankfurter, who had come to their aid first in an article published in the *Atlantic Monthly*[41] and later in a statement published in pamphlet form.[42]

The highly personal nature of Wigmore's attack, which appeared in two articles in the *Boston Evening Transcript*,[43] revealed that he was deeply stirred. He never referred to Frankfurter by name but called him the "plausible Pundit" or "contra-canonical critic," because of his alleged violation of Canon 20 of the American Bar Assocation Code of Ethics. It was not unusual for Wigmore to speak out in colorful language, for many of his criticisms were sharp and uncompromising. However, he had a great capacity for distinguishing between the issues involved and the participants concerned, and even when his feelings ran high they were usually quick to cool. Where there were strong personal differences of a continuing nature, they were generally one-sided, and if Wigmore was wrong he would usually acknowledge the fact upon giving the matter further thought.

Why, then, was this controversy not only acrimonious on his part, but sustained, while Frankfurter, in his replies, made no disparaging references and spoke highly of Wigmore in a public statement made at the time?[44] Although it is evident that the case evoked several strong emotional responses which no doubt reinforced each other, the overriding consideration seems to have been that the case was inexorably associated with the Communist movement, which at the time, was exploiting the Sacco-Vanzetti case to the full, by stirring up agitation about it all over the world. Communism was inimical to everything for which Wigmore stood. The agitation built around the Sacco-Vanzetti case was started "among various alien Communist circles; and this was extended to the general public"[45] by Frankfurter's articles. To Wigmore the effect of the articles was to undermine the orderly processes of the courts, and in his opinion for the Court to yield to public pressure in this instance would establish a precedent that would be fatal. Feeling as he did that Sacco and Vanzetti had had a fair trial, Wigmore was apparently incapable of appreciating the fact that, although Frankfurter, and many others, shared his great antipathy to communism, Frankfurter could nevertheless believe that because of the unpopularity of the defendants' views they had not had a fair trial.

As Wigmore saw the situation, Frankfurter's reflection of the record in the case was neither accurate nor fair, and he charged him with being guilty of "a gross libel" [46] against the honor of the courts of Massachusetts where he (Wigmore) had practiced after graduation from the Harvard Law School. Furthermore, he maintained that Frankfurter was not only misleading the public, but had also violated Canon 20 of the American Bar Association's Code of Ethics which "condemns newspaper publications by a lawyer as to pending or anticipated litigation." [47]

Wigmore so often criticized the courts that it is at first surprising to find him taking another to task for doing the same thing. The explanation seems to lie in the fact that, although Wigmore was a frequent critic of the courts and of legal institutions in general, he was essentially a reformer dedicated to the piecemeal improvement of these institutions — not to their destruction or replacement. We see him here in the role of champion and defender of the judiciary as an institution that he believed the communists were determined to destroy along with our entire system of government.

Even if Wigmore was right on the basic issue of fair trial (and on this not even the perspective of time has brought agreement), unquestionably he unfairly identified Frankfurter's position with that of the communists — as an attack on the judiciary. Wigmore completely overlooked the fact that honest men sometimes reach different conclusions even from an examination of the same facts, and in this instance there was not even agreement on the facts. [48]

The aftermath of the controversy, so far as the personal relationship between the contenders was concerned, was quite different from that which occurred between Wigmore and Holmes in the Waterman and Abrams cases. The latter created a momentary hiatus at most. On the other hand, the Sacco-Vanzetti case brought Wigmore's friendship for Frankfurter to an abrupt end. Although Frankfurter resented Wigmore's attitude in the Sacco-Vanzetti case, [49] and disagreed sharply with some of his views, he never publicly displayed any antipathy to him. Over the years Frankfurter made several attempts to heal the breach and continued to speak of Wigmore's scholarship in the highest terms. Indeed, almost his last utterance to appear in print was a tribute on the one hundredth anniversary of Wigmore's birth. [50] Wigmore, however, never relented.

It would have been surprising if Wigmore — with his strong convictions on the subject of freedom of speech — had not sooner or later locked horns with the American Civil Liberties Union. And this occurred when he was invited to debate the issue of free speech with Roger Baldwin, a representative of the American Civil Liberties Union, at a meeting of the Chicago Forum under the auspices of the Adult Education Council of Chicago on

January 11, 1931. Wigmore heatedly declined because Baldwin, in testimony before a Senate investigating committee, had upheld the right of a citizen or alien to "advocate" the overthrow of the government by force and violence, adding that it is "the healthiest kind of a thing for a country, of course, to have free speech unlimited." Baldwin reinforced his position, in answering a later question, by including advocacy of murder or assassination "if it is mere advocacy."[51]

For Wigmore this was far too much, and he not only did what he could to prevent the debate but stated his own case in the pages of the *Evanston News-Index*.[52] To Wigmore the issue was simple. Baldwin's public support of the right freely to advocate murder or assassination[53] was beyond the pale.

It was inevitable that the opinion in the case of *United States* v. *Macintosh*[54] would evoke a sharp response from Wigmore, even though once again this position involved disagreement with Holmes. In this case, an application for citizenship was denied by a majority of five to four because Macintosh would not promise in advance to bear arms in defense of the United States unless he believed the war to be morally justified. Holmes joined the minority in an opinion written by Charles Evans Hughes.[55] Wigmore supported the majority opinion in a comment in the *Illinois Law Review* in which he said that both opinions were disappointing.[56] His own observations reflected his strong feelings with respect to military service, and, in the opinion of one contemporary commentator, they were unjustifiedly dogmatic.

Equally provocative for Wigmore was the trial by general court-martial of Colonel William Mitchell. Wigmore strongly disapproved of Mitchell's vehement advocacy, while still in the service, of an independent air force and a unified control of air power when both were opposed by the army general staff and the navy. As to the merits of the case he said that Mitchell had testified falsely before the congressional committee,[57] but that the basic question was that an honorable man should not "stay inside an organization and yet be publicly damning it."[58] He said this position was applicable to any organization — commercial, religious, educational, etc. — but especially to the army, "where discipline is the backbone of success in its function of protecting the nation by armed force."[59] In short, Wigmore felt that Mitchell should have resigned if he had wanted to go to the public with the issue.[60] This trial also gave him another opportunity, which he no doubt eagerly accepted, to declare that the Federal military court procedure was the most modern of any penal system in the country and should make the "civilian bar blush for shame at the contrast."[61] Wigmore was so disturbed by the misrepresentations in the press that he took the trouble to set straight the facts as he saw them in a comment in the *Illinois Law Review*, hoping at least to reach some of the members of the bar.[62]

So much for these reflections on the impact of Wigmore's service during World War I. That he had always been a loyal citizen is beyond question, but his experience in Washington had introduced a new element, that of fervor, and this continued without abatement. In the longer perspective it is interesting to note that when as a young man, upon the recommendation of David Starr Jordan, he had been invited to join the Society of American Wars "organized to promote love of country and flag," he had seen no reason at that time for supporting such an organization.[63]

The various strands of Wigmore's life, interrupted by his absorbing wartime experiences, must now be picked up and pursued as the Law School once again becomes the base and focus of his activities.

11

New Law School
on Lake Michigan

On his return to the Law School after World War I Wigmore found urgent problems requring his attention, and he realized that the long-distance supervision that had sufficed during wartime was now totally inadequate. Under these circumstances General Crowder's requests for Wigmore's assistance in Cuba, where he was serving as a special representative of the United States, and where he hoped Wigmore would eventually succeed him did not attract him in the least.[1] He did, however, respond by letter to Crowder's appeals for suggestions and problems. Indeed, what he needed, in fact, was a complete rest, and for this he received a leave of absence from the university for the second semester of the academic year 1922–23, a month of which he spent in Washington, going on from there to the Mediterranean.[2]

But before any leave of absence could be considered, much had to be done. First and foremost, a determination had to be made on the much debated issue of whether to move the Law School to the Evanston campus or to keep it in or near the center of Chicago. For many years Wigmore had contended that the Law School had outgrown its quarters and should be moved to the Near North Side of Chicago, and when Nathan William MacChesney, elected to the Board of Trustees in 1913, shortly thereafter proposed a Chicago campus for all of the professional schools, located on Lake Michigan at Chicago Avenue, Wigmore became a strong supporter.

In 1917 the necessary options had been obtained for much of the land on which the Chicago campus is now located, but when the United States entered the war, the negotiations had to be dropped. However, MacChesney, William A. Dyche, (the imaginative and highly constructive business manager of the university), and Philip Shumway, a member of the Board of Trustees, had kept the options open, and after the war the battle for the downtown campus was resumed.[3] Meanwhile, on the first Monday after his return from Washington in May 1919, Wigmore secured an option from Arthur Farwell on the particular portion of land on which the Law School now stands, an option that was signed by Wigmore and seven graduates of the Law School.[4] This portion was within the area under consideration for the Chicago campus as a whole. On June 5, 1919, the Law School faculty voted in favor of locating the Law School on the Near North Side, and adjacent to the other professional schools if possible.[5]

The principal reasons advanced by the Law School faculty for this decision were that the location of the school in the center of a metropolis made it distinctive, that its removal to Evanston would deprive students and faculty of contact with most of the members of the legal profession, and that it would lose two-thirds of its present students without any substantial compensation from other sources. In addition, it was clear that Chicago citizens would not make financial contributions for a Law School located in Evanston.

As to the curriculum, it was believed that a Near North Side location would make available the services of many qualified lawyers, often without compensation, who could offer practical courses applying the principles of the law to everyday problems. The Law School faculty also believed that, if the school were moved to Evanston, the University of Illinois or some other university would promptly take advantage of the opportunity to locate its law school near the center of Chicago.[6]

In assuming reluctantly the responsibility for raising funds, Wigmore was himself uncompromising as to the location of the school. In a letter to the president of the university, written before a decision had been reached, he said, "virtually not a dollar can be raised from Chicago people for an institution which has not at least one foot in Chicago,"[7] and he stated that the Alumni Committee would proceed to raise the $1,500,000 Endowment and Building Fund "on the assumption that the new Law School Building will be located on North Side land now under option, without waiting for final decision of the Trustees to concentrate the other three professional schools on that sight." That he was deeply concerned about this matter is revealed by the following letter to President Lynn H. Hough:

> My conviction, to be sure, has always been that the best way for scholars to build up their University is to stand by it loyally, regardless of temporary obstructions and disappointments; and I have never supposed, at any time since 1902, when Dr. Harper [William Rainey Harper, president of the University of Chicago] nearly annihilated our School, and I saved it, that anything could ever drive me to desert the structure which meant so much to my colleagues and myself. But the case would be very different if that structure were to be deliberately destroyed by its own controlling authorities. A captain's duty binds him to stick to the ship, however threatening the storm; but I never heard that he was expected to stay and go down with a waterlogged wreck.
>
> That is what this issue means to me — I suppose that I could apply for a Carnegie pension, or vegetate in some Washington Law School. But, at any rate, I should have to go somewhere afar that would bring a forgetting of the wreck.[8]

Because of the tenor of this letter, it should not be concluded that Wigmore's general relationship to President Hough was strained, for such was not the case. Although it was no doubt intended to make his position perfectly clear to the president, it was also written for the president's use in discussing the matter with the Board of Trustees if he desired to do so.[9]

Thus, once again, Wigmore had to pit his prestige and the threat to resign against the power of the Board of Trustees, some members of which were never entirely sympathetic to, or understanding of, the problems of the Law School. Again he asked nothing for himself. What he wanted was the freedom and support needed to develop the Law School and its program as he conceived them. In this instance, his success in achieving the Near North Side location also assured the Chicago campus for the other professional schools. Encouraged by gifts and pledges of more than a million dollars, the trustees voted on June 15, 1920, to purchase the lakefront property. With twenty-nine members present only three voted in the negative.[10]

With his accustomed vigor Wigmore threw himself into the necessary fund-raising campaign, which he planned in meticulous detail and supported with his own enthusiasm and encouragement at every turn. Reflecting his usual breadth of approach, the plan envisioned Chicago as a great cultural and scientific center, with the university occupying a position of leadership, especially through the development of the Chicago campus, and with the Law School playing an outstanding role in legal education and in the work of the legal profession as well.[11]

The goal for the Law School was a building and endowment fund originally set at $1,500,000 and later raised to $5,000,000,[12] to replace quarters which were totally inadequate as to size and posted a constant fire hazard to the law library, which was not only the best by far in the Middle West, but at the time was excelled only by the collections at Harvard and the Library of Congress.

The drive proceeded under the slogan: "This Fund shall be raised *for* the Law School, *by* the Alumni, *from* the Alumni."[13] Wigmore himself contributed a campaign song, which was sung to the tune of "Oh! How I Hate to Get Up in the Morning."[14] The first line of each verse read, "Oh! how I hate to go after the money!" And the last verse went as follows:

I hope that Heaven has got its endowment,
Before I go there I mean to know.
If Gabriel runs a fund campaign,
He won't find me in the Angels' train;
Oh! — well, I'd rather go down below!

In closing his remarks to the Alumni Advisory Committee, in which he stressed the importance of the role of the legal profession, Wigmore pointed to his personal commitment: "I have worked for this Law School and this community for more than twenty-five years. I have never worked under any other school or university in this country. I want to see this great thing *done* while I am alive and in harness. Knowing you as I do, I *know* that you *can* do it. And I have faith that you *will* do it."[15]

The campaign had seven major objectives for support: (1) research concerning modern commercial and industrial law, (2) a bureau of legislative research, (3) a laboratory of applied criminal science, (4) a legal clinic for the poor, (5) the study of world law, (6) the study of jurisprudence, legal history, and philosophy of law, and (7) the study of international law.[16]

Even before the land was acquired, a committee of Law School alumni began a drive for building and endowment funds and, at the school's sixtieth-anniversary dinner, William Jennings Bryan, class of '83, spoke to promote the drive. Although a vigorous campaign among alumni produced pledges of about $200,000, the amount was of course far short of what was needed even for the buildings alone.[17] It was clear that considerable reliance would have to be placed upon the support of several major contributors.

Among the possible major donors was Elbert H. Gary, class of '67, who had for a number of years made annual contributions for the purchase of books for the library which totaled more than $100,000, and a further gift in 1923 of $100,000 for the purchase of additional books and for binding.[18] Although Judge Gary continued to express pride and interest in the library, he had accepted no moral obligation to make further contributions and would not permit Wigmore to take up the question of an endowment contribution. However, Judge Gary was aware of the fact that the library had carried his name all over the world, and it seemed natural that he would want to assure its future. At Wigmore's suggestion the president of the university asked a committee of the Board of Trustees to present the library proposal to him! Wigmore estimated that $400,000 would be needed for the building and $600,000 for endowment.[19] Finally in 1925 Gary agreed to give a further sum of $150,000 to build the new Elbert H. Gary Library.[20]

The first major benefaction to be received had been a gift of $500,000 given in 1923 by Mrs. Levy Mayer for a law-school building in memory of her husband, a distinguished Chicago lawyer. The gift brought the amount contributed to $1,600,000, leaving less than $3,500,000 still to be raised.

Wigmore's role in the raising of funds took much of his time and effort, and he found soliciting major donations distasteful.[21] His own contributions were generous: he gave $1,000 to the War Service Memorial in the Law School and assigned the salary he earned through teaching in the summers of 1919, 1920, 1921, and 1922 to the endowment fund.[22]

Although funds were now in hand to build the new Law School quarters, the goals established for research and endowment were not attained. Contributions that had been received for a John Henry Wigmore Chair of Evidence had to be merged into general endowment and the project abandoned. A John Henry Wigmore professorship was eventually created in 1966, and John C. Ritchie, dean of the Law School at the time, was the first appointee. However, several endowment funds of importance to the Law School were created. Among these was the James Nelson and Anna Louise Raymond Foundation which in 1926 established a substantial grant for legal-aid work. Mrs. Raymond also added funds for graduate fellowships and for loans to law students.[23]

Another important endowment was the Julius Rosenthal Foundation established early in the campaign and subsequently enlarged by gifts from a number of donors. Under the direction of the faculty the income is devoted to the publication of legal studies and the support of the Rosenthal Lectures, and the *Law Review.*

The income of the Charles C. Linthicum Foundation, established in 1926, is used for research, study, and instruction in the fields of patents, copyrights and trade marks, and other subjects relating to trade and commerce.[24]

Wigmore felt so strongly about the Law School building on which he had spent so much time and thought that he did not readily yield to suggestions for changes in his plans. On one occasion in a discussion with Robert W. Campbell, president of the Board of Trustees, it was suggested that the sizes of some of the faculty offices be reduced in order to bring the cubic-foot cost of the building in line with the funds available. Wigmore protested heatedly that the proposed offices would be too small. "Mr. Campbell observed that they were as large as his office, and asked why they needed more space. 'For books' said Wigmore. Campbell thinking of the Gary Library, off the same floor, asked 'why do they need books?' Whereupon Wigmore exploded and left in high dudgeon."[25] Walking three blocks to the offices of General MacChesney, he burst in upon him and said, "I have been insulted by the Board of Trustees and I demand an apology. Mr. Campbell evidently thinks we are not scholars and do not read." Mr. Campbell had considerable difficulty in explaining that he had intended no reflection on anyone.

Wigmore's interest in the library was unceasing, and he believed that every faculty member should do a certain amount of bibliographic work in helping to build up a well-selected collection. Although Wigmore probably never fully recognized the importance of the role of the staff in the administration of the growing library, he was eager to improve their size and overall professional competency.[26]

After the new building was completed Judge and Mrs. Gary were invited to come and inspect the object of their benefactions, and for their benefit Wigmore had put on display some of the choicest volumes in the library. MacChesney described the scene to Wigmore and "pointed out that each book had the distinctive book plate . . . 'The Elbert H. Gary Library of Law.' Mrs. Gary said nothing but quietly went to the shelves pulling out a half dozen volumes and looked at the bookplates. 'Humph,' she said, 'I thought perhaps you had planted these books for us but I can see they are all marked the same.' For a moment Wigmore was stunned — then said, 'Mrs. Gary, I assure you the only 'planting' that is done is in the minds of the faculty — and students I hope!"[27] Judge Gary laughed.

During the planning and construction of the buildings a battle royal developed over the allocation of space, the sizes of rooms, etc., and it became clear that all of Wigmore's ideas could not be carried out with the resources that were available. One economy that was suggested was the substitution of plaster for oak paneling in certain portions of Levy Mayer Hall. Wigmore fought to retain the paneling but both Mr. Dyche, the business manager, and the trustees believed the $16,000 cost should be saved.

Several years later when Wigmore

> heard of the possibility of a visit of the British Bar, he again urged that the oak paneling be put in as originally planned. The University hesitated for the reason stated. Wigmore went into action. One day the man in charge of the buildings called up Mr. Dyche and, in great excitement, told him that Dean Wigmore and a couple of students were breaking up some of the plaster panels along the corridor. Mr. Dyche got busy, talked to Wigmore, and consulted the trustees. They were taken aback but finally laughed, made a marital compromise, and Wigmore got the oak paneling before he retired and in time for the visit of the British Bench and Bar in 1930.[28]

But, Wigmore's troubles were by no means over just because the location of the Law School had been finally settled and the fund-raising campaign was well under way. Once again he was faced with a crisis in his relationship with the Board of Trustees — a crisis concerning the very existence of the Law School program. By 1921, Walter Dill Scott had succeeded Hough as president of the university. With a characteristic display of loyalty, Wigmore had told Scott, although he was not his first choice for the presidency, that now that he'd been appointed he was for him all the way.[29] His characteristic light and playful spirit clearly entered into the relationship with Scott which he enjoyed for the rest of his life. Welcoming him back to the university in the fall of 1923, Wigmore wrote to ask for an appointment: "I have no especial matter to take up; I am thinking merely of a general confabulation for the beginning of the new year."[30]

But the crux of Wigmore's conflict with the board developed when the board rejected his recommendations as to personnel and apparently reneged on a pledge made in 1916. Wigmore expressed his pique in a letter to Scott that was in fact never mailed

> providing for four senior-grade resident professorships and three junior-grade resident professorships, at salaries named. This resolution was in the nature of a formal pledge to me, made as a measure of efficiency for the School's future, and as an inducement to me to decline the pending Yale University offer to be Director of its new School of Jurisprudence.[31]

The same unsent letter also reflects Wigmore's reaction to a proposal of the Education Committee of the Board of Trustees to have a survey of the Law School made by experts employed from the outside.

> It is possible that I misunderstand the purport of the foregoing. But, as I read your letter, I am to celebrate the thirtieth year of my connection with the School, and the twenty-second year of my incumbency as Dean, by being investigated as to competency of administration; and my colleagues, resident and non-resident, who have all been members of this Faculty for periods of from five to twenty

years, are also to be investigated as to competency of instruction and soundness of scholarship. And meanwhile my recommendations as to personnel are to be shown such distrust that no action is to be taken upon them, — although I have had no opportunity to appear before the Board and to hear and answer the grounds for distrust. However, if my methods and personality are not so well known to the Board after thirty years that they speak for themselves, I presume that a hearing would be needless.

At any rate, it is obvious that the situation calls for my withdrawal from any further responsibilities as Dean of the Faculty, so that you and the Board can be free to choose a more satisfactory administrator.

It should not be concluded from the foregoing statement that Wigmore was opposed to an appropriate survey of the school, for he had made such a proposal on several occasions. In the midst of this discussion of a survey Wigmore asked the officers of the Board and the lawyer members to be his guests for dinner at the University Club in Evanston. They went and Wigmore was at his best as a host — which means that it could not have been more delightful. At the close of the dinner he said he had a matter that he wished to discuss with his guests and he took a long manuscript from his pocket and proceeded to read it. He reviewed the history of legal education, the role Northwestern had played in it, his struggles and his discouragements in developing and maintaining the Law School, the many offers he had declined to go elsewhere, all because of his loyalty to the Law School.

He acknowledged that there was room for improvement, and as to a survey as an appropriate step he had this to say:

But it must be made under conditions which promise that it will be of value. In the first place, it must be made by one who understands something of the subject, and of the difficulties of teaching law. In the second place, it must be made by someone who possesses accepted pedagogic standards. In the third place, it must be made by someone who can put himself in the position of the beginning law student. Therefore, the correct way is for a master of pedagogic standards to come to the School, and enter the first-year class, study the lessons, and attend the classes for the first semester, also attending the upper classes of the second year and the third year, so as to hear all the different instructors. My proposal to President Harris and to Professor Jones was that the College should lend Professor Jones to the Law School for one semester, full time, that he should make such a survey, and that his report should cover not only pedagogic methods in the abstract as applied to the teaching of law, but also comments on the personal shortcomings of the individual teachers; and the latter part to be kept confidential between the President, the individual teacher himself, and perhaps the Dean. Such a report would, of course, not have final value, in that a non-lawyer could hardly appreciate all the fine points that arise in teaching law. But it would have the primary value of applying general pedagogic standards to the teaching of Law.[32]

When Wigmore finished reading he put down the manuscript and said, "And how am I rewarded? By being investigated by the Board of Trustees!"[33] A dead silence followed as Wigmore strode from the room.

The guests were somewhat stunned. After about fifteen minutes, James A. Patton, President of the Board asked Professor Crossley, Secretary of the Law Faculty, to go and see if there was anything the matter with Mr. Wigmore. After some delay Crossley returned and said, not finding Mr. Wigmore, he had telephoned his house and Mrs. Wigmore had said he had gone to bed. Mr. Patton dryly remarked, "Gentlemen, I take it the party is over." We also then went home to bed.[34]

Another objection to the current survey proposal was that it emanated from a committee of the Board of Trustees rather than from the University Council, "the highest educational authority" under the statutes of the university.[35]

Wigmore's proposal that the survey be made by one not trained in law and experienced in law-school teaching was unusual. Visitations for the purpose of evaluating teaching and other aspects of legal education, whether for accreditation or on a voluntary basis, have traditionally been made by teachers or deans.

When a plan for the university survey, largely based on Wigmore's suggestions, was proposed by the University Council and approved by the Board of Trustees, Wigmore eventually yielded, although he did not consider the decision of much importance to the Law School. He felt he was under a "military order," and — as he put it — the "faculty and Dean of the Law School never conducted their relations with the University on the basis of military subordinates."[36]

Although a committee of five was appointed to direct the survey of the Law School, one member died and for various reasons the committee did not meet. Accordingly, the assignment was in effect under Wigmore's direction. In his letter of transmission to President Scott, Wigmore said, "It is believed that this report is the first comprehensive educational survey made of any American Law School."[37] Needless to say, it was a very useful document to the Law School and was praised highly by Leon Green, Wigmore's successor as dean.[38]

Its value, however, was limited by the fact that it was not made by someone outside of the Law School. A more objective analysis would have revealed the fact that Wigmore delegated too much authority to one individual, and one not qualified for the responsibilities given him. Furthermore, his loyalty to Wigmore and his judgment were limited. It appears that the undue proliferation of courses was in part due to the fact that they were sometimes handed out as favors by this individual. However, Wigmore did in fact favor a considerable amount of diversity, particularly within his conception of the four-year curriculum. That the outcome of misplaced confidence should continue indefinitely can be attributed to Wigmore's deep sense of loyalty, in this case a virtue carried to such an extreme that he declined, in spite of well-informed proddings by some of those around him, to make an investigation that would have brought the facts to light.

In all of his contests with university officials and with the Board of Trustees over support of the Law School, the faculty was an object of major concern, and Wigmore was unquestionably their champion in obtaining adequate facilities, better compensation, and academic freedom. The faculty minutes and Wigmore's correspondence with the university presidents clearly show that the faculty was constantly consulted on matters of interest to them and that their views not only influenced his decisions but were often accepted instead of his own. He showed no reluctance in changing his recommendations under such circumstances. On at least one occasion he declined an increase in salary and asked that the amount be divided among the members of the faculty.[39]

Although most of the faculty who served with Wigmore regarded him highly both as dean and as colleague, Wigmore did not have the undivided loyalty and support of every one of them. In fact a few found him difficult and some regarded him with antipathy. It was not surprising that a man of such pronounced convictions and untiring energy and determination often antagonized others. One such case involved a faculty wife who was also a student in a situation that Wigmore referred to in a letter as "unpleasant and yet amusing."[40] As a matter of fact, the behavior of the faculty wife, who severely criticized the teaching methods of several faculty members, had a demoralizing effect on both the students and faculty members. The latter, who were of course accustomed to student criticism generally, were placed in a particularly embarrassing situation in this case. Of Wigmore she said that out of three of his courses that she had taken, one did not seem "of any earthly good" and, as to another, "the examination was a joke."

On the question of academic freedom Wigmore had very definite views, and he embodied them in the Law School survey to which reference has already been made, "The tradition in this Faculty is one of complete freedom of the individual member to employ his own preferred methods in the conduct of his courses."[41]

Wigmore's reaction to a report of a faculty curriculum committee of which Professor Francis Philbrick was chairman indicated that this attitude was more than a matter of theory. One recommendation affected the sales courses taught by Professor Kocourek, who gave a regular, three-hour, case-method course and a one-hour, experimental course in alternate years. While considering the committee's recommendations that the regular three-hour course be offered each year, the faculty deliberations drifted off into a discussion of the merits of Kocourek's teaching.

To Wigmore, the issue then promptly transcended the technical curricular problem and became one of academic freedom. In a heated session, he read to the faculty a memorandum asserting that while the faculty as a whole had the right to determine the curriculum as such, the number of hours for each course and who should give the course, it had no right to infringe upon the "absolute" freedom of the teacher to teach the course as he sees fit. Academic freedom, he said, was the "obstinate cult of individualism" which had saved Oxford and Cambridge and must be protected not only against the public, the alumni, the trustees, the University officials and the students, but against the faculty itself. "Tyranny," he thundered, "is conceivably as possible under a democracy as under an autocracy.'' A subsequent memorandum by Professor Philbrick strongly challenged the assertion that any invasion of academic freedom had been intended. This, and the faculty's rejection of the proposed change, however, were both far overshadowed by the force of Wigmore's reaction. He was not an easy man to deter when pursuing a conviction, and he had many convictions.[42]

However, his desire to maintain an *esprit de corps* within his faculty and his eagerness to have faculty members keep in close touch with members of the bar did tempt him on one occasion to overstep his bounds as an administrator:

Memorandum for Members of the Faculty: (May 26, 1925)

I left here March 29, having attended a jolly lunch reunion at the C.B.A. [Chicago Bar Association] on March 24. I went there again today, and found our table no longer reserved. The superintendentess' excuse was that lately there had been only one or two of us coming, sometimes none.

I was pained. The facts may not be as extreme as she stated. But I had thought that enough of us appreciated the importance of social teamwork at least to hold a table. Living widely apart as we do, and performing our labors separately, what becomes of the "carry on" spirit of the institution if we can't foregather once in a while? The barracks life of a college campus is not the most admirable thing. But the opposite extreme is equally deplorable.[43]

It is not surprising that the memo drew an immediate polite but blunt response. Significantly, it came from a devoted and admiring colleague.

Memorandum for the Dean: (28 May 1925)

I have received your luncheon memorandum of the 25th inst., the contents of which distinctly hurt. So far as my own case is concerned, I have before explained that the exigencies of the Evidence Class made it necessary for me to utilize Tuesday as a "dies liber." But, quite apart from this, and looking at the matter from a general standpoint, I find myself reluctantly compelled to dissent from the implied premises of the memorandum. I agree that these meetings are interesting and enjoyable — no one, I think, has enjoyed them more than myself. I agree, also, that they are useful and valuable. I think, moreover, they ought to be encouraged and promoted by every appropriate means. I am willing to concede that, other things being equal, one's presence at them is a duty to the school and the University. But what I cannot admit is that this duty should be treated as resting upon anything other than the untrammeled volition of the individual. If, for example, anyone should feel that with John Henry Wigmore absent from the city, the gathering has lost its chief charm, and accordingly should withdraw from attendance, then, I say let the *un*erring brother depart in peace. In other words, I do not believe that we are dealing here with an official obligation. But, whatever its precise nature, I am quite clear, and I am moved to submit with all deference, that it is not an obligation whose infraction, excusable or inexcusable, should be made the text of a formal reprimand.

(Signed) Robert W. Millar[44]

On his return to Chicago, Wigmore had asked his War Department secretary, Sarah B. Morgan, to join him at the Law School when their service in Washington came to an end, and she had agreed. She describes her arrival in Chicago:

> Mr. Wigmore met me, looking very distinguished in a light gray suit, one of the ties, — lavender (in summer) or purple (in winter) — that he loved . . . and carrying a cane. Later I heard him say that when he carried a cane it showed he was not working, — and he always carried one on his travels, and on Sundays when he went out walking with Mrs. Wigmore and any guest who was visiting them. He took me to the YWCA where he waited in the parlor while I changed from my traveling clothes, and then he took me to the Law School and introduced me to everybody and showed me the office, took me to luncheon at Field's, and then escorted me to Evanston where Mrs. Wigmore was waiting for us at the North Shore Music Festival which was held in the old Patton Gymnasium. There they introduced me to all their friends, during the intermission of a very delightful concert (the first of many which I was to enjoy with them, little knowing that later I would sing in the chorus of that annual festival). After the concert they took me to their home for dinner, and then the Colonel took me all the way back into Chicago and saw that I arrived safely at the YWCA. Everything was done so naturally and quietly and I was made to feel so much at home that I did not realize until years later how much thought the Wigmores had put into making me welcome in a strange city.[45]

Miss Morgan, who would work most closely with Wigmore, was soon to discover what an excellent relationship existed between him and the four other women on his staff. Having noted his habit of making memos on any convenient piece of paper, they decided to recognize his birthday with a gift of colored memo pads and several colored pencils. The gift was accompanied by a verse signed "Office Fours." It was acknowledged with this verse by Wigmore:

Lines on Receiving This Paper, With Verses by Four Lady Friends

> The Muses *nine*, the Graces *four*
> In days of old there used to be.
> But, now that Woman, at the fore,
> Is changing all the rules of yore,
> Muses and Graces, both, are *four*.
> At any rate, upon *our* floor.

March 4, 1922   J.H.W.[46]

They were known as the "Office Fours" ever after, and the Wigmores returned from every trip with a gift for each of them.

Sometimes Wigmore used his own democratic attitude to teach a lesson to others. Among the many foreign visitors that came to call upon him was a professor from a Norwegian university. One day, taking his seemingly haughty guest into the hall where the janitor was polishing brass, he introduced him, explaining that the janitor was also from Norway and would show him around the Law School. The professor was quite taken aback, but there was nothing for him to do but follow. He asked the janitor how he came to be so well informed about the Law School. The janitor replied "that the opportunity of improving one's education was one of the principal advantages of being an American." Upon their return to Wigmore's office the professor was enthusiastic and appreciative of the information with which he had been provided. After the guest had left, Wigmore said to the janitor with a twinkle in his eye, "I think we gave the professor a little lesson in Americanism." [47]

With Wigmore the personal touch extended to all those with whom he came in contact. A warm greeting, a showing of interest, or an expression of appreciation met any workman who came to adjust a radiator, repair a lock, or perform some other assignment. Often a cigar would accompany the word of thanks.

Wigmore's responsibilities as dean were supplemented by his continuing role as a teacher. After the war he taught the courses in Evidence and Torts using his own casebooks, and his one-hour course based on *Principles of Judicial Proof* continued until his retirement as dean in 1929. Throughout this period he participated with other faculty members in offering a course entitled General Survey of Law, and from 1922 to 1924 he taught a course on Estoppel and Deceit. We have already noted that Wigmore believed that legal education should not be limited to the case method of instruction. His strong inclination to innovate inevitably reflected itself in his teaching. His teaching expressed both his broad scholarly approach to the law and his interest in its practical application. The courses entitled Codes, Revised Statutes and Compiled Laws; Office Briefs; Preparation of Transactional Documents; and Problems of Contemporary Legislation (given jointly with Eugene Harley) were offered several times during the postwar period. The courses in Public International Law, with Special Reference to the League of Nations; the World's Legal Systems; General Legal Literature; and History of the Bench and Bar (Legal Biography), which exemplified the scholarly approach were offered from time to time.

Wigmore's emphasis on biography can also be seen in his Course on Profession of the Bar. In 1931, addressing the Section on Legal Education and Admission to the Bar of the American Bar Association at its meeting in Atlantic City, Wigmore took the view that "A main problem of legal education is to awaken in the beginner the deep sense of becoming a member of a great professional fraternity, a fraternity with a past as well as a future, honoring duties as well as powers; and also [the problem is] to arouse the personal courage and ambition for the individual career in that profession." [48]

Wigmore conceded in his address that this could not be done directly but depended on something more than the atmosphere of the school and the attitude of the members of the faculty, important as they were. After twenty years of trial and error he had concluded that the objective could be achieved by a course containing the following elements: an introduction to the life stories of distinguished members of the bench and bar; an explanation of the organization of the bar and the accepted rules of professional behavior; a study of the problems with which the legal profession was actually concerned. Appended to the text of Wigmore's address was a list of suggested biographies, a list of course topics, and a list of books to be placed on reserve in the library.

In the General Survey course Wigmore would begin by asking each student to tell about himself and why he wanted to study law. He undoubtedly wanted to become acquainted with each student at the very beginning. One student answered the question of why he had chosen Northwestern by saying, "Because of you brother Wigmore."[49] Wigmore was obviously taken aback but said nothing.

On another occasion a student who had already elicited the disfavor of Wigmore by appearing without his waistcoat (a piece of apparel that was worn in Wigmore's time even on a hot day) gave the basic facts about himself and then said, "Many people thought lawyers were crooks; but he wanted to be a lawyer. Many people thought lawyers were knaves; but he wanted to be a lawyer." As he proceeded in this way the members of the class "listened in open-mouthed horror, half expecting the Dean to physically throw the offending student out of the room." However, Wigmore listened in silence and when the student finished the silence was painfully extended. Then Wigmore asked the student, "Have you read the statement by Abraham Lincoln which is on the wall just outside the door of this room?" The student replied in the negative and Wigmore said, "Suppose you go up, take the plaque off the wall and bring it in."

The student took the long walk up the steps and out of the room while the class waited in silence. When the student returned with the plaque, Wigmore said, after another painful moment of silence, "Read it." The student read it, including the words, if you "cannot be an honest lawyer, resolve to be honest without being a lawyer. Choose some other occupation, rather than one in the choosing of which you do, in advance, consent to be a knave." The student gulped, and blurted out, 'I apologize.'" Wigmore turned to the next speaker.[50]

In the course in Legal Literature Wigmore required the students to memorize passages from Shakespeare and the Bible. For the passage from the Bible one student chose Matthew 7:7: "Ask and it shall be given you; seek and ye shall find; knock and it shall be opened unto you." We continue with the student's own words:

> One day in Lowden Hall the Dean asked whether I was ready with my quotations. For a change I was prepared, so we went over in a corner, sat down, lit cigarettes, and I proceeded to recite. On finishing the passage from St. Matthew, he said: "Now, Mr. Wettling, what do you think that means?" Being somewhat nonplussed, I said, with a bit of embarrassment, "Well, frankly, Colonel, I hadn't given it much thought. I suppose it means just what it says." Then that inimitable smile came across his face and with the ever-present twinkle in his eye he said, "Well, I'll tell you what I think it means." (Of course, in giving his interpretation of the passage he exercised his literary

prerogative of changing it about a bit in order to make his point.) ''Knock, and it shall be opened unto you; seek, and ye shall find; ask, and it shall be given you — and very likely if you don't ask you won't get it.'' I have used that philosophy on many occasions with a high percentage of success for the past twenty years.[51]

In connection with the course in Contemporary Legislation Wigmore took his students to Springfield while the legislature was in session. A student who was Wigmore's roommate on one such occasion was startled to see that he stripped and did a ''daily dozen'' both at night and in the morning. The student was so impressed with this routine that he took up the practice and was ''proud to show that he himself was straight with no paunch.''[52]

One method that Wigmore used in class to harden the students to the realities of practice was to have students shuffle their feet on the floor while one of their peers was talking. Such distractions, he said, would have to be encountered in the municipal court.[53]

Sometimes Wigmore took full advantage of the immediate situation.

Once during a lecture on the law of Evidence, an exasperating and resounding hammering persisted on the floor above. The Dean (turning Colonel for the moment) called the class to attention, formed the student body into squads of eight, marched through the halls and up the stairs to a little carpenter, busy mending a window sash. The workman was confronted by the column in command of the Dean who stepped briskly forward, took the piece of lumber from the man's hands, held it aloft as a gladiator's sword and said, ''Gentlemen, this is real evidence.''

Dean Wigmore was far more than the cloistered scholar. He was a great natural psychologist. He knew the importance of techniques and that the advocate with a fine mind and a clear understanding of his case could not prevail unless he could create sympathy for his position and make himself heard and understood. In the middle of a class, a recitation presented in a weak voice would be interrupted. The Dean takes time out for a lesson in elocution, complete with sweeping gestures, booming voice, elaborate terminology, flights of fancy, deft figures of speech, metaphors, and stimuli to passion, greed and sympathy. The students were embarrassed, bored and amazed in turn, but secretly began practicing speaking in private.[54]

One episode worth recalling concerns final examinations. One morning when Miss Morgan came into the Law School on the train with Wigmore she called his attention to the fact that there was a student in a seat nearby. Wigmore got up to speak to him but stopped abruptly just behind him and returned to his seat. He shut his eyes, folded his hands, and did no more reading, and Miss Morgan thought he must not be feeling well. At the Law School Miss Morgan met the student who said jeeringly, ''I thought the Dean always read on the train.''[55] Wigmore had constantly urged the students to use every minute of their time. But the reason for Wigmore's unusual behavior soon became evident. He had noticed that the student on the train was reading a copy of an examination given many years before and one that Wigmore intended to repeat that year. After Wigmore substituted a new set of questions in the next examination, the student asked Miss Morgan if the dean had seen him on the train. She replied that he had and that he had also seen the examination he was reading, the very one the dean intended to use. The student exclaimed, "Gosh, and I thought he was asleep."[56]

Wigmore was convinced that grades provided a necessary incentive and that superior students were entitled to know that they had distinguished themselves. He believed that letter grades rather than percentage equivalents were sufficient.[57] Although many students were under the impression that Wigmore gave high grades and seldom failed any one in his courses, it is clear from the records available that he gave relatively few As and Bs. It does seem to be true, however, that he seldom failed anyone,[58] and there is some evidence that he grew more lenient in his later years.

As Wigmore's casebooks were not always acclaimed by his fellow teachers, an appraisal by a student is of considerable interest.

> Hence the Dean's casebooks were delightful in their frequent resort to unexpected authorities — — Aesop's Fables, the "Mabinogian," the "Chronicles of the Cid," Shakespeare's "Henry IV," Sheridan's "School for Scandal," Boswell's "Life of Johnson," Herman Melville, Victor Hugo and Balzac. Philosophers and economists were represented in numbers. Thomas Aquinas and Machiavelli both appeared. Herbert Spencer may arouse some contemptuous looks in certain places today; Karl Marx was *not* quoted, but Edward Bellamy was. These were the only casebooks in my own experience which were interesting reading. They more nearly succeeded in relating the decisions of judges to the whole life of society than any others given us.[59]

The casebooks were, of course, consistent with Wigmore's belief that it was necessary to search beyond the acts of legislatures, the decisions of the courts, and the comments of textbook writers, to ascertain the living reason behind the rule.

Wigmore's desire to continually enrich the curriculum was just one aspect of his vigorous effort to raise educational requirements and support the four-year curriculum that had gone into effect at Northwestern University in 1919. In several years during the 1920s the number of courses offered ran as high as 60 to 75. Although the students were allowed a great deal of freedom in selecting courses, the faculty saw to it that the students took a reasonable number of subjects which developed leadership and breadth of view and qualified them to render better public service.

Wigmore's continued advocacy after the war of the four-year curriculum was destined for ultimate failure in spite of the fact that he had the support of the faculty and of the Section on Legal Education of the American Bar Association. The program was not favored by the president of the university[60] or by the Association of American Law Schools[61] from which he sought formal approval,[62] and he stood alone in the association's Curriculum Committee.[63] The onset of the depression made the four-year course too much of a luxury, and in 1935 the three-year course was reinstated.[64]

In spite of Wigmore's multitudinous responsibilities he continued to have time for the students. His office was continually open, and his graciousness was appreciated. He went out of his way on his students' behalf, by providing financial aid through scholarships or other means, and by conferring with them when they were having difficulties with their studies. Illness always evoked a warm and often helpful response. Indeed, he had a hospital committee in each class to ferret out such cases, and "woe unto the committee that neglected its task."[65] He not only visited sick students but periodically wrote cards and letters to show his continuing interest. In one case he persuaded the doctor of an extremely ill student to permit him to return to the Law School temporarily to take his final examinations and receive a degree.

From a hard-pressed student came this response, "Your letter came as one of the happiest surprises and greatest inspirations of my life . . . I never knew that I could merit such kind thoughts, but to do so has given me a new incentive to greater achievements."[66]

Foreign students were especially appreciative of his interest, and they realized that his outlook transcended national boundaries. Filipino students expressed their appreciation as follows:

> The undersigned Phillipino students of Northwestern University school of Law, knowing that you will leave us pro tempore on a leave of absence to go to Europe for a vacation this winter, we wish you a pleasant journey. We also sincerely hope that you will have a most delightful time in visiting those historical countries in Europe, France and Italy.
>
> We dedicate this brief message to our beloved professor, Hon. John H. Wigmore as an expression of good will and fellowship, and we will look forward to his speedy return to us in this great institution of Northwestern University.[67]

Although he felt that the Northwestern commencement exercises were as good as those of any university, he suggested that "the organist abandon the idea that it is a church service or a musical recital, and substitute hereafter some cheerful and inspiring music. At the time of the march around, a genuine rhythmic march should be played, such as the Priests' March from Aida, or Athalile, or Pomp and Circumstance."[68]

Arthur Goldberg, a graduate of the Law School, expressed his regard for Wigmore as follows:

> Of all the recollections which crowd my memory of the gladdening and warming experience of our association as teacher and student, one is foremost in my mind. Dean Wigmore, in his charming and gracious way, accompanied our law class to Springfield for bar admission ceremonies. In the course of an animated and spritely conversation about our futures, he told me and my fellows something I have always carried with me.

"What law you practice is not important," he said; "any specialty can be interesting and sometimes rewarding, but *how* you practice is of key importance. And I urge you above all else to practice law in the *grand* manner." Holmes expressed the same thought in other words when he said that "every calling is great when greatly pursued." [69]

Although Wigmore's influence on his students was characteristically effected by kindness and consideration, he could exhibit an uncompromising firmness when this was required. Sometimes it would be expressed by a notice posted on the bulletin board. On one occasion the students were confronted with the following:

January 14, 1927:

Last evening, on leaving the school, an automobile said to belong to a Law student, was found parked exactly opposite the entrance walk, at the only place of exit from the two foot snow drift.

Other instances of such parking have recently occurred. I am astounded at the mean, selfish thoughtlessness that leads to such acts: I do not want to know the perpetrators' names this time, for I could not refrain from language of personal contumely. But I register the conviction that any one who repeats such an act, after attention called to its antisocial nature, is in much more pressing need of moral education than of legal education, and is not a promising candidate for an altruistic profession.

(signed) John H. Wigmore
Dean [70]

On another occasion the bulletin board displayed the following:

Special Course in Damages   February 2, 1927

From information received through the janitor, it is apparent that the eager devotees of learning, who are using the study rooms on the fourth floor, are spending a large part of their time in conducting a special course in Damages to the chairs. The score was yesterday two chairs, matched today with three chairs. Beginning 24 hours from the posting of this notice, a tally will be kept. Unless the record progressively diminishes to nothing, we shall reluctantly be obliged to remove all chairs from those rooms, so that the eager student may pursue his study as in the Orient, viz. by sitting on the floor.

John H. Wigmore [71]

In a happier vein is his expression of appreciation to the Class of 1928 for their gift upon his retirement as dean.

To the Class of '28
I take with pride the golden pen
    That now adorns my writing-den
To frame the wish, with grateful heart,
    That though our ways may sometime part
The loyal class of Twenty-Eight
    May find the road both broad and straight

> That brings the clients to the door
> And ends in bank accounts that soar!

September 10, 1929   John H. Wigmore [72]

Year after year Wigmore kept up his interest in music and in student musical events at the Law School. He even tried to keep up with the popular music prevalent at the time. His appreciation of it, however, had limits. In 1929, when he was making arrangements for some music at a forthcoming reception, he wrote to a faculty member in the Music School for suggestions: "It has been our custom on such occasions to make use of the Dental School orchestra for music, but their jazz programs the last one or two times have proved too much for us." [73]

Stuart S. Ball gives these glimpses of Wigmore's musical activity during his sojourn in the Law School as a student.

> The Dean had the rare ability to mingle with us man to man without conde-scension, and to do without loss of respect what others would have appeared undignified in doing.
> The last barriers to friendship and affection between my generation of law school students and the Dean were broken when the Dean made a not-too-serious attempt to organize a law school glee club. This was the excuse for several of the song-fests in which the Dean delighted — events which stripped the law of the last of the Olympian trappings in which we had first invested it. [74]

Even as late as 1941, when Wigmore was seventy-eight, he was still promoting songfests for the students. [75] Stuart Ball was convinced that Wigmore's "love of the piano and of irreverent parodies, must necessarily have been in part responsible for the [Chicago] Bar Association's annual shows, the composing of jocular songs about those who address the city's professional groups, and the songs sung at the annual outings of those groups." [76]

For Wigmore, music revolving around the piano continued to be an important interest. He went through some finger exercises and practiced every day, long after arthritis in his fingers made this difficult and inter-fered to some extent with his performance. [77] When the Wigmores enter-tained at home, he frequently both played the piano and sang with others participating. And often after attending an opera Wigmore would play all of the arias by ear.

Wigmore's interest in the students did not end upon their graduation, nor did their interest in him. He did his utmost to see that they were success-fully started on their careers, frequently assisted them in finding better openings, and often strongly supported them when they ran for public office. And of course faculty members, students, and graduates all enjoyed the graciousness of the Wigmore hospitality, both individually and in groups. [78] According to Miss Morgan:

> The Wigmores liked to have traditional parties like the smoker each year for the graduating class. . . . They had brought some very beautiful Japanese

lanterns from Japan and used them year after year. They would hang them around their home on the beautiful bridal wreath and barberry bushes and, with some on long thin sticks, on each side of the walk that led to the entrance. It was distinctly an affair for the graduating class, no members of their families being invited. After greeting the guests, Mrs. Wigmore and I kept out of sight and the Colonel entertained them with the help of the men of the faculty. Occasionally there were girls who were graduating, but the party was conducted in the same manner.

Another traditional affair with the Wigmores was a luncheon after the morning commencement exercises. To this they invited the recipient of the Honorary Degree of LL.D., all the faculty and their wives and the Law School office staff. The luncheon was served on the porch overlooking Lake Michigan and the affair lasted until late afternoon.

In respect to all their entertaining, and indeed their other recreation, Mrs. Wigmore often said that they lived on her husband's salary and played on the royalties from his books. However, the "playing" included "lending" a helping hand financially to others.[79]

After dinner Wigmore would usually play the piano, but he was also very fond of giving dramatic readings. One favorite was the impersonation of an old man walking back and forth, throwing out his shoulders, and exclaiming, "I am just as young as ever. I am just as young as ever." Then, suddenly clutching his hip, he would cry out in pain and say, "Oh my rheumatism, oh my rheumatism."[80]

Another of Wigmore's recitals was "The Seven Ages of Man." This he practiced early in his career, along with voice exercises that had been suggested by the dean of the School of Speech when Wigmore consulted him about what he regarded as a personal inadequacy in delivery. As they grew older Mrs. Wigmore said the last age of man was becoming too realistic and she persuaded him to give up the whole recitation.[81]

Another glimpse of the Wigmores as hosts has been preserved by Wigmore's sister Beatrice:

My sister-in-law was so hospitable and so lovely, she was often called the Duchess. Their house was the place we liked best to go, to meet their friends, to have music, to take our children to see them, and to hear talk of their wide interests — the countries they had traveled in, the people they knew the world over, and that included those in every walk of life, — janitors, taxi-drivers, maids, and the man in the street, as well as titled men in many lands, cabinet members, and supreme court justices. . . . at their house on Thanksgiving day, the table laden with fruits and flowers, the traditional turkey preceded, accompanied, and followed by so many eye-filling and mouth-watering things that we were hardly able to play the games that Harry delighted in. These ranged from quizzes that needed an intellectual approach, to a lower level such as the one I remember called "Murder," a kind of "Who dunnit" in which all the lights were put out, screams were heard, and when the lights were turned on we had to determine *who* had murdered the male or female that lay on the floor. There was never a dull moment at their house.[82]

One niece remembered long afterward how Wigmore had encouraged her as a child to go on and develop her poetic talent, and later, after she married, how Dean Wigmore had delighted her children by playing games with them or suitable pieces on the piano. Indeed, if children were present they were likely to engage his first attention.

But Wigmore's generosity was not limited to relatives, personal friends, and academic colleagues. When he discovered that a cab driver they had employed on a number of occasions had bought his own car, they employed him whenever they needed taxi service. One day the cab driver mentioned that he needed a new cab but didn't have the money. After Wigmore was assured that the car he wanted to buy was a bargain he gave the driver a check for the full amount. When the driver reported that he had bought the car Wigmore asked him if he had received a clear title, only to learn that the dealer had said that titles were not given on second-hand cars. Wigmore immediately phoned the dealer and told him the deal was off unless he supplied a clear title. When the dealer got saucy and said he had the check and the deal was closed, Wigmore replied that he had stopped payment on it. The title was promptly produced.

Shortly thereafter, when the Wigmores went to Europe Wigmore took the title with him for safekeeping but changed his will so that the car would go to the driver. Upon their return from Europe he returned the title.[83]

The goal toward which Wigmore had worked so assiduously was attained in 1926, and the long-anticipated move to the new Law School building took place on December 1. For Wigmore it was the realization of a dream and he clearly planned to make the most of it. His flare for the dramatic, the influence of his military experience, and his ever-present sense of humor are all reflected in his written instructions to the students which were entitled "Memorandum in re Transfluminal Juralistic Trampo-Campo Day." Students were given specific instructions as to when to report at the old Law School, how to tie up and tag the contents of their lockers, when to report to class monitors, where to secure penants, etc. The memorandum concludes:

8. At 11:00 o'clock Marshal Otis Lowell Hastings will call attention. The student body, in formation, will be facing west at this time.

9. At a signal from Marshal Hastings, the Color Guard will proceed down the stairway and out of the Dearborn Street entrance, followed by the Faculty and Guests. The students will remain at attention until a signal from Marshal Hastings. The Fourth Year Class, in column of twos, will then march out of the north entrance, followed by the Third, Second, and First Year Classes, in order.

10. Students will entrain in buses at the corner of Wacker Drive and Dearborn Street, having marched there in the order indicated above.[84]

Fortunately, the reaction of one student, Marshal Otis Lowell Hastings, has been recorded.

The famous old building at 31 West Lake Street had served its day and, to put it mildly, was in bad shape. Even the ceilings were cracking and falling. Col. Millar, among others, would have been able to testify to that fact, for he was struck on the head and shoulders by a generous piece of plaster while he was explaining to some of us about the demurrer ore tenus, or something more complicated. . . .

Manifestly, the members of the faculty and the student body did not change on December 1, 1926. They simply moved to a greatly improved environment which, I like to think, made them better teachers and students. The spirit of the School did not change, for that spirit was Dean John Henry Wigmore. Both the old building and the new buildings housed "Wigmore's Law School."

. . . the move went off as planned and in an air of all good humor. I doubt whether Stu or I have ever felt more honored than we did when we led that distinguished faculty and our fellow students down Michigan Avenue with a motorcycle police escort, horns blowing and pennants waiving.[86]

But as one student who was soon to graduate testifies, the move was not the only event that evoked the peculiarly Wigmorian touch:

The few months we were fortunate in spending in the new building did not dim our enjoyment of it. The Dean had a rare gift of finding occasions to bring us together in some light-hearted ceremony, which generally had thought-provoking undertones — the gathering to pay respect to the donors; the student meetings in the smoking room; and, in our last week, the mock pageantry of the sun-dial dedication with the university's professor of astronomy solemnly checking the noon reading with his sextant while a student dressed to represent an ancient astrologer roared out an abracadabra.[87]

To grace the occasion of the dedication with an aura of distinction and to endow it with an international flavor, Wigmore secured Sir William Holdsworth, Vinerian Professor of English law at Oxford University, as the dedication speaker. Because of Wigmore's great interest in legal history a warm friendship had developed between the two men, and Wigmore had been instrumental in securing funds in the United States to assist in the publication of Holdsworth's monumental work *A History of English Law*.[88] In expressing appreciation for Wigmore's assistance Holdsworth said, "I am sure that I have to thank you for helping to get this grant. It is a great satisfaction to me to feel that so eminent a legal historian as yourself thinks my work so well worth publishing. It is moreover an equally great satisfaction that your country should have had some share in its publication."[89]

Holdsworth's trip to the United States fulfilled a multiple purpose; he inaugurated the Rosenthal Lecture Series at Northwestern University and was the guest speaker at a meeting in his honor given by the Chicago Bar Association.

We know from Holdsworth's friend Arthur Goodhart, with whom he was staying at the time he received an honorary degree from Cambridge University, that Holdsworth was not entirely preoccupied with the preparation of his Rosenthal Lectures prior to his visit to the United States. In a letter to Wigmore, Goodhart said, "He [Holdsworth] is looking forward to his visit to America, and is studying American slang. He hopes that he will be able 'to put across' his lectures and that no one 'will pull a gun on him.' He finds 'attaboy' difficult to pronounce but is improving with practice." [90]

Holdsworth's Rosenthal lectures were entitled "Some Lessons From Our Legal History," and they were given on March 23, 24, and 25, 1927, and subsequently published under the same title. Contemporary appraisers characterized the lectures as "delightfully written" and "abundantly interesting and instructive from cover to cover." [91]

Holdsworth's presence in Chicago provided the Chicago Bar Association with the opportunity to be the first professional association to welcome the scholar in the United States. In introducing Holdsworth, Wigmore called attention to the fact that at one time the law of France was the law in Chicago. He continued by pointing out that, for a thousand miles to the south, it was Blackstone's *Commentaries on the Laws of England* "that proved to be the greatest influence that saved America for the Common Law." For this reason Wigmore said, "And I think, therefore, we may believe that the shade of Sir William Blackstone, the first Vinerian Professor, is watching with gratification this latest Vinerian Professor visiting in person that vast area that was conquered by that book." [92]

The lighter, playful, and humorous touch that characterized the program was accentuated by the Association Glee Club which sang several parodies especially prepared for the occasion, undoubtedly in large measure if not entirely by Wigmore. Among these were "When Bill Was a Lad He Served a Term," based on *Pinafore*, and "Who Takes the Seat of Vinerian Professors, When Vinerian Professors are Elsewhere" suggestive of the lines of "Who takes Care of the Caretaker's Daughter." [93]

The degree of Doctor of Laws was conferred upon Holdsworth when he returned to Chicago on June 16 to give the address at the dedication of Levy Mayer Hall and Elbert H. Gary Library, the connecting structures that formed the Law School plant. On the same day dedication ceremonies were conducted for the entire McKinlock Memorial Campus which also included new quarters for the Northwestern University Medical, Dental, and Commerce schools.

The move was a great occasion for Wigmore, for the new Law School building was the result of years of effort and the most meticulous attention to detail. Every design on the walls, ceilings, and windows symbolized some feature or aspect of legal history or tradition. Wigmore had collected the pictures for years from all over the world. They included numerous prints "ranging from very early wood-cuts, through the great periods of steel engraving and mezzotints and aquatints, to the most modern dry points." The stained-glass windows in Lincoln Hall have an interesting origin. When visiting the University of Padua in Italy, Wigmore saw the coats of arms of former students lining the walls. This suggested to Wigmore the desirability of having stained-glass windows in Lincoln Hall, and he suggested that each class give such a pane. Wigmore's proposal has been followed by many classes, each new pane identifying the donor class and embodying in its design some event or figure important to the school or in the development of the law.[94]

The lecture rooms and halls were given the names of distinguished persons formerly connected with the school, but "the building is really John Henry Wigmore's monument."[95] To many of his friends it was a source of regret that no part of the building bore his name. Many years later the large office he occupied after his retirement as dean was fittingly designated the John Henry Wigmore Room.

Jan. 12, 1932
207 Lake Street,
Evanston.

Dear Judge Holmes,
Today's dispatch,
about your retirement, brings most
sensibly to my mind your long-ago
kindness to my young man's doubts,
your standard of learning in "The
Common Law" which gave the first
push to my latent urgings, and your
continued confidence ever since,
which has been a valued stimulus.
Your public services others can and
will sing. I am just thinking of how
much you influenced
Yours devotedly
John H. Wigmore

A LETTER FROM WIGMORE TO HOLMES, JANUARY 12, 1932

NORTHWESTERN UNIVERSITY LAW SCHOOL TODAY

NORTHWESTERN UNIVER-
SITY LAW SCHOOL AND THE
DOWNTOWN UNIVERSITY
CAMPUS

WIGMORE IN MATURITY

COLONEL WIGMORE DURING WORLD
WAR I

THE WIGMORE APARTMENT IN THE LAKE SHORE CLUB IN CHICAGO

MR. AND MRS. WIGMORE

WIGMORE'S PUBLISHED VOLUMES. MORE THAN FIFTY OF THEM, INCLUDING HIS CASEBOOKS AND OTHER COMPILATIONS, WERE ORIGINAL WORKS. OF THE REMAINDER, HE WAS THE GENERAL EDITOR

12
Retirement as Dean

With the Law School firmly established in its new quarters it would seem reasonable to assume that Wigmore, now sixty-three, would be about ready to pass on the leadership to a younger man. Now he had the opportunity to free himself from the almost constant quest for funds that had been the major source of friction with the Board of Trustees, and pass on to a successor the numerous administrative matters that inevitably go with deanship. He was not only deeply involved in scholarly writing but was increasingly recognized as a leader in many fields. He certainly did not lack outlets for his talents.

However, he had no inclination to give up his stewardship. In the early years of his service he had saved the Law School from disaster and foregone a number of promising alternative opportunities. But now some rearrangement of his responsibilities was inevitable because administrators were usually retired at sixty-five, and he expressed a strong preference for the retention of the deanship with a reduction in his teaching load.[1] He urged the president to consult the faculty and some outstanding alumni in his behalf. He added in a postscript to a letter to the president: "I wish that you would ask my wife what she thinks; I believe that she has views on the subject and ought to be heard."[2] But it became clear that relinquishing the deanship could not be postponed, and he actually took the first step well in advance of the formal action by the Board of Trustees on July 8, 1929, establishing a mandatory retirement age of sixty-five for all deans and other administrative officers.[3] In a letter to President Scott in April 1928, he declared his intention to resign as soon as his successor was selected and a suitable arrangement could be worked out regarding future monetary compensation.[4] It is evident that the relationship between Wigmore and President Scott continued to be cordial and involved mutual respect in spite of differences of opinion between Wigmore and the Board of Trustees in which, to some degree at least, Scott sided with the board. Scott definitely wanted Wigmore to continue with the Law School in some manner,[5] and Wigmore, in a letter concerned with the controversy, referred to Scott's "incumbency" as the best thing that ever happened to the university.[6]

But neither the acceptance of the necessity for a change nor the warm working relationship with the president brought peace of mind. Wigmore objected strenuously to the proposal that he be reappointed to the faculty on an annual basis, saying that this would require him to come begging every year.[7] When Scott pointed out that there were several other faculty members in the same situation in respect to retirement, and that any exception would be regarded as unfair discrimination,[8] Wigmore retorted,

> Did anyone else organize an alumni campaign for building and endowment, the first ever made for any law school in the country, which ultimately secured the funds for a building and the endowment of it? Did anyone else single-handedly secure funds for a library which put our University on the map in the library world?[9]

Wigmore reminded Scott of another sore point in the history of his relationship with the university:

> . . . the point is that in 1902 when I rejected the University of Chicago offer, and stayed here at a lower salary, Dr. James and Dr. Sheppard[10] promised me a University house rent free, and plans were drawn; but later, after I burned my bridges, I was told that the University had changed its policy, and the most I could have was this Lake Street residence at a rental of $60.00.[11]

Another source of anxiety for Wigmore was his concern that the university would not allow him to control the disposition of the funds he had raised. He also pointed out that he had spent $1,000 on entertainment during the past year and needed funds to entertain the new dean when he arrived.[12]

As time dragged on Wigmore was particularly indignant at the fact that no final decision had been reached by the Board of Trustees in respect to his future status and the recommended salary increases for the faculty. In August 1929, he began a letter to George A. Mason, president of the Board of Trustees, with the statement, "Why am I treated by your honorable Board like a child? The plain fact is that a month ago, at the close of the School year, on 24 hours notice, I was legislated completely out of office, as dean and professor."[13] Wigmore expressed his views in no uncertain terms and pointed out that, even though the board's own committee had adopted recommendations that he was clearly willing to accept, it took no action. Wigmore concluded, "I am relying on you to get that prompt action. Unless you can now assure me of it, I am going to ask the President of the Law Alumni Trustees to call a meeting, at which I can explain the situation confidentially and ask their advice. I see no other course." Wigmore implemented this "threat" by sending copies of the correspondence relating to his reappointment not only to the law alumni trustees but to all members of the Board of Trustees and to the officers of the Law School Alumni Association for their "confidential information." He signed his letters "John H. Wigmore, Professor for 1929–30 only."[14]

A month or so later, when no definite action had been taken, Wigmore wrote to Mason as follows:

My Dear George Mason:

I enclose a copy of my recent letter of August 29th to the President.

It is my last word on the subject.

I have *never*, since being Dean, *asked* the Board for anything for *myself* financially. It has always been *offered* to me; ask Messers. Dyche and Mac-Chesney,[15] who know the history. What I have *asked*, I have asked for the others.

And now, the first time I really do ask for something for myself — and a very simple and just thing — the Executive Committee hems and haws and holds back, and at last refuses.

I am astonished and chagrined at this unfriendly treatment, after (if I do say it myself) faithful service to the School. I am simply tired of this long-drawn out struggle to get justice for myself from the Board. Now I am quite reconciled if I am to be forced out on a year's notice to settle down somewhere else, where things will be offered to me promptly and cordially.

Yours truly,[16]

At long last the controversy was brought to a close when the Executive Committee of the board adopted a resolution providing for an "annual appointment," "the same to be terminated at the end of any academic year upon the request of the professor involved or the University upon six months notice from either to the other."[17]

No doubt many of Wigmore's colleagues and friends as well as students and alumni were unhappy over his retirement as dean. Louis B. Wehle must have spoken for many when he wrote, "The news of your retirement as dean seemed incredible. Somehow you have become more of an institution than the School itself and there has been a violation of the realities."[18]

During all of this controversy about his own future status Wigmore continued to participate actively in the selection of his successor. The two men, both suggested by him, who received the most serious consideration were Justin Miller, dean of the Law School at the University of Southern California, and Leon Green of the Yale Law School, formerly dean of the University of North Carolina Law School. Although Wigmore originally believed that no resident member of the faculty would be willing to take his place, one of them, Edward F. Albertsworth, did express an interest and Wigmore included his name in his submission to the president. However, he preferred Miller, Green, and Albertsworth — in that order.[19]

Green, who was eventually selected,[20] had known and admired Wigmore for some years. He was one of the young teachers periodically rounded up by Wigmore for a luncheon at the University Club during meetings of the Association of American Law Schools in Chicago. "Many of my contemporaries," Green had written, "came to feel as I did that he was the friendliest of the big men of the profession of that period."[21] But the relationship had involved more than an occasional luncheon. In 1927, writing to Wigmore about some of his own work, Green had said, "You have done me so many good turns, which made me acceptable in such a promising field, that I should not blame your feeling that I had not lived up to my opportunities."[22]

Green's first formal association with Northwestern University had been in 1924, when he taught in the summer school. In 1926 Wigmore had invited him to become a member of the faculty but he declined. In the spring of 1929, Green was invited to come to Chicago to meet with the committee appointed to find a successor to Dean Wigmore.[23] Green, who was then at Yale, and, in his own words, "as happy as a young teacher could well be," accepted the invitation completely without enthusiasm. "If it had not been for the many good turns Mr. Wigmore had done for me and for the great affection that I had come to have for him, I would not have accepted the invitation."

When Green met with the committee his mood was what he later recalled as "unforgettable."

> My text was the shabby treatment Northwestern had given Mr. Wigmore, the brightest luminary in the law school world — how the University had starved the school financially — lost one by one of an unsurpassed galaxy of great scholars and teachers . . . how he had fostered the greatest production of legal scholarship in America and had brought together one of the great collections of foreign legal literature of the country — how with the aid of a few loyal friends of the Chicago bar he had obtained gifts for the first modern law school building of the country and a library building to house the great collection — how he had been forced to accept students who had been excluded from the great eastern schools in order to maintain the school's enrollment — how the University's attitude towards the school would have to be reversed and a whole new policy of support . . . would have to be put in operation in order to give the school the primacy it deserved and must have to sustain the reputation Mr. Wigmore had given it.
>
> Much more was said along this line in making specific suggestions about salaries and other expenditures. At the end of the day I felt rather surprised at my boldness, if not effrontery. I went back to New Haven safe in the thought that I had struck a blow in behalf of a friend, that I would hear nothing more about the deanship and was altogether relieved.[24]

This, however, proved not to be the case. Green described the events that followed:

> Late one hot afternoon, while buried by books in a small office in old Hendry Hall, a tall gaunt gentleman appeared in my office door, and without a second's hesitation said: "Well, I have come to tell you that all your terms will be met." He saw the look of wonderment on my face and quickly added: "I'm Walter Dill Scott of Northwestern." I unloaded a chair and asked him to have a seat. He did, but continued to talk very rapidly, saying that he had to catch a train for New York and he would like to have my answer by the next morning . . .
>
> When I had caught my breath I asked him if the University would do all the things for the school that I had suggested. "Yes and a lot more. We have got to have the best law school in our part of the country and we want you to develop it along the lines you talked about to the committee." We briefly reviewed the situation and what he had in mind about the "more" he had mentioned. It seemed at that time Northwestern was receiving some very large gifts and

expected others. He proceeded to take me to the mountain top, although he had to catch a later train.[25]

Leon Green arrived at the Law School late in August 1929 to assume the role of dean, but not until there had been an exchange of letters between him and Wigmore which reassured him that there would be a harmonious transfer of the deanship.[26]

One outward evidence of the attempt to achieve continuity was a reception given by Wigmore for the Greens in Lowden Hall in the Law School. Green's recollection provides a glimpse into the relationship at the time:

> . . . it seemed . . . all Chicago was invited. It was my first striped trouser affair, but not the last, for Mr. Wigmore had numerous distinguished foreign visitors and had provided the school with all the equipment for high level receptions, and I was delighted that he and Mrs. Wigmore were so generous in planning and directing such affairs. Some of the trustees thought that I was permitting Mr. Wigmore too big a hand in running the show . . .[27]

Green soon discovered why Wigmore had urged him during the negotiations to get all commitments in writing, for he became aware of "more tensions than I had ever dreamed could exist" — tensions that had developed as the result of many past disagreements and deep resentments on Wigmore's part.

As has already been indicated, Wigmore's troubles with the board were largely financial. He had felt impelled to raise funds himself, and his success inevitably aroused jealousies in some quarters. In consequence, Wigmore believed that the various organizations he promoted should be kept outside of the Law School and under his control. This, obviously, engendered further opposition. To repeat, another factor was that he gave so much time to scholarship and promotion that he delegated matters of administration almost entirely to others, in some cases to persons not qualified or responsible. He was thus vulnerable to attack and criticism. But the board's concerns were a result more of a lack of understanding of Wigmore's objectives and concerns about financial support than of personal considerations.

Unfortunately, the depression soon followed, and its adverse impact on the financial situation aggravated and increased the tensions.

> Nevertheless, President Scott, Mr. Dyche, a most understanding and generous hearted Business Manager of the University, together with such trustees as General MacChesney, Melvin Traylor, President of the First National Bank, Mr. Oates, Mr. Bertram Cahn and others gave the School and me all the support within their power, and within a few months most of the tensions had disappeared. Merited increases in salaries were made, new faculty members were added in quick succession . . . and then the full force of the depression hit Chicago and with it cuts in salaries and other retrenchments.[28]

This extremely difficult transition for Wigmore was eased not only by the sympathetic and constructive attitude of his successor but also by the support of his colleagues and friends.

Undoubtedly, one member of the Class of 1929, the last to graduate during Wigmore's deanship, spoke not only for himself but for many of his classmates when he wrote to his father:

> I was glad to hear that you had had a visit with Dean Wigmore. He is a most unusual and remarkable man and I am very fortunate in having had the privilege of being under him while at law school. Merely knowing him, with his combination of brilliant intellect and high idealism, was an education in itself. The more I see of the average lawyer and his selfish outlook on life, the more I respect Wigmore for his interesting efforts to instill into the hearts of his students his own high conception of the moral obligation of an attorney, not only to his client, but to his community as well. We all owe him a great debt of gratitude.[29]

The abundance of good will and affection culminated in a testimonial banquet given by the alumni and students of the Law School in the Union League Club on November 21, 1929 (the Northwestern University General Alumni Association having already expressed appreciation for Wigmore's contribution to the University as a whole). The ticket to the banquet included a small photograph of the guest of honor and the inscription "Thou Art My Guide, Philosopher and Friend," and testimonial letters to be read at the banquet came from far and wide — from Chief Justice Taft, Justices Holmes and Brandeis, Judge Cardozo, Elihu Root, Newton D. Baker, George W. Wickersham, Harlon S. Stone, Roscoe Pound, Henry M. Bates, Robert M. Hutchins, Harry A. Bigelow, John Bassett Moore, Antonio De Bustamente, and others. At the banquet Wigmore was presented with a handsomely embossed and bound resolution of appreciation[30] containing "the hope that he will continue with us for many years as teacher and as friend." Most fittingly the occasion included a touch of the Gilbert and Sullivan spirit in which Wigmore delighted. He had made musical satires an integral part of the life of the Law School and of the professional groups to which he belonged, including the bar of Chicago. Among the songs which were no doubt sung lustily was one entitled "John Hen — re — y Wigmore,"[31] sung to the tune of Lord Jeffrey Amherst. This amusing account of Wigmore's career concluded one verse with the following chorus:

> Oh! Wigmore, Dean Wigmore,
> You're a leader who is tried and true,
> Oh! Wigmore, Dean Wigmore
> Old Northwestern should be proud of you.

The next verse extolling his "astounding scroll" on Evidence concludes with the lines:

> Although no one can read it and know what its all about,
> It is a useful book to me and you,
> 'Cause when the other fellow opens volume one and starts to spout,
> You can find him over-ruled in volume two.

Oh! Wigmore, Dean Wigmore
You're the master of a style that's hard to understand,
But if we will dig more,
We may some day start to comprehend.

The day after the banquet Lawrence D. Egbert, a good friend of the Wigmores, told Mrs. Wigmore how deeply he had been moved by all the well-deserved tributes. Mrs. Wigmore smiled and replied, "You should have heard the maid on that subject. She was very annoyed that all these people who did not 'really know' the Dean had said so much about him, all formally, when she could have told them 'right at the start that he was simply the grandest, truest, finest man in the world.' " [32]

Thus Wigmore closed his career as dean in an atmosphere of appreciation and praise. He even felt hopeful about the relationship of the Law School to the university administration. What had been lacking, he felt, was the "complete confidence and liberal support of our Board; but I believe that we are now entering on a new era in that important respect." [33]

Nor did Wigmore forget President Scott amidst all this adulation and praise. To him he wrote:

> In closing this period of twenty-eight years as dean, and thirty-six as professor, during which I have served under five presidents and four acting presidents, I am impelled to record candidly my conviction that yourself is the ablest all-around president this University has ever had, indeed is ever likely to have. I express the hope that my successor will learn to share these convictions; and that your administration will continue to be blessed with the same solid progress in all departments that has marked its record to date. [34]

13

Dean Emeritus

Retirement was for Wigmore a decidedly frustrating experience. His erect carriage and his "brisk and rapid stride"[1] were the outward signs of a man with undiminished vigor and capacity. To see the Law School to which he had devoted so much of his life under the direction of another, however competent, was not easy. Although Wigmore continued to teach, had an office in the Law School, and was free to carry on his scholarly pursuits without abatement, he was unavoidably deprived of the platform upon which many of his activities as a leader had rested. Indeed, he won only disapproval from the university for his efforts to continue some of his pursuits independently. In any event, the depression actually made it necessary for him to bring several of his own projects under faculty and university control, as they inevitably lost their outside support and became "financial waifs on the school's doorstep."[2]

The *Illinois Law Review*, which had been operated jointly, for a time though with only nominal support, with the law schools of the University of Illinois and University of Chicago, was eventually taken over by the Northwestern Law School and operated with a subsidy from the university. The American Institute of Criminal Law and Criminology had to be abandoned, but the *Journal of Criminal Law and Criminology* and the *Journal of Police Science*, which it had sponsored, were combined and continued as a Northwestern Law School publication. Responsibility for the *Journal of Air Law* was shared with the School of Commerce. The Scientific Crime Detection Laboratory, a costly pilot project which had demonstrated its value to the Federal Bureau of Investigation and to the police administrations of the larger cities, was more of a burden than the university could carry and was sold to the city of Chicago. That the *Journal of the American Judicature Society* was not retained within the Northwestern family was due to the erroneous impression of Herbert Harley, its editor, that the *Journal* represented an undue financial burden. While definite plans were being made to provide financially both for him and for the *Journal*, he quite suddenly and without notice moved to the Law School of the University of Michigan, taking the *Journal* with him,[3] a step that was a great disappointment to Wigmore.[4]

In spite of these readjustments and retrenchments, the situation was by no means entirely negative. Wigmore's successor, far from trying to displace him merely because he had taken over the deanship, not only recognized what an asset Wigmore was to the Law School and the university, but facilitated and encouraged him in his participation as a member of the faculty. Wigmore was moved into an attractive and comfortable office on the ground floor with windows opening to the south and into the courtyard of the Law School, and his secretary was retained as a regular member of the staff.

As one of the faculty he continued to teach several courses, including International Law and Evidence. In some offerings in the latter field, he used his *Principles of Judicial Proof.*

Wigmore never lost interest in the library. From time to time he made donations from his own library and spent many hours cataloging the Japanese books he had acquired both by gift and by purchase. At that time he wrote to a correspondent in Japan, "our Law Library now has a very comprehensive collection of Japanese materials, both historical and modern, — more extensive, I believe, than those of either the Harvard Law Library or the Library of Congress." [5] Because of his known interest in the library Wigmore was appointed a member of the Committee on Law Library Standards created jointly in 1940 by the Association of American Law Schools and the Association of American Law Libraries — a committee on which he served through the year 1942. [6]

He attended faculty meetings regularly, playing his part in serving on committees, including important chairmanships. He frequently lunched with other faculty members at the Pearson Hotel near the Law School, and he excelled as a conversationalist. Although he seldom talked politics, his mind "ranged far and wide with great rapidity and there never was a topic to which he did not contribute something." [7] He and Mrs. Wigmore continued to be welcome and important figures in social activities. However deference and consideration could go too far. When Wigmore heard that a proposal had been made for his portrait to hang in the space occupied by that of Chief Justice Jay, he strenuously objected. [8]

Retirement as dean did not diminish Wigmore's opportunity to enjoy the close personal friendships that had developed over the years. General Crowder now lived at the University Club in Chicago and frequently came to the Law School for a visit and lunch with Wigmore. Another close friend was Frank J. Loesch, at one time president of the Chicago Crime Commission, and a near neighbor after the Wigmores moved to the Lake Shore Club. Loesch's important role in dealing with the problem of crime in Chicago inevitably brought the two men together. Wigmore kept in touch with a wide circle of friends in all parts of the world either by correspondence or as they came through Chicago. He wrote to Holmes between occasional visits to Washington, and to Holdsworth, with whom a mutual interest in legal history had provided the basis for such a warm friendship extending over many years.

Wigmore continued to assume responsibility for the entertainment of foreign visitors, and he received members of the British delegation to the

American Bar Association meeting in Chicago in 1930 in his new office, which had already become a focal point for visitors from near and far. This role as host for foreign visitors led him into one experience that is best described in his own words in a letter to Margaret G. Belknap, a lifelong friend.

> Speaking of Max Hayford [ticket manager of Northwestern University], I applied to him for two tickets to the Notre Dame Game, Oct. 10, so as to show our French visitor that unique (to him) sight. Max got us two excellent seats. That I should go made a sensation in our circle. But the astonishing thing is that, for the sake of hospitality to a guest I sat through *one hour* of a continuous smashing thunderstorm of rain — buckets and barrels and tanks of rain, drenching everybody — and was none the worse for it! But — never again! [9]

Among the Wigmores' many foreign visitors were Lord Macmillan and his wife who, in 1938 spent several days with them. The Wigmores were characteristically attentive. Lord MacMillan's address before the American Bar Association [10] occurred on July 27, 1938, his thirty-seventh wedding anniversary, with Lady MacMillan present, and the Wigmores thereafter remembered this occasion. In acknowledging this regular anniversary greeting in 1942, Lord MacMillan wrote, "I have been greatly enjoying the *Holmes-Pollock Letters*, now published in this country. What a delightful pair of correspondents! I wish it had been my privilege to have had a correspondence like that with you through the years." [11] In the same letter he spoke of the destruction in London (including their own home) from the air raids and continued, "If anything were needed to confirm us lawyers in our determination to extinguish the curse of Nazism, it would be the announcement in 'The Times' this morning of Hitler's appointment of a Minister of Justice [sic] 'with power to set aside all written law.' Now that your great nation is united with us in a bond of brotherhood pledged to the cause of righteousness it can only be a matter of time till victory is gained."

Wigmore's cordial relationship with President Scott continued, although now on an informal basis. Indeed, Wigmore was consulted from time to time and took some part in fund-raising, a task which he greatly disliked and which interfered with his writing. He felt considerable concern about his eyes, which were "beginning to show signs of age," and he believed he "ought not to delay using them on the research which will require entirely personal eye-work," [12] the preparation of a third edition of the *Treatise on Evidence*. Wigmore's office, as always, was open to the many students and graduates who enjoyed the warmth of his welcome. As a natural consequence the Junior Bar Association continued to ask him to speak from time to time or to introduce the speaker of the day.

When in 1934 Wigmore reached the faculty retirement age of seventy, another crisis arose with the Board of Trustees. Some of them felt strongly that he should leave the Law School, in complete disregard of the fact that he was "the greatest asset the School had and its financial setbacks were hard enough to withstand without casting away the valuable asset the School and the University had in him."[13]

Dean Green, in order to secure "an arrangement satisfactory to him [Wigmore] and which left him all the freedom and participation in the school's affairs that could be expected under the stringent conditions that then prevailed,"[14] had to indicate to the trustees rather emphatically that if Wigmore left he would leave as well.

When in May 1934 it became known that Wigmore was to be retired at the end of the academic year, Green had the support of the student body. A petition signed by 210 students was presented to the president and the Board of Trustees urging his retention "until such time as he [Wigmore] believes himself no longer able to profitably continue."[15] And there is no doubt about the loyalty and appreciation of the graduates of the Law School. One evidence was a dinner given in 1934 by the class of 1914 in honor of Wigmore and attended by many of his former students and other distinguished guests.[16]

One incident occurred in the midst of all this adulation and show of support that indicates not only Wigmore's sensitivity but the depth of his feeling regarding his enforced retirement. As his secretary recounts the episode, when he returned to his office after his last faculty meeting as an active professor, he was very much let down because no one had taken note of that fact.[17] This was no doubt only an oversight. Knowing that he was to remain with the Law School, his colleagues probably assumed that he would continue to attend faculty meetings. Not only Green but such long-time loyal and devoted colleagues as Kocourek and Millar would certainly have made some point of the occasion had they realized that it had any particular significance.

But a beautifully embossed tribute recognized the contributions Wigmore had made during his forty-three years of service to the university: "The lustre that your career has shed upon the University will attend it for all time to come, and the unremitting devotion to its interests with which that career has been accompanied will be appreciated so long as the University endures."[18]

In time the university recognized Wigmore's eminence by awarding him an honorary doctor of laws degree in 1937. Honorary degrees, it will be recalled, had come to Wigmore much earlier from the University of Wisconsin and from Harvard University.

Wigmore's long association with the university was recognized in 1934 when at the age of seventy he was designated a "veteran member" of the University Club of Evanston, to which he had belonged since 1901 when he attended the first meeting.[19]

Such scholastic honors were matched by recognition of Wigmore's diverse contributions as a leader. In 1941, writing to Newman F. Baker, a relatively new member of the Law School faculty at Northwestern, Herbert Harley said:

I wonder if you have known of the book of appreciations given him long ago, to celebrate, with a dinner, his completion of twenty-five years association with the Law School. Perhaps the period is not correct, but I remember so well that after the dinner there were tributes by twenty-five speakers, representing twenty-five public service organizations for which the Dean had performed some special services. I doubt if any of the 150 or more present could have named more than five such organizations.[20]

Amidst all this he still found time to devote to local causes. He displayed an undiminished propensity to speak out when he deemed it advisable, whether in his own behalf or in behalf of others. Both in Evanston and Chicago he urged appropriate action, including the use of mufflers, to lessen the noise of the outboard motors close to the lakeshore — the "bigger the noise," he felt, the more the owner conceived of himself as a "bigger fellow."[21] He urged the Park District Board not to remove the trees between the traffic lanes on Lake Shore Drive in Chicago. It is doubtful that his action had any effect — but eventually most of the trees did disappear. However, more than thirty years later (in 1968) new trees were planted in a long stretch that includes the site of the Lake Shore Club and the Northwestern University Chicago Campus. Long before air pollution was a matter of general concern Wigmore was calling attention to excessive smoke coming from the chimney of an Evanston hotel.

But the episode that most clearly demonstrated Wigmore's strong sense of social responsibility (even when it might run counter to his personal self-interest), was his opposition to the proposal by the city of Evanston to (in effect) prohibit the use of Evanston parks by citizens of Chicago — a response to the increasing number of persons crowding the parks along the suburban lakeshore. As the Wigmore home in Evanston abutted on one of the lakeside parks, he knew the situation firsthand. Yet the crowds at that time were largely made up of family groups who were orderly and not unduly noisy. His attitude that the streets along the lake were public thoroughfares that should be available to all and to which the adjoining owners had no special rights was further evidence of his unselfish attitude.[22]

Wigmore's involvement in his community was most appropriately recognized when, in 1941, the Art Institute of Chicago included his portrait in an exhibit those of men and women who had helped to make Chicago great.

Now formally retired both as dean and as a regular member of the faculty, Wigmore was nonetheless retained as an advisor and lecturer on public and professional relations. He still had his office in the Law School and was provided with secretarial assistance. His writing alone would have kept him busy but he by no means became a recluse. In a letter written to Albertsworth in 1939 he said, "In my own line of activities which are numerous, I find plenty to occupy my time and interest. In Washington at the time of the American Law Institute meeting, I must attend five different committees and almost every day brings a pile of letters calling for correspondence on a variegated list of subjects."[23] Wigmore's life was certainly not cloistered and, with his writing continuing unabated, he was exceedingly busy.

But formal retirement at seventy not only involved vocational readjustment but precipitated a crisis on the domestic front when the Wigmores' "shattered income" made it impossible for them to continue living at 207 Lake Street in Evanston.[24] However, even before the move to the Lake Shore Club in Chicago, only a short block from the Law School, Mrs. Wigmore had recognized the advantages for her husband of substituting a two-minute walk for two hours a day in elevated and surface cars. The actual move could only be an ordeal, for it was not easy to leave a home in which they had spent so many happy and fruitful years together for a three-room suite, even though it occupied the tenth floor with a magnificent view of Lake Michigan. Though their most important possessions were still around them, in these more restricted quarters they did have to give up their concert grand piano. This was not an easy parting as Miss Morgan records, "One of the most heart breaking moments I ever had in sympathy with others was when the Colonel's piano was taken from the house . . . They both went upstairs and left me to take care of the removal, and the Colonel sang funny songs. But they did not sound funny."[25]

Once settled, Mrs. Wigmore was able to write, "I wish you could come and see us in our new surroundings . . . I do not think either of us has had a moment of regret . . . we have a glorious view of the Lake . . . very different from that of 207 Lake Street . . . like the Riviera. . . . All our treasures being collected in three rooms make a very impressive showing."[26] Soon Wigmore was donating books to the Lake Shore Club library. Later when he served as chairman of the club's Library Committee, he made a special effort to increase the size of the collection. Wigmore also served as a director of the club and a trustee of the Lake Shore Corporation, turning over his fees for a special library fund.

Once again Wigmore's loyalty expressed itself. He prepared a double postcard suitable for mailing. The statement "*Evidence* from Col. John H. Wigmore" was on the side for the postage and the name of the addressee, and on the other side of the card was a fulsome message praising the club — its management, members, and employees — and closing with the statement, "To become a member and live at Lake Shore is an unique privilege." The message was "Unanimously signed, John H. and Emma H. V. Wigmore." Of special biographical interest is the following excerpt from the larger statement, "After thirty years of housekeeping in Evanston, it was an uprooting for us to come to Lake Shore: and of course we wondered how the change would turn out. We are comfortable and contented. We are in clover. We like our surroundings, the constant view of noble Lake Michigan and the 'high life' on the tenth floor. When I come home from the office, I hum Manrico's song in 'Il Trovatore,' 'Back to Our Mountain Home'!"[27]

Entertaining was not inhibited by the more restricted quarters. On one occasion when a small group was assembled Wigmore read from a book of seafaring tales that he thought had been lost during the move. "He selected one with a sea captain, his daughter and a bosun's mate lover of the daughter for characters. He gave a dramatic rendition of the story, roaring the denunciations of the sea captain in full voice; giving the daughter's responses in falsetto, and the bosun's mate's in mild tones.'' On such occasions Wigmore ''read with abandonment and great enjoyment.'' His audience was reduced to tears from laughter, and they ''wondered as to what the impressions of the chance passers by along the club corridor might be.''[28]

In spite of his fears, Wigmore's enforced retirement at seventy did not substantially alter his relationship to the Law School, and on balance the move to the Lake Shore Club proved to be advantageous. However, the loss of salary was a legitimate matter of concern, and there was in fact some justification for their financial anxieties. As Wigmore saw the situation, the ''collapse of savings-investments, torpidity of the book-market and the modest limits of the University retirement allowance,''[29] necessitated some form of professional income-producing work.

Quite naturally he turned to Newton D. Baker, among others, for the warm friendship established during World War I days had continued unabated. Baker, who was in practice in Cleveland, thought well of Wigmore's idea of associating himself with some large firm as a consultant. George A. Mason, formerly a member of the Board of Trustees, who was in practice in Chicago also favored this plan, but no such arrangement ever materialized. To Mason, Wigmore submitted another possibility as follows:

> But, secondly, I am much attracted by the notion of establishing an office in Chicago as arbitrator for lawyers. I happened to be called in, two or three times during recent years, in that capacity, and I rather liked the experience. What I have in mind is not to act as arbitrator for businessmen in the ordinary way, but to act as judicial arbitrator in cases *already in the hands of attorneys*, who desire a decision on law and fact without the delay and expense of a trial in court. At a moderate per diem charge by the arbitrator, one would suppose that clients and attorneys alike (in this metropolis) would take to this solution. But, as yet, it seems to be a novelty. And the question is, Would the attorneys in fact avail themselves of it?[30]

Mason was of the opinion ''that the bar is not quite ready''[31] for this, and such proved to be the case. Wigmore, therefore, set himself up independently as a consulting counsel. His card included the statement that his services were available as arbitrator in matters submitted by members of the bar, and he let it be known, generally, that he was available on such a basis. He also registered with the Illinois Bar Association under its new ''Experienced Lawyers Service.'' Although R. Allan Stephens, its secretary, thought that Wigmore would be in great demand,[32] he received only a limited number of assignments. This was not surprising in view of Wigmore's lifelong practice of answering questions gratuitously, particularly concerning the law of evidence; nor was it likely that he was greatly disappointed, for he was certainly fully occupied and his income proved to be more adequate than he and Mrs. Wigmore had anticipated.

Wigmore had not overlooked the possibility of further academic service.

In December 1933, he sent a letter to the deans of all the law schools saying in part "that I should like to take advantage of my freedom by spending one semester in lecturing at other universities, giving some of the courses which have been my specialties." [33] Once again the result was disappointing. The only concrete proposal was from Harvard. In October 1934, Pound wrote:

> Would you consider coming here some time during the school year for a month to answer such questions as students might put to you, especially with respect to Evidence, and generally give our student body for that time the benefit of consultation with you on questions of law in which you and they are interested. I should like to try some such experiment and I am sure no one could do this sort of thing as you could. [34]

Wigmore replied that he would be glad to come but that he thought a period of two weeks was long enough, and to this Pound agreed. [35] Accordingly, late in February Wigmore appeared at the Harvard Law School for a two-week assisgnment which, as finally arranged, had become somewhat more formal than the format originally proposed. [36]

In the first place, he gave a series of five lectures entitled Problems and Prospects in the Law of Evidence (1935) [37] and four lectures on the Panorama of the World's Legal Systems, illustrated with his lantern slides. Taking advantage of the fact that he was regarded as having a penchant for long words, he asked Pound if it would be "out of place to intrude any semi-humorosity in place of dignified solemnity," [38] and apparently with Pound's approval he gave one talk to the students on how to teach and study law under the title Pragmatic Postulates in Nomologic Pedagogy. [39] But aside from the title and perhaps some introductory remarks, Wigmore's offering was not humorous. He began by pointing out that Langdell's postulates no longer prevailed unchallenged, and Wigmore, to offset the probable assumption that, because of his age, his ideas were necessarily conservative, called attention to the numerous innovations he had suggested over the years "which are now accepted or are being accepted in various quarters." [40]

Beginning with prelegal education, on which he acknowledged there was no unanimity of opinion, Wigmore said that, after vacillating because of the difficulties involved, he had concluded that the essentials were mathematics, logic, Latin, English speech, and physical demeanor. [41] By the latter, Wigmore said that he meant "A manly bearing, a clean and trim attire, a physical fitness, — in short, the finished appearance of the man of the world," [42] subjects not taught in college. To make his point Wigmore quoted with approval from Winston Churchill's autobiography:

> The whole atmosphere of Sandhurst was very unlike Oxford and Cambridge. Everyone was taught to be clean, smart and punctual. . . .
> I should like after my experience of life and affairs to introduce a little Sandhurst discipline at our great universities. . . . Some of the universities at the

present time seem to be forcing beds of sloppiness and slouching, both in body and mind. Indeed the prevailing fashion seems to be long hair, untidy clothes and subversive opinion.

To the expected reply that these students were beyond the age of college students, Wigmore said that it was never too late for self-education. He then turned to his theory of the law-school curriculum. "Law as a subject of thought and activity, has several distinct categories, or modes of being." "Education is training in modes of thinking about law. . . . Hence the curriculum of legal education" should be based on five "distinct mental processes and should attempt to develop each process adequately." [43] They were: (1) the analytic, or thinking about law as it is; (2) the historic, or thinking about law as a becoming; (3) the legislative process, or the law as it was made at the time and as it has become important now; (4) the synthetic process, the process of generalizing legal rules and building them up into a consistent system; and, finally, (5) the operative process, the actual working conditions and results of any rule of law whether substantive or adjective.

Wigmore felt that the fact that these processes are not of "equal frequency or importance in the career of the practitioner" [44] should be taken into account in preparing a curriculum. He concluded by pointing out that two important factors: "What the teacher gives out through his personality" and what "the student puts in through his personality" could not appear in the curriculum. [45] The latter, he said, was the most important, and the shortcomings of the professor were no excuse for the student; he should merely work harder. To be thrown back on himself might result in greater profit.

It was quite natural that he should close his remarks to the students on this occasion with a quotation from Holmes, "the Nestor of our judiciary," whom he had just seen in retirement in Washington: "We have learned that whether a man accepts from Fortune her spade and looks downward and digs, or whether he accepts from Aspiration her axe and cord and will scale the ice-peaks, the one and only success which it is his to command is to bring to his work a mighty heart." [46]

Wigmore again spoke to students in March, in this case to the students about to graduate, taking as his topic, "Advice of a Veteran to Young Lawyers," [47] and pointing out that in the forty-five years since he graduated he had observed the careers of hundreds of lawyers and "followed with interest the careers of many of the several thousand law students" [48] who had studied with him. He divided his subject into two topics; the ideals and the methods to be followed in continuing their training for a successful career. In turn he divided ideals into personal ideals and professional ideals. As to personal ideals, he said that since they required refreshing or they would fade, he recommended reading a few concise philosophies of life, among them the parables of Jesus, the wise sayings in the Proverbs of Solomon and in the Book of Ecclesiastes, and two or three speeches from Shakespeare. Among these he suggested:

the one in Hamlet, uttered by Polonius when he advises young Laertes how to behave himself on his travels; "Beware of entrance to a quarrel; but being in, bear it that the opponent be aware of thee. Give every man thine ear, but few thy voice," and so on. And the one in Henry VIII, when Cardinal Wolsey, after his own ruin advises young Cromwell how to succeed in his career, "Let all the ends thou aims't at be thy country's, they God's, and truth's," and so on.[49]

Lastly Wigmore stressed Emerson's essays. "Read a page of Emerson every day; and commit to memory the other passages I have cited. You will never regret it." In Emerson's words: "The one virtue for accomplishing a purpose, is concentration, and the one vice is dissipation," meaning dissipation of energies.

Wigmore emphasized the constant enlargement of the knowledge of the law, development of greater skill in expression, both oral and written, an expanding mastery of general facts with which cases may be concerned, an understanding of human nature, and the development of a wide acquaintanceship.[50]

As was so often the case, Wigmore included some purely practical suggestions.

Most of all, when you start out, list on cards every person — *every* person — who knows you or your family, and who might remember that you exist, and send him your card announcing that you are now a lawyer.

Now the secret for accomplishing this and the things I am recommending, is to do only a *little at a time* but *regularly* and *inexorably*. Prepare a schedule for each of these undertakings and check off each stage as it is finished.[51]

Admitting that no prospective lawyer had all the desirable qualities in the highest degree, he said the practice of law was so diverse that success could be achieved by the man who possessed these qualities in various degrees, with some stronger than others. Accordingly, his closing advice was, "Take courage; analyze your native qualities; develop your strongest ones; improve your weak ones; and you will find that the legal profession has a welcome place and an honorable career awaiting you."[52]

But Wigmore's activities while in Cambridge were not confined to the Law School or to legal circles. He spoke at the Harvard Medical School on "Topics of Mutual Interest to our Two Professions."[53] After acknowledging that the medical profession was substantially ahead both as to organization and education, he called attention to a number of ways in which some doctors impeded the administration of justice. Since without them "ambulance chasing" would be impossible, he considered this problem to be the joint responsibility of both professions. He said that the canon of ethics that prevented one doctor from testifying against another left an injured person helpless in any state where expert testimony was required. Wigmore also criticized the rule of evidence adopted at the instance of the medical profession which does not allow a doctor to testify as to his patient's condition, saying that, although justified in a few instances, in most cases the privilege was used to impede the administration of justice.

Wigmore also called attention to the complaint that doctors as expert witnesses were frequently subjected to ''hectoring examination'' by counsel and that the other side of the problem was the prevalence of medical witnesses who were charlatans and had to be exposed. As a remedy, he suggested that medical witnesses be prepared for such questioning by consulting in advance with reputable trial lawyers. As to hypothetical questions and the issue of insanity, Wigmore said that no altogether satisfactory solutions had been found, but he did offer some constructive suggestions. Wigmore also dealt with expert witness fees, the proof of heredity, the great need for reform in the office of coroner, and the role of scientific crime-detection laboratories, in which the medical profession should also be interested. Finally, he described the legal-aid program in Chicago as a possible model for the medical profession in dealing with what he then described as ''socialized medicine.''[54]

These various formal appearances by Wigmore were, of course, interspersed with small group gatherings and various forms of entertainment. Although the honoraria received went only a short way in meeting Wigmore's financial needs, his most cordial reception made this return to Harvard a happy and rewarding occasion.

Pound's satisfaction with Wigmore's performance in this brief assignment at Harvard was evident: ''His attractive personality, cordial desire to help, and ability to put at their ease those with whom he talked, even more than his encyclopaedic knowledge of the subject, made the project succeed even beyond my expectations.''[55]

Wigmore returned briefly to Harvard the following year, having gladly accepted Pound's invitation to participate in a series of lectures on ''The Future of the Common Law'' as one feature in the celebration of the Tercentenary of the Founding of Harvard College. In accepting the invitation Wigmore wrote, ''The subject is particularly interesting to me, and the principal speaker [for the session involved], Sir Maurice Amos is even more so. We thought he was the most interesting Englishman at the Hague in 1932.''[56] It was Pound's wish that Wigmore, ''as the first legal scholar of America,'' be the initial speaker in the informal discussion on the opening day of the conference as he would ''know best how to lead the discussion of the subject so as to direct it into profitable channels.''[57] Wigmore accepted this assignment.

Wigmore also returned to Harvard for class reunions when he could, and he was one of the speakers at the fiftieth anniversary of his college class, the class of '83. He went with enthusiasm, armed with music for his classmates to sing (he had been their accompanyist when in college) and was considerably let down when his exuberance was not matched by theirs. He reflected this disappointment in a letter to Holmes as follows: ''This winter I went nowhere, except to my 50th at Cambridge. But, to my dismay, most of the fellows were *old*, — I mean, in Spirit; there was no unbending, — no spirit like that described in your distinguished father's ode to 'The Boys.' ''[58] In reporting to Mrs. Wigmore on his return, he said, ''they had sung, but he did not think they were interested'' and continued, ''Why, Emma, do you know they were really old men!''[59]

Although Wigmore and Dean Green had in common a deep conviction that there was an urgent need for substantial improvements in the law and its administration and were, therefore, both leaders in efforts to bring about reforms, they differed greatly in their political outlooks, and the extent of these differences became more evident with the passage of time. However, in 1935, when it was proposed that Green fill a vacancy in the United States Circuit Court for the Seventh Circuit, Wigmore was not deterred by such differences from addressing a strong letter of recommendation to the attorney general, closing with the statement, "We should regret to lose him here, but we should congratulate the Federal Judiciary."[60]

Political differences came into sharpest focus several years later when Green, a liberal, in an article in the *New Republic*, supported Roosevelt's "Court-packing plan" on the ground that the Court was already packed with conservatives and needed unpacking.[61] Twelve members of the faculty responded by issuing statements opposing President Roosevelt's plan.[62] The gap between the political views of Wigmore and Green was certainly not narrowed when in a second article in the *New Republic* Green supported the sit-down strike.[63]

But eventually differences of opinion between Wigmore and his successor were not confined to political questions. The large measure of agreement as to legal education that had existed at the beginning gradually eroded. New faculty appointments obviously tended to reflect the views of Dean Green and those who served him. A little later, in writing to Frederick D. Fagg, Jr., soon to become vice-president and dean of faculties at Northwestern University, Wigmore characterized the Law School faculty as overstaffed and spoke adversely of the trend in the Law School during the last ten years.[64] Wigmore hoped for the correction of the situation by the departure of Green and the appointment of a successor. However, disturbing as the situation was to him, he apparently resisted every effort to become involved in any attempt to secure the removal of Green.[65] And to the very end, Green generously supported Wigmore in his drive for continued participation in the instructional program, sometimes in collaboration with another faculty member. He taught his courses in Profession of the Bar and in International Law, in which he emphasized American authorities. His lectures on the World's Legal Systems were offered almost every year, and during the summer sessions he gave a course on the Principles of Judicial Proof based upon his own book of the same title. Wigmore was invited to appear before the class in Evidence so that every student might have this opportunity to meet the author of the monumental *Treatise*.

This periodic exposure to the students was but a small aspect of Wigmore's relationship to them during his later years. His interest was in no way diminished either by his retirement or by the reduction of his teaching. During World War II Wigmore, then near the end of his career, revived the practice he had followed during World War I of keeping in touch with Northwestern Law School men in service. He kept a list in his own handwriting "and would send postcards again and again to the entire list, inditing ten or twelve at a time."[66] These personal approaches were supplemented by a "War Newsletter" edited by Miss Morgan, his secretary.

Another evidence of Wigmore's significance to the students occurred on his eightieth birthday when a group gave a party for him at the Law School. One of the students had baked the cake and there were candles and all the usual trimmings. He was presented with fifty red roses, in recognition of long years of service to Northwestern University.[67] Wigmore was, of course, pleased, and this was evident to all as he was "one of the liveliest members of the group."[68]

At a luncheon meeting of the Northwestern University Associates, a group of leading citizens in the Chicago area, he received further recognition when he was greeted "by prolonged applause and an encomium by President Franklyn Bliss Snyder."[69]

"Each year is better than the last — could that be possible?" wrote Mrs. Wigmore to Margaret Belknap. "Won't it be fine if we have our fiftieth?"[70] They did, and because their friends knew that their Lake Shore apartment was full to capacity with the things they treasured, and that more possessions would be a burden, they "conspired" to have a shower of golden anniversary letters from far and wide to demonstrate the affection and esteem with which the Wigmores were regarded. When it was learned that Wigmore was acknowledging each message with a personally written note, he received "A protesting apology for having brought all that labor upon him."[71] "Don't be disturbed about the writing of those acknowledgments," answered Wigmore. "It was not only a small return to make for the nice messages, but the compliments received in consequence of your conspiracy would have made up for a thousand letters to write. To have acknowledged in print-type would have been too inadequate and impersonal. So it was all to the good."

14

Administration of Justice

In the three foregoing post-World War I chapters, Wigmore's Law School activity has been traced through to his eightieth birthday and almost to the close of his career. Yet, even in his later years, the institution to which he had such a deep commitment was only one facet of the broad arena in which he played a number of important roles. His activities following World War I were so extensive and so diversified that they will, for convenience, be treated in three separate chapters: Administration of Justice; A Continuing Leadership: Law, Public Service, Religion; and World Community.

It will be recalled that a concern for improvement in the administration of justice was the focal point for a considerable part of Wigmore's activity and scholarly writing before World War I. He had thus created a broad base for future efforts in this field, and it was inevitable that a beginning should be made with his second edition of the *Treatise on Evidence.*

It had been perfectly clear to Wigmore that the *Treatise* published in 1904–5 must eventually be revised, and that the supplementation which had been provided by single volumes in 1908 and 1915 [1] would no longer suffice. The time came when he felt he must give the revision a major portion of his attention, [2] and by an arrangement with the university in 1923 the dean began spending Wednesdays and Saturdays working on the revision at home. He personally examined all of the later decisions and reexamined virtually every authority cited in the first edition of the *Treatise* and its supplements. He now had stenographic and secretarial assistance as well as the invaluable nonprofessional help that Mrs. Wigmore had always provided. During the period of intensive work at home Miss Morgan, his secretary, lived with the Wigmores, and again the books he needed were regularly shipped from the Law Library to his home in Evanston. According to Miss Morgan:

> When the Colonel worked at home, he got up early in the morning, had breakfast upstairs in the sitting room part of their bedroom, while Mrs. Wigmore read bits from the local morning paper to him while she sipped warm milk. Later in the day he would read the *New York Times* which was his favorite newspaper. After breakfast he would go to his study or, in summer, to the big

porch which overlooked Lake Michigan which he loved. (I wonder if it did not remind him of his boyhood view of the Bay in San Francisco), and starting at seven o'clock, he worked a full day on his book. Many times when I was working on the second edition of the Evidence Treatise, I would take my working materials from the workroom allotted to me (an extra guestroom, turned into a workroom for the time being) and go out on the porch; the Colonel would stop his work and greet me, perhaps remarking that the Lake looked like dancing diamonds that morning. One summer, the Colonel asked me if I would like to come down fifteen or twenty minutes earlier than the hour for starting work and take up the study of French with him to coach me. Mrs. Wigmore gave me a book on perfect French pronunciation and would give me suggestions in the afternoon, as she was an excellent French scholar. The memory of that pleasant summer will linger long in my heart.[3]

As with all his writing, Wigmore had a system for checking every step he took. He made charts of the sources to be examined, reporters, statutes, law reviews, etc., and noted carefully the progress made so that at all times he knew how much he had accomplished and how much remained to be done. He continued to use as guides the cards containing the numbers of the sections made in 1905 in connection with the preparation of the first edition.[4]

The painstaking character of Wigmore's work and his determination to bring his research as nearly to date as possible is also illustrated by his study of every page of a bill pending in the United States House of Representatives to consolidate, codify, and re-enact the general and permanent laws of the United States.[5] In consequence of Wigmore's thorough study of the bill, he was in a position to support William L. Burdick, who, after it had been passed by the House, pleaded for its prompt adoption by the Senate, in spite of an unfavorable report by the Senate's Select Committee. Wigmore declared the bill to be "entirely satisfactory."[6]

All of the arduous labor on the *Treatise* came to fruition in 1923 when the second edition, completely rewritten, and extensively revised and enlarged, appeared in five volumes.[7] That Wigmore had not rested on his laurels with the publication of the first edition is confirmed by the following statement from Zechariah Chafee's review of the second edition:

> The abundant harvest from a twice ploughed field has been brought home. The host of practitioners and law teachers who have eagerly awaited Mr. Wigmore's second edition can welcome it with the same praise that Mr. Beale nearly twenty years go bestowed on the original work: "It is hardly too much to say that this is the most complete and exhaustive treatise on a single branch of our law that has ever been written. . . . For greatness of conception and patience of execution, for complete collection of authority, and for fullness and vividness of treatment, this treatise cannot be too warmly commended. . . . When we come to the subject-matter we find it admirable in every way. The historical discussions are illuminating, the statement of doctrine is clear and sufficiently precise, and the argument is always enlightening and usually convincing. . . . This is, and must long remain, the best treatise on the common law of evidence."
> Even when he is cited only to be rejected or is followed only in the dissenting

opinion, it is no cause for disappointment, for it shows that he has become a force to reckon with. . . . The young men whom he has inspired are striving to crystallize his ideas in statutes. It is too early to say that Wigmore found the law of evidence built of brick and left it marble, for many of the old ramshackle structures still stand, but signs of demolition and rebuilding are everywhere about us.[8]

The second edition could no more be expected to escape all criticism than the first edition, but the criticisms related to particulars, and there were few readers, if any, who would not have endorsed Chafee's general appraisal. Wigmore was neither submerged by, nor overwhelmed with, the mass of details and their antecedents; ". . . we see again and again the reformer, whose common sense has been whetted, not dulled by scholarship."[9]

On one occasion, Miss Morgan was consolidating some indexes and the Kellys and the Kelleys became badly mixed. When she told Wigmore at the end of the day that she would have to start with the task of straightening out this "mess" the next morning, he was sympathetic. However, after dinner he sat down at the piano "and played a rollicking Irish air about the Rileys, the Kellys, the O'Shaughnessys, etc., being no match for the brave McIntyres, and for days," she reported, "he would make us laugh by singing it on the least provocation, emphasizing the Kellys."[10]

The Wigmores celebrated the completion of the manuscript for the second edition of the *Treatise* by a much needed rest along the Riviera, but this "prodigiously energetic" man characteristically ended his sojourn there with a month's study of some of the archives, collecting photographs for a course on the law of Rome, Greece, and other ancient places. They then went to Switzerland where, as a member of the Committee on Intellectual Cooperation, Wigmore observed a meeting of the Council of the League of Nations.[11]

As a by-product of his work on the revision of the *Treatise*, Wigmore prepared, from 1920 when he returned to the Law School as dean until his retirement in 1929, an article, twenty case comments, and two notes on the law of evidence for the *Northwestern University Law Review*.[12] His succint statement on the law of evidence which was embodied in Article I of his "Creed for the Nation," an address delivered at an annual Law School alumni dinner, had a typically Wigmorean flavor.

> I BELIEVE in the Anglo-American system of Evidence, for jury trials at common law. The general rules are based on shrewd experience in human nature. And they have contributed many fundamental principles to the World's knowledge of just procedure. But the ten thousand details which now form our law of evidence represent a system dried up and gone to seed. They should be thoroughly pruned and reformed. And, especially, they have no place in the inquiries of administrative tribunals, such as State Industrial Commissions, which investigate and decide without a jury. The Federal Land Office, the Federal Patent Office, the Federal Customs Court, and the Federal Commerce Commission, have disposed of millions of claims involving billions of dollars,

with satisfaction to all interests and without observing the strict rules of jury trial evidence. The State Industrial Commissions and Public Service Commissions should now be allowed to do justice, in their spheres, with the same freedom of method. Therefore, the recent attempts of Supreme Courts, as in Illinois, New York and California, to fix upon industrial commissions the incubus of our technical jury trial rules of evidence, are misguided, and should be abandoned.[13]

Thus, in spite of Wigmore's preoccupation with the law of evidence and, therefore, with the regular judicial system, he early recognized the important role that administrative tribunals would play. He praised Justice Floyd E. Thompson of the Illinois Supreme Court for the constructive statement embodied in a decision of that court: "Now is the time for magnanimity on the part of the incumbents of the regular tribunals. It is for them to take the lead in recognizing and publicly acknowledging the trend of events and the worthy status of the new tribunals."[14] As early as 1916[15] Wigmore was among those who recognized the emergence of a new field — industrial law — and in 1920 he hailed the creation of the Kansas Industrial Court for the settlement of labor disputes as "epoch-making." He regarded the principle as sound and incorrectly predicted that its extension was only a question of time.[16]

However, Wigmore's many relatively modest writings in the field of evidence which accompanied or followed the preparation of the second edition of the *Treatise*, apparently in no way interfered with the task of bringing his other major works in this same area up to date. In 1931 the second edition of his *Principles of Judicial Proof*[17] made its appearance. The revision of the *Principles* was so thorough and so carefully rewritten that it was virtually a new book and a distinct improvement over the first edition (1913), except that many of the extended quotations from trials had to be omitted to allow for the enlarged text. For this reason Chafee, who had described the first edition as "one of the most delightful books in a law library," believed that both should be readily at hand.[18] And although the book was primarily written for lawyers and law students Chafee believed it should be of interest to logicians, scientists, historians, detectives, and "the large and apparently growing public which loves murders and legal mysteries." In spite of the fact that it was obviously the kind of book that would have to be carefully studied to be fully appreciated, Edmund Morgan regarded many of its pages as "fascinating enough to make good summer reading for the tired lawyer."[19]

Most authors aged sixty-seven might appropriately have regarded such a work as a final effort at revision. However, refusing to allow the rapid pace of events to render his efforts obsolete for long — even in part — Wigmore brought forth a third edition in 1937 under the title *The Science of Judicial Proof as Given by Logic, Psychology, and General Experience and Illustrated in Judicial Trials*. Wigmore dedicated this volume to the memory of Hans Gross, formerly of the University of Graz, "who did more than any other man in modern times to encourage the application of science to judicial proof.'' The object of the new third edition was to take account of the notable scientific advances that had taken place in the intervals. So numerous were these that the new edition involved the complete resetting of the type. Wigmore acknowledged his indebtedness to the staff of the Scientific Crime Detection Laboratory of Northwestern University for assistance in describing the details of the progress made.[20] Once again Wigmore's effort in this field received widespread approval and substantial criticisms were few. One reviewer believed that ''certain portions'' of the book were ''unduly formulary,'' and another doubted the value of the use of complicated symbols in ''balancing the conflicting evidence to sustain or disprove the existence of a fact,'' but both spoke well of the book as a whole.[21] From the psychological point of view, Robert H. Gault said, ''Each edition . . . contains a great many references to scientific literature over practically the whole range of psychology. . . . Academic walls between areas of subject-matter have not restrained Wigmore — the roving scholar.''[22] Finally, a more recent commentator believed that Wigmore paved the way for the use of the computer in law, something that no one else had yet suggested.[23]

Another step taken by Wigmore in order to keep his writings up to date was the third edition of his *Select Cases on the Law of Evidence*, published in 1932. This involved the substitution of about 200 cases and abstracts, footnotes citing about 150 leading case comments drawn from 40 law reviews, and several new appendices. The appendix titles included ''A Program of Instruction, Now Used by the Editor'' [Wigmore], which he believed would be useful to the ''teachers who are still in the 'trial and error' state of mind''; ''Topics for Research in Unfamiliar Fields,'' which could serve to ''broaden the outlook of ambitious and diligent students''; and ''Problems from Bench and Bar,'' containing many ''puzzles that will furnish both debate and entertainment.'' Wigmore thought that the latter was perhaps the most interesting feature of this new edition.[24]

Mrs. Wigmore, who was always her husband's close assistant, was obviously relieved when this task was done: ''Today the Case Book on Evidence went to the printer, and I hope there will be a little less strenuousness in the atmosphere.''[25]

As with prior editions of the Case Book, contemporary appraisals were mixed. For example, one reviewer regarded it as ''the finest case book . . . ever examined,'' a volume that from the point of view of the teacher ''would seem to be the fulfillment of wishes hardly to be dreamed of.''[26] Although others found substantial merit in the book, they pointed to shortcomings: some believed it attempted to cover too much ground;[27] others felt that there was no proper allotment of space between topics[28] and that the subdivision of subjects was too minute.[29]

At long last Wigmore supplemented his case book with a student text. *A Students' Textbook of the Law of Evidence* appeared in 1935 and was published in Braille in 1939. The book was keyed to the *Treatise* and was ''written both in a present and in a forward-looking spirit.''[30] It met a real need and received a warm welcome. The *Students' Textbook* not only served as an elementary text but also gave students easy access to Wigmore's classification and general approach. It was declared to be "much better than any other small book on the subject for the use of the student." [31] Not often does a textbook win such high praise as the following: "Individuality sparkles through these pages and one is never unmindful that insight and critical judgment have informed every statement." [32]

But its utility did not end there. One reviewer, Ralph T. Catterall, who described the book as the "exegesis of the great text by the master himself," gave it especially high praise: "If all trial lawyers would put this little textbook on their shelves beside the little volumes of the American Law Institute, and would undertake the not impossible task of mastering its contents, it would be a long step in the desired direction" and would reduce the economic loss caused by lawyers arguing over the rules of evidence. In his opinion, such an achievement would be as significant as finding the cause of the common cold, and "the gratitude of the nation to anybody who could cure a cold ought not to exceed the gratitude owing to anybody who could make lawyers stop wrangling over the rules of evidence." [33]

During the same year (1935) Wigmore somehow managed to revise his *Code of Evidence.* [33] It will be recalled that the original edition, published in 1910, had been warmly welcomed, and the new edition received a similar reception. [34] Indeed, Lyman P. Wilson believed that the *Code* meant that any activity on the part of the American Law Institute would be "needless supererogation," [35] and Charles T. McCormick was prompted to declare, "In any event, whatever the group responsible, and whatever the method followed, when the rules of evidence come to be refashioned, the genius of Wigmore will light the council-table." [36]

A third edition of the *Code* came out in 1942 [37] in order to accommodate it to the third edition of the *Treatise*, to be discussed at the end of this chapter.

In spite of the frailties of human nature and the shortcomings of the rules of evidence at their best, Wigmore was an ardent supporter of the jury system. When in 1925 William Lyon Phelps declared the jury "a bad thing which continues to demonstrate its uselessness," [38] Wigmore rose to the challenge but began his defense by asking the question: "What is the American Bar going to do about it?" [39] The main purpose of his comment was to arouse the bar to remedial action in an appeal for "first aid to trial by jury" lest the cause "will soon be as good as lost."

A more extended treatment of the subject was given in a 1929 article entitled "A Program for the Trial of Jury Trials," appearing in the *Journal of the American Judicature Society.* [40] After discussing the demerits of trial by jury, real and alleged, Wigmore noted four reasons why it nevertheless remained superior to judge trial. In his view jury trial (a) prevents popular distrust of official justice, (b) provides for the necessary flexibility in legal rules, (c) educates the citizenry in the administration of the law, and (d) improves the quality of the verdict because it is based upon the reconciliation of varied temperaments and minds. [41]

In a 1935 lecture at New York University, Wigmore made an attempt to predict the future of jury-trial rules during the following century.[42] He prefaced his remarks by asking if the rules had progressed or degenerated during the preceding century. His answer was that they had done both: they had progressed in the sense that they had in theory become rationalized; yet at least in the United States the practice of the rules had degenerated.

> The employment of the rules no longer is marked by referring "articulately and definitely to the end" which they subserve, viz., the ascertainment of the truth. They have swelled into a mass of details that have no relation to that end. They are used as tactical weapons for unrelated ends. They are incidentally fought over with irrelevant snarling and yapping — as if two packs of eager hounds on their way to a hunt were allowed by their masters to spend the morning in a public dogfight, and thus to spoil the purposes of the hunt. Their mass has become so voluminous and unmanageable that only a few judges and practitioners are able to master them and to use them correctly.

Wigmore did not believe that the situation could be improved by direct measures, for he thought that the causes were external to the law of evidence.

> They are due to other and larger conditions — the misguided constitutional notion that a jury's verdict is sacrosanct; the separation of the appellate tribunal on high, controlling the trial bench only on rules of law and not on facts; the partisan political selection of judges, and their brief terms of office, resulting in lack of respect by the bar for the rulings of the trial bench; the hoypolloyization of the bar, resulting in misuse of evidence rules by crude or by unscrupulous upstarts and (last but not least) in bad manners, worthy only of a cockpit or a monkey house and not of the courtrooms of a Mansfield and a Marshall.
>
> While these conditions prevail uncured, the jury-trial rules of evidence cannot be radically reformed. One might as well expect a modern hospital or a chemical laboratory to be properly used when donated to a tribe of African bushmen.[43]

But in Wigmore's view this did not mean that the solution lay in the abolition of the jury-trial rules, because they were necessary to an effective determination of the truth in litigation. His belief that the practice of the administrative agencies might in time provide helpful conclusions based on actual experience has already been mentioned. He also thought that trials by juryless judges might develop simple rules that, if the external conditions changed, might be used in jury trials as well.

In conclusion, Wigmore submitted for debate his own summary of evidence principles for a nonjury trial so that others might offer "rival formulations"[44] to the end that a model summary might emerge. However, he introduced his own summary with the reply of Solon when he was asked by the Athenians if the *Code* he had prepared at their request was the best he could devise: "Yes," Solon said, "that is the best that they could endure."

Wigmore once again rose to the challenge when the United States Senate had before it a bill that would forbid a federal judge to express his opinion as to the credibility of witnesses or the weight of the evidence. He condemned the action as one that would destroy a prerogative that had existed for centuries and had "helped to make jury trial survive successfully against the juryless procedure of the Canon law, which spread victoriously over the rest of Europe four centuries ago." [45] In Wigmore's opinion, the abandonment by most courts in the United States of the right of the judge to express his opinion as to the credibility of witnesses "as a part of a democratic and demogogic movement . . . was one of the greatest mistakes the American people ever made." He continued:

> The grand solid merit of jury trial is that the jurors of fact are selected at the last moment from the multitude of citizens. They cannot be known beforehand, and they melt back into the multitude after each trial.
> This is the vital feature. But to save justice from the consequences of using untrained jurors, there must be judicial control. *The judge must be the thirteenth juror.*
> The present trouble with jury trial is due, not to any inherent defects, but to the defects that have been allowed to accrue on the orthodox institution that originally attained fame and reverence. By piling up these accidental defects, we have discredited jury trial needlessly. [46]

Obviously, Wigmore's zeal for the reform of the rules of evidence not only involved the jury system but embraced changes in the judiciary as a whole. In 1916 Wigmore advocated the creation of a new judicial office, "a chief judicial superintendent" [47] whose responsibility it would be to detect failures in judicial transactions and work out improvements which would prevent their recurrence. In one example he cited a case that had involved five trials, four appeals, and nine years of litigation. [48] As he pointed out, although the lawyers, trial judge, jury, and appellate court may each have done its part appropriately, each had a limited function and none had the authority to deal with the botched-up situation as a whole. [49] In an editorial, Wigmore's article was described as a "plea for light, order, system and direction for the administrative side of the judicial function." [50]

Wigmore was opposed to the popular election of judges, and he had to look no further than his own Cook County to see the system in operation. He spoke out emphatically against judicial support of candidates for political office, a not uncommon practice, [51] contending that, even when campaigning in their own behalf, judges should observe two perfectly practical standards: they should take part only in elections where judicial office is involved, and should speak only in defense of their own or another judge's past conduct or principles without making any pledges for future beliefs or action. Sitting judges, he stated emphatically, should not hold any official position in a political party. [52]

In an editorial in the *Illinois Law Review* he said that a popular election

> forces the judges to be vote-seekers. It obliges the candidate to go upon the public platform with claptrap and irrelevant arguments. It tempts him to seek constantly the ephemeral notoriety of newspaper mention. It attracts the tem-

peraments to which such unjudicial conduct is congenial, and puts a handicap upon those whose truly judicial disposition cannot stomach such practices.

In short, the system of popular election not only is false objectively in committing the selection to unqualified voters, but is subjectively suicidal by tending to repel the fit and to attract the unfit.[53]

In an earlier editorial he had cited the conduct of Pilate in "truckling to the demand of the multitude."[54] Of the popular election he said: "This system has not yet begotten for us any obvious Pilates. But its natural tendency is to do so."[55]

It is thus not surprising that Wigmore became an active participant in the work that led to the creation of the "Missouri Plan" for the selection of judges. Wigmore believed it should have been called the "Chicago Plan" because it was worked out in Chicago under the auspices of the American Judicature Society under the leadership of Albert Kales, who effected a compromise between the extremes of executive appointment and popular election.[56]

However, Wigmore had some additional suggestions of his own, which he submitted to the members of the Chicago Bar Association in an address in 1938. His suggestions were designed to insure that nominees for the federal Supreme Court and for the state supreme courts would not only be qualified for their respective offices but would be selected irrespective of political affiliation. Wigmore proposed two lists of eligible nominees, one for the federal Supreme Court and one for the state Supreme Court, consisting of persons recommended by the legal profession.[57] These lists were to be given wide publicity and would provide an authoritative source from which a consensus would emerge. They are effective today as well in reducing "political" appointments, and making it mandatory for an appointing officer to rely on the lists or risk the severest criticism.

At a much earlier date Wigmore had been concerned with the Senate's role in the performance of the courts at the federal level. He was greatly irked by the behavior of the Senate in respect to certain nominations made by President Taft, and he sounded forth in the colorful terms for which he had such a strong proclivity when he was aroused. Among other things, he referred to the Senate "with its feet in the political trough, [which] has sullenly refused to cease munching the husks of partisan provender."[58]

Over the years Wigmore had become aware of the fact that some courts performed better than others. Inevitably, he believed that this insight should be used to further the improvement of the administration of justice. For this purpose, he embodied his ideas in an article entitled "Grading Our State Supreme Courts: A Tentative Method," which appeared in the *American Bar Association Journal*.[59] As the title indicates, Wigmore regarded his approach as tentative and he recognized its limitations. However he thought a start should be made,[60] because such an evaluation, if objective and reliable, could be an important factor in increasing the prestige of the courts and in turn making judicial offices more attractive to those who should occupy them.

It was because only the law of evidence was involved in Wigmore's approach that he regarded it as tentative. However, he said his approach could readily be broadened by examining the performance of the courts in dealing with other important subjects, thus overcoming the obvious inadequacy of a narrow approach. In his own words the "method claims the merit of at least attempting to find a rational, comprehensive, and semiscientific basis for professional judgment." [61]

The foregoing plan for grading the supreme courts was only one of many ways in which Wigmore worked to improve the administration of justice both in the state of Illinois and throughout the country. He asserted that a legislative body (federal or state) had no power to impose rules of procedure upon the courts unless expressly or implicitly prescribed by the constitution. [62] Therefore, when the United States Supreme Court, in its preliminary draft of the Rules of Civil Procedure, resumed "its natural power and duty" to formulate its own rules, he regarded this "as the most important event in a hundred years for Federal Justice." [63] As for the draft, however, Wigmore saw some room for improvement, and he submitted specific suggestions to the American Bar Association at its meeting in 1936. [64] His criticisms fell under three general headings, and he suggested that the Advisory Committee give them further study:

1. A reopening of the whole question of Article 50 to consider the possibility of dealing adequately with the subject of evidence.

2. The incorporation of all statutory rules on any subject so as to make them into a compact code.

3. The breaking up of sections into manageable size, numbered according to the expansible method already in use in many states. [65]

The Advisory Committee considered all of Wigmore's proposals and made some of the changes suggested. [66] He also considered it important to achieve uniformity between the rules of the federal and state courts and hoped that there would be collaboration at least so far as the state supreme courts, which already had rule-making authority, were concerned. [67]

In 1928 Wigmore had spoken vigorously on the subject in the *Illinois Law Review* in an editorial entitled "All Legislative Rules for Judiciary Procedure Are Void Constitutionally." [68] He not only contended that his position was sound as a matter of constitutional law, except when there was an express constitutional provision to the contrary, but also considered that the courts were in far better position to formulate rules of procedure.

Wigmore's "Creed for the Nation" also contained a third statement relating to the judicial branch of government in which he used the state of Illinois as an example. Article III:

> I BELIEVE that all courts of a state, without exception, should be unified into a single state system, with supervised decentralization, and with flexibility of personnel and jurisdiction. Within that system, a metropolis, like Chicago, should have a single unified system, subject only to the State Supreme Court. Therefore, the proposed judiciary article, now reported to the Illlinois State Constitutional Convention, is defective, in that it proposes to maintain three

distinct courts for Cook County instead of a single court. This defect is so serious that it calls for rejection of that article, even if we have to wait another generation until we get a better one.[69]

Wigmore's criticism of the courts and of many of their opinions certainly did not incline him to agree with those who, in the face of the ever increasing mass of court reports, advocated the elimination of written opinions. He contended that court decisions should be justified in writing, and he supported his position by a quotation from Edmund Burke.[70] However, he did not gracefully accept excessively long opinions, particularly when the issue involved was in no way complex. Such was the opinion, he felt, in *Anderson* v. *Fidelity and Casualty Co.* of New York:[71]

> The question before this court is whether the taxicab in which the plaintiff received his injury is a "public conveyance provided by a common carrier for passenger service within the meaning of the policy sued upon." With this language the Court prefaces a long opinion. . . . Will someone explain why it required a long opinion [17 pages] to justify a decision that the Yellow Cab service is that of a common carrier of passengers? In these days of mountainous masses of judicial lucubrations, when the courts (in Judge Winslow's neat phrase) are feeding the paper mills, cannot more discrimination be used in the length of language dedicated to the demonstration of the indubitable and the exegesis of the evident.[72]

Once again, as so often in the past, Wigmore showed an interest in practical problems. In this situation he was concerned over the inaccessibility of the rules of court. In the December 1938 issue of the *Journal of the American Judicature Society*,[73] he pointed out that to provide a service whereby the rules of court would be made available would be a significant contribution for some university. He also suggested that probably the best solution would be an additional unit of the *National Reporter System*. He closed his statement by appealing to readers to submit suggestions. Although no solution of the problem as to state court rules followed Wigmore's suggestion, the *National Reporter System* did in 1941 commence publication of a new unit, the *Federal Rules Decisions*, which met the problem so far as the federal courts are concerned.

The same interest in the practical led Wigmore to attack the problem created by the proliferation of administrative agencies with no central source of information about their rules. When two eminent practitioners in administrative law expressed great interest in this problem, he corresponded with some forty agencies and elicited many responses. The "Replies — usually prompt and accommodating — brought such a copious supply of novel information that I believed it worth while to offer it immediately to the profession in concise though (I daresay) dry form."[74] This he did in an article in the January 1939 issue of the *American Bar Association Journal*, again inviting corrections and suggestions which duly appeared in the next issue.[75]

After the passage of the Federal Register Act, Wigmore again was impelled to play a practical role when it became evident that the legal profession as a whole was not aware of the usefulness of the *Federal Register* and the *Code of Federal Regulations*, and how to use them in locating rules of federal administrative agencies. This was perhaps not surprising, as the American Bar Association had not even been represented in support of the bill that provided for these two publications. Wigmore's article[76] stimulated a much greater interest on the part of the bar.[77]

One admirer who had found Wigmore's utilitarian articles of great value wrote:

I cannot understand how a man so richly endowed could do such uninteresting and detailed work for the benefit of the bar as you have done. . . . Men with such wide accomplishments rarely have the capacity to work out such vexatious details.

May you live for a thousand years to continue your labors for the benefit of mankind and particularly of the bench and bar.[78]

Wigmore's close identification with the administration of justice rested upon a keen interest in both the civil and criminal aspects of the judicial process. It will be recalled that Wigmore's first contribution as an author in the area of criminal law was his "Circumstantial Evidence in Poisoning Cases" for which he was awarded the first prize by the Medico-Legal Society.[79] He was the sponsor (as recorded in Chapter 7) of the pioneer National Conference on Criminal Law in 1909, the virtual founder of the American Institute of Criminal Law and Criminology and the *Journal of Criminal Law and Criminology*, the general editor of the nine-volume Modern Criminal Science Series, and on several occasions concerned himself with the military aspects of the subject during his tour of duty in Washington.

After the war, Wigmore turned his attention once again to the American Institute of Criminal Law and Criminology, and he became active in the American Bar Association in support of the creation of a Section on Criminal Law. In his advocacy he pointed out that: "For forty years the American Bar Association gave no sign, by committee or otherwise, that the great branch of Criminal Law existed."[80] Wigmore was of the opinion that the organized bar had a very useful function to perform and was determined that it should assume this responsibility. His efforts and the work of a limited number of others eventually culminated in 1920 in the establishment of the Criminal Law Section.[81]

Contrary to the view expressed by some of his colleagues in the institute, Wigmore believed that the section would not supplant the American Institute of Criminal Law and Criminology but would "develop the field of the law as applied to crime, just as the medical men, the psychologists, and others, have developed their respective specialties. To coordinate the results of all these independent branches is the function of the Institute."[82]

However, the institute, since its organization in 1909, had worked very closely with the American Bar Association, assuming, to some degree at least, a part of what might logically have been its responsibility.[83] After the section was established, the institute, although it continued to operate, gradually lost the support that was needed to make it effective. When the depression hit, it had to be abandoned.[84] However, the *Journal of Criminal Law and Criminology* continues today as a leading publication.

Although the institute held no annual meeting after 1921, as late as 1927–28 it was one of the active sponsors of *The Illinois Crime Survey*, a study that had widespread support.[85] The 1,100 page report was prepared under the supervision of an advisory committee of which Wigmore was a member. In his editorial preface he said in part: "The main feature of what is wrong may be put in one word — Inefficiency. No one part of the system of Criminal Justice works to maximum power and most of them to less than moderate power, — Insufficiency everywhere."[86] In answering the question of why this was so he said, "My guess is that they [the reasons] are all reducible ultimately to *one* prime cause; and that cause is: the Selfishness of the Ordinary Citizen (the O.C. as Arthur Train calls him)."[87] Wigmore's interest in criminal law also found an outlet through membership and active participation in a committee of the Association of American Law Schools on Survey of Crime, Criminal Law, and Criminal Procedure.[88]

Wigmore finally had another opportunity to do something practical and concrete with respect to scientific crime detection. Burt A. Massee and other business leaders in Chicago who were disgusted by the ineffectiveness of the investigation in the St. Valentine's Day gang massacre became interested in contributing to the rectification of the situation and raised the funds to establish the Scientific Crime Detection Laboratory in 1929. It was located near the Law School and affiliated with Northwestern University.[89] This was the first institution of its kind in the United States.[90] The venture attracted wide attention and exerted a great deal of influence, producing such a large mass of materials on new methods of proof in court, most of them from the Crime Detection Laboratory, that Wigmore found it necessary to prepare a new edition of his *Science of Judicial Proof*. When Wigmore was pressed by those who questioned the necessity of having the Crime Laboratory affiliated with the university, he declared that such an arrangement not only reflected favorably on the university, but was preferable to having it attached to a police department, where it would be subject to political pressure. The only way it could be operated honestly, he felt, was for it to be connected with a university. Wigmore was also a pioneer in the movement to provide special training for police work at all levels. Assessing Wigmore's role August Vollmer wrote, "no one . . . can estimate the dynamic and vast influence that he has exerted during his life time in placing recruit and pre-employment training schools on a solid foundation."[91]

The psychological aspects of the crime problem also engaged Wigmore's attention, and he believed there was important work to be done. In the words of Winfred Overholser:

It would be difficult to exaggerate the debt which forensic psychiatry owes to Wigmore. His championship of a scientific study of the criminal, coming as it did from a leader in a field which traditionally had claimed to be the *fons et origo* of all knowledge of how to deal with the criminal did much to encourage the leaders in the psychiatric field, such as William A. White, Adolf Meyer, and Bernard Glueck, to prosecute further their studies of criminal psychopathology.[92]

Wigmore's receptivity to the application of psychology to the crime problem did not include the notion of some psychiatrists that punishment was merely revenge, an attitude that overlooked the factor of deterrence. In support of his view he quoted Chief Justice Taft, who said, "We must never forget that the first and chief object of prosecution of crime is its deterrent effect upon *future would-be criminals* in the protection of society."[93] Wigmore concludes, "Some . . . psychiatrists may propose to do away with 'punishment and other criminal terminology,' and still keep people from being criminals."

Perhaps no case (except the Abrams and Sacco-Vanzetti cases) evoked a more emphatic response from Wigmore than Loeb-Leopold,[94] the case that attracted such widespread attention at the time and also came back into the news in 1958 with stories of Leopold's reformation. It will be recalled that the case involved the coldly planned and executed kidnapping and murder of Robert Franks by the two defendants, aged eighteen and nineteen.

On several occasions Wigmore contributed characteristically forthright comments concerning this case. In one, he commended the parents who, in spite of their wealth, declared that they would not spend an excessive amount for the defense.[95] However, he criticized the experts involved in the trial for using the nicknames "Dickie" and "Babe" subtly to influence the jury.[96] Wigmore also criticized "the vicious method of the Law which permits and requires each of the opposing parties to summon the witnesses on the party's own account."[97] He took the position that, while the parties should have the right to request certain witnesses, "expert witnesses" should be paid by the state and called by the court, and both parties should be provided with the opportunity to consult them.

Wigmore was also goaded into action by the sentence of the court in this case which, in his view, contained two "astonishing pronouncements."[98] The court declared that it was moved to impose less than the extreme penalty chiefly because "of the *age of the defendants* — boys of 18 and 19 years . . . in accordance with (1) the progress of criminal law all over the world and (2) the dictates of enlightened humanity." The opinion adds that the life-imprisonment penalty may well be "the severer form of retribution and expiation."

In his comment Wigmore took advantage of the opportunity to state his own position succinctly. He declared that the basic aims of the penal law were four — retribution, reformation, deterrence, and prevention. The first had long since been discredited, and the last — prevention — required general social measures and did not depend on the law of the courts. He

again stated, ''the deterrence theory is the kingpin of the criminal law.'' [99]
He took sharp issue with the experts who suggested that, on the basis of the
theory of determinism, the court should be lenient on the defendants, both
of whom were, in his opinion, completely beyond the possibility of re-
habilitation.[100] As to the relationship between reformation and deterrence
he said, ''As doctors and friends, let them sympathetically 'help the criminal to get through the situation' by all means. But as advisors of a criminal
court, let them learn that their Determinism is out of place, and that
Society's right to eliminate its human weeds is not affected by the pre-
determined character of the weeds.'' [101]

The foregoing case comments and, indeed many others, suggest that
Wigmore was more readily aligned with the conviction of the guilty than
with the protection of the guilty at the expense of the innocent. In this
connection, it should be kept in mind that his extensive reading had
brought to light countless cases where the administration of justice had
been thwarted by the interposition of all sorts of technicalities. In his view
the crime rate was entirely too high for any kind of complacency. In
addition, his great interest in scientific crime detection may have tended to
focus his attention on identifying and convicting the guilty. At any rate, by
1923 Wigmore felt impelled to include the following statement in the
second edition of the *Treatise:*

> The maudlin sentimentality of judges in criminal cases must cease. Reverence
> for the Constitution is one thing, and a respect for substantial fairness of proce-
> dure is commendable. But the exaltation of technicalities of every sort merely
> because they are raised on behalf of an accused person is a different and a
> reprehensible thing. There seems to be a constant neglect of the pitiful cause of
> the injured victim, and the solid claims of law and order. All the sentiment is
> thrown to weight the scales for the criminal — that is, not for the mere accused,
> who may be assumed innocent, but for the man who upon the record plainly
> appears to be the villain that the jury have pronounced him to be. . . .
>   This much had to be said here, in order to redeem the law of Evidence from
> that reproach which belongs rather to the law of new trials.[102]

Wigmore had no doubt as to the importance of the fear motive in the
reduction of crime, and he dealt with it most explicitly in an editorial in the
Journal of Criminal Law and Criminology in 1931.[103] For him

> the most fundamental and justifying rationale of the Criminal Law is found in the
> *crimes that are not committed.* . . . it is the criminal law, in a large proportion of
> occasions, that clamps an inhibition on our will and represses our illegal act. Take
> off that repressive influence, and the community would become a seething sham-
> bles, in which the most self-willed and unscrupulous ones . . . would be preying
> daily upon the life, liberty and property of the others. Not until the millennium
> arrives, when love of Fellow-Man shall be the universal motive, can we afford to
> relax the fear motive of the criminal law.[104]

Although Wigmore was certainly in favor of prison reform and played an
important part in bringing about needed changes, it is not always clear how

he felt on specific issues. However, we do know that earlier he was uncertain as to the propriety of using the whipping post as a form of punishment. In response to a request for his opinion he said in a letter:

> I really have not formed an opinion on the subject. Hence, I cannot say anything, one way or another. I suppose I have a general notion against Whipping Posts. On the other hand, I know that there are some fiends who ought to be tortured in retaliation. As it is possible that there is something to be said on both sides, and as I have no duty to enter into the question, I simply have no opinion on the subject.[105]

At one time Wigmore felt a similar uncertainty about the death penalty. He then referred to it as "that great problem which has been haunting our civilization for more than a century past — indeed ever since Beccaria, about the time of our American Revolution, wrote his 'Crimes and Penalties' — namely, the wisdom of the death-penalty for crime. . . . We trust that . . . this great subject will soon receive practical consideration as a problem of the times."[106]   In spite of the fact that in much of Wigmore's writing the emphasis was on catching and convicting the criminal·rather than protecting the innocent, such was by no means always the case, and, notwithstanding his statements to the contrary, he did recognize that there were practices that worked undue hardship on persons accused of crime or resulted in miscarriages of justice. Furthermore, he recognized that, in the nature of things, many innocent persons were accused of crime and suffered loss of freedom, income, and reputation pending their acquittal and that some were even convicted erroneously. As early as 1913 he strongly favored legislation to provide compensation for the latter,[107] and in 1932 he reviewed Edwin Borchard's *Convicting the Innocent: Errors of Criminal Justice* most favorably and commended "the author on the final appearance of a book which will do much to promote the reform that he has so long advocated with such devotion."[108]

In 1931 Wigmore supported a bill authorizing county boards in Illinois to establish the office of public defender. He said, "it represents a long-delayed performance by the state of a part of one of its fundamental duties — the duty to make justice obtainable by all and without price."[109]

Concentration on these important but restricted areas of the criminal law and preoccupation with particular cases never obscured the broader view, and Wigmore had quite definite ideas about the general administration of criminal justice. Another notable reform was suggested in his "Creed for the Nation," which has already been mentioned:

> I believe that every State should have a superintendent of criminal justice. The suppression and prevention of crime is a single complex task, which needs direction and supervision. Laws and courts alone, without effective administration, are like a factory with an independent operator at each machine. The machinery of criminal justice is now working day and night without any responsible overseer. Let us install a state superintendent of criminal justice, with the power and duty to inspect the operation, to report upon the product, and to devise improved means of making criminal justice effective and just.[110]

Thus for more than half a century Wigmore's interest in matters concerning the administration of criminal justice ranged far and wide. His over-all contribution was succinctly summed up by his colleague Robert W. Millar in the following words: "In this field [criminal law] many men have had their part in the general advance, but the part of none has been more incisive or on a wider scale than that of John Henry Wigmore."[111]

Attention must be given to Wigmore's lifelong interest in and support of the legal-aid movement. Although this aspect of his work has necessarily been referred to from time to time, his support was so substantial and so sustained that it requires separate delineation. He believed that legal aid was essential in a democracy.[112] His commitment went beyond its role in the Law School curriculum and his activities in writing and speaking out in its behalf. At the local level he served on the board of directors of the Bureau of Justice of Chicago in 1904 and as a director or vice-president of the Legal Aid Society of Chicago beginning in 1907 and for many years thereafter.[113] Securing funds, primarily through subscriptions, to keep the society going was one of his important services. Wigmore also assisted in integrating the clinic with the Legal Aid Bureau when it merged with the United Charities of Chicago because he recognized that many clients also had social problems.[114]

But Wigmore's active interest and influence were national in scope. In 1922 he was selected as a member of a distinguished group known as the National Committee on Legal Aid Work, whose duty it was to draft a constitution and by-laws for an organization that would be more effective than the National Alliance of Legal Aid Societies. The following year in Cleveland the constitution and by-laws were adopted with minor changes and the National Association of Legal Aid Organizations was created.[115] Funds provided by the Carnegie Foundation made possible the employment of an executive secretary. Wigmore was elected one of two vice-presidents.[116]

Wigmore, however, did not stop at the national boundary. In 1923 he proposed to the League of Nations that it promote an international service, and some preliminary work was done before the league disbanded.[117] However, "the seed was planted," and "It bloomed in 1960 as the International Legal Aid Association."[118]

In 1963, a tribute giving recognition to Wigmore's work in this field, concluded with these words, "The professor who became dean exemplar left an imprint in many areas of the law. On the centennial of the birth of Dean John H. Wigmore, we spotlight here only the heritage we find in Legal Aid. We pause, proud to point it out, and we take courage in its indestructibility."[119]

More than thirty years after Wigmore had produced the first edition of the *Treatise on Evidence*, he confronted for the second time the task of bringing up to date the work that had brought him early renown as a scholar. The second edition had in its turn become inadequate. Indeed, the new edition had to be projected in terms of ten large volumes instead of the six that had sufficed at the time the second edition had appeared.

Once again Wigmore — now in his seventies — worked at home, his secretary, Miss Morgan, at the typewriter and Mrs. Wigmore offering whatever help she could. Through Miss Morgan we can get some conception of how the pressure mounted:

> I worked on Saturday afternoons for several years, probably from about 1937. As the deadline for sending the manuscript to the publisher drew near, I worked two and then three nights a week additionally for two or three hours, and finally on Sunday afternoons also. For all of this Mr. Wigmore paid by the hour.[120]

While work was without doubt the order of the day (and often the day was long), it was not to the exclusion of either the wit or music that were such an inseparable part of Wigmore's being. The two women were fond of teasing him over the fact that, in response to a question, he seldom said he did not know, a natural consequence of his extremely wide reading. Occasionally, when he did admit that he did not know, they would shout with one voice that "we should put it in the book" that you said you do not know, and they would all have a good laugh.[121]

In 1940 all this effort became a reality — the third edition of the *Treatise on Evidence* in 10 volumes.[122] This superseded not only the second edition but also the 1934 supplement, a volume which reflected careful consideration of the criticisms that had been made of the second edition, although the author did not, as some had hoped, reexamine some of the doctrines advanced by him but questioned by others.[123]

Even in purely quantitative terms the third edition was a stupendous undertaking. The first edition contained about 40,000 citations to judicial decisions, the second approximately 55,000, and the third about 85,000. Statute citations in the third edition totaled about 20,000. In addition, there were numerous citations to "valuable literature from learned thinkers . . . occasionally differing with the views expounded in this *Treatise*," reports of bar association committees and reformatory commissions, and "scores of quotations of anecdote and comment from recent professional memoirs."[124] The third edition alone had 7,324 pages, and the three editions and their supplements came to a total of 19,358 pages distributed among 22 large volumes which occupied four and one-half feet of shelf space. Standing before them one inevitably recalls the somewhat facetious but nevertheless effective words of Robert T. Donley, written in 1934 and some years before the third edition of the *Treatise* appeared: "The amount of research, thought and physical labor which must have been necessary for the production of this [the *Treatise*] and the other works of Dean Wigmore is simply appalling: ample to have developed round-shoulders and quarrelsomeness in any dozen professors of law."[125]

However, the third edition involved far more than the addition of later materials. Revision was thorough and the entire text was brought up to date. Among the anecdotes that were quoted was one of Wigmore's favorites, Frank Hogan's account of Theodore Roosevelt as a character witness. Instead of responding briefly to the appropriate questions as is customary, Roosevelt entered into an extended delineation of his own career, followed by a similar treatment of the life of the person to whose character he was to testify, undeterred by counsel on either side or by the judge.[126]

Apparently, Wigmore's review of the more recent cases provided him with the basis for a reasonable degree of optimism. In 1933, when he was completing his work on the 1934 revision, he was concerned over the prevalence of the "same meticulous wrangling over petty details."[127] Now he detected a "new phase in the profession's attitude toward the rules of Evidence, viz. a disposition to reconsider the rules' weaknesses, and a willingness — even a determination — to improve that body of law in every possible part.[128] Wigmore attributed this "changeful trend" to three separate influences: (1) the generally skeptical disposition of the times, (2) the popular dissatisfaction with "obstructive technicalities," and (3) a more direct influence of the demand for a fair and simple set of rules to be used by administrative officials. These influences put the jury-trial rules on the defensive.[129] He did not add — but he might have — that a fourth influence was the highly constructive impact of his own work in the field.

In spite of Wigmore's preoccupation for fifty years with the numerous rules of evidence and his great influence on the law, he did not lose sight of the broader considerations involved. In what was probably his last statement on the subject, he said:

> But after all, it is the spirit that gives life to the rules: *All the rules in the world will not get us substantial justice if the judges and the lawyers have not the correct living moral attitude toward substantial justice.*
>
> What the law of Evidence and Procedure, nowadays most needs is that the men who are our judges and our lawyers shall firmly dispose themselves to get at the truth and the merits of the case before them. Until they become of this disposition, the mere body of rules, however scientific, however sensible, however apt for justice, will minister to them in vain.[130]

For the third time Wigmore's major scholarly effort was exposed to the scrutiny of his admirers and his critics — ten large volumes dealing with innumerable matters of detail. Comments were numerous and extensive, but for the sake of brevity only three will be given consideration here.

In his appraisal, Charles T. McCormick said that "the greatest legal treatise ever written" would have been "greater still" if Wigmore had not underestimated the value of the law-review materials and if he had resisted the temptation "to lash the judges — the men he is seeking to lead — with the whip of scorn."[131] Although McCormick regarded the latter as an obvious weakness, he continued, "Perhaps sparks of invective that fly astray are part of his ardent energy, an accompanying manifestation of the genius that shows itself in the gift for luminous description, and the passion for order, which have brought light and guidance through the tangled under brush of evidence-law. We take the bitter with the sweet."[132]

Wigmore did, indeed, sometimes lash the judges as the following typical examples graphically illustrate: "Much depends upon whether the perverse stolidity of the juristic mind can be compelled by a few statutory words to leave its accustomed ruts;"[133] "the logic chopping in such cases as the present seems a pitiable method of getting at the truth about a murder, — pitiable, that is, when one reflects that it is the method used by able men administering a great legal system and fancying themselves to be doing its proper service;"[134] "the quiddities of the Court's reasoning are not worth setting out here; it is a good example of the anachronistic Cokianism which has become nauseous, and naturally excites popular distrust of the Courts;"[135] "a wondrous cobweb of pedantry is here woven to occupy the jury's simple mind and the trial judge's tongue."[136] Another example was the case of Anderson v. Crawford[137] involving assault and battery, where the defendant was discharged in a habeas corpus proceeding because of what Wigmore called a sample of "falsity." Wigmore said that, regardless of the pro and con,

> the general fact staring out from the case is that our criminal law is being administered by the courts up in a sky-parlor of logical quiddities which have nothing to do directly with either justice or efficiency. Read again Aristophanes' play of the Birds, and amuse yourself with his satiric description of Cloud — Cuckoo-Land. It was written for twenty-five centuries ago, but it fits our courts of today. They twitter away seriously with their pretty logical antiphones; but their twitterings do not have any genuine relation to [t]he seething affairs of mankind below on the earth of reality.
>
> When the legalistic minds of the lawyers on the criminal bench substitute for legalism some standards of justice or efficiency, or both, we shall have a respectable system of criminal justice; but not before.[138]

The frequent use of this sharp and uncompromising language in regard to decisions about which Wigmore felt strongly tended to create the impression that his comments were always critical, which was by no means the case. On many occasions his comments praised the courts for forward-looking decisions, particularly where the applicable case law was unsound historically or not in touch with the realities of the situations involved. Neither McCormick nor anyone else knew that Wigmore wrote hundreds of personal letters to individual judges, praising them for particular opinions or commending them for the quality of their work on the bench. Upon retirement or in recognition of an anniversary, many a judge was the recipient of a personal commendatory letter from Wigmore.

In contrast, the evaluation of Albert S. Osborn was typical of many specialists who had been stimulated by and received encouragement from Wigmore. As an expert in the disputed-documents field he gladly recorded that

> John H. Wigmore . . . did more than any other man in applying scientific methods to the discovery and proof of the facts in questioned and disputed document cases. . . .

Professor Wigmore wrote appreciative introductions for all three of the author's previous books and his helpful encouragement was highly appreciated in the dark days when there was wide misunderstanding of the work of the questioned documents examiner.

This distinguished legal author had the satisfaction of seeing all of his proposed reforms, regarding the legal procedure relating to questioned documents, adopted in every state in this nation.[139]

In Edward M. Morgan, Wigmore had both a critic and an admirer — Morgan's approach to the *Treatise* was in the best tradition of the scholar. His own contributions to the law of evidence had been substantial, and some believed that to these Wigmore had not given enough attention. Morgan disagreed with Wigmore in some important particulars and expressed regret that Wigmore had not, in the preparation of the third edition, made a reexamination of the entire subject rather than, in effect, bringing the second edition down to date. He conceded, however, that many changes and additions in the text were a testament that this had been thoroughly done and that "no important published study of problems of evidence seems to have been overlooked. In a word, these ten volumes bring the second edition of Wigmore down to date, and do it in the Wigmorean manner."[140]

Wigmore gave two reasons for not undertaking the complete reexamination of the subject that Morgan suggested: (1) that the changes in the arrangement that would be involved would be inconvenient for those who were familiar with the present work, and (2) that he did not have time (here, it should be sufficient to point out that he was at the time a dean emeritus in his late seventies).[141]

As to the criticism that the work was too long, it must be kept in mind that the relevant materials were extensive and that Wigmore believed a thorough examination of the entire subject was essential. In his own thinking an important part of his task was to set forth "by excerpts, the most influential, the most lucid, and the most carefully reasoned passages anywhere recorded in judicial annals — the best things that have been said upon the rules of Evidence."[142] He also regretted the length of the book, but from the following passage it is clear that Wigmore placed the blame elsewhere. "It is a pity that the book has had to be so large. But if Legislators will continue so copiously to legislate, and if Judges still refuse to justify with jejunity their judgments, shall not Authors continue assiduously to amass and to annotate these luciferous lucubrations for the benefit of the Bar, so long as the Bar incumbently bears this burden?"[143]

Morgan concluded his excellent appraisal with the following statement:

> Disagreement with Mr. Wigmore's theories in some particulars and mild dissatisfaction with his treatment of some topics does not imply lack of appreciation of his sound scholarship or of respect for his views or any want of profound admiration for his accomplishment. In this day of freely flung challenges to debate this reviewer offers to support the following proposition against all comers: Not only is this the best, by far the best, treatise on the Law of

Evidence, it is also the best work ever produced on any comparable division of Anglo-American law.[144]

All of the previously mentioned appraisals were made at or about the time of publication. What has been the effect of the perspective of time? More than twenty years later Justice Felix Frankfurter went even further in his praise, for he not only agreed fully with Morgan as to the outstanding character of the work in this field of law, but he said of the *Treatise:*

It is not only a great treatise on the law of evidence, but it is a masterpiece of scholarship, conveyed through a distinguished style of writing . . . I would make his treatise compulsory reading in every university that has the ambition to turn out its graduates as competent masters of the English language, not merely for the original parts written by Wigmore himself but for the marvelous collection of otherwise unavailable quotations.[145]

15

A Continuing Leadership: Law, Public Service, Religion

||||||||||||||C3||||||||||||C3||||||||||||C3||||||||||||C3||||||||||||C3||||||||||||C3||||||||||||C3||||||||||||C3||||||||||||C3||||||||||||C3|||||||||

After World War I, Wigmore's interests and activities followed the pattern that had developed earlier; now, however, his concerns went far beyond his interest in the administration of justice, massive as his contribution to that field had been. For convenience, consideration will be given here to pursuits related to the national scenes, leaving until the next chapter a discussion of Wigmore's role in the broader international arena.

In the field of law close identification with the work of the Association of American Law Schools and the American Bar Association continued unabated. In the former organization Wigmore served on a number of committees and took part in round-table programs concerned with criminal law, curriculum, evidence, jurisprudence, legal history, a juristic center, legal aid, legal procedure, library problems, memorials, professional doctorates, torts, and the review of law books.[1]

In 1921 Wigmore read a paper at the annual meeting of the Association of American Law Schools entitled "The Job Analysis Method of Teaching the Use of Law Sources."[2] Although fully appreciating at that time the value of the case method of instruction, Wigmore recognized that the widespread use of case books, no matter how necessary and useful, deprived the student of experience in finding the sources for himself. This deficiency in research training was not recognized by many of Wigmore's contemporaries — nor is it understood by many law teachers today. As a result of Wigmore's experience during the war as a member of the War Department Committee on Education and Special Training,[3] he sought to apply the techniques developed there to training in legal research. The extensive report made by the Curriculum Committee in 1944 evaluated the recommendation that Wigmore had made in his paper: though "too complex for effective general use, it offers a fine starter for any teacher's thought."[4] In spite of the fact that Wigmore had worked year after year for the raising of the standards of the Association of American Law Schools and for the improvement of the quality of legal education generally, he vehemently opposed the adoption of a resolution that would require a minimum number of full-time faculty members at every member school. His chief objection was that such a requirement would amount to an abridgement of the schools' freedom. He also was critical of the assumption that practitioners were less competent as teachers, pointing out that Papinian, a great practitioner, was the first official professor of law and that a thousand years later Bartolus was the most famous professor of his day.[5] Wigmore seems to have overlooked the fact that the proposed minimum of three full-time faculty members and in no case "fewer than one for each 100 students and fraction thereof,"[6] was in fact a modest requirement and would in no way have prevented a member school from including practitioners on its faculty.

Of course Wigmore continued to be a leader in providing entertainment for the Law School Association meetings, frequently in company with Roscoe Pound.[7] He usually selected the songs to be sung — and frequently the program included his own words or music.[8] "He distributed mimeographed copies of the words, and he was the major domo of the chorus."[9] On more than one occasion Wigmore played the piano while Pound "sang the 'Dives of Lazarus' to the delight of their hearers."[10] A common sight at the annual dinner was Wigmore accompanying the audience in some of his well-known lyrics. The following verses are a sample:

> All the Law
> > We ever saw
> > We've banished from our sight;
> Nunc pro bunk,
> > The Law is junk,
> > We've scrapped it for tonight;
> Contracts, Pleading
> > Cases leading,
> > Codes, and all, taboo;
> Every Prof. can have this night off,
> > To be gay clear through![11]

Wigmore's activities as a member of the American Bar Association also continued. He was a member of several committees (1) the Joint Committee on Improvement of Criminal Justice (American Bar Association, American Law Institute, and Association of American Law Schools), which submitted a significant report in 1931;[12] (2) the Special Committee on the Improvement of Procedure in Trials of Rate and Public Utility Cases;[13] and (3) the Committee on the Development of International Law Through International Conferences.[14] Of special importance was Wigmore's role as chairman of the Section of Judicial Administration's Committee on Improvements in the Law of Evidence, to which he rendered an invaluable service. This report[15] was characterized as "the most progressive and open minded survey of needed reforms since the report of the Commonwealth Fund Committee in 1927."[16]

In his press release [17] before the annual meeting in 1938 in Cleveland, Wigmore as chairman used as an illustration the story of David Harum and his setter. Asked why he did not do something about the dog's fleas, David's reply was, "A reasonable amount of fleas is good for a dog. They keep him from broodin' over being just a dog." Wigmore applied the anecdote to the law of evidence:

> Now the fact is that our law of evidence has been so troubled with fleas, I mean petty technicalities, that the system has spent most of its time scratching for those technicalities, and it has not had time enough to remember that it is really *a system of evidence* — that is, a system for the efficient investigation of facts. So this committee has caught some of those fleas of technicalities, and is proposing that we get rid of them, and give the system of evidence a chance to be more often conscious that it is really a system of efficient investigation of facts.

Although Wigmore was primarily concerned at the Cleveland meeting with the law of evidence, a local committee of lawyers took advantage of the occasion to honor him for his much wider contribution to the work of the legal profession by designating a special collection in the Cleveland Public Library — "The Collection of Jurisprudence Established in Honor of John Henry Wigmore." The collection included about six hundred books on jurisprudence, legal history, legal biography, classics of legal literature, and a number of works in closely related fields. Also included were a representative collection of portraits, etchings, and prints of famous legal personalities and historical buildings, and some manuscripts relating to the early history of Ohio law. The extent to which the collection was used by the public testified to the belief of the sponsoring committee that such a collection had a fitting place in a public library. [18]

Another way in which Wigmore shared in the work of the American Bar Association was his appearance in two of a series of nationwide radio programs sponsored by the association and entitled "The Lawyer and the Public." On March 19, 1933, he discussed the topic, "Should the Public Distrust a Lawyer." [19] On December 29, 1933, he participated in a discussion called "Modern Methods of Crime Detection," [20] in which the other participant was Leonarde Keeler, psychologist of Northwestern University's Scientific Crime Detection Laboratory. [24] Wigmore received many letters of commendation for his performance. At the request of the American Bar Association, Wigmore also gave a lecture on evidence which was filmed for general use. Afterward he expressed great sympathy for the motion-picture actors who had to endure the heat of the strong lights. [22]

It will be recalled that before World War I Wigmore made several strenuous efforts to improve the effectiveness of the American Bar Association. In 1923 he had the opportunity to work toward further improvement when he was appointed a member of its Special Committee on Coordination of State and Local Bar Associations. This committee unanimously recommended an amendment to the constitution of the association providing for the nomination of members of the ABA Council by each of the state bar associations — a step, at least, toward the federation that the committee believed was not yet feasible.[23] However, even such a modest beginning was rejected by the members.[24]

However, Wigmore had an additional opportunity to press for federation as one of the speakers at the National Conference of Bar Association Delegates in 1929. In his remarks he supported Chairman James Grafton Rogers's plea for a reorganization of the ABA. Regarding the creation of the Delegates Conference as the most significant development in his thirty-six years of membership in the association, Wigmore viewed it as a step toward the united organization which was absolutely essential if lawyers were to perform their primary function of administering justice.[25]

Wigmore felt impelled to revive his original plan for federation, and with the assent of the *American Bar Association Journal* he submitted an article (to which he appended his original proposal) reviewing the history of the movement to strengthen the American Bar Association.[26] Although the goals he had envisioned had by no means been fully realized, it must have given him considerable satisfaction to be able to say: "It will be just eighteen years ago in August that the first formal proposal was made to nationalize the power of the American Bar. That proposal, failing at that time, has now become an inevitable movement, which only awaits for its realization the discovery of an acceptable practical plan."

In the interval many improvements had been made, but the "power" which Wigmore believed required federation of the state bar associations with the national body was still unrealized. Therefore, in his view, "What the Association as a body still lacks, and ought to have, is the power to represent, actively and rationally, the convictions of the entire legal profession in our country."[27]

And so it went. Wigmore, ever watchful for improvements in performance, suggested that a supplement be added to the *Journal* to be edited by a committee of the Junior Bar Conference "to summarize the news of importance to members of the Bar from various localities of the country."[28] A resolution to this effect was adopted in 1936. Finally, when World War II involved the United States, he was appointed a member of the Criminal Law Section's Committee on Courts and Wartime Social Protection.[29] As another response to the war Wigmore drafted an explanation of the Soldier's and Sailor's Civil Relief Act,[30] giving an account of its history and showing how it was derived from the Act of 1918 in which he had played an important part. Some years before, indeed in 1927, he had advocated legislation that would facilitate preparedness, pointing back to the delay and inefficiency that had hampered the nation in World War I.[31]

Although Wigmore's major effort in the work of the organized bar was directed toward the ABA, he never lost touch with professional activities at the state and local levels. He obviously enjoyed his personal associations with practitioners and not only took part in formal meetings and assumed committee assignments but also was often present on less formal occasions. He frequently had lunch with fellow lawyers at the Chicago Bar Association's dining room and was received with special warmth by his former students.[32]

An example of how Wigmore characteristically seized every opportunity to make himself effective is told by George Anderson, a graduate of the Law School and a member of the Chicago Bar Association. On one occasion, in 1922, when in a conversation Anderson mentioned Wigmore's "One Hundred Legal Novels," Wigmore pointed his finger at Anderson and said, "George, I charge you with the duty of starting such a collection for the Chicago Bar Association." Shortly thereafter Wigmore became a member of the committee that was assigned the responsibility of selecting the books. He served on this committee as long as he lived.[33] Stuart Ball felt certain that Wigmore added significantly to the lighter side of bar association activity by promoting the annual shows and composing jocular songs.[34]

"Beautiful Ships in the Blue,"[35] for example, was prepared especially for a meeting of the Illinois Bar Association in 1936 under the sponsorship of its Section on Aeronautical Law. The chorus reflects the spirit of the title, but the verse was a lament over a dilatory Congress: "No product of their lucubration on Air Law is yet aught but air."

Having so strongly advocated higher standards for legal education and admission to the bar, Wigmore was obviously pleased when Illinois was the first state to respond affirmatively in 1922 to the recommendations of the American Bar Association raising minimum requirements for legal education[36] to two years of a liberal education at college and three years of study at a law school.[37]

Several years later, when an anonymous pamphlet was circulated by the commercialized law schools opposing with extravagant charges the two-year college requirement, Wigmore countered with a vigorous statement.[38] Because far more young men were now in college, he said, the requirement would impose no hardship. Probably one-half of college or law-school youths, he contended, were earning or had earned money for their education. "If they have not pluck enough to do that where necessary, they have not ambition nor staying power enough to succeed at the bar. . . . The only right that this pamphlet really stands on is the alleged right to become an incompetent lawyer. Nobody else ought to want to stand on that platform."[39]

At a much earlier date Wigmore had given a talk before the Law Club of Chicago entitled "The Eighteen Jobs of the Lawyer,"[40] which left little doubt about the diversity of skills required and the importance of adequate preparation.

Wigmore constantly advocated better preparation for admission to the bar in order to raise the general level of intellectual capacity and character. He thought "that the number of lawyers should be reduced by one-half" as the only "rational and beneficent measure for reducing hereafter the spawning mass of promiscuous semi-intelligence which now enters the Bar."[41] In his address at the Annual Alumni Dinner in 1921 he said:

I BELIEVE that law is a profession, not a trade. Therefore, it is not too much to demand that entrance to the profession of law, as well as to those of medicine and engineering, shall be universally prepared for by a substantial college education. Ten years ago there were only 200,000 young men and women in all our colleges; today there are 600,000. To require a college preparation today means no more relatively than it meant to require a high school education ten years ago. The legal profession will continue to furnish the shapers of our fundamental laws and institutions. They must be wise for the times. With college-educated men permeating the business world, it follows that college-educated men must set the pace in the legal world.[42]

In 1925 the Illinois Legislature defeated a bill which would have granted the Supreme Court the power to draft rules relative to practice and procedure in courts of record. Wigmore regarded this bill as "the greatest single measure calculated to relieve our civil justice from the reproach of delay, expense and confusion." When all but five of the lawyer members of the legislature voted in the negative, Wigmore was scathing in his criticism, saying, "So that is where those lawyers locate themselves — firmly on their hauches, ears pointing forward, reluctant to help pull out of the mire the Ambulance of Civil Justice."[43]

In a tribute to both Wigmore and Pound, Leon Green has summarized as well as anyone Wigmore's great contribution to the work of the legal profession:

Take the American and state bar associations. Prior to the day of Wigmore and Pound, these associations were little more than social affairs for railroad attorneys. These two young scholars began their pioneering, which has proved so valuable in building professional organization, in the early 1900's. Wigmore, on the one hand, through enlisting cooperative efforts of scholarly talent, opened for the lawyer vast stores of foreign legal literature, legal history, legal philosophy, in the lawyer's own language; promoted legal periodicals for the purposes of current legal literature; organized institutes and societies devoted to the development of special fields, sponsored various group interests which later grew into sections of the American Bar Association; in the meantime, personally setting the high water mark of legal scholarship for American lawyers — all of which have profoundly affected the professional attitude, professional organizations and their programs.[44]

For this broad and massive contribution as well as for his great service to the American Bar Association, Wigmore was awarded its most significant honor — the Gold Medal.[45] Pound was prompted to write: "How much I rejoice to see the ABA medal awarded you. No one could have deserved it so much."[46]

Although Wigmore gave his loyal support to the American Bar Association at the national level and firmly believed that the state bar associations had very important roles to play within their respective jurisdictions, he recognized other organized channels as well, and his role in the work of the American Institute of Criminal Law and Criminology in his earlier days and his support of the American Judicature Society are testimony. His interest in the American Law Institute began in 1910, when a proposal was made for the creation of a complete and comprehensive statement of the entire body of American Law — A Corpus Juris. He felt the proposal very much missed the mark, however, and he gave his reasons in a letter to the editor of the *Green Bag*,[47] the periodical in which it had originally appeared. His reasons were, briefly, as follows:

1. The proposal was untimely because American law was passing through a period of radical change and the perspective of a generation was necessary before an accurate statement could be made.

2. There were at present fifty distinct bodies of law, and it would be scientifically false to state a Corpus Juris until uniform codification had removed a larger part of the differences.

3. There were as yet not enough scholars to produce such a work in terms of the ideals set forth.

4. Such a Corpus Juris would permanently fix upon the law an untested and premature juristic analysis and method. "This would be, juristically, a calamity for our law."

As to the latter Wigmore said, "The opinion that it would be a calamity is shared by several well-known legal thinkers with whom I have discussed the matter before now. In making public this firm conviction, I am moved (as those who know me well will understand) only by a sense of respect for the scientific needs of our law, and not by any desire to show disrespect for the learned authors of the project."

In a letter to William Howard Taft and a number of other persons who had endorsed the original proposal by James DeWitt Andrews, Wigmore advanced another objection, namely, that the proposed organization was not properly initiated. On this point Wigmore said

> that it is a mistake for him [Mr. Andrews] to attempt to secure beforehand an endorsement of his theories from a distinguished list of legal brethren who are good-natured enough to sign their names to a plan for a high-purposed Society; and that his purpose can be equally served, to its legitimate extent, by publishing his juristic theories and his other legal views on his own separate responsibility.[48]

Because of such strongly held views Wigmore did not attend the meeting held at the Association of the Bar of the City of New York on May 10, 1922, at which time the Committee on the Establishment of a Permanent Organization for the Improvement of the Law was created. However, he did, with a number of other persons, later join the committee which led to the organization of the American Law Institute.[49] It should be noted that nearly a decade had elapsed since Mr. Andrews's proposal had originally been submitted. The mere passage of time tended to minimize one of Wigmore's objections, and the approach adopted was substantially different from the early one for official codification. At any rate, open opposition had changed to somewhat reluctant approval.

Although Wigmore rendered some assistance in the preparation of the Restatement on Torts and served on the American Law Institute's Advisory Committee on Criminal Justice, his main concern was with the Code of Evidence. In that undertaking Wigmore served as chief consultant to Edward M. Morgan, the reporter,[50] and in this role he received each part of the draft, at every stage, for his comments. It will be recalled that in respect to the subject of evidence the objective was not to restate the law but to formulate a set of rules reflecting what the legal profession thought should be the law.[51]

At the beginning of the undertaking Wigmore submitted six postulates on which to establish a consensus,[52] but when the first tentative draft was submitted, Wigmore took the position that it "failed substantially to conform to any of the six Postulates." However, Morgan and his advisors believed that the rules as submitted did substantially conform to all except the fourth, with which they did not agree.[53]

The chief substantive difference between them was that Wigmore favored a formulation much like his own Code of Evidence — a formulation that would contain "a definite affirmance or repudiation of each concrete rule that has been passed upon in the majority of jurisdictions, rather than a group of generalized statements." Morgan and his advisers, on the other hand, favored a more general set of rules.[54]

Wigmore, no doubt anticipating that there might be differences of opinion, had accepted the assignment as consultant, with the distinct understanding that his name was not to be associated with the code in any way and that, when it was finished, he should be free to express his views as he liked. Accordingly, he put his position on record in an article in the *American Bar Association Journal* in January 1942, entitled "The American Law Institute Code of Evidence Rules: A Dissent."[55] He prefaced his discussion by acknowledging that he might be presumed to be biased in favor of his own code, but stated that nothing in the three years of discussions of the rules had altered his convictions. Having often been reproached in the past as being too radical, he now appeared to be too conservative. Aside from the general objection discussed above and the fact that some of the rules were too radical to be practical, Wigmore objected to the draftsmanship which he said was inappropriate for a legislative measure. In his opinion, this was a sufficient ground for rejecting the institute's code. And it was primarily this objection to which his article was directed.

Although Wigmore acknowledged that some of the ambiguities in the text of the rules were cleared up by the comments that followed, in a draft for legislative purposes, as distinguished from a restatement, one cannot rely on comments to cure shortcomings in drafting. He continued:

> Have not the Institute draftsmen, in thus entering the (to them) novel field of Codification, forgotten the radical and practical difference between a Re-Statement which is a treatise by unofficial jurists, and a Code, which is a self-contained legislative enactment? In a treatise the distinction between text

and comment is little more than a difference of typography. But in a Code, when the text ends, the *law ends*. . . .

This Code, as a legislative proposal, must stand or fall by its text, not by its draftsmen's comments.

Reviewing this cumulation of shortcomings, on the whole might not a cold-hearted-critic describe this Draft Code somewhat as follows: This is an academic composition, meritorious as a record of aspirations, and highly significant as a symptom that Bench and Bar are ready for considerable progress; but not meriting legislative favor, first because its advanced proposals are far too radical at the present time, and secondly because its imperfections in the formulation of the rules render it quite unfit for practical use.[56]

Although a majority of the members of the institute were opposed to Wigmore's views and endorsed the views recommended by Morgan and his assistants,[57] Wigmore was not without support. Statements by both Leon Green and Jerome Hall[58] indicate that they, at best, had been in agreement. In Hall's opinion the American Law Institute's program suffered from the fact that it eliminated differences that were valid and worthwhile and sometimes obtained the support of members who had only superficial knowledge of the subject. Hall also thought that Wigmore should have stated his position on criminal law before withdrawing when he found he was in disagreement with the majority.[59] Wigmore believed that he should have been more frequently consulted and that, if he had been in an eastern law school where the control of the institute lay, he might have been given a greater share in its work. However that may have been, there is no doubt that he disagreed sharply with some of the institute leaders and that such differences may have prevented a greater degree of participation.

In sharp contrast with Wigmore's experience with the American Law Institute was his role in the uniform law movement. Immediately after World War I Wigmore had resumed his active role in the work of the commission. It will be recalled that he received his first appointment to the National Conference of Commissioners on Uniform State Laws in 1908. Through successive appointments he continuously served as a member from Illinois until 1924, when he was not reappointed by Governor Lennington Small. Small's action can no doubt be attributed to the fact that Wigmore had attended a meeting to protest an acquittal of the governor under suspicious circumstances on a charge alleging misconduct during a previous term as state treasurer. Wigmore's service on the commission was revived in 1933 when he was appointed by Governor Henry Horner to fill a vacancy due to the death of Ernest Freund.[60] Thereafter, he represented Illinois until his death in 1943. His most important early assignment was to serve as chairman of the Special Committee on Compacts and Agreements Between States, a responsibility he had first assumed in 1920.[61] Wigmore contended that the interstate compact could and should be more extensively used and that this was one way to minimize the tendency to turn to the federal government for the solution of all problems involving more than one state.[62] As chairman of the committee, he came forward in 1921 with an extensive report dealing with all aspects of the subject.[63] This report recommended the greater use of interstate compacts to deal with the "extraordinary inconvenience and obstruction, due to independence of State Laws and to consequent complexity and disharmony of action or inaction; that these conditions are in urgent need of remedy; and that the most feasible and promising remedy for them seems to be found in the use of inter-State Compacts."[64]

The report was so thorough that the committee found no need for supplementation in subsequent years. In addition, the report was rather widely distributed and was, therefore, presumably available to all to whom it might be of interest.[65] Accordingly, the committee concluded that it had no further role to play in relation to interstate problems. One conclusion in the committee report that Wigmore supported strongly involved the role of the interstate compact in international commercial transactions[66] in areas where the United States government did not have sole authority. Wigmore's work on interstate compacts, although substantial, was but one aspect of his contribution to the work of the National Conference of Commissioners on Uniform State Laws. He was involved with a number of facets of the law of evidence as well as with other aspects of state legislation: acknowledgment of instruments, aeronautics, criminal statistics, depositions and proof of statutes of other states, interstate comity, judicial assistance, property, trusts, and uniform statutory enactments. Wigmore also served on the commission's Committees on Cooperation with the American Law Institute, and the American Institute of Criminal Law and Criminology. He was vice-president of the commission in 1936–37, a member of the executive committee from 1936 to 1940, and chairman of the Executive Committee's Sub-Committee on Scope and Program from 1937 to 1940.[67] During the years 1926 and 1927, when he was not a member of the commission, he was, nevertheless, identified with state legislation as a representative of the American Bar Association.[68]

Wigmore's ardent support of the work of the commissioners not only rested on his firm belief in the process involved but was reinforced by his strong opposition to the development of uniformity by action of the federal government. It is for this reason that he was disturbed by the fact that the state legislatures were not more responsive to the work of the commission. In writing to Nathan W. MacChesney, president of the Conference of Commissioners, in 1925 he said:

> The time has now come when the States should be upbraided severely for not making more systematic and rapid progress in avoiding the threatened Federalization of everything by acting promptly on the voluntary adoption of Uniform Acts. How needful is this stimulus may be seen by the following calculations based on your table. The 30 Acts of the Conference, beginning with the first and ending with the last one enumerated have taken 276 legislative years to adopt. Divided by 30 this gives 9.2 legislative years per State per act on the average; which would give us complete uniformity long after the present generation is gone. Take another point of view. The total legislative acts necessary to make uniform the law on those 30 subjects is 1,500, but only (359) have been passed, or only one-quarter of the necessary number.[69]

The issues of long delay and even disregard of the careful work of the commissioners came to a head when Wigmore, as vice-president, presented in the absence of Alexander Armstrong, the president, four acts to the House of Delegates of the American Bar Association for its routine approval. For the first time in forty-eight years, it declined such prompt approval and referred the matter to the Board of Governors with power to act.[70] This prompted Wigmore to suggest that every act be prefaced by ''a full explanation, both of history and of policy, so as to win, if possible, the support and approval, in principle, of everyone in whose hands the printed act may come.''[71]

During the conference in Cleveland in 1938, Wigmore was taken ill while debating with great intensity certain provisions concerning air law. He was forced to return to Chicago and was accompanied by his friend Nathan MacChesney who said that Wigmore's principal concern was that Mrs. Wigmore, who suffered from high blood pressure, not be alarmed. When MacChesney returned to the conference the next day, he reported that Wigmore had had a ''heart attack'' but that he was comfortable and hopefully would be all right.[72] MacChesney reported a conversation that was indicative of Wigmore's state of mind. Wigmore said he was reminded of the story about a consultation of several physicians concerning the condition of a patient who was very ill. As the patient was eager to know their conclusion, he called a Negro boy he had in his employ and said: ''Sam I want to know what these men really think. They are going to talk downstairs, and you stand behind the curtain and you come back and tell me what they say.'' Presently the boy came back and reported as follows: ''Well, Master, they talked and they talked and they talked, and they argued and they talked and they talked and they argued, and they used a lot of words that I didn't know the meaning of; but they all agreed on one thing, and that was what the autopsy would show.''[73]

Wigmore's disinclination to be overcome by illness was also demonstrated by his eagerness to know what action the commission had taken on his two ''pet projects'' at that time, the Aeronautical Code and the Presumption of Death Act.[74] Happily Wigmore's condition at the moment proved not to be serious and he was soon at work again as usual.

The attitude of the commissioners toward Wigmore's illness is reflected by the statement of the president, Alexander Armstrong, that in making committee appointments Wigmore was to be treated as if he were ''a perfectly well man with an expectancy of some fifty or a hundred years.''[75] Some years later, after her husband's death, Mrs. Wigmore wrote, ''Of all the many associations that he belonged to, the Uniform Law Commissioners was his favorite for it seemed to be founded not on theories but on common sense . . . that all success may attend the work of the Commissioners and that the state legislatures may recognize the worth of their work has always been the hope of John H. and Emma H. V. Wigmore.''[76]

Through the years Wigmore was the central figure in closing the work of the commission each year with fun and song. He often wrote words appropriate for the location of the conference or for the nature of its work that year. Quite appropriately the list of songs each year was called the "Tentative Report of Committee on Uniform Act to Promote Vocalization and Conviviality."[77]

The Cincinnati *Times* gave an account of a musical finale to the 1921 meeting:

> Dean John H. Wigmore of the Northwestern University Law School, Chicago, celebrated the final session of the National Conference of the Commissioners on Uniform State Laws with his "Doxology" which was sung to the tune of "Smiles" with great glee at the end of the last session, even the extremely dignified president, Judge Henry Stackbridge of the highest court of Maryland, joining in with laughter in his voice:
> There are laws which need amendment;
> There are laws which make us sigh;
> There are laws whose obvious intendment
> Is to make us permanently dry:
> There are laws whose legislative craftsmen
> Have been quite deprived of legal sense,
> But the *laws* of which we are the draftsmen
> Make the rest look like thirty cents.[78]

The following song zestfully closed the meeting in San Francisco in 1922.

Ah, me! now I know
Why the judges love us so;
Uniformly less will grow
The law they need to know!
Ah, me! now 'tis plain
Judges bless our widening reign;
We're the gents that took the dents
From out of Precedents![79]

Although Wigmore never sought public office and, apparently, only twice indicated that he would accept such an assignment (in 1920 as solicitor for the Department of State[80] and in 1935 to fill a possible vacancy in the International Court of Justice),[81] he had, as we have seen, a lifelong interest and a desire to participate in public affairs.

It will be recalled that as a youth he had been active in organizing the Municipal Reform League in San Francisco, had participated in the Republican party in Cambridge, and had concerned himself in a number of his early writings with political issues. Indeed, although he was not permanently identified with any political party, Wigmore had no hestitancy about speaking out, either on public issues or political candidates, throughout his life.

Wigmore was of course aware of the tendency of parties to succumb to the control of a small group more concerned with the exploitation of the government, to achieve selfish ends, than with the furtherance of the interests of the public at large. In his opinion, "Such combinations are and always have been based on the philosophy that you can fool all of the people all of the time. But we must cherish rather the courageous and inspired utterance of Abraham Lincoln, who pronounced that principle false."[82]

Nevertheless, because of his conservative attitude on some political issues, it was assumed by many of his friends that he was a Republican. Although he supported his local congressman, a Republican,[83] while living in Evanston, and agreed to assist in securing the attendance of Lord Mac-Millan (when in the United States) at a meeting of the Executive Committee of the Republican Program Committee on a purely informal basis,[84] this apparently was as far as his identification with the Republican party went. Indeed, when in December 1937 he was named in the press as a candidate for the chairmanship of the Republican Program Committee he replied: "In the first place, I have not been in communication with the Republican organization meeting at St. Louis. In the second place, I have no connection with the Republican party. I voted for Roosevelt and Gov. Horner and by all the rules might be rated a Democrat. Furthermore, I am not interested in taking part in any Republican program."[85]

And finally, in March 1937, Wigmore chose to annotate his favorable reference to Franklin D. Roosevelt having gone off "on a hard-earned fishing vacation," by quoting Will Rogers's observation at the time: "Well, Congress thought they knew more about how to run the country than the President, so the President decided to go fishing. The trouble is, the wrong one went fishing."[86] As a matter of fact Wigmore's first vote was cast for Grover Cleveland, and he "supported the principles and the nominees of the [Democratic] party whenever reconcilable"[87] with his convictions. When it came to state and local candidates he certainly made his selections on the basis of merit, being, as he was, a constant opponent of corruption and an advocate of reforms of one kind or another although the reforms were sometimes cast in a conservative pattern.

As to the two major political parties Wigmore had quite definite views, at least in 1921. He felt that the greatest need of the Democratic party was for a leader, and he apparently did not see one in sight. He continued by asking whether there was a leader "who can translate into concrete practical proposals the universal readiness for a progress which shall change without destroying? Anyone who is not so much of a demagogue as Hiram Johnson nor so much of an intellectual as Elihu Root?"

As to the Republican party at that time, his principal concern involved the question of whether the leadership would be in the Senate or in the White House.

The greatest records of party performance in the last generation — Cleveland, Roosevelt, Wilson — have been made by a White House absolutely free. A Senatorial oligarchy, pulling the strings of a puppet, marked the darkest periods of past history for Rome, Italy, France, Germany, England and would signify the same for our history. The greatest political conundrum today is whether we are for the next four years to have the policies of our country guided by a White House absolutely free.[89]

As Wigmore's attitude toward broad social questions inevitably underlay the approaches that he took to specific political issues, his own words in Article VIII of his "Creed for the Nation" provide an important summary of his basic philosophy:

> I believe in the sacredness of human individuality. Each of us must be treated for himself and by himself. And yet in the large mass-relations of government and society the lamentable tendency is to deal with the mass, for good or ill, and to forget the merits or demerits of the individual. . . . Modern psychology reveals the infinite variety of the human soul, yet our popular prejudices are vented alike on all colored men, all aliens, all capitalists, all labor unions, all Jews or gentiles, or Catholics or Protestants, and so on, by classes, as if every man in the class was of identical merit or demerit. It is un-American, un-ethical and unscientific, to support any movement which favors or boycotts or opposes a whole class and makes no discrimination between the individuals in that class.[90]

Wigmore clearly recognized, however, that the rights of individuals should yield where their exercise would impair the rights of others. He gave this recognition an emphatic expression by citing his pronounced but not generally held views on the automobile: "The reckless gunmen and the heedless motorist are equally a public menace. . . . I anticipate with equal calmness the prospect of being assassinated by a hostile burglar while opening my cash-till and by a friendly motorist while crossing the street."[91] How strongly Wigmore felt about the automobile driver is shown by his contention that every motorist should be "responsible in full damages for every death caused, regardless of fault." He also thought that driver's licenses should be revoked for a year on a presumption of negligence. And it is striking to note that a man who was on the whole a political conservative actually worked out and proposed a system of rent control by declaring that the business of renting homes for hire "be impressed with a public interest," placed under the police power of the state, and regulated by an administrative commission.[92] Such a policy, he felt, would protect the home-seeker from extortion and stifle the housing profiteer.

Throughout his life Wigmore demonstrated a complete absence of either religious or racial bias. He mingled freely with persons of all backgrounds and went out of his way to assist Negroes confronted with discrimination, although in his day such assistance was extremely difficult. He considered anti-Semitism "baseless, un-American, cruel and dangerous," but he pointed out that Jewish discrimination against Gentiles had preceded anti-Semitism and had been a stimulus to it. "A taboo on marriage outside of the clan touches the most sacred relations of life, and deep down beneath the surface, modern anti-Semitism is a Gentile reaction against that taboo. Once the Jewish group itself frankly abandons this taboo, anti-Semitism will disappear like fire without fuel; we shall no longer have Jews and Gentiles, only Americans."[93]

It is likely that Wigmore would have been in the vanguard today of those favoring the removal of all barriers based on racial discrimination. The attitude he expressed in 1921 must, therefore, be considered in the context of conditions as they existed at the time. The "social boycott of the colored people as a class [was] ungenerous and dangerous," he said; the Civil War was fought to put an end to "legal discriminations based on color"; and the "white race should for its part recognize that its racial prejudice is ungenerous and snobbish, and should seek not to leave it as an inheritance to the next generation." Wigmore regarded the questions of labor and housing at that time as potential sources of trouble and believed that the colored race "should recognize the unpleasant fact as it exists, and should by rigorous self-restraint avoid precipitating an issue which is at present hopeless, following the noble example of their great leader, Booker Washington."

That Wigmore's concern for the individual did not lead him to the conclusion, common among the conservatives with whom he was often classed politically, that the less government the better was demonstrated by an address he gave to the Chicago Bar Association in March 1937 entitled "Bureaucracy and Dictatorship: What Are They? and Why?"[94] Wigmore began by isolating three notable features of American political life: absenteeism — "the unwillingness of competent citizens to undertake public office as a public duty and career";[95] parasitism — the tendency to think of government "merely for personal purely selfish profit"; and sycophantism — the tendency of any person elected to public office to act in such a manner as to secure his re-election.[96] Wigmore claimed that although not all citizens exhibited these tendencies the net result was detrimental, especially upon the legislative branch where "parliamentary government has virtually broken down — judged by the standard of efficiency." European countries, he observed, were no better in developing political character.[97]

Wigmore also discussed the words "liberty," "democracy," "bureaucracy," and "dictatorship." The ideas developed by John Stuart Mill in his essay on *Liberty*, (in which Wigmore had thoroughly believed) were, he felt, no longer political facts. Since Mill's day a vast network of regulations had been placed on the state statute books. The federal legislation under attack was not essentially new. The real question was whether the federal government should undertake such regulation of liberty.[98]

In discussing "democracy" Wigmore called attention to the wide range of governmental forms that the term covered on federal, state, and local levels. Wigmore felt that it was the Italian leader Giuseppe Mazzini who had put forth the most apt definition: "Democracy is the progress of all under the *leadership* of the wisest and best."[99]

In dealing with the term "bureaucracy" Wigmore used the term in its orthodox sense as "the exercise of power by the *Executive* and his administrative departments, instead of by the legislative branch." Wigmore stated emphatically his contention that, in this sense and on the basis of his extended experience in Washington, bureaucracy was "far more efficient than the legislative branch."[100]

The word "dictatorship" Wigmore suggested, contained an implication that is apt to be overlooked. Democracies do need leaders, and it is regrettable that the development of leaders has not been encouraged because of the fear of dictatorship.[101]

In this connection, it is interesting to recall Wigmore's impression of Mussolini's very early efforts.

> We spent three months in Italy, and every day I read the Popolo d'Italia, the Fascist newspaper, and talked with Italians of all classes. Fascism has saved Italy — there is no doubt about that. It began as a union of defense against bolshevism and the sabotage of factories. It showed its capacity for greater political duties. Last December, it came into power. It has suppressed beggary and petty graft. It has sent everybody to work. It has cut down public extravagance and restored the national finances. Mr. Mussolini may be termed the Roosevelt of Italy. He has been called a dictator; he is hardly that. But you would have some idea of what Fascism means in Italy if you could imagine the American Legion, the American Federation of Labor, the American Farmers' Federation, and the Rotary Clubs, all merged into one nation-wide, semi-military organization, with our Charles Dawes at the head![102]

Wigmore's low regard for the role played by Congress, which he originally based upon its performance during World War I, continued without abatement. Feeling as he did, it is not surprising that a characteristically forthright statement should find its way into his "Creed" as Article XI.

> I BELIEVE that the Legislatures of America, compared with all other bodies of team-workers having a specific service to render, are the most inefficient bodies of men in all America. Their job is the worst done job in the Nation. And among them the most inefficient of all is the Federal Congress. It is not because of dishonesty, — not because of individual incompetency. It is because of four things, — excessive egoism, subservience to popular opinion, anxiety to appear as public saviors, and antiquated methods. The egoism holds back needful legislation endlessly until each individual member is satisfied to approve. The subservience deprives members of any courage of personal conviction on public policies. The anxiety to appear as public saviors drives Congressmen to spend most of their time in investigating the shortcomings of the Executive Departments, who are the men that really do things for the Nation; and this leaves Congress little time to devote to its own proper duty of Legislation. And the methods are so antiquated, that no business house which refused in like manner to improve its methods could survive for thirty days. The first three qualities are perhaps irremediable. The fourth will be remedied when a bold genius comes to Washington who will break the idols of tradition and lead the Congress to reform itself, as the best and the first measure for reforming the Country.[103]

Since few public issues stirred Wigmore more deeply, some additional examples of his attitude toward Congress are worth citing.

When Congress had before it the codification of the laws of the United States, and the House had already acted affirmatively, Wigmore waited four years for Senate action and then could keep silent no longer. In a typically Wigmorian editorial entitled, "Are Senate Delays of Justice Due to Rules that Safeguard Debate or to Rules that Fortify Egotism?,"[104] he cited a number of examples of unreasonable delay or complete inaction, in disregard of the public interest. He concluded, "The Senate today, in its rules and in the consciousness of its members, is an iron-clad fraternity *bent on becoming the primary organ of national government* to the exclusion of the House and the executive."[105]

In another editorial comment Wigmore asserted that, because of the *"single senatorial veto"* and the *"grand jury inquisitions of senatorial committees,"* the "most serious single drawback to national happiness and progress today, in the realm of law, is the legislative inefficiency of the federal Senate."[106]

Wigmore was incensed about the abusive treatment often accorded witnesses appearing before congressional committees. In another editorial comment he condemned the practice of some congressional committees in assuming the role of a grand jury and abusing witnesses. For this propensity to investigate, Wigmore coined the word "scopotropism" which he justified as follows:

> A "tropism," the medical dictionary tells us, is the "innate tendency of an organism to react in a definite manner to external stimuli," and the root "scop —," of course, signifies "to look, to inquire, to spy into"; and a "scopotropism" is an incurable mania to investigate for the mere sake of investigating. The "external stimulus" which causes this particular Senatorial tropismic reaction is any notorious event out of which a Senator can obtain political capital by posing as a public patriot.[107]

Commenting on Wigmore's coined word, one newspaper wrote, "That's one advantage professors have over those who know only how to swear."[108]

Wigmore also pointed out that to a large extent many of the same criticisms applied to the state legislatures. Indeed, he declared that "the breakdown of legislative efficiency is one of the marked political phenomena of our times."[109] In order to alleviate the situation in the states Wigmore proposed a model constitutional amendment.

Briefly stated, the amendment provided that the governor alone could convene the legislature, either as a whole or in part, make administrative appointments from among the legislators, and appoint an advisory legislative drafting board. The amendment also provided for a federal House of Governors in which the governor would have legislative power, subject to subsequent ratification by the legislature. The Supreme Court, under the amendment, would have the power to make rules of procedure for stages of litigation and would be authorized to appoint an advisory Judicial Council. Finally, the attorney general, as superintendent of the administration of law and justice, would, among other things, make inquiries into the need for proposed legislation and the effect of existing legislation, when requested to do so by the governor.[110]

Another approach to the problems of state government in which Wigmore took a great interest was the short ballot, which in his opinion, had worked well at the national level from the beginning:

We groan under the duty of voting ignorantly for a long list of twenty to one hundred offices at each local election. We have as much chance of correct selection as a blind man would have at a restaurant in choosing from a menu card handed to him by a deaf waiter. Let us reduce the state elective offices to three, governor, senator, assemblyman, and the local officers to two, mayor and councilman. This would reduce the total of elective offices to nine. The short ballot would be as great a boon in state and local government as it has been in national government.[111]

In spite of his varied and absorbing interests Wigmore never lost touch with events in his own state. One of the problems to which he applied his zeal for reform was the drafting of a constitution for Illinois which was submitted to the voters for ratification. Wigmore was greatly concerned because the ordinary voter, as well as many of his friends, was disposed to vote against its adoption because of dissatisfaction with some particular provision. He said the question before the voters was, "Is this proposed new Constitution *better than the Constitution under which we now live?*" And his answer was, "Yes — far better — *fifty years better!*" He concluded, "Let us be grateful for the good things offered us by the gods . . . and then let us proceed to concentrate on the single improvements which to each faction of us seem most important. For the new Constitution's cardinal boon is the readiness and speed with which change of institutions is henceforth to be permitted to the people of Illinois."[112]

Nor did Wigmore neglect the city of Chicago, to which he was so greatly attached. He did not hesitate, however, to make a critical appraisal. In 1921 he said that its excellent location was "the only thing about it that is yet just right. It is still dirty with smut and smoke, noisy with needless noise, congested by inadequate traffic ways, disunited by inadequate commercial and industrial rivalries, stinted in public donations, infested with unpunished criminals, tardy in solving its civic problems, commonplace in political methods, and weak in aggressive courageous leadership of good causes."[113]

Wigmore favored Chicago's commercial and industrial supremacy but contended that the city should also be a center of legal research. The Bologna of one thousand years before "still rings down the ages for two things — its sausage, and its law school. Why not also Chicago."[114]

So much for Wigmore's active concern as a citizen at different levels of government. What was his attitude toward the controversial question of the relationship between the federal government and the states? His loyal support of the work of the Commissioners on Uniform State Laws rested on his conviction that uniformity should be achieved by cooperation between the states and not through coercion or by federal legislation. He felt equally strongly that federal power could not be marshaled to solve issues that did not attract popular support in some states: woman's suffrage, child labor, equal rights for women, and prohibition, for example. Although in 1915 he was not in favor of state-wide prohibition in Illinois,[115] in 1921 he accepted federal legislation upon the adoption of the Eighteenth Amendment, believing that "on the whole" it was a good thing and had come to stay, in spite of the fact that it became law without the consent of a majority of the citizens. He recognized the cynical attitude of many toward the law, but he thought "genuine and general abstinence" was not to be expected until the younger generation "that knew not Bacchus" grew to manhood.[116] Nevertheless, like many of his contemporaries he was ultimately disturbed by "an enactment which had convulsed the national life for more than a decade past," and by 1933 he was not in favor of dealing with the problem at the national level.[117] On the other hand, not long thereafter when the depression deepened, Wigmore was favorably disposed toward the NRA Codes,[118] formulated under the National Industrial Recovery Act, though they attempted to regulate industry on a nationwide basis and regardless of state boundaries.

As we shall see later in this volume, Wigmore's stand on the extension of federal power was put to a crucial test in the field of aviation, in which he was greatly interested. From his own experience he knew at first hand that the federal government had to exercise broad regulatory powers, yet to him this did not mean that it should assume responsibility in respect to matters which were of purely state or local concern. He said:

> I am opposed to any form of State aid by the Federal Government. The main trouble with the country today is that the States and the Municipalities have lost their backbone and have not the courage to perform their own constitutional duties. If a State or a Metropolis wants to have air traffic patronize its locality, let it devise its own facilities by its own efforts and finances; if it does not do so, it deserves to lose the traffic. Moreover any of these recent forms of State aid which give the Federal Government a grip on State control and thus tend to centralize all administration and initiation at Washington, are ill-advised.[119]

When the national government, under Franklin D. Roosevelt, attempted to deal with the depression through congressional action, Wigmore attempted to justify his reluctant support:

> I was deeply impressed four years ago, in the former drought of the Middle Western States, 1933 and 1934, in a table published in the Chicago Tribune which showed that there were thirteen states badly affected by the drought, but eleven of those states, in the January meeting of their legislatures, passed resolutions, without having appropriated one single dollar to help their own people in their own states, begging the Federal Congress to do something for their people. I remember Kentucky was one of the states.
>
> It is that attitude, in my conviction, which has led to the situation since 1933. We talk about the inalienable rights of the states, but we have forgotten all about the inalienable duties of the states. In my opinion, it has been the duty of the states, all along, to take care of their own miseries and their own problems, and you know what condition many states' legislatures are in. They have not done it. That situation having arisen, it was inevitable, as a force of nature, that, if leadership arose in the federal region, something should be done to fill up the No Man's Land which the states could have occupied and did not occupy.[120]

Wigmore's lifelong interest in public affairs eventually impelled him to serve the federal government in the role of a specialist in the field of air law.[121] He had previously engaged in many activities that had prepared him for this departure.

In view of the fact that Wigmore had pioneered in so many fields it is not surprising that he recognized the new challenge created by the development of air transportation and the need to cope with the many difficult legal problems that it would be creating. Wigmore's response to this challenge was the establishment in 1929 of the Air Law Institute at the Northwestern University Law School shortly before his retirement as dean. Frederick D. Fagg, Jr., a new member of the Law School faculty and a specialist in the field, was appointed managing director. His appointment was a notable example of Wigmore's propensity to give encouragement and support to a promising young man. In this case, as will become apparent, the younger man played an important part in providing a new role for Wigmore just as his retirement as dean was freeing him from the responsibilities of the deanship.

The funds needed to launch this venture and operate it for three years were secured by Wigmore. The initial subscribers included the Daniel Guggenheim Fund for the Promotion of Aeronautics, and Robert R. McCormick, Earle H. Reynolds, Edward D'Ancona, Elias Mayer, Melvin Emerich, and Martin Straus.[122] Thereafter the institute was supported by Northwestern University, and despite the rigors of the depression years the basic program was kept alive.[123] Wigmore was not just the promoter of the Air Law Institute — he followed with interest its cooperation with developing state legislation, the activities of the state aviation commission, and the work of the recently organized National Association of State Aviation Officials.

One of the objectives of the institute was to develop, on an international basis, a special collection of books and other materials dealing with the broad legal aspects of the field.

> The whole body of property laws must be reconsidered with regard to the air. Everything that is happening on earth soon will be rehappening, under different conditions, in the air. The law, as it relates to aviation, is chock full of problems that must be worked out. These concern the liability of carriers, whether the owner of a ship or the pilot is responsible, the licensing of pilots and airplanes and other problems. It took 200 years to work out the liability of common carriers. Similar laws must be worked out for air carriers.[124]

The institute sought to fulfill its role as a clearinghouse for information on aeronautical law by establishing the *Journal of Air Law*, which issued its first number in January 1930.[125] *The Journal of Radio Law*, which the Northwestern Law School also established under the sponsorship of the Air Law Institute and which began publication in April 1931, was discontinued with the issue of October 1932, which completed volume 2. Wigmore contributed to the *Journal of Air Law* from time to time and served as associate editor from 1935 until 1942, when publication was suspended. Publication was resumed in 1947.

In the summer of 1930 the institute offered the first international course of lectures on air law in connection with a two-week program for lawyers and law students during the regular Law School summer session. The course of instruction included lectures on American, English, French, German, Italian, and international law by domestic and foreign experts, as well as round-table discussions.

However, Wigmore did not confine his interest in air law to the Air Law Institute. He was a vigorous participant in the controversial discussions of air-law questions in both the American Bar Association and the National Conference of Commissioners on Uniform State Laws,[126] and he had several tours of duty as an advisor to the federal government on aeronautical questions.

At the suggestion of Frederick D. Fagg, Jr., who was at the time secretary of the National Association of State Aviation Officials, Wigmore was invited to serve as an advisor to the Federal Aviation Commission, a five-man body appointed to study aviation problems, and to recommend a national policy. To Wigmore this was a new challenge, and he gladly accepted. He knew little of the physical laws of aerodynamics, but he thoroughly understood the economic and legal problems confronting the nation because of the rapid development of aviation. He himself had never flown, not because of concern for his life but because of the effect on his income-protection for Mrs. Wigmore.

The members of the commission soon realized that Wigmore's eminence was matched by his competence, and they were more than willing to have him as an advisor and usually accepted his advice on controversial matters of law. In addition, his name brought support and prestige to congressional legislation embodying the commission's recommendations.

When the commission members assembled to report to President Roosevelt, they were considerably surprised when the president requested a private interview with Wigmore beforehand. Afterward Wigmore explained that the president had discussed his own legal education and particularly his difficulties with the law of evidence.

The commission recommended the creation of an independent agency of government to deal with both the economic and safety aspects of civil air transportation — a recommendation they assumed would be acceptable to the president. It was, therefore, with consternation that the group, as they leaned forward in their congressional balcony seats, heard the president say, "In this recommendation [for an Air Commerce Commission] I am unable to concur."[127]

Instead, the president recommended that the authority be vested in the Interstate Commerce Commission. Thus the work to which Wigmore had contributed was quickly shelved for the ensuing three years.

On February 2, the Federal Aviation Commission offices were closed, and planes and trains leaving Washington were scattering its staff throughout the country. The experience, though disappointing, had given Wigmore an opportunity to renew many friendships in Washington, and he had demonstrated that he could encompass the intricacies of a new and difficult field at seventy years of age. He also greatly enjoyed working with the young and vigorous aviation group.[128] But not everyone with whom Wigmore worked in Washington was imbued with such a youthful outlook. Of one man who was inclined to be obstructive, Fagg gives this account, "I remember so well the piercing look of Dean JHW as he examined the directory chart in the corridor. As he stood there under his iron hat (the derby worn in D.C.), I heard him say: 'The man's mind is filled with *dubitative* bugaboos!' For a fellow who wouldn't permit himself an oath, this was going far."[129]

In order that the two Chicago legal advisors (Wigmore and Fagg) might have convenient quarters during their stay in Washington (December and January, 1934–35) Wigmore arranged for a twin bedroom at the Cosmos Club. According to Fagg, Wigmore

> explained that his choice of quarters was due to the fact that this exclusive hostelry served "a *fourth* pancake" for breakfast, but his companion, who knew his habit of eating sparingly at all times, was not hoodwinked. . . . the Cosmos Club offered a meeting place for scientists in many fields of endeavor. Most seemed to know the Chicago jurist.[130]

For Wigmore, as for many others, the Cosmos Club did, indeed, play an important role, and he only gave up his membership, which extended over a period of twenty years, in 1941, when it was evident that he would no longer be able to travel.

Fred Fagg also gives us some interesting personal glimpses of Wigmore's life while in Washington on this assignment.

> JHW had a sweet tooth and, around midnight, would suggest a stroll and a cup of hot chocolate. Learning that JHW avoided movies, and learning also that there was an excellent feature picture at a nearby theatre, FDF lured him inside one evening just as the newsreel started. JHW sat quietly through the parade of current events and, just as the feature was about to start, exclaimed: "Well, that's that. Now let's go get a cup of chocolate!"[131]

But midnight was by no means necessarily the end of his workday. "Many were the two and three a.m. awakenings, to find JHW writing home to his 'Emma'."[132] Mrs. Wigmore had been reluctant to see her husband go to Washington and thought he was overworking at a task that was not sufficiently rewarding, for a man of his achievements particularly, since it did not add appreciably to his income, which needed replenishing.[133] She believed that once he had given the much younger Fred Fagg, for whom the assignment promised a real opportunity, the valuable initial support he needed, her husband should come home.[134] Meanwhile she was no doubt happy about the companionship of the two, and in one of her letters she wrote, "Tell Mr. Fagg that I have paid him the highest compliment in my power by handing to him my privilege of taking care of you."[135]

The new day was always introduced by "setting-up" exercises so vigorous that the "younger legal advisor pondered the fact that his own earlier participation in college contact-sports had not resulted in matching qualities of endurance."[136]

Soon after Wigmore's arrival in Washington he and Fred Fagg went to hear an argument before the Supreme Court.

> Promptly at the appointed hour, the members of the court filed in. The justices seated themselves, glanced around the room and, one by one, noted the presence of the author of the great treatise on the Law of Evidence. There were rustlings, pages were summoned, and scribbled messages were delivered. JHW read each one and then handed it over to FDF. Invitations to tea or dinner were sent from seven members of the court. FDF was so intrigued by the interruption of the work of that august body — in recognition of its distinguished visitor — that he could not later recall how many justices were present. He was alert enough, however, to realize that — if he needed proof of the eminence of the Dean Emeritus of the NU School of Law — he had received it in full measure.
>
> JHW received his welcome with customary modesty, later conceded his gratification, kept his tea and dinner dates, and returned to his duties in Chicago with a feeling of warm satisfaction arising from his first Washington aviation experience — despite the fact that the President of the United States had kicked some of his handiwork in the teeth.

Although the airlines had established a new safety record, four passengers lost their lives in scheduled airline flights from January to June, 1935. One of them was Senator Bronson M. Cutting, who was killed on May 6, 1935. The Senate sprang into action, and a subcommittee of the Senate Committee on Commerce was authorized to "do something as quickly as possible."[137] Very soon after this committee was organized Wigmore and Fagg were again asked to serve as advisors, and regular train trips started to Washington once more. Although the immediate duty of the committee was to determine the cause of the accident, the two legal advisors set to work on the long-range assignment of preventing similar accidents in the future and examining the role of the Bureau of Air Commerce and providing valuable historical perspective. The "prestige of Wigmore slowed the forces that were eager for 'immediate results'." "When JHW and FDF returned to Chicago they were convinced that, when the proper time came, there were at least five Senators who had a good understanding of the basic problems of national aviation policy. The second Washington tour of duty ended in the Spring of 1936 and JHW had enjoyed every minute of it."[138]

In June 1936, Wigmore and Fagg were invited by Assistant Secretary of Commerce Johnson to come to Washington to make a thorough revision of the federal aviation regulations, and they began work on June 16 on an assignment that they expected would take a year. On this occasion, Mrs. Wigmore accompanied her husband.

While weeks passed during which the existing regulations were being collected, Wigmore and Fagg agreed upon the scope and form of the new regulations. In this work Wigmore's unusual organizational ability and experience were of great value. It was a substantial undertaking, and it was seventeen months later when the first twenty-seven chapters of the Civil Aeronautics Regulations were issued on November 1, 1937. Other chapters were added at a later date, and in 1938, less then a year later, the Civil Aeronautics Board was established by law. Since the board adopted the Bureau Code verbatim, it was unwittingly assumed by many that the board itself was its originator. While in Washington on this tour of duty Wigmore was also concerned with negotiations for transoceanic air lines and with the drafting of the State Uniform Aviation Liability Act.

Fred Fagg gives us this further insight into Wigmore's role:

> Perhaps there are some persons who think of JHW as a ''lone wolf'' (and certainly his outstanding publications in many diverse fields attest his personal capacity) but few realize what a wonderful ''team-worker'' he was. In the long venture of the air regulations, JHW joined hands with engineers, pilots, airline presidents, Bureau technicians, and countless other persons, in making possible a body of revised rules for the safe conduct of aeronautical affairs. His ability, enthusiasm, capacity for long hours of fruitful work, continually boosted the productivity and morale of all his co-workers. No man was more respected in Department of Commerce halls. No man was held in greater affection by his colleagues there.[139]

That Wigmore enjoyed the experience is evident from the words that Mrs. Wigmore inscribed on the flyleaf of Wigmore's copy of the *Civil Air Regulations*: ''Some of the Happiest days of Harry's life were spent . . . in Washington . . . on this work.''[140]

Finally, it should be noted that Wigmore was delighted when the bill he helped draft in 1934–35 [the Lea Bill] for the Federal Aviation Commission was at last taken off the shelf and its best features incorporated in new proposals. This time President Roosevelt agreed to reverse his recommendation of February 1935, and he signed the Civil Aeronautics Act of 1938.

As in World War I days, Wigmore's counsel and advice were sought in connection with many matters not directly concerned with his specific official assignment. And ''so it went in many fields of endeavor where few, if any traces'' of his ''footprints may be found.''[141]

But life in Washington was not all work, even for someone as tirelessly dedicated as Wigmore. He and his wife enjoyed many social events and had an opportunity to renew many friendships. On one occasion, after they had accepted an invitation by the Faggs to spend an evening at the Normandy Farm Inn in Rockville, Wigmore dropped into Fagg's office on the preceding morning to express his regret that since Emma was indisposed they would not be able to come. According to Fagg, Wigmore was evasive and ill at ease, but at any rate it was clear that the engagement was off. However, when Fagg called Mrs. Wigmore to express his regret and wish her well she said, ''I'm fine — but *Harry's got the chiggers!*''[142] The secret was out. Mrs. Wigmore explained that after sitting on Wigmore's brother's lawn in Virginia the day before, her husband had come away with the unwanted trespassers!

That evening they did join the Faggs for the drive out to Maryland, and as a way of teasing Wigmore for his failure to "confess his sins," Fagg and Mrs. Wigmore spent the evening discussing how much fun it would be to eat outdoors at Normandy Farm. Whether Wigmore squirmed from the chiggers already acquired or from the prospect of a new attack is in doubt, but his blood pressure dropped appreciably when he found that the four-some were to eat at a table indoors near one of the fireplaces. Soon afterward the Wigmores left for a visit to The Hague, from which Fagg received a post card with this laconic comment: "Chiggers gone. Hide also. JHW."

When Wigmore died in 1943, Mrs. Wigmore offered his beloved friend and collaborator Fred Fagg the academic gown he had "worn so jauntily and with such distinction." For Fagg, its significance was evident:

> That resplendent silk gown has been worn by its recipient — sans the ermine appurtenances and other decorations accorded JHW by numerous foreign universities . . . at every Northwestern or University of Southern California commencement exercise since 1943. . . . Who really sees all the facets of a diamond? Who really comprehends all the evidences of genius? The wearer of the gown humbly concluded that he should be most grateful for the limited number of days he had been privileged to share with a good and great man. He was extremely pleased . . . that he had not flunked his first JHW course in "Elementary Law."

Although a good deal can be said with certainty about Wigmore's attitude toward religion generally, it is more difficult to pinpoint the nature of his personal beliefs and convictions. It will be recalled that he was brought up in the Episcopal church under the tutelage of parents who were ardent Episcopalians. However, his affiliation with that church ended when he reached maturity. Although Wigmore went to Japan under the auspices of the Unitarian church and did a considerable amount of writing on religious topics as a part of his responsibility to that group, there is no evidence of any deep commitment.

Just why Wigmore did not continue his connection with the Episcopal church, must, in the absence of any definite information on the subject, remain largely a matter of speculation. It does, however, seem likely that the intolerant attitude of both of his parents on that subject, and the complete inability of Wigmore's mother to willingly permit him to develop his own identity and independence from parental control were significant factors. Certainly the young Wigmore had to make a complete break with parental authority (and, as we have seen, this was most difficult) not only in respect to religion but also in his selection of both bride and vocation. His courtships of Emma Vogl had brought him in touch with a family who were Unitarians and whose views were much less dogmatic than the views of his parents. Also, his wife's family accepted him heartily, recognized his potentialities, and supported him in his efforts toward goals of his own choosing. In any event, Wigmore apparently avoided any permanent prejudice in respect to the exercise of parental authority, however much he may have been disturbed at the time. In 1921 he believed that the "most marked danger sign of an approach of pure state communism was not government regulation but the "subtle influence of the American parents"[143] in abdicating parental responsibility and authority and leaving more and more to the schools and the state.

We know very little about Wigmore's attitude toward organized religion during his early manhood, but we do know that after their marriage neither he nor Mrs. Wigmore was ever formally affiliated with any religious group. In 1911, when writing to Holmes about the growth of Harvard, he said, "The traditional asceticism of the Scholar has gone; and Harvard will experience the fate of success, like the Church; it will grow fat and sleek, and cease to serve."[144] By 1921, when Wigmore was fifty-eight years of age, he set forth some very definite views on both Protestantism and Catholicism. Of Protestantism Wigmore said:

I BELIEVE that Protestantism is no longer a religion; it has become a merely social institution. Ecclesiastically, it represents self-determination gone to seed. Four centuries of religious self-determination have ended in placing the individual pastor at the mercy of the individual congregation, both financially and morally. Few Protestants have any genuine religion. They give much money to teach the heathen to say prayers, but they do not say their prayers themselves. Every other religionist but the Protestant says his prayers in public. The rationalization of the creeds has relaxed the intellectual and moral control of the Church as a body over the religion of the individual. What Protestantism now needs is organization, amalgamation of the united forces of its separate sects. Thus alone can Protestantism as a religion regain its intellectual and moral power. And when it has done this, and then only, can it compete with Catholicism. But if it should do this, it will not be essentially different from Catholicism.[145]

And of Catholicism:

I BELIEVE that the Catholic religion is the most endurable and admirable form of Christianity, — strong enough to lift the weak, loose enough to satisfy the independent, broad enough to admit all, and devout enough to satisfy the universal religious emotions. But the Catholic religion is universal while the Catholic ecclesiasticism is Roman, and that is its one great defect. Its government is centralized in a foreign country, under 72 men, only 3 of whom are Americans and 50 of whom are Italians. That the religious life and actions of the American nation should be dictated from a foreign country is not natural nor wholesome. The political intrigues of Europe and the world inevitably affect the policies of the Roman Pontificate in its mandates to America; and thus religion becomes subservient to politics, which is un-American. The American Catholic Church must be totally independent of Rome, if it is to achieve its just position in American religious life.

Although these appraisals are not altogether objective they do help to explain, if not necessarily justify, his failure to give his formal support to any religious group. However, there is certainly nothing in them that suggests opposition to the fundamental teachings of Christ, and his behavior was regarded by his friends as reflecting to a high degree the life of a Christian. In the first place, his interest in the Bible was substantial and enduring. Not only did he give the New Testament that he received in 1883 the most meticulous study, but over and over again he called particular passages of both the New and Old Testaments to the special attention of his students. In 1914 he said that the aim of a college education should be "to develop wholesome traits of character and mind every gentleman and Christian should have." [146] In his study of foreign languages he translated the New Testament from Welsh and Gaelic.

In their social relationships the Wigmores numbered among their best friends ministers, priests, bishops, and other religious leaders. From time to time, Wigmore appeared as a speaker at one church or another, and he had a most friendly relationship with the Garrett Biblical Institute on the Evanston campus of Northwestern. An example of the warm friendships that developed with church dignitaries is reflected in the following passage of a letter from Bishop William F. McDonald at a time when he was about to leave Evanston for a rest to recover his health. "I cannot go away without telling you how dear your friendship is and will ever be; how grateful I am for kindnesses beyond measure, and how I thank God for the relations which have come to me during the dozen years of my life here. They are beyond price." [147] Even in his music Wigmore did not ignore the religious emphasis. He composed the music for "Wider Wider Yet," a processional, and "While Shepherds Watched Their Flocks," both of which he included in his *Lyrics of a Lawyer's Leisure.* "Wider and Wider Yet" was also included in the Sunday school hymnal of the Methodist Episcopal church.

If Wigmore had any religious preference it was apparently for Catholicism. He was one of the promoters of the Red Mass for lawyers celebrated in the Holy Name Cathedral in Chicago on the feast day of St. Thomas More, and he wanted this revival of the old English and French custom to be "a general celebration, semi-official for the bar and bench, as nearly all-inclusive as it could be made." [148] Indeed he once hoped to secure the attendance of a "few Rabbis . . . preferably venerable old men, with beards, who should sit in the front pews." He had a strong interest in St. Ives as the patron saint of the law, and this will be discussed in some detail in the following chapter. Not long before Wigmore's death, when Nathan Mac-Chesney was discussing his own religious views, Wigmore said to Mac-Chesney's surprise, "If I were a Catholic I should be quite content; I would never leave it." [149] He had indicated to his friend Edward Harriman, however, that he and Mrs. Wigmore did not believe in personal immortality but did believe in some relationship between the human and the divine. [150]

Albert Kocourek recorded that Wigmore had "attempted to sound the depths of metaphysics" as a substitute for religion only to conclude that he "was not congenitally apt to much of that material." Kocourek concluded "We know of no man of like or comparable eminence in the modern age whose whole life was so purely an embodiment of what is best and most workable in Christian doctrine as applied to an industrial era." [151] Harriman, whose close friendship with Wigmore was not diminished when he left the Law School to go East to practice, made this appraisal: "It has been said that all sensible men are of one religion; but what that religion is, they never tell. If there is any truth in that statement, the Wigmores undoubtedly shared that mysterious religion, to which they were sincerely devoted; for their conduct was most exemplary, and they could show anyone their faith by their works." [152]

As was indicated at the beginning of this chapter, consideration has been given to Wigmore's post-World War I activities concerned with the national scene. In scope, his interests were so broad that, for convenience, the discussion has been divided into several topics: law, public service, and religion.

16
The World Community

IIIIIIIIIIC3IIIIIIIIIIC3IIIIIIIIIIC3IIIIIIIIIIC3IIIIIIIIIIC3IIIIIIIIIIC3IIIIIIIIIIC3IIIIIIIIIIC3IIIIIIIIIIC3IIIIIIIIIIC3IIIIIIIIIIC3IIIIIIIIIIC3IIIIIIIII

In the last two chapters attention has been given to a number of Wigmore's
post-World War I activities — involving matters largely of domestic concern. Attention must now be given to his role in a much larger arena — the
world community. In this connection two questions inevitably arise. What
were the effects of the war and his heightened sense of patriotism on his
wide-ranging interests? Did Wigmore emerge with a highly nationalistic
outlook and the isolationism that so generally followed? That this was a
common expectation is suggested by the recollection of Stuart S. Ball:

> A few of us who took a course under the Dean innocuously labeled Interna-
> tional Law II saw a side of his thinking which was very surprising to us. At that
> time (the middle 1920s) the disillusionment which followed World War I had
> made college students especially susceptible to propaganda about the "mer-
> chants of death," the presumptive falsehood of all atrocity stories, the inno-
> cence of our former enemies, the guilt of our allies, and the moral wrongness of
> military training in any form. To some degree most of us were influenced in our
> thinking by the prevalence of these dogmas. To that extent we looked upon the
> Dean, with a feeling of tolerant superiority, as a reactionary. He was proud of
> his contribution to the Army in the war, and of the rosette of the Legion of
> Honor.[1] He was pleased when he was called by his wartime title of "Colonel."
> He maintained a touch of near-military discipline in his classrooms. He adopted
> and praised the military practice of numbering the paragraphs of his papers. All
> these things which we saw helped to stamp him in our minds as a lover of the
> pomp and circumstance of war, and as an emotional ultranationalist.
> The Dean's approach to the subject-matter of the course in International Law
> II was proof of the callowness of this judgment. The course was a study of the
> League of Nations, its history, its structure, and the effectiveness of its
> functioning. Under the Dean's guidance, we who took the course found to our
> amazement that the League was at that time, contrary to general belief, a
> functioning and vital organization, not on the broad scale of its initial concep-
> tion, but an effective start to the solution of many international problems. This
> was the Dean's view; and he convinced us.[2]

What the students did not know and what even many of Wigmore's
friends and associates only vaguely appreciated was the extraordinary

breadth of Wigmore's background and outlook. His three-year stay in Japan had been followed by many summers spent in Europe, "some years settling down in a quiet small town and studying the language of the country. Other years they travelled about rather freely and more than once were hosts for the vacation trip to some couple of whom they were fond, and who could not otherwise have had such a pleasurable event."[3]

Wigmore's secretary was a guest on a trip to Scotland and England. She recalls that

> They had a certain routine of their own. They always had their breakfast brought to their room (at home or traveling) and did not appear until later in the morning while traveling. Hence a guest could take his or her breakfast downstairs in the hotel and go out on private expeditions. We would meet at lunch or at an hour necessary for any planned trip for the day. In the afternoon they usually rested for a short while before dinner. Then a dinner meeting and reading in the evening if a theatre party (or some such entertainment) was not planned.[4]

Wigmore's propensity for travel invariably led to the study of maps, and each country visited was studied in advance: its language, history, and the places worthy of attention, including art galleries, churches, universities, courthouses, and other public buildings.[5] His travels reflected his thoroughness in preparing for any assignment he undertook. The trips enriched his store of information and his understanding of various peoples and their laws and institutions and also enabled him to develop a wide circle of friends with whom he maintained an extensive correspondence. According to his secretary, "He used to read his foreign language on the train, whispering the words to himself, in spite of looks from the other passengers (and I really do not believe that he saw the looks, as he was thoroughly engaged in what he was doing, but he wouldn't have cared if he had seem them)."[6]

On one occasion a fellow passenger finally asked Wigmore why he pronounced the words out loud. When Wigmore explained that he remembered the words much better that way, the passenger said, "I am an Egyptian butcher." To this Wigmore responded, "You are exactly the person I want. I have heard that Arabic and Egyptian are pronounced about the same. I will count one, two, three, etc., in Arabic and you do it in Egyptian." When the two pronunciations agreed, Wigmore was delighted.[7]

> When he [Wigmore] decided to go to Morocco and Algeria, he thought he should know something about Arabic, — so he started studying alone from a French-Arabic grammar (there being no English-Arabic grammars), and he was in his seventies at the time! Then through the French Consul in Chicago, he got in touch with a priest in a Syrian church in Michigan City, Indiana, and paid him to come to Chicago[8] once a week and give him an hour of spoken Arabic. This went on for about two years so that he could at least read the titles of law books and make a presentable effort at polite conversation with jurists over there.[9]

Upon entering Wigmore's office the priest would bow very low and utter some such phrase as "Allah be with you," and Wigmore would respond in Arabic.[10]

The war effort did not narrow his outlook in any significant way. He not only continued to foster international cooperation, but he was equipped to play a constructive role in its development and opposed the kind of nationalism that was an inevitable obstacle to collective action.

Although Wigmore had been greatly impressed by Mussolini's early domestic policy, as had many others,[11] he roundly condemned him in 1923 for resorting to the use of force against Greece in demanding reparations regardless of Italy's obligations as a member of the League of Nations.[12] As to the fascist leaders, Wigmore wrote in 1938: "The only consolation that I can see just now is that neither Hitler nor Mussolini can last forever, and that maybe the thumb of the Lord will be turned down in mercy and the angel of fate will touch them on the shoulder. The only trouble about this solution is that when the angel came down last month and took off Attaturk he touched the wrong fellow."[13]

Nor did Wigmore spare the United States. The dispute with Mexico over the effect of its oil and land laws on American property was, he felt, purely a matter of international law. Here was a perfect case for the International Court of Justice. In his view, the threat to use force was "the most sadly shameful announcement made by this government in two generations."[14]

In 1924 Wigmore favored the draft treaty for the pacific settlement of international disputes[15] as a move in the right direction. He also thought that extraterritoriality should eventually be abandoned in China,[16] as it had been in Japan, but not until China had more adequately "occidentalized its organization of justice,"[17] the failure of which was the only excuse for extraterritoriality.

Another area that engaged Wigmore's attention was his concern over the problems which arose when naturalized Americans were still claimed as citizens by the countries of their birth, such as Germany, France, and Italy. He insisted that the only solution was the universal acceptance of the right of voluntary expatriation and citizenship based exclusively upon domicile, as exemplified by the several states in the American Union.

> Do we realize that, in this as in some other principles, the organization of our United States of America may well become the model for the United States of the World? The history of the fundamental principle of limited federal jurisdiction, developed from colonial days into our Constitution of 1787, foreshadows the gradual imitation of that splendid example in the jurisdiction of the World Court.[18]

Not surprisingly, Wigmore felt strongly about the exclusionary effect of American immigration laws as they related to the Japanese, along with other Orientals, and about California's alien land laws (1921) which precipitated a caustic and graphic statement:

I BELIEVE that the Japanese nightmare should be banished by all rational Americans. I was born and brought up in California and I understand the Californians. I lived for some years in Japan and I understand the Japanese. The real people of Japan are as peaceful as our own real people; they merely have a group of party politicians, as we do, who try in public to play upon patriotic sentiment for party purposes. The Japanese are a patriotic people, and so are we. They are sensitive about their farmers being discriminated against in California, just as we ourselves are sensitive about our oil-producers being discriminated against in Mesopotamia and in Mexico. Do not support the extreme claims of the California propagandists. The people of that fortunate State are apt to be, on occasion, as egotistic as children. They have to have hysterics every decade or two, so as to remind the rest of the country that California is in the United States. The solution of the California land question is very simple, viz., let California forbid land ownership by any *alien*, without specifically discriminating against the Japanese. This will entirely accomplish California's purpose, and will also satisfy the Japanese. Then the rest of us can go on attending peacefully to the Nation's business, while California plays with its rattle in its cradle.[19]

He was equally explicit on another burning issue, the Irish question. While he acknowledged that he was partly of Irish ancestry, Wigmore said that the Irish "should substitute evolution by parliamentary persuasion for devolution by assassination [and that] the South Irish readiness to abandon democratic England and join imperial Germany in the bloody world-war [I] was the saddest instance of political lunacy that history has ever recorded."[20] As to the Irish immigrants Wigmore said: "If the men of the Irish stock in America would devote to the cause of good government *here* one-tenth of the interest which they are devoting to the cause of political unrest in the land they have left behind them the 'Wearing of the Green' might become the national American Anthem!''

In this connection, it is of interest to note that Wigmore regarded President Wilson's slogan of self-determination as plausible and perhaps inevitable at the time it was uttered. He was convinced, however, that with the passage of time it had become evident that it was a misguided principle and had become a justification for war in a dozen parts of Europe. He had come to believe that "What the people of the world needed in 1917 was not self-determination, but liberty to reconcile national ambitions by peaceful rational methods, instead of by superior military strength. The nations' real slogan should be, not self-determination, but the Rule of Reason as the arbiter of equal opportunity for all."[21]

This attitude coincided with Wigmore's staunch advocacy of the League of Nations, and he contended that the covenant should have been ratified with or without reservations. "He was black and thunderous over criticisms of the League of Nations in 1919, that dimmed the prospects of its success. He wanted no more of neutrality."[22]

Although Wigmore recognized that the league was not much more than a forum for debate, he thought that such an outlet was what world politics most needed and that America's membership would have a steadying influence. In 1921 he said:

> It may well be affirmed that had we joined promptly we should not be witness-ing the present pitiable situation of Europe — factions fighting, governments bankrupt, people starving, ships idle, industry paralyzed. By staying out we have hurt the world far more than we have hurt ourselves. And we have lost forever the most unique opportunity of world leadership that destiny ever of-fered us.[23]

Wigmore not only supported the league through his writing but was a member and officer of the League of Nations Non-Partisan Association and made many talks on its behalf, some of them before members of the bar, even though, as he put it, "there are many lawyers who can't stand the mention of that dreadful subject."[24] Frequently his talks were illustrated with lantern slides. He also served on the league's Committee on Intellectual Cooperation. That he was not free from strong emotions himself became evident at the first meeting of the committee when he at first declared that he would not even sit in the same room with distinguished intellectuals of the defeated nations. "The Colonel was obviously still bent on winning the war."[25] However, he finally settled into the work with enthusiasm and made a substantial contribution. In 1923 Wigmore called attention to the fact that the United States was cooperating increasingly with the league, and he predicted that it would become a member.[26]

In spite of the league's limitations, which Wigmore fully recognized, it had his unqualified support with respect to the vital but limited role it could and should play. However, he was by no means an advocate of world government. He closed an article in which his position is succinctly stated, and in which he makes an interesting comparison between the procedures of the league and the National Conference of Commissioners on Uniform State Laws, with the following words:

> I challenge anyone to read faithfully the Official Journal of any year's proceed-ings [of the league] without experiencing a thrill of cosmic pride in the percep-tion that the world's politics are for the first time being discussed and settled in a free, central and universal forum.
> The League is the arrival of the rule of reason. And this means, sooner or later, the exit of the rule of force.[27]

When Wigmore heard that the University of Michigan had refused to permit George W. Wickersham, counsel of the League of Nations Non-Partisan Association, to speak there, he sent a telegram on behalf of the faculty of his Law School asking that Wickersham give an address at Northwestern on the date thus vacated. In his telegram he said in part:

> That University [Michigan] like most others purports to exclude discussion of current partisan politics, but to confuse political science with partisan politics, is an error of the first magnitude and imparts danger to free university research for

the truth. The motto of Northwestern University is "qua cumqua sunt vera." The faculties and not the regents or trustees are the custodians of educational research and when they placed in the curriculum the subjects of political science and international law, they did not conceive the range of discussion to be limited to such matters as the hours of county commissioners or the treaties of Louis XIV.[28]

While in Europe in 1932 Wigmore went to Geneva to meet some of the members of the League of Nations staff, and he looked in on the Disarmament Conference. His appraisal was that "It moves as slowly as a glacier."[29] Later, as he saw the league's effectiveness decline, he no doubt fully appreciated a comment from his friend Hugh R. Wilson, then in Berlin as ambassador to Germany, but formerly in Geneva, who said, "I had been in Geneva for years and had seen the League of Nations roll over and put its paws in the air over the Ethiopian matter."[30]

Wigmore believed that, even if the United States did not join the League of Nations, it should not desert its allies; German reparations should be measured by the amount of damage done, and ability to pay should no more be a consideration in international law than in the law of torts. Similarly, he believed that the needs of the Allied peoples for aid should be fully satisfied before any allocations were made to Germany.[31]

As an ardent advocate of a World Court Wigmore was jubilant when the Permanent Court of International Justice was created. In an editorial he wrote:

It should have given to every lawyer a thrill of cosmic vibration to learn on Wednesday, September 14, 1921, that an International Court of Justice had come into existence, by vote of the Council and Assembly of the League of Nations, sitting at Geneva. For the first time in the history of mankind a genuine World Court of Justice exists. The dreams of past centuries are realized, and the persistent practical efforts of the last twenty years, for a time fruitless, have at last reached success.[32]

Accordingly, he strongly supported every effort to secure ratification of the treaty creating the court by the United States Senate. However, when at last the Senate's price for ratification appeared to include acceptance of the fifth reservation,* which would in effect substantially inhibit the court's consideration of any issue in which the United States had an interest, Wigmore thought too hard a bargain was being exacted. Therefore, although he had been willing to accept reservations applying to the League of Nations, he balked with respect to the court.

We register the hope that *no nation at all* will accept this reservation; for (1) it is arrogant, (2) it is insulting, and (3) it represents merely an attempt by a few selfish Senators to maintain the stranglehold of those 96 veto-powers on the legal life of the people of the United States. . . . We prefer to stay out of the Court

*Of a number of reservations proposed, this was the fifth.

until we can break that stranglehold, by our own courage and the vice-president's.[34]

In the interval Wigmore received whatever satisfaction he could from the fact that one of the judges was an American. He congratulated John Bassett Moore on his election in 1921, and in 1929, on the election of Charles Evans Hughes, he concluded his congratulatory statement with these words: "The only dark feature in the picture is the humiliation that should be felt by the American people to realize that, after forty years of effort to establish the Court, the American nation should be refusing to make good its high principles by adhering to the Court treaty."[35]

In view of Wigmore's great interest in the Permanent Court of International Justice and his strong advocacy of American participation, it is not surprising that, when he and several friends were denied admission to the Peace Palace at the Hague on September 10, 1923, (although the Court was in session), he was "shocked beyond measure."[36] It was not reassuring for him to find that the Peace Palace was open to visitors only on Sundays from 2 to 5 P.M. He and his party were obliged to move on in their travels and miss their only convenient opportunity. Characteristically, he did not let the matter drop, for he was convinced that the court would never command the public confidence that it deserved if it held secret hearings. In what Manley O. Hudson described as a typical "Wigmorian blast"[37] he said in part:

> Let the Court-room even be packed full with eager hearers if they are interested to come. Are the Directors apprehensive of the dignity of the Court? Are they afraid that some muddy feet will soil the marble pavements of the corridors? Do they regret to see some manual worker appearing informally in his rough garments of daily toil? These things are nothing in comparison to the cause of World Justice. If you can interest the people of the Earth visibly in the proceedings of that Court, and make it known to them as a real institution of Justice, you will do much to advance the great Cause for which it is founded.[38]

In his inquiry, Wigmore encountered great difficulty in determining whether the restrictive policy on admissions was a requirement of the court, of the Dutch government, or of the Carnegie Institution, which was set up to operate the Peace Palace that had been built with Carnegie funds. However, he strongly suspected that the attitude of the registrar of the court, the only year-round resident, was an important factor, as he was a Swedish practitioner. Wigmore had visited most of the supreme courts of Europe, except in Russia, and had encountered difficulty in gaining admission only in Sweden, where admission had been denied to him even though he had presented a letter from the American secretary of state addressed to the minister of justice in Stockholm.[39]

For this reason, Wigmore was not completely reassured when he was advised that the rules had been somewhat relaxed; nor did the defense of the admission policy contributed to the *American Bar Association Journal* by Manley O. Hudson[40] assuage his anger, for access was in fact still surrounded with formalities. Wigmore contended that under Article 46 of the court statute, "The hearing in Court shall be public, *unless the Court shall decide otherwise* or unless the parties demand that the public shall not be admitted."[41] As he saw it, under this rule, restriction of admission was the exception and must be declared by the court in each case. In addition, Wigmore said, "It is a fundamentally wrong rule. I do not like to see the Permanent Court of International Justice starting off on a so unwise, illegal and erratic a precedent as the Swedish precedent. And I shall continue respectfully to voice my protest wherever I can, until that Court is just as easy to attend as any national Supreme Court outside of Sweden."[42]

But Wigmore's tenacity, as we have seen, was not confined to the issue of having the court open and available to the general public. It also applied to his support of the court as an institution and to his advocacy of participation in it by the United States. That his distaste for the fifth reservation would continue was not surprising. Several years later, in 1931, in writing to Manley Hudson, he said "that he would not care to see the United States go into the Court unless it can go in man size without any such childish, silly, cowardly conditions which only make us a laughing stock. This is not an opportunist attitude but a matter of principle."[43] However, in responding to Hudson's request that he join other American law-school professors in signing a statement in favor of United States adherence to the court, he said, "If you think that I should, nevertheless give in on this occasion, I will do so, but not otherwise." But if he was really ready to yield at all as to the fifth reservation because of his great respect for Hudson, his acquiescence was not of long duration, for four years later he wrote:

> The results of the Senate's attitude, first in misrepresenting and then misleading the American people, have been tragi-comic. In making our people behave to the Court like an ignorant big boy frightened by his naughty nurses bugaboo, the spectacle has been a world-comedy. And in making them refuse to take their part in using the most notable and hopeful instrument for international justice, the spectacle has been a world-tragedy.[44]

While Wigmore's preoccupation with the court was limited to support for the institution and United States participation, many of his friends believed he was eminently qualified to serve and they determined to do something about it. Early in 1930, while Wigmore was traveling in France and Morocco, a group of his friends and admirers, acting as the Wigmore World Court Nomination Committee, and without Wigmore's knowledge, solicited funds to promote his name as a nominee for the International Court of Justice. Under the direction of a managing committee consisting of Silas H. Strawn, chairman; General Enoch H. Crowder; Benjamin P. Epstein; James J. Forrestal, and Charles H. Watson, a suitable memorial was prepared and about 1,800 copies were distributed widely.[45] Among the recipients were the members of the International Court of Arbitration, the members of the Council and Assembly of the League of Nations, the chief executives of all of the member states, their prime ministers, and other important officers and leading newspapers around the world.[46] The memorial contained the names of 131 prominent persons as endorsers, including 17 college and university presidents or chancellors and 42 law-school deans. The Northwestern University Law School faculty formally recommended Wigmore for the appointment at its meeting on April 14, 1930,[47] and it became increasingly evident that the proposal had wide support. Manley Hudson wrote from Geneva: "Your fame extends all over the world and any such recognition of it is bound to warm my heart."[48] There was, however, some disapproval, probably for reasons expressed in an editorial in the *Nation*:

> It is to be hoped, however, that the choice may not fall upon Professor John H. Wigmore, of Northwestern University, who has been strongly urged for the position. Professor Wigmore has high standing as a legal writer, but his attitude toward pacifists and radicals during the time, 1916–1920, when he was attached to the Judge Advocate General's office was so openly hostile as to unfit him for Judicial honor.[49]

Wigmore's insistence on withdrawing his name came as a great shock to his friends and supporters.[50] Albert Kocourek, among others, made every effort to persuade him to change his mind but to no avail. Nevertheless, Wigmore was in fact nominated by the national groups from the Dominican Republic and Panama for the full nine-year term, and by the national groups for Belgium, Bulgaria, Luxembourg, Portugal, and Panama for the vacancy left by the resignation of Charles Evans Hughes. Apparently, Wigmore had several reasons for withdrawing.

In writing formally to the secretary-general of the League of Nations to withdraw his nomination, Wigmore merely stated that he was not in a position to accept, adding, "I only add at this time that the Permanent Court membership is deemed by me to be the highest international honor that can fall to anyone, and that I regret deeply that circumstances close that avenue to me."[51] Writing to Kocourek at the time, Wigmore said that he must decline the nomination because he wanted to complete his "system of scientific proof,"[52] but to Hudson several months later he said, "The main reason why I declined to let my name be considered as a nominee was the requirement of the new protocol of spending the time from October to June at The Hague. If that requirement is not adopted, that would have made a difference in my attitude."[53]

It is evident that he would have been receptive five years later, for, when he was leaving for Japan for three months, he said in a letter to Newton D. Baker, "The reason was that I thought it would be both improper and futile for me to be a candidate in rivalry to Mr. Kellogg. Should a similar situation arise again I should *not* take that view. I mention this simply because I am about to be away from the country for three months."[54]

So much for Wigmore's personal and possible official involvement in the work of the court. As has already been made evident, the reasons for Wigmore's criticism of the Senate went beyond its attitude toward the

International Court and the League of Nations. It will be recalled that he castigated the Senate for its attitude toward the League of Nations and that his ire had been first aroused during World War I when the Senate procrastinated for months in passing the Soldier's and Sailor's Civil Relief Act[55] while the men in uniform worried about their personal affairs at home. Indeed, his criticism extended to what he regarded as the Senate's uniformly obstructive role in the general conduct of foreign affairs: "collective power is, by Senate Rule 22, loaned to each individual Senator whenever he asks for it." He said that Rule 22 was wholly unconstitutional and should be abolished.[56]

In 1932 the chronic backlog in the Senate was once more too much for Wigmore to tolerate in silence, and he began an editorial in the *Illinois Law Review* with these words, "When the curtain rose last December on the third session of the 71st Congress, it revealed in the stage-setting one feature as changeless as usual, viz., the Senate table covered with papers representing the nation's international interests, unattended to."[57] Included were two treaties that had been pending for five and six years respectively, three for three years, three for two years, and one for one year. In addition, there were nine other pacts, not technically treaties. The president had urged prompt action on all of these. To further emphasize the dilatory tactics of the Senate, Wigmore cited an earlier item — an annual appropriation of not more than $250 for the United States's share of the expense of the International Technical Committee of Aerial Legal Experts. About this item there was no controversy; the House had approved the expenditure in four days, but the Senate had taken nearly three years to act.

Pointing out that the Senate was at the time "absorbed in its most favored occupation, viz., bargaining for offices,"[58] he concluded:

> It is not a spectacle pleasant to dwell upon. We refer to it here because until this period of feverish bargaining has elapsed, there is no prospect of any action being taken in the twenty pending treaties urged by the President for prompt action.
> Buzzards look like eagles, and may well be mistaken for them, when soaring far aloft in the vast void of the empyrean. But on close inspection, as they sit wrangling around their prey, one is disillusioned.
> Senators look like statesmen, in the lofty and lucid ambient of the text of our Constitution describing their duties. But in their performance of those duties under that Constitution, what do they look like?[59]

Wigmore's interest in international law reflected not only his belief in its importance from a broad social point of view but his view of its relevance to the work of the legal profession. This conviction once again prompted him toward the end of his career to renew his attempts to convince members of the bar "that international law is not merely a foreign subject, nor just a parlor subject, but is an *American* subject, and withal a practical subject, i.e., one whose knowledge will enable the practitioner to earn a fee."[60]

Congressional responses to the gathering clouds and threats of World War II, coupled with a host of executive orders and regulations, helped to make Wigmore's point more evident. Finally, the declaration of war and "another batch of Statutes and Executive Orders and Regulations suited for a state of war,"[61] made it imperative for the American lawyer "to know some elementary American international law."

Wigmore did not seek to convince solely by argument; he undertook to provide American lawyers with books that would serve as tools in their work. The first consisted of two booklets donated to the legal profession and published by the American Bar Association. Part I concerned international substantive common law, and Part II the law for a state of war.[62]

The second volume, *A Guide to American International Law and Practice*, although somewhat more ambitious, was still elementary in its approach. As has already been indicated the book was published in 1943, and in a copy presented to Northwestern University on the author's eightieth birthday he "characterized [it] . . . with almost boyish pride as 'My last — no, I mean my latest — work'."[63]

Both of these books reflected Wigmore's interest in making useful information available, especially in an area where lawyers were not sufficiently informed. In order to accentuate the significance of the "American" component in international law and to make these books useful to practitioners, they were based primarily on American materials. They were not meant to be scholarly works. They reflected Wigmore's zeal in interesting the regular practitioner, an objective that clearly overrode any intention he might otherwise have had to make a substantive contribution to the field. International law had never received his sustained attention *as a scholar*, nor was that his concern now. In Manley Hudson's words:

> In his later years, international law became a great bond between us. Not so interested in exploring the subject, Wigmore wished to arouse the legal profession to appreciation of its significance. When he could stand the apathy no longer, a crusade had to be organized and the Colonel got out his lance to lead it. With ceaseless industry he scoured the libraries; untiringly, he scanned the daily press for items to cull; voluminously, he tried out his ideas on his friends in correspondence. Everything was grist to his mill in such a moment.[64]

Paralleling Wigmore's keen interest in international law was his enthusiasm for comparative law. Therefore, after World War I, he continued to serve as a member of the Council of the Comparative Law Bureau until 1928 when he submitted his resignation,[65] but he was later elected again for the year 1932–33.[66] While acting in this capacity he saw the possibility of strengthening the role of the American Bar Association in this field as well as in two others in which he was an active participant — the International Law Committee and the Society of Military Law. In consequence, he became a leader in a movement to consolidate the work of these three groups. The Law Committee, the Comparative Law Bureau, and the Society of Military Law, which bore fruit in 1934 through the creation of the

American Bar Association Section of International and Comparative Law. With Wigmore as chairman, the first annual meeting was a "wedding feast of intellectual fare and good fellowship," and he had "injected newness of life into International and Comparative Law with the completion of this first successful year."[67] He continued to give the section his active support until his death in 1943, by serving as a member of the council and by assuming a number of committee assignments.

A closely related activity was his role as chairman of the American Bar Association's Special Committee on International Bar Relations, and he made his personal views clear in an article in the *American Bar Association Journal* entitled, "Should the World's Legal Profession Organize?"[68] Wigmore's own scholarly interests and his personal associations with individuals in many parts of the world convinced him that "all who belong to the legal profession — judges, teachers, legislators, prosecutors — have a common fund of tradition and experience in all countries." As usual he came forward with specific suggestions, embodied in a plan worked out in considerable detail. In his supporting argument he pointed out that the legal profession was "almost the only profession or occupation in the whole social sphere that is not yet so organized." He documented his argument by pointing to the *Handbook of International Associations* published by the League of Nations which in sixty pages or more listed hundreds of occupations. "All occupations are there, from the astronomers to the zoologists. The cooks are there; also the poultry-instructors and seed crushers. Among the technically trained professions there are the accountants, the dentists, the physicians and surgeons, the chemists, the geographers, the librarians, the pharmacists, the psychologists — and so on."

After two years in which Wigmore, as chairman, corresponded with the bar associations in nearly every country, the committee concluded that "the time is ripe for some sort of affiliation between the organized Bars of all nations," and that "the most suitable nucleus for such an affiliation is the existing body known as the International Union of Advocates, formed by delegates from the organized Bars of 15 nations of Europe and Latin America."[69] Wigmore was appointed a member of the special committee[70] which in 1935 recommended that affiliation be approved, and its recommendation was adopted by the association.[71] When affiliation shortly followed, the step was warmly welcomed by the International Union of Advocates.[72] However, Wigmore favored and actively advocated, as a further step forward, a call by the American Bar Association of a "World Congress of Bar Associations" to be held in Washington, D.C.[73]

But Wigmore's determination to broaden this horizon of the members of the bar was not satisfied merely through affiliation with the International Union. He had long maintained that there should be more collaboration with the lawyers of Latin America, and he was, therefore, a prime mover in the creation of the Inter-American Bar Association in 1940, following the adoption of a resolution by the American Bar Association authorizing the Section on International and Comparative Law to explore the possibility of establishing such a group.[74] In 1942, when the little that had been accomplished so far on a worldwide basis collapsed because of the war, Wigmore was all the more strenuously advocating the development of a stronger Inter-American Bar Association.[75]

Wigmore's conception of the world community embraced far more than the League of Nations and the International Court or even the development of an international regime of law and order to govern the conduct of the nations of the world in their relationships to each other. He contended that members of the legal profession should also have some understanding and appreciation of the internal laws of countries other than their own. Accordingly, Wigmore continued vigorously to support the study of comparative law, an approach that had from the beginning been reflected in much of his writing. This interest was one of his most important bonds with Holmes, to whom he wrote in June 1924: "I have been straying back into the field of my early and defeated aspirations — Comparative Law . . ." Even earlier he had reported to him: "I am become a genuine 'fan' on the History of Laws in Pictures" and "I am working on a new idea, an impressionist construction of the World's Legal Systems . . . with pictorial panorama and monologue."[76]

Articles, notes, book reviews, and translations flowed from Wigmore's pen.[77] However, the most ambitious effort during this period was *A Panorama of the World's Legal Systems*, copiously illustrated, which appeared in three volumes in 1928.[78] The *Panorama* was the outgrowth of lectures given by Wigmore not only to students but also to lawyers all over the United States. In all he appeared before almost 10,000 persons.[79] The lectures were illustrated with 150 colored lantern slides, for he was convinced that much comparative law could be taught pictorially.[80] Wigmore's first appearance in the series was at the annual meeting of the Law School Alumni Association on June 12, 1924, to which graduates were invited to hear their "beloved dean" present "The thrilling march of ancient, medieval and modern men and measures beautifully illustrated."[81]

In responding to Holmes's welcome to Washington, on the occasion of Wigmore's lecture at the Cosmos Club, of which he had been a member since 1918, he wrote, "the truth is, I have wished to show you, more than anyone else, what I am trying to do to awaken the Bar to an interest in the world of law outside us, as your book first did for me."[82] This wish was unfortunately not realized because Holmes was by this time not going out at all in the evenings. However, 175 persons attended the lecture.[83]

Wigmore's sojourn in Washington on this occasion was not devoted exclusively to lecturing. As a matter of fact his eight-day visit (accompanied by Mrs. Wigmore) included a dizzying round of activities, including visits with numerous government officials, among them Justices Holmes, Stone, Butler, and Brandeis. There was, of course, a reasonable amount of social activity which included Mrs. Wigmore.

An incident during this stay was subsequently used in class to demonstrate that one must take the initiative if one wants to succeed. Nelson Wettling, one of Wigmore's students, reports the episode as follows:

He [Wigmore] and his wife went into the dining room in the Powhatan Hotel in Washington one morning for breakfast. They were seated at a table and proceeded to wait for a long period of time without anyone paying the slightest attention to them. As the Dean expressed it, "The dining room might just as well have been closed so far as we were concerned." His patience became taxed to the limit and then exhausted. Finally, in that deep, resonant bass voice of his (and he showed us in class just what he meant) he bellowed out, "I want some service." Everyone in the dining room, of course, looked around. The head waiter came running over. Following closely on his heels was the bus boy, and bringing up the rear of this procession was a waiter. He declared that he never had better service in his life.[84]

In connection with his lectures in San Francisco, Wigmore was honored by the local bar association both as a scholar and as a native son. During the dinner his mother had the seat of honor at his right and Mrs. Wigmore sat to his left. That his mother's dictatorial attitude toward her son had not changed is evident from the following exchange on this festive occasion:

MOTHER: Harry, drink your water.
WIGMORE: No thank you Mother, I do not care for it.
MOTHER: Harry, drink your water.
WIGMORE: No thank you Mother, I do not care for water with my meals.
MOTHER: Harry, drink your water.
WIGMORE: No thank you Mother, I do not care for it.
MRS. WIGMORE (*leaning over and whispering in her husband's ear*): Oh Harry, drink the water if it kills you if it makes her happier.

Wigmore complied with his wife's request by taking a few swallows. Later when his wife told this story in Wigmore's presence, he broke into a broad grin.[85]

The *Panorama* was quite generally received with approval and won such appraisals as "perhaps the most attractive set of law books ever published";[86] a book in which a scholar has humanized the law successfully "without loss of dignity to himself or to the profession";[87] a book in which the author has succeeded in converting "the dry history of the law into a fascinating story";[88] "one of the most stimulating scholarly works which has appeared in a long time";[89] a "significant permanent contribution."[90]

But the *Panorama* also elicited some highly critical responses. These included the view that the early records would signify nothing to those for whom the book was intended, the belief that there should have been "fewer curiosities" and more of "Dean Wigmore's learning,"[91] the assertion that the translations were poor, that some of the illustrations were imaginary, that the text was "needlessly uncritical at times,"[92] and that, although the book was good for the general reader, it was "a less serious work than either H. G. Wells' Outline of History or Durant's The Story of Philosophy."[93] Finally, A. L. Goodhart and Theodore F. T. Plucknett[94] believed that Wigmore overemphasized the importance of "a highly trained professional class" when he identified it as the primary consideration in "the rise and perpetuation of a legal system."[95] Holdsworth apparently agreed with Wigmore. At any rate account should be taken of the fact that Wigmore advanced this generalization not as a final conclusion but as a mere hypothesis "thrown out as worthy of inquiry." Holdsworth also thought that some of the reviewers had failed to grasp the magnitude and originality of Wigmore's contribution.[96] One reader, Ben Atkinson Wortley, upon reexamining the set over thirty years after its publication, did so with the "greatest pleasure" and said it deserved a fresh edition "to bring it to the notice of young men of the world of the United Nations who contemplate a career in the law or in administration."[97]

Although some of the criticisms unquestionably have merit, it seems only fair to add that they do not always take account of Wigmore's clearly declared objective. The book itself, he said, was meant to be a popular outline of the sixteen legal systems, past and present, for the general reader and not for the scholar, "a temporary flight above the earth" so that one may "look down upon the globe, and there watch the Panorama of the World's Legal Systems unroll before us."[98] Judged in these terms the book achieved its objective, for it did succeed in presenting "in perspective for the legal profession (and the general public) a true impressionistic whole."[99] In 1936 the *Panorama* was republished in a one-volume "Library Edition" with some amplification.[100]

Some years later, in 1941, the *Kaleidoscope of Justice* appeared.[101] An anthology of 142 trials which in effect complements the *Panorama*, it was designed to provide informational entertainment rather than to reflect scientific research. That Wigmore succeeded was generally agreed, and Arthur Train declared in a review, "For sheer entertainment this book equals the Arabian Nights, Cellini's Memoirs or Sherlock Holmes."[102]

Among other writings in the field of comparative law, three at least should be mentioned. In "Jottings on Comparative Legal Ideas and Institutions,"[103] Wigmore discusses the Mesopotamian, Chinese, Hindu, Greek, Roman, Japanese, Mohammedan, Celtic, Slavic, Germanic, maritime, canon, and Romanesque legal systems. *Comparative Juristic Corporeology* (1931) was dedicated in "homage" to Del Vecchio and "his career of leadership in juristic science." "The Pledge-Mortgage Idea in Roman Law: A Revolutionary Interpretation"[104] discusses the significance of the substitution of hypotheca for fiducia in the *Digest*, thus bringing up to date Wigmore's article "The Pledge Idea: A Study in Comparative Legal Ideas" which had been published in 1897.[105]

In his far-flung efforts to broaden the outlook of the members of the bar, Wigmore did not overlook the value of bringing people together from time to time to consider problems that transcended national boundaries. As the American member of the Board of Councilors of the International Association of Penal Law, Wigmore vigorously supported the call for an International Congress of Penal Law held in Brussels in 1926. Among other things, he strove with characteristic enthusiasm to develop interest in the congress in this country and to encourage attendance and active participation in this organization of which the American Institute of Criminal Law and Criminology was the American affiliate.

Although an International Congress of Comparative Law was scheduled to be held in Europe in 1932, Wigmore recommended that the congress be postponed for a time to permit better planning and held at a later date at The Hague.[106] His recommendation was adopted. In his effort to promote participation by the United States he assumed the chairmanship of a committee of the Conference of State Bar Delegates[107] and, in that role, addressed the September 1931 meeting of the American Bar Association's Conference of State Bar Delegates.[108] An intensive correspondence campaign directed by Wigmore reached all of the 800 faculty members of the American law schools, and the presidents and secretaries of the 1200 state, county, and city bar associations, supplying relevant information and urging them to appoint representatives.[109] In this connection, Wigmore submitted an article to the *American Bar Association Journal* entitled "An American Lawyer's Pilgrimage on the Continent," which described places of special interest to lawyers.[110] He arranged with a travel agency for special rates for package tours, and in doing so he incurred costs of about $400, which he obviously assumed himself.

This was an immense promotional undertaking, as the following excerpt from a letter to a friend indicates: "You see, when I told the European Committee, two years ago, that I would try to arouse interest among our bar, I didn't realize what I was getting into. Now it is a case of not being able to let go of the bull's tail. Having done so much propaganda for the Congress, I *simply have to go* — even if it bankrupts us."[111]

As a result of this tremendous effort, when Wigmore registered for the congress he did so as a member of the National Committee for the United States, as chairman of the Committee of the Conference of State Bar Associations, and as a representative of the Association of American Law Schools, the Illinois Bar Association, and Northwestern University.[112]

Wigmore seized upon the opportunity to address the congress in order to push the idea that was uppermost in his mind, and he said in part:

> First, this Congress, no matter how valuable its proceedings, must not adjourn without *making provision for a permanent future in periodic meetings.* It must not be a mere ephemeris, a beautiful juristic butterfly. It must make, out of itself, a permanent organism, with a perpetual self-renewing life. I am old enough to recall three such Congresses of the past. In 1893, at the Columbian World's Fair in Chicago, there was a World Congress of Lawyers, though its attendance was small and local. Again in Paris, in 1901, at the World Exposition, there was a Juridical Congress, attended mainly by European delegates. And again in St. Louis in 1904, at the Louisiana Purchase World's Exposition, there was a World Congress of Science, with a Department of Jurisprudence; I myself read there a paper on Legal History, but there were few delegates from outside of the United States. Nothing permanent resulted from either of those three Congresses. This record of three ephemeral phenomena, covering forty years, must not be repeated. *This* time a living organism *must* be the result. And so, I adjure you, to conceive firmly of this Congress as only the embryo of that future organism, and I urge you to take suitable measures accordingly, before adjournment. The lesson of the past and the needs of the future, make this our duty. . . .

So, now that we are assembled here, for the first time, from nearly every country of the world, it is unthinkable that we should neglect this opportunity.

Let us foster some plan for our permanent fraternization throughout the world. The occasion is unique. It points to a broader mission, an unavoidable destiny. Let us fulfill it.[113]

But Wigmore was not merely satisfied with a clarion call for action. He had prepared in advance "A Plan for a Permanent World Wide Co-ordination of the Legal Profession,"[114] in which he set out (1) the aims to be avoided, (2) the aims to be included, and (3) the general principles of a concrete plan. Unfortunately, Wigmore did not win the support of the delegates for his proposal although provision was made for another congress. As usual, he was ahead of his time.

One American delegate summed up his part in the congress. "You were the 'Star' at the Hague Meeting and we Americans were very proud."[115]

Although the goals set by Wigmore have not been realized to this day, some progress has been made. Today the International Bar Association embraces 63 constituent groups from 45 countries which represent more than 250,000 individual lawyers. Attendance at the regular biennial conferences ranges from 1,250 to 1,600 persons. Among the objectives of the association is the promotion of the principles and aims of the United Nations "in their legal aspects." It cooperates with and promotes "coordination among international juridical organizations having similar purposes"[116] and has been accorded consultative status with the United Nations.

The World Peace through Law Center, which was established in Geneva, Switzerland, in 1963, would certainly have merited Wigmore's support. The center sponsors biennial conferences and carries on a variety of activities involving many members of the legal profession for the purpose of fostering the development and expansion of transnational law and transnational legal structures for world peace.

However disappointed Wigmore may have been over the fact that his proposal for a permanent world-wide coordination of the legal profession was not adopted, this did not blind him to the value of the more modest achievements of the congress. He in fact regarded it as "the greatest assembly of the kind ever held by our profession,"[117] in spite of the gross inadequacy of physical arrangements due to limited funds, lack of experience, and an unexpectedly large enrollment. The three prior congresses — in Chicago, Paris, and St. Louis — were but small and ephemeral beginnings in comparison. In his report of the congress, Wigmore described its significance with enthusiasm:

The significance of the Congress lay, not merely in the number of delegates and the range of countries represented, but in the quality of the personnel. The reports presented for debate had been prepared by known experts in each topic, specially selected. The delegates attending to debate them were fully representative (on the whole) of the most competent talent in each country.

As a milestone of the world's juridical and professional progress, the Congress was emphatically a success beyond all expectation. As a beginning toward permanent world-wide cooperation of all branches of the legal profession, it was a forecast of a great future. And as a demonstration of the capacity and willingness of the United States profession henceforth to take its proper part in such a movement, it was eminently encouraging.[118]

The congress provided Wigmore with an opportunity to pursue a long-standing special interest in St. Ives (1252–1303), generally recognized as the patron saint of the law. In 1913, during one of the Wigmores' trips to Europe, Baedeker's *Northern France* had brought to his attention a reference to the fishing town of Tréguier, and the cathedral which contained a monument to St. Ives. The Wigmores decided to stop over for a few hours, and the visit "was enough to arouse a deep interest in this wonderful man who in real life had set a standard — an unattainable one, perhaps for our profession."[119] As one outcome of this abiding interest, Wigmore headed a committee appointed during the meeting of the International Congress to visit Tréguier, pay homage to the patron saint, and present to the cathedral a handsome tablet bearing the arms of the family of St. Ives, with the following inscription:

HOMMAGE
DES AVOCATS DES ETATS UNIS
D'AMERIQUE
AU PATRON DE LEUR PROFESSION
SAINT YVES

EN SOUVENIR DE LEUR VISITE

21 AOUT 1932[120]

In making the presentation Wigmore said, "I come here, with my friends, as delegate from the Bar Association of the United States of America (now numbering more than 30,000 members), to pay respect to St. Ives, patron of the lawyers, not only of France and of the United States, but of all countries of the world."

The curé then responded by expressing great appreciation for the gesture by the American lawyers:

It so happens, sir, that the curé who now speaks to you was during the Great War attached as interpreter to the Seventh Regiment of American Infantry in France, and that he was wounded, on Oct. 5, 1918, at Cierges, in the terrific combat around the fortress of Montfaucon, while with your doughboys, — those boys who freed the soil of France. I am therefore one who is least likely to forget what the United States did on our behalf; for it was their entry on the scene, with all their great strength, that brought victory.

But may I venture to express the hope that this gift is but a welcome presage of a greater blessing to us? For it has long been my cherished dream to restore, in this superb cathedral, the stained-glass windows which were destroyed by the mob at the time of the French Revolution. You have mentioned that your bar association has some 30,000 members. Would it not, sir, be easily possible, and well worthy of the dignity of your Association, to place here, in this chapel, a window depicting St. Ives rendering justice to the distressed. . . .

I must confess indeed to some chagrin when I reflect that you Americans would be the first to do this; for our lawyers of France have not yet undertaken the like tribute to our saint. But I am persuaded that they too would be spurred by your example and would soon do likewise.[121]

This was the kind of a challenge that a man like Wigmore could not resist. Thus he became the chairman of an unofficial committee of the American Bar Association authorized to secure funds for a memorial window which it was hoped would represent the bar in every state in the Union.[122] Wigmore took the major responsibility for raising the $1,200 that was required, a particularly arduous undertaking on account of the desire to have every state represented. Somewhat later, when Wigmore was urging a colleague to continue his efforts to raise funds for another purpose, Wigmore wrote, "Please keep it up, recalling the motto of the Ayer Advertising Company of Chicago, which has often kept me going, 'Everlastingly keep at it wins success.' You know it took me four years to raise the total amount with which we installed that window to St. Ives in Brittany."[123]

Wigmore also took a great interest in the designing of the memorial window and kept in close touch with the subcommittee in Paris which was in charge of making the arrangements for the installation. Presentation of the window by the American lawyers was made on May 19, 1936, the traditional day of the pilgrimage to the Shrine of St. Ives, in the presence of a crowd estimated at 40,000. The presentation was made by Pendleton Buckley, European chairman of the St. Ives Memorial Committee. The program included a letter from Wigmore in which he paid tribute to St. Ives and expressed regret that he could not attend.[124]

In 1927 Wigmore was given an honorary LL.D. from the University of Louvain in Belgium. His lifelong interest in France and his admiration for French culture were unquestionably appreciated by her countrymen. He received an honorary degree from the University of Lyons in 1938. In responding from Paris to a congratulatory letter from Henry Seldon Bacon on behalf of the Association des Juristes Estrangers, Wigmore wrote,

I was proud to be selected by the University of Lyon for that distinguished ceremony, but it adds a particular pleasure to know that my compatriots in Paris took notice of it and were kind enough to send me their expressions of good will.

I have no doubt that, taken altogether, that event and others like it do help to hold together the peoples of the two countries.

I for one see no reason at all, in spite of what the timid politicians think, why France and Great Britain and the United States should not form a back to back alliance to safeguard their interests against the pressure from ambitious autocratic leaders in other countries.[125]

In academic circles at least, Wigmore was not quickly forgotten. Twenty years after Wigmore's death a member of the faculty of Northwestern

University who was visiting universities in France was impressed that whenever he met any one connected with the law, the immediate response would be, ''Northwestern University, Oh yes, that was Wigmore's University.''

Though Wigmore was vigorously involved in a variety of activities for which Chicago was his base of operations, he quite unexpectedly received — through the Japanese consulate in Chicago — an invitation from the Society for International Cultural Relations and Keio University to return to Japan to organize the completion of the translation and editing of the records of justice in Japan covering the Tokugawa period, 1600–1860, a project that, it will be recalled, he had started when he was in Japan in 1889–92. Although Wigmore was glad to assist in the completion of his first undertaking in comparative law, his commitments in the United States allowed him to accept the invitation only if his stay could be limited to two months.[126] In March 1935, Wigmore accompanied by Mrs. Wigmore, he left Evanston to fulfill this assignment, and he reached Yokohama on April 4.[127]

The materials to be translated were a selection from about fifteen volumes compiled from a great mass of supreme court records from the period when Japan was self-isolated from the rest of the world. In Wigmore's view and in that of other scholars the undertaking was important because such isolated development was unique among modern countries and provided valuable data for the comparative study of the evolution of law, and because the original records in hundreds of volumes had been largely destroyed by fire after the earthquake of 1923. The revival of interest in this project in Japan arose from the fact that the Society of International Cultural Relations founded in 1934 (somewhat similar to the Carnegie or Rockefeller Foundations) wished to use it as an illustration of the intellectual achievements of Japan.

A glimpse of Wigmore's approach to his task is provided by Mr. Shinzo Koizumi, president of Keio University:

> His professed aim of visiting us again was far from such a conventional one as feasting his eyes upon the superb scenery of the land. So, on the day after his arrival at the port of Yokohama, he put in an unexpected appearance at the office of the Bunkwa Kyokwai in Tokyo, and immediately set about formulating a plan for the completion of the translation. . . . From that time on, he was never found off this arduous self-imposed duty of his, and unceasingly engaged in supervising a staff of translators selected for the purpose. Each time we planned a pleasure trip for his recreation, taking advantage of the very best season in our country, in which he was brought over here, he resolutely turned down the proposition, saying that his sense of duty did not allow him to indulge in this sort of enjoyment. Thus, eventually he had to leave our country even without seeing Nikko or Kyoto. He is really a ''solid man'' (*katai hito*).[128]

The translation embraced five branches of law — persons, property, contracts, commercial law, and procedure. To aid him in this undertaking, Wigmore had an assistant, six translators, and three skilled typists. Aside from providing general direction of the project, Wigmore (though he was not too familiar with Japanese generally) knew the legal terms of the Tokugawa period in Japanese and their equivalents in English and was able to put the final draft of the translation into correct form. Although the entire task could not be finished in two months, a model portion for each of the five branches of law, in a style suitable for printing, was completed. Wigmore continued to work on the manuscript after he returned to the United States and made every effort to find a publisher, for he believed the publication would find an important place in the law libraries of the world. He was greatly disappointed that this massive undertaking, which he had had to abandon forty-three years earlier and to which he had returned "with all the vigor of an enthusiastic youth," found no publisher during his lifetime.[129] Eventually, however, the Japanese government recognized the importance of this material and determined to support the undertaking by providing the necessary funds for publication.[130]

The translation assignment was not the only activity to capture Wigmore's attention during his stay in Japan. By invitation he had brought his 800 colored lantern slides to illustrate his series of six lectures on "A Panorama of the World's Legal Systems." Wigmore had the lantern slides so carefully packed and kept such a vigilant eye on them during the journey that Mrs. Wigmore facetiously dubbed the package "Lady Lantern Slides." By arrangement, three of these lectures were given at Keio University and three at Tokyo Imperial University. They were given in English, and a translation in Japanese by one of the professors followed. Typically, Wigmore was received by a committee before each lecture, and tea and elaborate refreshments were served in the anteroom.

Wigmore also gave a lecture at Keio University on "The Present Condition of Air Law, National and International," and another at Tokyo Imperial University on "The Evolution of Law." In the latter, he used a balloon and a gyroscope to illustrate his planetary theory of legal evolution.[131] He also spoke on various subjects at a Keio University faculty dinner, and at the Kojunsha Club, the Imperial University Law Faculty Dinner, the Tokyo Association, the Pan-Pacific Club, the Asiatic Society of Japan, and elsewhere.

Wigmore was deeply touched by his welcome back to Japan, especially at Keio University, where a great deal was made of the work he had accomplished during his initial visit in 1889–92. In retrospect, however, his own contribution seemed to him limited. In his own words: "My share in the initial task of starting the University departments was a very limited one. Moreover, as I look back on it, I can see how many mistakes I made and how much better I could have done had I been as intelligent as the situation required. My only excuse can be the fact of my youth and of the novelty of the enterprise for an American coming to Japan."[132]

Although the faculty and all of the officers had largely changed, the president, Dr. Koizumi, was the son of the president who had been in office during Wigmore's first visit, and among those who welcomed him was Torajiro Kambe, a former student of Wigmore's and later professor and dean of the Law Faculty. In addition, Wigmore was taken in charge by Haruzo Minegishi, professor of Anglo-American Law, who had studied at Lincoln's Inn and in Germany and had lectured at Keio University on the law of evidence.

Wigmore's loyalty to Keio University derived not only from his personal associations but also from its long traditions. It had been founded in 1858 as the first independent college, and through the years it had maintained a unique spirit of educational independence as the best privately endowed university of the time and one that was unrivaled in France, Germany, or Italy. It had introduced into Japan the spirit of "alumni fraternity and institutional loyalty" that was so characteristic of the United States and so lacking in the universities of Continental Europe.

During this visit Wigmore was interested in securing information about developments in specified branches of Japanese law. In aviation he obtained a copy of the 1921 Civil Aviation Act and sent to Northwestern University a translation for publication in the *Journal of Air Law*. He also secured articles on recent developments in air law and pursued his interest in police science by visiting the Criminal Investigation Bureau of the Metropolitan Police Department of Tokyo. At that time he found it, over all, "pretty well up to date in the application of science to the detection of crime" and its laboratory, "though not so extensive as the Northwestern one, . . . more varied in apparatus than the Federal one in Washington."

Finally, Wigmore made a search for law books to complete the collection of Japanese modern law in the Northwestern University Law School Library, and for volumes on Japanese political science for the Deering Library on the Evanston campus of Northwestern. In all of his assignments while in Japan, Wigmore was indebted to Dr. Kenzo Takayanagi, a member of the Law Faculty of Tokyo Imperial University, for his "assiduous attention." Wigmore's high regard for Takayanagi is evident from the following incident. After the attack on Pearl Harbor one of Wigmore's former students, now in uniform, came to say good-bye to his "old master" before going to the Pacific Theater. Wigmore gave him a message to give to Takayanagi should the student reach Tokyo. In due course the message, "War now separates us, but will not affect our friendship," was delivered in person, and Takayanagi was moved to tears.[133]

This brief and strenuous Japanese visit did not leave much time for sightseeing and recreation. The Wigmores' only trip outside of Tokyo was to Miyanoshita, when they were fortunate to get a perfect view of Mount Fuji, "the world's peerless mountain peak." In Tokyo they attended the emperor's famous cherry-garden party in one of the beautiful Imperial parks and sampled three varieties of theatrical entertainment, including the Spring Tournament of professional wrestling matches (a sport greatly enjoyed by Wigmore during his first visit to Japan) where 20,000 school boys of all ages in the top gallery cheered their favorites like spectators at a college football game. They also attended a baseball game (Wigmore was an avid fan) with an attendance of 60,000, recalling that Wigmore himself had "played shortstop, away back when, on the first team ever organized in Tokyo,'' a team that ''must have helped to start the vogue of baseball in Japan.''

As the time for departure approached there was a round of farewell parties ''and parting gifts, which signified friendly feelings and good wishes for the homeward journey, and embarrassed the recipients with a sense of their demerits.''

> To crown all, a delegation of friends assembled at the Tokyo railway station to say farewell, and at the steamer-pier in Yokohama another large delegation, representing the various institutions. The paper-ribbons of friendship were cast across by the departing passengers to the crowd of hundreds of friends on the piers, forming a woven network like a gorgeous cobweb between ship and pier. A group of Keio students gathered at the outermost end of the pier, singing their College song; and as the steamer glided off down the bay, the final and moving token of good feeling was the Keio students waiving their flags, giving the college cheer, and shouting, ''Banzai, Wigmore.''[134]

But this was not all, for after their return to the United States the Wigmores were showered with tokens of friendship sent by societies, groups, and individuals. Among the gifts were ''cloisonne vases of extraordinary beauty packed in boxes of fine workmanship lined with padded silk which themselves were beautiful objects, exquisite silken fabrics and a great 'book of remembrance' made up of photographs of the American visitors and their surroundings at the many entertainments and receptions given in their honor.''[135]

The climax came on November, 1935, when at a dinner in Chicago, Hirosi Saito, Japanese ambassador to the United States, formally decorated Wigmore with the Order of the Sacred Treasure conferred upon him by Hirohito, the emperor of Japan.[136]

Wigmore's visit to Japan fully reassured him in his conviction that the Japanese were an industrious, cooperative, and peace-loving people, but he strongly disapproved of the dominant role played by the military leaders. However, he believed that our relations with Japan could be substantially improved if we would accept the principle of racial equality, since the widespread resentment toward the United States in Japan, he felt, played into the hands of the military leaders. He was among those who declared that the problem could be easily solved by placing Japanese immigration on the quota basis applicable to other foreigners, which would in fact permit the entry of relatively few persons. Because of his concern over the deteriorating relations between the United States and Japan, Wigmore carried on an extensive correspondence through which he endeavored to secure acceptance of his own deeply held view that discrimination against the Japanese was the principal obstacle to friendly relations. Toward this end he urged the secretary of state to eliminate discrimination in future treaty negotiations with Japan by repealing the present exclusion law and substituting the usual quota arrangement.[137]

Wigmore also endeavored to think of ways to counter military influence in Japan. For this purpose he proposed a meeting of the Association of

American Universities in Japan, believing that an invitation could easily be arranged.[138] On the other hand, when Warren A. Seavy urged Wigmore to write letters to his congressman and senators and other influential persons, urging them to legislate against trade with Japan because of her military activities in China, he declined. He said that, although he agreed with Seavey's position, and, although he knew that the Japanese with whom he was working on the translation of the historical materials were not sympathetic with the present military aggressiveness, he "could not afford to hurt their feelings by public utterance."[139]

Even after Pearl Harbor, Wigmore strove to preserve the distinction between the attitude of the vast majority of the Japanese people and the military leaders who were in complete control. Consequently, Wigmore was disturbed when Nathaniel Peffer, in an article in *Asia*,[140] contended that the entire trend of Japanese political thinking had for centuries shown a tendency to dominate the Orient, and that nationalistic policies were not new to the military party in control at the present time. To offset this article Wigmore wrote a long letter to Hallett Abend urging him to refute this erroneous doctirne in his projected book to be entitled *The Pacific Charter*.[144]

Finally when Arthur Krock, in an article in the *New York Times*,[143] took the position that the envoys Admiral Kichishuro Nomura and Mr. Saburo Kurusu, who were in Washington at the time of the Pearl Harbor attack, knew of the military plans, Wigmore wrote Krock indicating that he believed this was not true. Wigmore said he did not know Admiral Nomura well enough to be certain, but he was convinced from long acquaintance with Mr. Kurusu that he had not been aware of the military plans. Arthur Krock acknowledged the letter with appreciation and agreed that Wigmore was probably correct.[143]

It was not long after Wigmore's return from this visit to Japan that he resumed a leading part in arranging for another International Congress to be held at The Hague in 1937. Roscoe Pound, who was also interested, promised to help in any way that he could. He wrote, "But as you have had experience in this sort of thing, if you are willing to undertake it I should be rejoiced if you would carry out the plan suggested in your letter."[144] Accordingly, Wigmore "in full vigor" and with "the tide of his enthusiasm . . . running strong"[145] assumed the chairmanship of the American Committee which was delegated to obtain papers contributed by American scholars.[146] Wigmore had been greatly disturbed at the 1932 congress because, although many of the papers were read in French, arrangements for immediate translation had not been made despite his strenuous efforts. Accordingly he resolved that he would "not raise a finger to cause anybody else to attend" if American delegates would again have to sit around in despair most of the time. Characteristically, he set to work to see that this mistake would not be made again and to assist in securing funds for this purpose. Wigmore kept in constant touch with the academy at The Hague and participated actively in the development of the plans.[147] Although the attendance in 1937 was not as large as it had been in

1932 (240 as against 305) and although the representation from the United States was also smaller (47 as against 72), Wigmore characterized it as "an unqualified success." Altogether it was another skillful but time-consuming effort.[148] In his report to the Section of International and Comparative Law Wigmore said, in the

> representative character of the delegates, in the practical purport of the topics discussed, and in the active discussion of those topics by well qualified participants, this Congress was far superior to the First, in 1932, and left nothing to be desired. The list of judges, and lawyers and professors, whose reports on the various topics were on file, represented a varied and competent and cosmopolitan aggregation of juristic talent such as has never before been assembled in any country on any occasion.[149]

An action by the congress which Wigmore actively promoted and which he regarded as of great importance was a resolution adopted with unanimity concerned with a "long-pending proposal for an international Faculty of Comparative Law." Now, however, it was modified to make it "ambulatory" so that it could meet in different places,[150] an action that was subsequently approved by the American Bar Association.[151] Wigmore regarded this modification with favor, since it would make it possible for the United States to share in the benefits of such an institution.

Wigmore's role in the 1937 congress was seen through the eyes of Jerome Hall, one of the American delegates:

> Mr. Wigmore was responsible for the large American delegation and for the publicity given to that conference in this country. I had been designated general reporter on *Nulla Poena sine Lege*, and it seemed advisable to attend the meeting partly to present my views but mostly, to respond to the Dean's alluring presentation of what was in store. For most of the American delegation, this was the first visit to Europe and the first attendance at such a congress. I do not believe there had been any formal appointment of representatives of our group, but it is certain that all turned, almost instinctively, to Mr. Wigmore as leader of the Americans. He knew many of the foreign scholars well and was most accomplished in making them generally acquainted. Mr. Wigmore excelled in an unusual capacity for social intercourse. He handled such situations easily and effectively. But, of course, he was essentially the great scholar with a particular interest in international collaboration by lawyers. It was characteristic that he aimed at the large body of practitioners in the various countries, rather than at specialized groups. At least, so his conduct at the Hague in 1937 seemed to indicate.[152]

Wigmore had for some time been thinking of a World Congress of Bar Associations in Washington, D. C., to be held in 1938 or 1939.[153] He was named, along with Louis Wehle of New York, to an informal committee to nominate other Americans who would assist in preparing plans for such a congress.[154] But the gathering clouds of World War II brought all such activity to an end for the time being.

Participation in the 1937 congress was not the last association that Hall was to have with Wigmore. Before long Wigmore became interested in the publication of a second series of translations in the field of legal philosophy, and he was largely responsible for success in securing the sponsorship of the Association of American Law Schools.[155] A committee on a Twentieth-century Legal Philosophy Series was appointed with Jerome Hall as chairman and Wigmore as honorary chairman.[156] Wigmore's status would have permitted him to remain more or less inactive, but characteristically he chose to participate in all important committee meetings and decisions. The practical difficulties in carrying such a project through to completion were greatly aggravated by the war, but Wigmore assisted materially in securing funds and dealing with other practical problems. His vast expertise was frequently sought by Hall. What was the relationship between Wigmore, a man in his late seventies with a well-merited international reputation in the field, and his younger colleague? According to the latter:

> Mr. Wigmore held very definite opinions on many subjects, as was only natural; he may sometimes have given the impression to those who did not know him, that he was dogmatic on certain issues. But I can report that I never sensed the slightest trace of dogmatism in him. He was emphatic in the expression of some of his opinions; but he was willing to discuss any of them and to state his reasons, in detail. Even more to the point, he was willing and able to change his mind if the evidence warranted. That this is not conjecture could be definitely shown — for I know of specific instances where he first took a very strong stand and later, in the light of additional facts, modified his position radically. Moreover, and perhaps of greatest significance, is that Mr. Wigmore never, in any of my numerous meetings with him, exhibited the slightest inclination to impose his views. There was never the attitude of the authoritarian, never the slightest intimation, even when the discussion related to matters on which he was the most recognized of all experts, that his views should prevail by virtue of his authority in the field. He was, of course, a warm and vigorous advocate of his position; he was persistent and resourceful in maintaining it. But never for a moment did he depart from the canons of courteous rational debate. It was evident that Mr. Wigmore's sensibilities in such matters transcended codes and creeds.[157]

Although, as the foregoing pages clearly indicate, Wigmore was devoting a great deal of time and effort in pursuit of his lifelong interest in comparative law, he now followed with great concern the deterioration of the international situation, and as the war clouds gathered he gave more and more attention to the problems connected with the maintenance of international peace. At the time of his untimely death in 1943, he had begun the development of a plan for the use of an economic boycott (which he considered preferable to an international police force) to maintain peace among nations. The essence of Wigmore's plan, based on his handwritten notes and elaborated by his colleague Albert Kocourek, appeared posthumously in the *American Bar Association Journal*.[158]

In essence Wigmore's argument was that an economic boycott was preferable to the use of military force because it would avoid mutual "slaughter," "the miserable aftermath of national feuds," it would be "cheaper in money cost," and "the disturbance to international economic relations would much sooner subside."[159] Wigmore, of course, recognized the necessity of overcoming what would otherwise be a fatal flaw — namely, the opposition of the trade and industrial groups in the countries that would be affected by a boycott. Wigmore's remedy was the use of insurance, already so widely applied to other kinds of losses.[160] To make this plan effective, assessments were to be levied against the participating nations, and awards were to be paid to the claimants, with the culpable nation being required to issue bonds or pay cash for the total damage.[161] As Wigmore's notes were obviously both fragmentary and tentative, it is impossible to know what his fully developed plan might have embodied. Unfortunately, subsequent events have demonstrated that nations continue to prefer the sacrifice of human lives to the loss of economic advantage and that, in any event, reaching agreement as to what constitutes aggression has so far proved to be an almost insuperable problem.

But important as Wigmore regarded the economic boycott to be, he was deeply concerned with the broader problems involved in establishing some kind of international regime after the war. He believed that his profession had a special responsibility in respect to the legal aspects of such problems and should be prepared to make a contribution to the over-all effort. In order to do this he urged lawyers to begin at once to prepare themselves, and to this end he wrote an article for the *American Bar Association Journal* entitled "Constitutional Problems in the Coming World Federation,"[162] in which he attempted to raise the basic legal questions without presuming to provide any answers. In his opinion, these problems fell into five groups: (a) the basis of representation of states, (b) the rule for decision (unanimity or majority), (c) the scope of legislative powers, (d) the executive power, and (e) citizenship. A brief analysis of each of these topics was followed by a list of books and articles dealing with some aspect of the particular problem.[163]

It is obvious that Wigmore was giving these questions careful attention. For him it naturally followed that he should share the information acquired and that he should urge members of the bar to take seriously the responsibility for the legal aspects of such international problems. He himself did not favor a superstate, if only because such a surrender of national sovereignty could not be expected "for another century or so."[164] He believed that the powers of the League of Nations were adequate, that many activities involved in world-government proposals could be voluntarily coordinated under the league as needed, and that the machinery provided for the use of the economic boycott was adequate "*if used.*"[165]

Had Wigmore lived he would certainly have articulated his thinking more fully, and it would probably have undergone modifications in response to the course of events. However, he would undoubtedly have been an ardent supporter of the United Nations as he was of the League of Nations.

17

Epilogue

On April 19, 1943, according to Mrs. Wigmore, her husband "was dismissed by his throat-and-nose specialist as in perfect condition, and he then went out and was fitted to what the salesman called a 'joyous' tweed suit, scorning a quiet, grey suit as 'too appropriate.' On the 20th his regular physician pronounced him in fine condition, and he left at noon for a business luncheon, looking so gay, so straight and young."[1] The luncheon was a meeting of the editorial board of the *Journal of Criminal Law and Criminology* at the Chicago Bar Association, and Wigmore was merely following his regular practice of attending. John W. Curran, a former student, took note of the fact that Wigmore wore his "kind spirit and infectious smile"[2] during the meeting as he had many years before when he was a student in his classes. He was vivacious, told stories, discussed books, and upon leaving "volunteered to assume responsibility for a small journalistic matter and bade us all good day."[3]

After the meeting Wigmore took a taxi to return to his home. In Mrs. Wigmore's words: "He disliked taxis and always told the driver to be very careful. But the other driver broke the law by trying to cut in front of a streetcar. Harry must have been thrown against something sharp, perhaps the door knob, for there was no blemish on him, except a deep cut into his brain, and the brain specialist said it was fatal."[4] In Kocourek's words, "But for a stupid mischance he [Wigmore] might have lived into his nineties like his senior contemporaries, Holmes and Pollock. *Fata abstabant*. In a short hour the world of legal science shrank to a small and poorer dimension."[5]

At the time of Wigmore's death there were conflicting instructions as to his burial. A memorandum in his own handwriting asked that his brother-in-law, Joel D. Hunter, who was a minister, conduct the funeral service, and also that his ashes be put in Lake Michigan off the coast of Evanston. However, in a note, a copy of which he had sent to George Craig Stewart, bishop of the Episcopal Diocese of Chicago, he expressed the desire to be buried in the Vogl lot in Cambridge, Massachusetts, with Bishop Stewart conducting the funeral service. Mrs. Wigmore objected to burying him in the Vogl lot, saying "it was a place of very gloomy remembrance for her."[6] She chose a brief private service at a funeral parlor in Chicago, which was conducted by Joel Hunter on April 23, 1943, with a minister from St. Luke's Episcopal Church in Evanston participating.[7]

A large number of persons came to "give silent testimony of their respect and affection," and "among those who signed the register were not only prominent judges, lawyers and physicians, former students and colleagues of Mr. Wigmore, but also stenographers from the office of his publishers, bell-boys and elevator operators from the hotel where they lived [the Lake Shore Club], the dressmaker who made Mrs. Wigmore's clothes after their return from Japan forty odd years before. Many were people whose contacts with Mr. Wigmore had been slight, but who, because they had experienced his unique gift of genuine interest in all whose lives he touched, felt their loss as greatly as did those who had been his intimates."[8]

At the suggestion of close friends and with Mrs. Wigmore's approval, Wigmore's ashes were buried with military honors in Arlington National Cemetery in Washington on April 28, 1943, near the grave of his friend and wartime chief, General Crowder.[9]

The selection of the Arlington National Cemetery as a final resting place not only corresponded with Mrs. Wigmore's wishes but gave recognition to Wigmore's wartime service and took account of the fact that he sometimes seemed to feel a greater pride as "Colonel" than as the author of *The Treatise on Evidence.*

A memorial service held in Thorne Hall at Northwestern University on June 11, 1943, gave recognition to Wigmore's "genius and accomplishments"; it was attended not only by his associates in the university, but by members of the legal profession. Tributes were offered by representatives on the bench, the bar, the Board of Trustees,[10] the faculty, and the university.[11] In his tribute on behalf of the Law School faculty, Robert W. Millar most aptly said: ". . . we seek and find the monument of John Henry Wigmore — by turning to the wide-spread departments of life and law which he touched and in touching adorned."[12] The National Conference of Commissioners on Uniform State Laws also took special note of Wigmore's long and constructive service as a member at a memorial service held in connection with its regular meeting in Chicago in August 1943.[13]

How the Wigmores' relationship appeared to their contemporaries is suggested by the words of Jerome Hall: "Despite the lack of any direct expressions by them, it was plain that through the many years of a long marriage they had preserved a rare and delicate affection that was a joy to see. . . . To us, the Wigmores seemed in many ways an extraordinary couple who had trod the same paths together for many years in an inspired companionship."[14]

The character of the union which endured for fifty-three years was evidenced in many little ways. Wigmore's deep affection and attentiveness were revealed by his characteristic propensity to use written notes as reminders of ideas and events. Almost unfailingly he remembered special occasions such as birthdays and other anniversaries with flowers or other gifts. Often, Mrs. Wigmore was prepared for such welcome gestures, not only because they were so generally forthcoming, but because she would find her husband's reminders in various parts of the house. Mrs. Wigmore's affection is touchingly demonstrated by the following note, with its revealing signature, written shortly after her husband's death:

> Dear Margaret:
> In spite of doctors orders, I was going to write you a long birthday letter, but I find I am too tired. Uncle Harry and I were too much one person and when that taxi-cab killed Uncle Harry, he [*sic*] killed Aunt Emma, all but a mere fragment that is trying, not very successfully, to carry on and do the many things that have to be done. But remember always that you are our Margaret . . .
> Your Uncle Harry and Aunt Emma.[15]

Mrs. Wigmore, who had been ill for some time prior to her husband's death, survived him by only four months. On August 22, 1943, her ashes were buried beside his, bringing to a close the final chapter in what was an exceptional matrimonial partnership.

How was Wigmore occupied when his activities came to such an untimely end? Although he was eighty years old he was still young at heart. He could no longer travel or take on arduous assignments, but within these limitations he was still at work. He pursued various interests at home, as, indeed, he had always done to some extent. His secretary would bring his mail and, on occasion, run some errand for him. Physical restrictions did not narrow the range of his interests, and he continued to read widely, with the subject matter ranging from wit and humor to the most pressing problems of the day. He regularly scanned the numerous legal periodicals for items of special concern. For example, he noticed one day in the current number of the *India Law Journal* a quite inadequate version of "How to Give an Orange," an amusing account of a simple gift that was couched in the most stilted legal language. This was a humorous item with which he had long been familiar. Believing that the correct version should be in the record, he used one of the quickest outlets available to him, the *Illinois Bar Journal*, for a letter to the editor in which he set out the original and much more effective version.[16]

As usual he was always looking ahead, and he recognized that a crucial postwar issue would revolve around the American naturalization law. In a discussion in the *American Bar Association Journal*[17] he considered the meanings of the terms "equality of races," "white persons," and "Aryans." He pointed out that the racial question would be an issue after the war, and he realized that the United States would not be willing to place the question of American citizenship in the hands of an international agency. Accordingly, he proposed that the existing quota system be continued but that it apply also to nationals who were then excluded. At the same time, Wigmore was giving thought to ways of enforcing international decisions. A draft of his article, "Bullets or Boycotts: Which Shall be the Measure to Enforce World Peace" was published posthumously.[18]

His publications continued to be supplemented by a flow of correspondence and by an interest in the active life around him. In a letter to Judge Lobinger dated April 19, the day before his death, he discussed his *Guide to International Law* and made comments on the work of the American Bar Association Section on International and Comparative Law in a manner indicating that he was conversant with its current activities.[19]

What would have caught his attention, and what he might have accomplished had he lived longer is largely a matter of speculation. That his efforts would have been constructive seems certain, and it cannot be doubted that in his personal associations he would have continued to be helpful and encouraging to many.

More feasible and more appropriate now is an attempt to appraise his life and achievements in the perspective of the thirty-three years that have elapsed since his death. How about the Law School to which he had devoted so much time, thought, and effort? What has been its evolution under the leadership of succeeding deans (Leon Green, Harold C. Havighurst, John Ritchie, and James A. Rahl) and their respective faculties? A full record belongs, of course, in a history of the Law School. Here, account can be taken of only a few developments that are especially relevant to the present assignment. Certainly significant is the fact that the Law School quarters have been doubled in size by completing the quadrangle, although not exactly in accordance with Wigmore's conception.[20] This expansion, together with the alterations made in the old quarters at the same time, has permitted an enlargement of the faculty and an enrichment of the curriculum in ways that would have been gratifying to Wigmore. And doubling the size of the library quarters brought it in line with his original conception, frustrated in his time only by the lack of funds. As one outcome of this expansion and remodeling of the Law School quarters, one portion of the structure was at last to bear his name. The attractive office he had occupied after his retirement as dean was named the John Henry Wigmore Room. This space has not been assigned the role of a "shrine" — it serves a functional purpose. It has been used as the office of the Air Law Institute and as a seminar room, and it is presently the office of the placement service.

Turning from physical facilities to program, attention should certainly be called to the increased emphasis on legal aid and moot court — areas that Wigmore regarded as integral parts of the educational process. The greatly broadened horizon reflected in the interests of the faculty and in the curriculum would have been a delight to John Henry Wigmore.

Although the more recent developments are, of course, the products of the leadership and the labors of Wigmore's successors, they rest on the firm foundation laid by him and his colleagues. Did Wigmore's dynamic influence cease with his death? Was he largely forgotten? The record makes the answer to these questions perfectly clear. The loyalty and affection of Wigmore's many students have had an enduring quality that emerges whenever they have been called upon for support. After World War II, when the funds available for the purchase of books were hopelessly inadequate, alumni members and their friends raised a special fund of $140,000, known as the John Henry Wigmore Fund, as a substantial start on the rehabilitation of the collection. Today thousands of books in the library are identified by the John Henry Wigmore bookplate.

In the task of raising funds for the enlargement of the Law School, the name of Wigmore has played a significant part. The dynamic leadership of this drive, of course, has had new loyalties to draw upon, but for many the name of Wigmore still played an important part and for some it was no doubt decisive.

In 1963, during the centennial celebration of the birth of Wigmore, the John Henry Wigmore Club was organized to raise funds on a continuing basis for the support of the Law School. Though some might believe that fund raising represents a crass exploitation of the Wigmore name, the dean himself would probably not have agreed. Much as he disliked the task of fund raising, he was never hesitant to assume the responsibility when necessary. To see others assuming it in his name would certainly be a source of gratification.

The award of the Wigmore Key has been made since 1949–50 by the Junior Bar Association to the member of the senior class who has done the most to preserve the traditions of the school. The Lowden-Wigmore prizes were established by Frank O. Lowden of the class of 1887. Income from the fund is used to award prizes annually ''on the basis of competitions designed to test the ability to marshall authorities, to present arguments effectively in written form and to speak lucidly and convincingly in public.'' The John Henry Wigmore Honorary Scholarships are given annually to students of exceptional ability and promise who do not need financial assistance. In the faculty a special chair has been created in honor of Wigmore. The appointee, and it is an honor, is designated the John Henry Wigmore Professor of Law.

So much for the Law School. What of Wigmore's achievements as a scholar? Any intelligent approach must first take account of the fact that he was not a recluse but an extremely active man. And yet, his productivity as a writer was astonishing — so astonishing that no appraisal of his achievements would be complete without taking it into consideration. According to a computation (counting only last editions and excluding supplementary volumes) made shortly after his death,[21] Wigmore produced 46 original volumes, including his published casebooks and other compilations, 38 edited volumes, and 16 volumes on the law of the Tokugawa Shogunate (1603–1867) — a grand total of 100 books. When his writings in pamphlet form and his articles, comments, editorials, and translations are considered, the total comes to nearly 900 titles.[22] The sheer magnitude of the achievement is almost impossible to appreciate fully until one sees the nearly eighteen feet of shelf space it occupies — an entire section of standard library shelving. The text of the memorial published by the Association of American Law Schools compares Wigmore's scholarly production with that of both legal and nonlegal authors and concludes with the statement that "no great law writer or even any great novelist, such as Scott or Dumas, . . . appears to match Dean Wigmore in the volume of published achievement.[23] Although there might be disagreement on some elements of the above computation, when account is taken of the fact that much of Wigmore's revision was extensive and many of his books contain a large number of pages, this computation is in all probability conservative.

When it comes to a qualitative appraisal of Wigmore's achievements as a writer, it should first be pointed out that no useful evaluation can be made without considering a factor heretofore referred to, but often overlooked. Broad as were the fields to which he devoted his scholarly pursuits, scholarship alone was never an adequate objective to engage the entire attention of this talented and dynamic figure. He was essentially a reformer and an educator for whom the long-range effect of his scholarship was not enough. Quite deliberately, he often turned aside from his scholarship to comment on some current development, for he could not resist the impulse to make himself heard, to throw his weight in favor of improvements in the administration of justice or against practices that were not in keeping with the best traditions of the legal profession. And over and over again he took up the task of making useful information available when no one else seemed disposed to do so.

Wigmore's writings simply cannot all be fitted into the category of scholarship. Some are informative and are intended to be no more; some are educational in character; others are editorials. Because Wigmore achieved such a high standard as a scholar, his critics have sometimes tended to apply the standard of scholarship even to writings to which he ascribed other objectives.

When these distinctly different tests are appropriately brought to bear upon his writings, there is surprisingly little that can be regarded as trivial, and even less that, because of some temporary emotional reaction, can be regarded as irresponsible. Wigmore was a writer whose scholarship never separated him from the life around him. His writings, like his relations with his fellow men, described a very wide circle indeed. He was perfectly at home with the scholar in many fields and in many countries, but he was by his own choice accessible to all, and there is ample evidence to demonstrate that he thoroughly enjoyed this wide span of personal relationships. Hence, it is not surprising that as a writer he was never satisfied to confine his efforts to the narrower arena. What is remarkable is that Wigmore could make such a massive contribution at the highest level and yet produce so much of a more popular character.

Albert Kocourek believed that one explanation for Wigmore's enormous industry and output was that his life was carefully reasoned and planned — although no specific plan has been discovered.[24] Another explanation is certainly his loyalty for or commitment to an undertaking once he assumed responsibility for it. The Law School is no doubt the outstanding example, but so is the law of evidence which he pursued relentlessly throughout his life, in spite of a variety of other major interests.

When it comes to Wigmore's role as a leader there is no doubt about the fact that, as Herbert Harley so aptly said, "He invented a way of multiplying his accomplishment by taking hold only when an emergency arose, and others were unable or unwilling, to do what was needed." Unlike many leaders who identify the causes they espouse with themselves, Wigmore identified himself with any cause he supported, and the cause and not his personal aggrandizement became the goal toward which he strove. Consequently, he had no interest in and felt no need to be assigned the formal role of titular leader when another was at hand and willing to serve in that capacity. That he was a genius is beyond question. To repeat, "At work he reminded one of the easy motion of the long driving shaft of a powerful machine resting on oil bearings. He had lived beyond his 80th year and he had escaped the torque of genius — that twisting of mind, body, character or behavior which often afflicts men of great productive powers."[25] When on his eightieth birthday a friend in writing to congratulate him remarked "that he had been a favorite of the gods" — he reported that Wigmore "admitted with feeling that the statement was true."[26]

Underlying much of Wigmore's achievement is an attribute that is impossible to measure fully: his relationships with others. The number who testify to his personal influence is legion. One of these, Sheldon Glueck, has suggested that, for many men, Wigmore is enshrined in their hearts more as a person than for his many published works.[27]

In spite of Wigmore's extraordinary capacity for scholarly work, a capacity that Holmes characterized as "unequaled" and "unapproached in fertile suggestion and massive achievement,"[28] he was never content with the cloister. "He looked upon ignorance as an evil. Valiant, colorful, resourceful, courageous, he was a personality first and a scholar afterward. The facets of that personality were so numerous and so varied that the legend of Wigmore must long live in the lore of American law, alongside his great contributions to the science of law."[29]

Notes

||||||||||⊏⊐||||||||||⊏⊐||||||||||⊏⊐||||||||||⊏⊐||||||||||⊏⊐||||||||||⊏⊐||||||||||⊏⊐||||||||||⊏⊐||||||||||⊏⊐||||||||||⊏⊐||||||||||⊏⊐||||||||||⊏⊐||||||||

U nless otherwise indicated the unpublished materials referred to in these notes can be found in the Wigmore Collection in the Northwestern University Law School Library. In addition to the letters and papers, the collection includes: *Opera Minora* consisting of a selection of Wigmore's lesser writings, *Miscellaneous Writings* in typed or near-print form, and an unpublished manuscript entitled *Recollections of a Great Scholar and Superb Gentleman, a Symposium*, edited by Albert Kocourek. References to *Opera Minora* are made only when the item cited would be otherwise difficult to locate. For the sake of brevity the manuscript edited by Albert Kocourek will hereafter be referred to as *Recollections*, and, since it is not paged continuously, the reference will give the name of the specific contributor and the page or pages of his contribution. For example: *Recollections*, Robert W. Millar, p. 3. The letters written by both Wigmore and his wife from Japan, 1889–92, have been gathered together and are also included in a typed transcription which is referred to as *Letters from Japan*.

All of Wigmore's original letters to Oliver Wendell Holmes are in the Wigmore Collection, and all of Holmes's original letters are in the Harvard Law School Library. However, the file of this correspondence has been completed in each library through the use of photocopies.

A complete *Bibliography* of John Henry Wigmore has been prepared by Kurt Schwerin and publication is forthcoming.

PREFACE

1. Wigmore to West Publishing Co., Jan. 17, 1941 (Wigmore Collection).
2. *Recollections*, Nathan W. MacChesney, p. 6 (Wigmore Collection).

CHAPTER 1. SAN FRANCISCO — BOYHOOD

1. *Recollections*, Beatrice W. Hunter, p. 2 (Wigmore Collection).
2. *Ibid*.
3. *Ibid*.
4. *Recollections*, Margaret G. Belknap, p. 4 (Wigmore Collection).
5. *Recollections*, Beatrice W. Hunter, p. 2 (Wigmore Collection). The school was sometimes referred to as the Urban Academy.
6. *Ibid*.
7. His brothers, all born in San Francisco, were George Herbert, Francis Marion, Hubert Llewelyn, and Cyril. His two sisters, Violet and Beatrice, were born in Cambridge, Massachusetts, while the family was living there.

8. *Recollections*, Beatrice W. Hunter, p. 1 (Wigmore Collection).

9. This paragraph is based on data in "Dictation of John Wigmore," Bancroft Library, University of California, Berkeley, and "Minute adopted February 5th, 1908, by the Vestry of St. Paul's Pro-Cathedral Parish," Los Angeles, California. For the death of Emma Hewitt Wigmore see "Interments in Lone Mountain Cemetery," *Daily Alta California*, San Francisco, Sept. 1, 1854, p. 2, col. 5.

10. Albert Kocourek, "John Henry Wigmore," 27 *J. Am. Jud. Soc'y* 122 (1943). See editor's note.

11. *Recollections*, Beatrice W. Hunter, p. 1 (Wigmore Collection).

12. "Minute, Feb. 5, 1908, Vestry of St. Paul's Pro-Cathedral Parish," Los Angeles.

13. *The Industries of San Francisco, California, a Review of the Manufacturing, Mercantile, and Business Interests of the Bay City Together With a Historical Sketch of Her Rise and Progress* (1889), p. 52. See also John S. Hittell, *Commerce and Industries of the Pacific Coast* (1882), p. 596, and "Minute, Feb. 5, 1908, Vestry of St. Paul's Pro-Cathedral Parish," Los Angeles.

14. Yda Addis Storke, *A Memorial and Biographical History of the Counties of Santa Barbara, San Louis Obisbo and Ventura, California* (1891), p. 508.

15. *Ibid.*

16. "Circular of the Urban School, established in A.D. 1864, and situated at No. 1017 Hyde Street, between Pine and Calif. Sts., S. F. California," p. 7, California Historical Society, San Francisco.

17. *Ibid.*, p. 21.

18. *Recollections*, Beatrice W. Hunter, p. 2 (Wigmore Collection).

19. For these and further details regarding the Urban School, see materials at the California Historical Society, San Francisco.

20. *Recollections*, Francis M. Wigmore, p. 1 (Wigmore Collection).

21. Sarah B. Morgan to the author, Feb. 12, 1962.

22. *Recollections*, Beatrice W. Hunter, p. 2 (Wigmore Collection).

23. Sarah B. Morgan to the author, Feb. 12, 1962.

24. Lilliam H. Guerin to the author, May 26, 1965.

25. Alfred M. Shafter, *Musical Copyright*, 2d ed. (1939), p. xv.

26. *Recollections*, Francis M. Wigmore, p. 2 (Wigmore Collection).

27. Sarah B. Morgan to the author, Feb. 12, 1962.

28. *Recollections*, Beatrice W. Hunter, p. 2 (Wigmore Collection).

CHAPTER 2. HARVARD

1. *Recollections*, Beatrice W. Hunter, p. 3 (Wigmore Collection).

2. *Recollections*, Francis M. Wigmore, p. 2 (Wigmore Collection).

3. *Recollections*, Beatrice W. Hunter, p. 3 (Wigmore Collection).

4. *Recollections*, Francis M. Wigmore, p. 2 (Wigmore Collection).

5. Wigmore, "Honor to Brains," pp. 1–2. Address at the College Honors Convocation, Oct. 21, 1931, Northwestern University (Wigmore Collection).

6. Harvard College Class of 1883, *Secretary's Report No. 1*, pp. 11, 12, 17.

7. Alfred M. Shafter, *Musical Copyright*, 2d ed. (1939), p. xvi.

8. Harvard College Class of 1883, *Fiftieth Anniversary* (1933), p. 339.

9. "Benefit Program" (Wigmore Collection).

10. "Programme" (Wigmore Collection).

11. Shafter, *Musical Copyright*, p. xvi.

12. Harvard College Class of 1883, *Secretary's Report No. 1*, p. 35.

13. *Ibid.*, p. 30.

14. Triennial 1883, *Secretary's Report No. 2* [1886], p. 76.

15. Lately Thomas, *A Debonair Scoundrel* (1962), p. 8.

16. As to the Municipal Reform League, see also Anne W. Lane and Louise H. Wall, *The Letters of Franklin K. Lane Personal and Political* (1922), p. 17.

17. Probably all of these early journalistic efforts appeared in San Francisco newspapers, and most of them in the *Daily Alta California*. However, although copies of all of them are in the Wigmore Collection, most of them are so incompletely identified as to date and newspaper that it has been impossible to confirm or complete the references. Although the daily newspapers of the period appeared in more than one edition, with variations as to contents, the files available in California did not include all editions. For copies see *Opera Minora*, 9:1-6.

18. *The New Testament of Our Lord and Savior Jesus Christ Translated Out of the Greek: Being the Version Set Fourth A.D. 1611 Compared With the Most Ancient Authorities and Revised A.D. 1881*, Oxford 1881.

19. *Recollections*, Preface [Albert Kocourek], p. 3 (Wigmore Collection).

20. *Recollections*, Sarah B. Morgan, p. 33 (Wigmore Collection).

21. Hollis Hall room list (Wigmore Collection).

22. Mrs. James H. Chadbourn to the author, April 10, 1968.

23. Arthur Sutherland, *The Law at Harvard* (1967), pp. 170–71.

24. "Memorial," *1943 Handbook*, Ass'n. Am. L. Schools, p. 239.

25. *The Centennial History of the Harvard Law School 1817–1917* (1918), pp. 42, 139–41.

26. "The Recent Cases Department," 50 *Harv. L. Rev.* 862 (1937).

27. *Id.* at 863.

28. *Centennial History of the Harvard Law School 1817–1917*, p. 140.

29. *Ibid.*, p. 262.

30. *Ibid.*, p. 42.

31. *Ibid.*, p. 140.

32. "Pow-Wow Club, Harvard Law School, 1870—1901" (Wigmore Collection).

33. *Recollections*, Beatrice W. Hunter, p. 3 (Wigmore Collection).

34. In Wigmore Collection.

35. In Wigmore Collection.

36. Wigmore to Holmes, March 18, 1902 (Wigmore Collection).

37. Wigmore to Holmes, June 7, 1924 (Wigmore Collection).

38. Sarah B. Morgan to the author, May 12, 1966.

39. *Recollections*, Francis M. Wigmore, p. 3 (Wigmore Collection).

40. "The Jewel of Consistency," Oct. 1, 1885, *Opera Minora*, 9:5 (Wigmore Collection).

41. (1885), 29:468; *Opera Minora*, 9:6 (Wigmore Collection).

42. 21 *Am L. Rev.* 509 (1887). Also 21 *Irish L. Times* 470 (1887).

43. 21 *Am. L. Rev.* 764 (1889). Also 22 *Irish L. Times* 56, 96 (1888).

44. Wigmore to George M. Bartlett, Nov. 10, 1904 (Wigmore Collection).

45. Nov. 7, 1887.

46. Mark DeWolfe Howe, *Holmes — Pollock Letters* (1941), 1:31.

CHAPTER 3. BOSTON

1. Ass'n Am. L. Schools, *Directory of Teachers in Member Schools* (1942–43), p. 199.

2. Wigmore, "Advice of a Veteran to Young Lawyers," p. 8. See also p. 7. Remarks at the Harvard Law School, Feb. 28, 1935 (Wigmore Collection).

3. Wigmore kept a "Diary of Work for Various Persons" (Wigmore Collection). His correspondence confirms the limited range of his practice.

4. Wigmore to Robert G. Pike, March 27, 1916. Quoted in Robert G. Pike, "Memories of Judge Doe," *Proceedings of Bar Ass'n. of State of N.H.* 463, 476 (1916).

5. *Id.*

6. Charles Doe to Wigmore, April 13, 1888 (Wigmore Collection).

7. Wigmore to Robert G. Pike, March 27, 1916. Quoted in Robert G. Pike, "Memories of Judge Doe," at 477.

8. Wigmore to Holmes, Feb. 6, 1916 (Wigmore Collection).

9. Wigmore, "Independent Research Work," p. 2. Remarks to the Northwestern University Law School Class of 1915 (Wigmore Collection).

10. Louis D. Brandeis to Wigmore, April 2, 1889 (Wigmore Collection).

11. "John H. Wigmore," *The Advocate: America's Jewish J.*, Oct. 17, 1941 (Wigmore Collection).

12. See the following letters to the governor of Massachusetts: Leonard A. Jones, May 18, 1888; John C. Gray, May 21, 1888; James B. Thayer, May 18, 1888. See also James B. Ames to Wigmore, June 9, 1888 (Wigmore Collection).

13. The full title is *A Digest of the Reported Decisions, Precedents and General Principles Enunciated by the Board of Railroad Commissioners of the Commonwealth of Massachusetts from 1870 to 1888.*

14. Wigmore prepared a news story describing the work of the commission and the purpose of the *Digest*. Copy in *Opera Minora*, 9:15 (Wigmore Collection).

15. Holmes to Wigmore, Sept. 8, 1888 (Wigmore Collection).

16. 6 *Medico-Legal J.* 292 (1888). Copy in *Opera Minora*, vol. 1 (Wigmore Collection). Wigmore also received honorable mention for "Admissibility of Medical Books in Evidence." See "Transactions," 6 *Medico-Legal J.* 332–33 (1888).

17. Paul G. Kuntz to the author, Jan. 30, 1968.

18. Feb. 13, 1888, *Opera Minora*, 9:13 (Wigmore Collection).

19. (1888), 22:890.

20. William S. Holdsworth, "Wigmore as a Legal Historian," 29 *Ill. L. Rev.* 448, 451 (1934).

21. The full title is *A Treatise on the Measure of Damages; or, An Inquiry Into the Principles Which Govern the Amount of Pecuniary Compensation Awarded by Courts of Justice*, 8th ed. (1891).

22. Charles Doe to Wigmore, March 30, 1889 (Wigmore Collection).

23. Agreement dated March 22, 1889 (Wigmore Collection).

24. W. H. Stevenson to Wigmore, April 24, 1889; May 1, 1889; May 7, 1889; May 13, 1889 (Wigmore Collection).

25. *Opera Minora*, 9:17 (Wigmore Collection).

26. *Id.* at 18.

27. (1889), 23:719.

28. Harvard College Class of 1883, *Fiftieth Anniversary* (1933), p. 337.

29. H. T. Terry to Wigmore, June 22, 1889 (Wigmore Collection).

30. H. E. Capen to Wigmore, June 20, 1889 (Wigmore Collection).

31. Kocourek and Wigmore, *Sources of Ancient and Primitive Law* (1915), p. xi–xii. Also *Evolution of Law: Select Readings on the Origin and Development of Legal Institutions* (1915), vol. 1.

32. Wigmore, "Jottings on Comparative Legal Ideas and Institutions," 6 *Tulane L. Rev.* 48 (1931).

33. Charles W. Eliot to Wigmore, July 12, 1889 (Wigmore Collection).

34. When the revision was completed Wigmore's contribution was acknowledged as follows: "The accumulation of cases for the new edition proved to be very great and in 1887, Mr. J. H. Wigmore, of the Boston Bar, who had begun the work of rearrangement, was compelled to abandon it. His suggestions, however, have proved of value to the present editors." Sedgwick and Beale, *A Treatise on the Measure of Damages; Or, An Inquiry Into the Principles Which Govern the Amount of Pecuniary Compensation Awarded by Courts of Justice*, 8th ed. (1891), vol. 8.

35. H. B. Adams to Wigmore, Oct. 26, 1889 (Wigmore Collection).

36. *Ibid.*

37. Franklin K. Lane to Wigmore, May 10, 1889; July 20, 1889; July 23, 1889; Aug. 14, 1889 (Wigmore Collection).

38. To Wigmore from W. P. Garrison, Sept. 5, 1889; C. R. Hiller, Sept. 5, 1889; E. L. Burlingame, Sept. 9, 1889; and Horace W. Fuller, Oct. 25, 1889 (Wigmore Collection).

39. Wigmore to Richard W. Gilder, Aug. 9, 1889 (Wigmore Collection).

40. Charles Doe to Wigmore, July 9, 1889 (Wigmore Collection).

41. Louis D. Brandeis to Wigmore, Sept. 3, 1889 (Wigmore Collection).

42. Julian Mack to Wigmore, July 26, 1889 (Wigmore Collection).

43. "Certificate of Marriage" (Wigmore Collection).

44. *Recollections*, Beatrice W. Hunter, p. 3 (Wigmore Collection).

45. Wigmore's father to Wigmore, n.d. [1889] (Wigmore Collection).

46. Wigmore apparently kept all the letters from his parents, but none of his letters to his parents have been located. However, their letters refer to a number of letters received from him while he was at the Harvard Law School.

CHAPTER 4. JAPAN

1. *Letters from Japan*, p. 3 (Wigmore Collection).

2. *Ibid.*, pp. 3, 9.

3. *Ibid.*, p. 8.

4. *Ibid.*, p. 18.

5. *Ibid.*, p. 37.

6. *Ibid.*, pp. 38–39, 119–20, 148, 204.

7. *Ibid.*, pp. 39, 102.

8. *Ibid.*, p. 102.

9. *Ibid.*, pp. 8, 84, 138.

10. *Ibid.*, pp. 243, 362.

11. Wigmore to Hallett Aband, Nov. 4, 1942 (Wigmore Collection).

12. Sarah B. Morgan to the author, July 30, 1965.

13. *Letters from Japan*, pp. 265, 295 (Wigmore Collection).

14. *Ibid.*, pp. 148, 238.

15. *Ibid.*, pp. 139, 298, 401.

16. *Ibid.*, pp. 129, 130, 136, 148.

17. *Recollections*, Helen K. McNamara, p. 1 (Wigmore Collection).

18. *Recollections*, Anne G. Millar, pp. 4–5 (Wigmore Collection).

19. *Letters from Japan*, p. 149. See also p. 93 (Wigmore Collection).

20. As to Wigmore's athletic interests see also *ibid.*, pp. 115, 150, 163, 333, 339, 344, 365, 399.

21. "Wigmore Revisits Japan" [1935], p. 8 (Wigmore Collection).

22. Wigmore to Frederick D. Fagg, Jr., May 13, 1940 (Wigmore Collection).

23. *Recollections*, Sarah B. Morgan, p. 3 (Wigmore Collection).

24. Agreement between American Unitarian Association and John Henry Wigmore (1889) (Wigmore Collection).

25. *Letters from Japan*, pp. 281, 298, 339 (Wigmore Collection).

26. *Ibid.*, p. 76. See also p. 75.

27. *Ibid.*, p. 140.

28. *Ibid.*, p. 144.

29. Boston Book Co. to Wigmore, Aug. 2 and 29, 1889; Feb. 13 and 19, 1890; April 11 and 16, 1890; May 6, 1890; Oct. 11 and 15, 1890 (Wigmore Collection).

30. I. Kadono to Wigmore, Dec. 4, 1890 (Wigmore Collection).

31. JHW diary, Sept. 25, 1891 (Wigmore Collection).

32. *Ibid.*, Sept. 26, 1891.

33. Kenzo Takayanagi, ''Jurisprudence: East and West — Wigmore's Remarkable Contribution,'' p. 3. Address before the John Henry Wigmore Club, Feb. 3, 1966 (Wigmore Collection).

34. *Ibid.*, p. 2.

35. *Opera Minora*, 9:25 (Wigmore Collection).

36. *Id.* at 28.

37. These are listed in the forthcoming *Bibliography* referred to in the Preface which has been prepared by Kurt Schwerin. Copies of the articles are in the Wigmore Collection.

38. *Ibid.*

39. W. P. Garrison to Wigmore, Sept. 26, 1890 (Wigmore Collection).

40. *Letters from Japan*, p. 295 (Wigmore Collection).

41. W. V. Keller to Wigmore, July 20, 1890 (Wigmore Collection).

42. (July–Aug. 1891), 10:33–51, 243–55. Copies in *Opera Minora*, vol. 3 (Wigmore Collection).

43. E. L. Burlingame to Wigmore, Feb. 19, 1891 (Wigmore Collection).

44. *Green Bag* (1892), 4:403, 478.

45. *Green Bag* (1893), 5:17, 78.

46. *Green Bag* (1892), 4:563; (1897), 9:359; (1898), 10:287.

47. (1891), 5:71. For a more extensive treatment by Wigmore see ''The Privilege Against Self-Crimination,'' 15 *Harv. L. Rev.* 610 (1902).

48. (1890), 24:874; (1891), 25:695; (1892), 26:390.

49. Leonard A. Jones to Wigmore, June 20, 1891 (Wigmore Collection).

50. Frederic C. Woodward, *Law of Quasi Contracts* (1913).

51. Regarding Wigmore's activities see the *Transactions* of the Asiatic Society of Japan, 19:501–4, xvi, xix, xxviii; 20:xi; 21:x, xi.

52. Published in *Transactions* (1891), 19:37–270. The table of contents is at the beginning of the volume. For minutes relating to this study see pp. viii-ix at the end of the volume. Wigmore also contributed a short comment to this volume (p. 501) entitled ''Note on the Eiraku-Sen.''

53. Arthur M. Knapp to Wigmore, June 27, 1891 (Wigmore Collection).

54. William E. Griffin to Wigmore, May 11, 1891 (Wigmore Collection).

55. Supplement to vol. 20.

56. *Transactions*, 21:xii.

57. *Ibid.*

58. *Japan Weekly Mail*, Feb. 11, 1893, pp. 169, 170 (Wigmore Collection).

59. Kenzo Takayanagi, ''Jurisprudence: East and West — Wigmore's Remarkable Contribution'' (1966), p. 5.

60. Wigmore to Holmes, Nov. 1, 1892 (Wigmore Collection).

61. Holmes to Wigmore, Mar. 25, 1895 (Harvard Law School Library).

62. *Letters from Japan*, p. 366 (Wigmore Collection).

63. Louis D. Brandeis to Wigmore, Aug. 30, 1891 (Wigmore Collection).

64. Charles G. Soule to Wigmore, July 30, 1891 (Wigmore Collection).

65. Joseph E. Beale to Wigmore, April 12, 1892 (Wigmore Collection).

66. *Letters from Japan*, p. 269 (Wigmore Collection).

67. *Ibid.*, p. 381.

68. *Ibid.*, p. 382 (Wigmore Collection).

69. *Ibid.*, p. 414.

70. Remarks in student's handwriting. Author not known (Wigmore Collection).

71. *Letters from Japan*, p. 414 (Wigmore Collection).

72. *Ibid.*, p. 415.

73. *Japan Daily Mail*, Dec. 17, 1892 (Wigmore Collection).

74. Takayanagi, "Jurisprudence: East and West — Wigmore's Remarkable Contributions," p. 2.

CHAPTER 5. NORTHWESTERN UNIVERSITY

1. Henry W. Rogers to Wigmore, Jan. 27, 1893 (Wigmore Collection).

2. *Ibid.*, June 16, 1893.

3. *Letters from Japan*, p. 382 (Wigmore Collection).

4. Henry W. Rogers to Wigmore, Mar. 3, 1893 (Wigmore Collection).

5. Holmes to Wigmore, Feb. 20, 1893 (Harvard Law School Library).

6. *Ibid.* See also Wigmore to Holmes, Mar. 10, 1928 (Wigmore Collection).

7. Wigmore to Holmes, Mar. 10, 1928 (Wigmore Collection).

8. *Ibid.*, Mar. 6, 1931.

9. Louis D. Brandeis to Wigmore, Feb. 21, 1893 (Wigmore Collection).

10. E. A. Harriman to Wigmore, Mar. 27, 1893 (Wigmore Collection).

11. Henry W. Rogers to Wigmore, May 19, 1893 (Wigmore Collection).

12. Nathan Abbott to Wigmore, May 9, 1893 (Wigmore Collection).

13. Julian W. Mack to Wigmore, Apr. 19, 1893 (Wigmore Collection).

14. Charles W. Eliot to Wigmore, May 16, 1894 (Wigmore Collection).

15. Nathan Abbott to Wigmore, Mar. 22, 1893 (Wigmore Collection).

16. *Recollections*, Helen K. McNamara, p. 10 (Wigmore Collection).

17. *Recollections*, Agnes F. Bradley, p. 2 (Wigmore Collection).

18. *Recollections*, Helen K. McNamara, p. 10 (Wigmore Collection).

19. For a more detailed account of the Law School than is possible here, see James A. Rahl and Kurt Schwerin, *Northwestern University School of Law — A Short History* (1960).

20. *Id.* at 8.

21. *Id.* at 9.

22. *Id.* at 14.

23. See especially Charles W. Eliot to Wigmore: Feb. 27, 1893; Apr. 15, 1893; June 27, 1893; June 30, 1893; Nov. 28, 1893; May 16, 1894; May 12, 1897; June 17, 1899 (Wigmore Collection).

24. Joseph H. Beale to Wigmore, Apr. 18, 1900 (Wigmore Collection).

25. See James B. Thayer to Wigmore: June 22, 1893; Aug. 22, 1893; Mar. 6, 1899; Sept. 23, 1899; Sept. 28, 1899; Feb. 1, 1900; Feb. 8, 1900; May 13, 1900; Sept. 19, 1900 (Wigmore Collection).

26. Ames wrote many letters to Wigmore between 1893 and 1910 (Wigmore Collection).

27. Joseph H. Beale to Wigmore, Mar. 8, 1894; Feb. 16, 1899; Apr. 18, 1900; May 6, 1900. See also James B. Ames to Wigmore, Sept. 26, 1893 and Oct. 30, 1893, and William A. Keener to Wigmore, Feb. 19, 1895 and Feb. 27, 1895 (Wigmore Collection).

28. James B. Ames to Wigmore, Feb. 23, 1894 (Wigmore Collection).

29. Joseph H. Beale to Wigmore, Feb. 20, 1894 (Wigmore Collection).

30. James B. Ames to Wigmore, Sept. 7, 1894 (Wigmore Collection).

31. Henry Recke to Wigmore, May 11, 1894 (Wigmore Collection).

32. Charles W. Eliot to Wigmore, Feb. 27, 1893; Apr. 15, 1893; June 27, 1893; June 30, 1893; June 17, 1899 (Wigmore Collection).

33. Charles W. Eliot to Wigmore, Nov. 28, 1896; W. O. Batchelder to Wigmore, May 6 and 21, 1921 (Wigmore Collection).

34. Frederick Nicholas to Wigmore, Apr. 13, 1895 (Wigmore Collection).

35. Seth P. Smith to Wigmore, Sept. 9, 1895; John Hollingshead to Wigmore, Aug. 1, 1895 (Wigmore Collection).

36. Blewett Lee to Wigmore, Aug. 15, 1893 (Wigmore Collection).

37. *Ibid.*, Nov. 22, 1900.

38. Charles C. Hyde to Wigmore, June 20, 1899 (Wigmore Collection).

39. James B. Ames to Wigmore, Apr. 18, 1893 (Wigmore Collection).

40. *Recollections*, Charles B. Elder, p. 2 (Wigmore Collection).

41. The courses taught by Wigmore were regularly listed in the *Bulletin* of the Northwestern University School of Law.

42. "The Tripartite Division of Torts," 8 *Harv. L. Rev.* 200 (1894).

43. 2 William Blackstone's Reports 892.

44. James B. Thayer, *Select Cases on Evidence at Common Law* (1892).

45. Simon Greenleaf, *A Treatise on the Law of Evidence* . . . Annotated by J. H. Wigmore (1899).

46. *Recollections*, Charles B. Elder, p. 1 (Wigmore Collection).

47. *Recollections*, Nathan W. MacChesney, p. 3 (Wigmore Collection).

48. Fred H. Bowersock to Wigmore, Oct. 5, 1897 (Wigmore Collection).

49. The last minutes signed by Wigmore as secretary were dated June 10, 1895.

50. Concerning the development of the library, see W. R. Roalfe and Kurt Schwerin, "The Elbert H. Gary Law Library of Northwestern University" 46 *Law Lib. J.* 219 (1953).

51. This forerunner of the *Illinois Law Review*, which became the *Northwestern University Law Review* in 1952, appeared monthly during the school year from January 1893 to May 1896 in four volumes.

52. University Trustee Minutes, June 11, 1895, p. 186.

53. *Ibid.*, p. 222. For a more extended discussion of this period in the Law School's history, see Rahl and Schwerin, *Northwestern University School of Law — A Short History*, pp. 12–18.

54. Henry M. Bates to Wigmore, Dec. 11, 1929 (Wigmore Collection).

55. J. W. Jenks to Wigmore, May 23, 1894 (Wigmore Collection).

56. Franklin K. Lane to Wigmore, Jan. 30, 1897; Feb. 7, 1897; June 16, 1897; Apr. 5, 1898; July 22, 1898 (Wigmore Collection).

57. A. S. Draper to Wigmore, Apr. 17, 1899 (Wigmore Collection).

58. 7 *Harv. L. Rev.* 315, 383, 441 (1894). Reprinted in *Select Essays in Anglo-American Legal History* (1909), 3:474–539. For a comment see 2 *Northwestern L. Rev.* 61 (1894).

59. 8 *Harv. L. Rev.* 200 (1894).

60. *Id.* at 377 (1895).

61. James B. Ames to Wigmore, Feb. 6, 1894 (Wigmore Collection).

62. "Responsibility for Tortious Acts: Its History — III," 7 *Harv. L. Rev.* 441 (1894).

63. Frederick Pollock to Wigmore, Mar. 23, 1895 (Wigmore Collection).

64. Wigmore to Holmes, Mar. 29, 1895 (Wigmore Collection).

65. *Ibid.*, Apr. 29, 1894.

66. Holmes to Wigmore, May 3, 1894 (Harvard Law School Library).

67. *Ibid.*, Mar. 25, 1895.

68. See page 15.

69. 27 *Am. L. Rev.* 819 (1893).

70. H. M. Knowlton to Wigmore, July 6, 1893; July 8, 1893; July 21, 1893 (Wigmore Collection).

71. 30 *Am. L. Rev.* 29 (1896).

72. 32 *Am. L. Rev.* 187 (1898).

73. *Opera Minora*, 11:1 (Wigmore Collection).

74. 30 *Am. L. Rev.* 481 (1896).

75. 32 *Am. L. Rev.* 713 (1898).

76. 33 *Am. L. Rev.* 376 (1899).

77. 38 *Am. L. Reg.* (N.S.) 337, 432, 683 (1899).

78. Simon Greenleaf, *A Treatise on the Law of Evidence (1899)*. Little, Brown and Company accepted Wigmore's recommendation that Edward A. Harriman, a colleague of Wigmore's on the Northwestern University Law School faculty, revise vols. 2 and 3, and Harriman undertook the assignment. Little, Brown and Company to Wigmore, July 15, 1898, and Edward A. Harriman to Wigmore, July 19, 1898 (Wigmore Collection).

79. Greenleaf, *Treatise on Law of Evidence*, 1:vi.

80. James B. Thayer to Wigmore, Sept. 28, 1899 (Wigmore Collection).

81. *Ibid.*, Feb. 8, 1900.

82. Henry W. Rogers to Wigmore, Sept. 19, 1899 (Wigmore Collection).

83. 13 *Harv. L. Rev.* 228 (1899).

84. Little, Brown and Company to Wigmore, Feb. 17, 1899 (Wigmore Collection).

85. *Ibid.*, Nov. 29, 1899.

86. Seymour D. Thompson to Wigmore, Jan. 3, 1898 (Wigmore Collection).

87. *Ibid.*, Mar. 13, 1899.

88. *Harv. L. Rev.* 10:321; 11:18 (1897). Reprinted in Albert Kocourek and J. H. Wigmore, *Evolution of Law: Select Readings on the Origin and Development of Legal Institutions* (1915), 2:456–77.

89. James B. Ames to Wigmore, Jan. 5, 1896 (Wigmore Collection).

90. Ernest Freund to Wigmore, Feb. 26, 1897 (Wigmore Collection).

91. *Recollections*, Roscoe Pound, p. 1 (Wigmore Collection).

92. Robert W. Millar, "On Behalf of the Law Faculty," 34 *J. Crim. L. & C.* 85, 87 (1943).

93. 36 New Series 437, 491, 571, 628, 714 (1897).

94. *Green Bag* (1893), 5:17, 78.

95. 17 *A. B. A. Rep.* 453 (1894).

96. *The Brief* (Phi Delta Phi) (1900), 2:124. Later expanded versions appear in 2 *Ill. L. Rev.* 574 (1908), 17 *Ill. L. Rev.* 26 (1922), 52 *Lib. J.* 189 (1927).

97. *Chicago L. J.*, June 10, 1898, p. 234.

98. *Green Bag* (1898), 10:394; (1899), 11:111, 176.

99. See the following letters: *Atlantic Monthly* to Wigmore, Jan. 21, 1898; *The Forum* to Wigmore, Dec. 2, 1897, Jan. 7, 1898, Feb. 24, 1898; Harper & Brothers to Wigmore, Apr. 4, 1893, Jan. 11, 1897, Dec. 10, 1897, Dec. 23, 1897, Jan. 18,

1898; Charles Scribner's Sons to Wigmore, Jan. 19, 1895, Dec. 14, 1897 (Wigmore Collection).

100. Harper & Brothers to Wigmore, Dec. 23, 1897 (Wigmore Collection).

101. Walter H. Page (*Atlantic Monthly*) to Wigmore, Jan. 21, 1898 (Wigmore Collection).

CHAPTER 6 — DEAN

1. Wigmore, "Remarks on September 8, 1922," p. 1 (Wigmore Collection).

2. E. A. Harriman to Wigmore, Sept. 11, 1901 (Wigmore Collection).

3. Blewett Lee to Wigmore, n.d. (Wigmore Collection).

4. On Sept. 16, 1901, the Executive Committee of the Board of Trustees recommended that Wigmore be appointed acting dean, and on Sept. 25, 1901, they recommended that he be appointed dean. University Trustee Minutes, Sept. 16 and 25, 1901.

5. Wigmore, "Remarks on September 8, 1922," p. 1 (Wigmore Collection).

6. May 16, 1902 (Wigmore Collection).

7. Wigmore, "Remarks on September 8, 1922," p. 2 (Wigmore Collection).

8. *Ibid.*

9. *Ibid.*

10. *Recollections*, Nathan W. MacChesney, p. 3 (Wigmore Collection).

11. Charles C. Hyde and Albert M. Kales were the men under consideration. See James A. Rahl and Kurt Schwerin, *Northwestern University School of Law — A Short History* (1960), p. 19.

12. Wigmore, "Remarks on September 8, 1922," p. 3 (Wigmore Collection).

13. *Ibid.*

14. Edward A. Harriman to Wigmore, June 6, 1902 (Wigmore Collection).

15. Wigmore, "Remarks on September 8, 1922," p. 3 (Wigmore Collection).

16. Edward A. Harriman to Wigmore, June 6, 1902 (Wigmore Collection).

17. *N.U. School of Law Bull.*, May, 1902, p. 40.

18. Nathan W. MacChesney, "On Behalf of the Board of Trustees," 38 *Ill. L. Rev.* 5, 6 (1943).

19. *N. U. School of Law Bull.*, May, 1902, p. 40.

20. *Id.*, Aug., 1903, p. 11.

21. For text of the dedication address, see Holmes, *Collected Legal Papers* 272 (1920). His other speech was printed at least in part in 17 *Chicago L. Rev.* 733 (1902). For a description of the inaugural exercises at the opening of the new quarters with Holmes's address see *N. U. School of Law Bull.*, Nov., 1902, p. 2.

22. Holmes to Lady Pollock, Oct. 24, 1902. In Mark D. Howe, *Holmes — Pollock Letters* (1942), p. 108.

23. Holmes to Wigmore, Oct. 24, 1902 (Harvard Law School Library).

24. *Ibid.*, Oct. 31, 1902.

25. *N.U. School of Law Bull.*, May, 1902, p. 39.

26. *Id.* at 35.

27. Confidential letter to Wigmore, Feb. 8, 1903 (Wigmore Collection).

28. (Wigmore Collection).

29. *Recollections*, Charles B. Elder, p. 4 (Wigmore Collection).

30. 30 *A.B.A. Rep.* (Pt. 1) 395 (1906).

31. Roscoe Pound to Wigmore, Nov. 10, 1906 (Wigmore Collection).

32. Paul Sayre, *The Life of Roscoe Pound* (1948), p. 153.

33. Robert E. Allard to the author, Nov. 20, 1963.

34. Wigmore to Holmes, Sept. 5, 1907 (Wigmore Collection).

35. Copy in Wigmore Collection.

36. Felix Frankfurter to Wigmore, Oct. 2, 1913; Wigmore to Frankfurter, Oct. 3, 1913 (Wigmore Collection).

37. *Recollections*, Charles B. Elder, p. 6 (Wigmore Collection).

38. A description of the course for 1914–15 and copies of the final-examination questions for 1909, 1910, 1914, 1916, and 1917 have been preserved (Wigmore Collection).

39. Wigmore to Ezra R. Thayer, June 12, 1914, Oct. 20, 1914, Oct. 26, 1914; Ezra R. Thayer to Wigmore, Dec. 12, 1913 (Wigmore Collection).

40. The courses taught by Wigmore were listed regularly in *N.U. School of Law Bull.*

41. For a description of the course see *N.U. School of Law Bull.*, Aug.–Nov., 1907, pp. 5–18.

42. 30 *A.B.A. Rep.* (Pt. 2) 34 (1906).

43. Wigmore to James H. Tufts, Oct. 7, 1914 (Wigmore Collection).

44. Wigmore to Felix Frankfurter, May 11, 1914 (Wigmore Collection).

45. Felix Frankfurter to Wigmore, May 24, 1914 (Wigmore Collection).

46. *Ibid.*

47. Ezra R. Thayer to Wigmore, Feb. 7, 1914 (Wigmore Collection).

48. Draft of a letter for general distribution, Sept. 15, 1914 (Wigmore Collection).

49. *Recollections*, Stuart S. Ball, p. 2 (Wigmore Collection).

50. *Ibid.*

51. *Ibid.*

52. *Recollections*, Hugh Green 2 (Wigmore Collection).

53. Henry J. Fehrman to Wigmore, Nov. 10, 1922 (Wigmore Collection).

54. 2 *Select Cases on the Law of Torts* 997 (1912).

55. Robert G. Howlett to the author, May 20, 1964, p. 5.

56. *Ibid.*, p. 6.

57. *Recollections*, Charles H. Watson, p. 5 (Wigmore Collection).

58. Wigmore (photocopy) to Samuel Levin, March 20, 1941 (author's collection).

59. Based on a statement made to the author by a student of Wigmore's.

60. *Recollections*, Stephen Love, p. 2 (Wigmore Collection).

61. Robert G. Howlett to the author, May 20, 1964, p. 3.

62. *Recollections*, Charles H. Watson, p. 3 (Wigmore Collection).

63. *Recollections*, John W. Curran, p. 2 (Wigmore Collection).

64. *Recollections*, Charles H. Watson, p. 4 (Wigmore Collection).

65. *Recollections*, Stephen Love, p. 4 (Wigmore Collection).

66. The complete title is *Conduct of Law Suits, Out of and In Court: Practically Teaching and Copiously Illustrating, the Preparation and Forensic Management of Litigated Cases of All Kinds*, 2d ed. (1912).

67. *Id.* at vii.

68. Based on a statement made to the author by a student of Wigmore's.

69. *Recollections*, John W. Curran, p. 2 (Wigmore Collection).

70. *Recollections*, Robert W. Millar, p. 1 (Wigmore Collection).

71. Nathan W. MacChesney, "John Henry Wigmore — A Personal Appreciation," 32 *J. Crim. L. & C.* 285 (1914)

72. [Wigmore], *Northwestern University School of Law Educational Survey, Report of the Dean* 286 (1927).

73. *Id.*

74. University Trustee Minutes, Jan. 20, 1908.

75. [Wigmore], *Northwestern University School of Law Educational Survey, Report of the Dean* 287 (1927). See also Wigmore's address to the Caxton Club, Mar. 21, 1936 (Wigmore Collection).

76. In a letter to Wigmore dated Feb. 7, 1905, Burt E. Howard says, "While both Harvard and Columbia have considerable material for a study of foreign law, you have undoubtedly the best collection in the country" (Wigmore Collection).

77. *N.U. School of Law Bull.*, May–July, 1908, p. 6.

78. Albert Kocourek, "John Henry Wigmore," *Green Bag* (1912), 24:3, 5; 13 *Ill. L. Rev.* 340, 343 (1918).

79. Northwestern University School of Law, *Book of Information*, 3d ed., n.d. (Wigmore Collection).

80. *Recollections*, Hugh Green, p. 3 (Wigmore Collection).

81. Edmund J. James to Wigmore, May 2, 1902 (Wigmore Collection).

82. Law Faculty Minutes, Feb. 14, 1903, and Feb. 19, 1904, pp. 140, 163.

83. Law Faculty Minutes, Feb. 2, Mar. 2, 1906, pp. 214–15.

84. In 1952 (vol. 47) the name was changed to *Northwestern University Law Review*.

85. "The Illinois Law Review," 1 *Ill. L. Rev.* 39 (1906).

86. 10 *Ill. L. Rev.* 129 (1915).

87. *Recollections*, Roscoe Pound, p. 3 and Elmer M. Leesman, p. 2 (Wigmore Collection). For examples of verses see *Opera Minora*, 13:67 (Wigmore Collection).

88. *Recollections*, Robert W. Millar, p. 4 (Wigmore Collection).

89. 58 *Law Q. Rev.* 61 (1942).

90. "Some Evidence Statutes that Illinois Ought to Have," 1 *Ill. L. Rev.* 9 (1906); and jointly with Henry C. Hall, "Compensation for Property Destroyed to Stop the Spread of a Conflagration," 1 *Ill. L. Rev.* 501 (1907).

91. 1 *Ill. L. Rev.* 43, 44, 113, 122, 397, 400, 478, 548, 549, 551, 618 (1906–7).

92. 1 *Ill. L. Rev.* 180, 253, 470, 606 (1906–7).

93. *N.U. School of Law Bull.*, May 1910, p. 24.

94. University Trustee Minutes, July 17, 1916, p. 51.

95. [Wigmore], *Northwestern University School of Law Educational Survey, Report of the Dean* 34 (1927).

96. H. E. Varga, "The Institute of the Cleveland Bar Association," 18 *A.B.A.J.* 317 (1932).

97. Rahl and Schwerin, *Northwestern University School of Law — A Short History* (1960), p. 29.

98. Law Faculty Minutes, Dec. 4, 1908, p. 270.

99. *N.U. School of Law Bull.*, Aug.–Oct., 1909, p. 3. For an account of the conference see pp. 3–10 and *Proceedings of the First National Conference on Criminal Law and Criminology, Called in Celebration of the Fiftieth Anniversary of the Founding of Northwestern University School of Law* (Union College of Law) (1910).

100. Wigmore to Holmes, Mar. 15, 1909 (Wigmore Collection).

101. Adolf Meyer, "Recalling the First Conference," 32 *J. Crim. L. & C.* 287 (1941–42).

102. For a brief account of Wigmore's administration see Nathan W. MacChesney, "The President's Address," 36 *A.B.A. Rep.* 963 (1911).

103. The proceedings of the annual meetings are published as follows: First, 1909, Chicago, bound separately with the title: *National Conference on Criminal Law and Criminology* (1909); Second, 1910, Washington, D. C., 1 *J. Crim. L. & C.*

515 (1910); Third, 1911, Boston, 2 *J. Crim. L. & C.* 583 (1911), same 36 *A.B.A. Rep.*, 956 (1911); Fourth, 1912, Milwaukee, 3 *J. Crim. L. & C.* 333, 592 (1912–13), same, 37 *A.B.A. Rep.* 1190 (1912); Fifth, 1913, Montreal, 4 *J. Crim. L. & C.* 553 (1913–14), same 38 *A.B.A. Rep.* 1077 (1913); Sixth, 1914, Washington, D.C., 5 *J. Crim. L. & C.* 322, 486, 744 (1914–15), same 39 *A.B.A. Rep.* 1092 (1914); Seventh, 1915, Salt Lake City, 6 *J. Crim. L. & C.* 594 (1915–16), same 2 *A.B.A.J.* 79 (1916); Eighth, 1916, Chicago, 7 *J. Crim. L. & C.* 162, 732 (1917), same 41 *A.B.A. Rep.* 789 (1916); Ninth, 1917, Saratoga Springs, 8 *J. Crim. L. & C.* 162, 322, 482 (1917–18), same 42 *A.B.A. Rep.* 42, 715 (1917); Tenth, 1918, Cleveland, 9 *J. Crim. L. & C.* 325 (1918–19), same 43 *A.B.A. Rep.* 573 (1918); Eleventh, 1919, Boston, 10 *J. Crim. L. & C.* 165, 423 (1919–20), same 44 *A.B.A. Rep.* 492 (1919); Twelfth, 1920, Indianapolis, 11 *J. Crim. L. & C.* 165, 328 (1920–21); Thirteenth, 1921, Cincinnati, 12 *J. Crim. L. & C.* 147, 149, 309 (1921–22) (Program but no Proceedings); 1922, Minutes of Executive Board only, 13 *J. Crim. L. & C.* 169 (1922–23); 1923, Detroit, 14 *J. Crim. L. & C.* 337. 480 (1924).

104. William E. Mikell, ''A Proposed Draft of a Code of Criminal Procedure,'' 5 *J. Crim. L. & C.* 827 (1915). For the publications of the institute see Augustus F. Kuhlman, *A Guide to Material on Crime and Criminal Justice* (1929).

105. *Recollections*, Robert H. Gault, p. 9 (Wigmore Collection).

106. Gault became editor beginning with no. 2 of vol. 3.

107. *Recollections*, Robert H. Gault, p. 8 (Wigmore Collection).

108. Roscoe Pound, ''John Henry Wigmore,'' 56 *Harv. L. Rev.* 988, 989 (1943).

109. Newman F. Baker, ''The Innovator,'' 32 *J. Crim. L. & C.* 263, 264 (1941).

110. Wigmore to Eugene A. Gilmore, Mar. 29, 1913 (Wigmore Collection).

111. *Ibid.*

112. Wigmore to Ezra R. Thayer, Apr. 25, 1915 (Wigmore Collection).

113. Joseph H. Beale to Wigmore, Apr. 2, 1902, Apr. 10, 1902, June 9, 1902 (Wigmore Collection).

114. Law Faculty Minutes, Sept. 24, 1902.

115. J. P. Hall to Wigmore, Nov. 12, 1914, and Walter W. Cook to Wigmore, May 20, 1916 (Wigmore Collection).

116. Harry P. Judson to Wigmore, June 17, 1916 (Wigmore Collection).

117. Nathan W. MacChesney, ''On Behalf of the Board of Trustees,'' 38 *Ill. L. Rev.* 6, 7 (1943).

118. From a draft of a note in Wigmore's own handwriting. The message may not have been sent. The correspondence clearly denotes a cordial relationship.

119. Abram W. Harris to Wigmore, Dec. 18, 1912 (Wigmore Collection).

120. Lynn H. Hough to Wigmore, Aug. 9, 1919 (Wigmore Collection).

121. William A. Dyche to Wigmore, Aug. 31, 1915 (Wigmore Collection).

122. *Ibid.*, May 26, 1916 (Wigmore Collection).

123. *Recollections*, Mary C. Goodhue, p. 1 (Wigmore Collection).

124. *Ibid.*

125. *Ibid.*, pp. 2–3.

126. *Evanston Daily News*, Apr. 3, 1912, p. 4.

127. W. H. Hamilton to Wigmore, Dec. 12, 1929 (Wigmore Collection).

128. Wigmore to Friends of Billy McKean, Dec. 12, 1929 (Wigmore Collection).

129. *Recollections*, Sarah B. Morgan, p. 35 (Wigmore Collection).

130. *Ibid.*

131. *Recollections*, Hugh Green, p. 2 (Wigmore Collection).

132. *Recollections*, Mary E. Goodhue, p. 2 (Wigmore Collection).

133. *Ibid.*, p. 1.

134. *Ibid.*, pp. 3–4.

135. Statement made to the author by a graduate of the Law School on May 1, 1963.

136. *Recollections*, Mary E. Goodhue, p. 3 (Wigmore Collection).

137. Copy in *Opera Minora*, 13:86 (Wigmore Collection). This volume also includes additional Wigmore songs.

138. Franklin K. Lane to Wigmore, Jan. 11, 1915 (Wigmore Collection).

139. *Recollections*, Edwin C. Austin, p. 2; Sarah B. Morgan, p. 20 (Wigmore Collection).

140. *Recollections*, Nathan W. MacChesney, p. 4 (Wigmore Collection).

141. *Recollections*, Hugh Green, p. 4 (Wigmore Collection).

142. *Recollections*, Stephen Love, p. 3 (Wigmore Collection).

143. *Recollections*, Stephen Love, p. 2 (Wigmore Collection).

144. See Wigmore's statement in a symposium on the honor system, 1 *Am. L. School Rev.* 369,375 (1906).

145. "Presentation Program," *Northwestern University Bull.* (Nov. 3, 1911), 12, no. 12.

146. *Celebration of the Twentieth Year of Service of Dean John Henry Wigmore to Northwestern University Law School* (1914) (Wigmore Collection).

147. Albert Kocourek was the editor, and three other faculty members, George P. Costigan, Jr., Frederic B. Crossley, and Robert W. Millar, constituted the editorial committee.

148. Albert Kocourek, "John Henry Wigmore," 27 *J. Am. Jud. Soc'y* 122 (1943).

149. George E. MacLean to Wigmore, Jan. 23 and Mar. 25, 1901 (Wigmore Collection).

150. Henry Schofield to Wigmore, Sept. 7, 1904 (Wigmore Collection).

151. Julien C. Monnet to president and fellows of Harvard University, Sept. 22, 1915; J.D.M. Ford to Wigmore, Oct. 29, 1915 (Wigmore Collection).

152. George W. Kirchway to Wigmore, Feb. 24, 1903 (Wigmore Collection).

153. Nicholas M. Butler to Wigmore, Mar. 2, 1903 (Wigmore Collection).

154. *Ibid.* See also George W. Kirchway to Wigmore, Mar. 3, 1903 (Wigmore Collection).

155. Wigmore to Robert D. Sheppard, Mar. 8 [1903] (Archives, Deering Library, Northwestern University).

156. George W. Kirchway to Wigmore, May 22, 1906 (Wigmore Collection).

157. *Ibid.*, Mar. 3, 1903.

158. Wigmore, "Remarks on September 8, 1922," p. 9 (Wigmore Collection).

159. University Trustee Minutes, July 17, 1916, p. 49.

160. Thomas W. Swan to Wigmore, Nov. 10, 1916 (Wigmore Collection).

161. Wigmore to Julien C. Monnet, Oct. 12, 1915 (Wigmore Collection).

162. The house located at 207 Lake Street, Evanston.

163. Wigmore to Holmes, Nov. 9, 1902. (Wigmore Collection).

164. Myron Hunt to Wigmore, Feb. 26, 1907 (Wigmore Collection).

165. *Ibid.*, Dec. 27, 1907.

166. *Recollections*, Francis M. Wigmore, p. 6 (Wigmore Collection).

167. *Ibid.*, p. 4.

168. *Ibid.*, p. 7.

169. *Recollections*, Sarah B. Morgan, p. 12 (Wigmore Collection).
170. *Ibid.*
171. *Recollections*, Margaret G. Belknap, p. 4 (Wigmore Collection).
172. *Recollections*, Agnes F. Bradley, p. 4 (Wigmore Collection).
173. *Ibid.*
174. *Ibid.*
175. *Ibid.*, p. 2.
176. Frank Simpson to the author, May 21, 1965.
177. Wigmore to Heath, Feb. 6, 1915 (Wigmore Collection).
178. Sarah B. Morgan to the author, Sept. 25, 1966.
179. *Recollections*, Robert W. Millar, p. 6 (Wigmore Collection).
180. *Recollections*, Sarah B. Morgan, p. 34 (Wigmore Collection).
181. *Recollections*, Mary E. Goodhue, p. 7 (Wigmore Collection).
182. *Recollections*, Sarah B. Morgan, p. 28 (Wigmore Collection).

CHAPTER 7. SCHOLAR

1. *Recollections*, Mary E. Goodhue, p. 4 (Wigmore Collection).
2. Wigmore to Adams Express Co., May 1, 1916 (Wigmore Collection).
3. Based on a statement made to the author by Mrs. Dean Atherton Eyre. See also Recollections, Sarah B. Morgan, pp. 11, 36 (Wigmore Collection).
4. *Recollections*, Jerome Hall, p. 6, and Sarah B. Morgan, p. 25 (Wigmore Collection).
5. *Recollections*, Charles H. Watson, p. 2 (Wigmore Collection).
6. Sarah B. Morgan, "Wigmore — The Man," 58 *Nw.U.L.Rev.* 461, 463 (1963).
7. "Sequestration of Witnesses," 14 *Harv. L. Rev.* 475 (1901); "Required Number of Witnesses; A Brief History of the Numerical System in England," 15 *Harv. L. Rev.* 83 (1901); "Expert Opinion as to Insurance Risk," 2 *Colum. L. Rev.* 67 (1902); "The Privilege Against Self-Crimination; Its History," 15 *Harv. L. Rev.* 610 (1902) (Revision of an earlier article in 5 *Harv. L. Rev.* 71 [1901]; "New Trials for Erroneous Rulings on Evidence; A Practical Problem for American Justice," 3 *Colum. L. Rev.* 433 (1903); "Putting in One's Own Case on Cross-Examination," 14 *Yale L. J.* 26 (1904); "A Brief History of the Parole Evidence Rule," 4 *Colum. L. Rev.* 338 (1904); "The History of the Hearsay Rule," 17 *Harv. L. Rev.* 437 (1904).
8. The full title is *A Treatise on the System of Evidence in Trials at Common Law, Including the Statutes and Judicial Decisions of All Jurisdictions of the United States.*
9. Albert Kocourek, "John Henry Wigmore," 27 *J. Am. Jud. Soc'y* 122, 123 (1943). Although Kocourek speaks of "10 years of monastic toil," Wigmore, in his dedication to Mrs. Wigmore, speaks of fifteen years of labor.
10. Albert M. Kales and others to Wigmore, Dec. 14, 1905 (Wigmore Collection).
11. *Recollections*, Nathan W. MacChesney, p. 43 (Wigmore Collection).
12. *Recollections*, Charles B. Elder, p. 5 (Wigmore Collection).
13. For book reviews see Anon., 8 *Colum. L. Rev.* 423 (1908); J.H.B., 21 *Harv. L. Rev.* 377 (1908); V.H.L., 6 *Mich. L. Rev.* 274 (1908).
14. For book reviews see A.M.K., 3 *Cal. L. Rev.* 512 (1915); Anon., 81 *Cent. L. J.* 355 (1915); William G. Hastings, 10 *Ill. L. Rev.* 673 (1916); E.W.M., 63 *U. Pa. L. Rev.* 916 (1916); Anon., 25 *Yale L.J.* 163 (1915).
15. Edwin M. Borchard to Wigmore, Feb. 7, 1916 (Wigmore Collection).

16. *Recollections*, Robert W. Millar, p. 1 (Wigmore Collection).

17. Ass'n Am. L. Schools, *1943 Handbook* (1944), p. 239; *Recollections*, Jerome Hall, p. 4 (Wigmore Collection).

18. Sarah B. Morgan to the author, May 25, 1961.

19. The special dedication to Mrs. Wigmore read, "E.H.V.W. devoted co-laborer for fifteen years without whose arduous and skillful toil this work could never have been completed."

20. Sarah B. Morgan to the author, May 25, 1961.

21. Concerning Wigmore's relationship to Charles Doe, see the discussion on pp. 13–14.

22. John P. Reid, *Chief Justice, the Judicial World of Charles Doe* (1967), pp. 297–99.

23. Roscoe Pound, *Formative Era of American Law* (1938), pp. 4, 30–31.

24. Willard Hurst, "Book Review," 115 *U. Pa. L. Rev.* 1020, 1022 (1967).

25. Holmes to Wigmore, Jan. 14, 1910 (Harvard Law School Library).

26. Albert Kocourek, "John Henry Wigmore," 27 *J. Am. Jud Soc'y* 122, 123 (1943).

27. 18 *Harv. L. Rev.* 478, 479 (1905).

28. *Id.* at 480.

29. Wigmore to Holmes, Sept. 10, 1915 (Wigmore Collection).

30. Morse v. State, 10 Ga. App. 61, 72 S.E. 534, 535 (1911).

31. 21 *Harv. L. Rev.* 377 (1908).

32. E. A. Harriman to Wigmore, June 3, 1907 (Wigmore Collection).

33. Ralph W. Gifford, "Book Review," 24 *Colum. L. Rev.* 440 (1924).

34. Felix Frankfurter, "The Law and the Law Schools," 1 A.B.A.J. 532, 538–39 (1915).

35. For other book reviews see Francis H. Bohlen, 44 *Am. L. Reg.* (N.S.) 142 (1905) and G.S.A., 14 *Yale L. J.* 124, 245, 415 (1904–5).

36. *Recollections*, Margaret G. Belknap, p. 1 (Wigmore Collection).

37. *Recollections*, Agnes F. Bradley, p. 1 (Wigmore Collection).

38. Reprinted in 1915.

39. For book reviews see K.T.F., 10 *Colum. L. Rev.* 494 (1910); Anon., *Green Bag* (1910), 22:247; R.P., 5 *Ill. L. Rev.* 190 (1910); J.W.C., 1 *J. Crim. L. & Crim.* 166 (1910); Anon., 3 *Lawyer & Banker* 52 (1910); H.E., 58 *U. Pa. L. Rev.* 452 (1915); Anon., 15 *Va. L. Reg.* 823 (1910); C.K.W., 19 *Yale L. J.* 393 (1910).

40. "Book Review," 15 *Va. L. Reg.* 823 (1910).

41. Holmes to Wigmore, Jan. 14, 1910 (Harvard Law School Library).

42. *Pocket Code* viii.

43. The full title is *A Pocket Code of the Rules of Evidence in Trials at Law, Massachusetts Edition, by Charles N. Harris, with Federal Citations by John Simpson* (1915). For reviews see Anon., 49 *Am. L. Rev.* 471 (1915); Anon., 21 *Case and Comment* 943 (1915).

44. George H. Harris to Wigmore, Sept. 22, 1921 (Wigmore Collection).

45. *Ibid.*, Mar. 12, 1924, and Apr. 11, 1924.

46. *Ibid.*, Mar. 22, 1927.

47. Sanford H. E. Freund, "Book Review," 40 *Am. L. Rev.* 956 (1906).

48. The second and third editions were entitled *Select Cases on the Law of Evidence*. For book reviews see Lyman P. Wilson, 18 *Cornell L. Q.* 473 (1933); Clarke B. Whittier, 27 *Ill. L. Rev.* 586 (1933); Paul L. Sayre, 18 *Iowa L. Rev.* 420 (1933); Leslie J. Tomkins, 10 *N.Y.U.L.Q. Rev.* 259 (1932); Scott Rowley, 81 *U.Pa. L. Rev.* 496 (1933); Robert T. Donley, 40 *West Va. L. Q.* 300 (1934); E. W. Hinton, 42 *Yale L. J.* 465 (1933).

49. The full title is *The Principles of Judicial Proof as Given by Logic, Psychology, and General Experience and Illustrated in Judicial Trials.*

50. 1st ed., p. 1 (1913).

51. N.M.T., "Book Review," 48 *Am. L. Rev.* 313 (1914).

52. E.R.T., "Book Review," 27 *Harv. L. Rev.* 692, 693 (1914).

53. *Id.* at 694. For the experience of one such teacher, see letter of George D. Ayres printed in Ass'n Am. L. Schools, *Handbook 15th Annual Meeting* (1915), p. 119.

54. See Charles C. Moore, "Book Review," 20 *Case and Comment* 432 (1913), and Wigmore to Charles C. Moore, Oct. 16, 1913 (Wigmore Collection).

55. For the title of these writings see the forthcoming *Bibliography* by Kurt Schwerin referred to in the explanatory statement at the beginning of these notes.

56. "Responsibility for Tortious Acts: Its History," 7 *Harv. L. Rev.* 315 (1894); "The Tripartite Division of Torts," 8 *Harv. L. Rev.* 200 (1894); "A General Analysis of Tort Relations," 8 *Harv. L. Rev.* 377 (1895).

57. See Chap. 00, p. 00.

58. William S. Holdsworth, "Wigmore as a Legal Historian," 29 *Ill. L. Rev.* 448, 452 (1934).

59. "Contributory Negligence of the Beneficiary as Bar to Administrator's Action for Death," 2 *Ill L. Rev.* 487 (1908); "Responsibility for Tortious Acts: Its History (Revised)." In *Select Essays in Anglo-American Legal History* (1909) 3:474; "The Right Against False Attribution of Belief or Utterance," 4 *Kent L. J.*, no. 8 p. 3 (1916); "Justice Holmes and the Law of Torts," 29 *Harv L. Rev.* 601 (1916).

60. For the titles of these writings see the forthcoming *Bibliography* by Kurt Schwerein referred to in the explanatory statement at the beginning of these notes.

61. *Recollections*, Roscoe Pound, p. 1 (Wigmore Collection). For an appraisal of the book as a whole see Leon Green's statement on p. 225 and Wesley N. Hohfeld's observation in "A Vital Jurisprudence and Law," Ass'n Am. L. Schools *1914 Proceedings*, pp. 76, 101–2.

62. Wigmore, *Select Cases on the Law of Torts* ix (1911).

63. In this connection see Wigmore, "Justice Holmes and the Law of Torts," 29 *Harv. L. Rev.* 601, 607 (1916).

64. John P. Reid, "Experience or Reason: The Tort Theories of Holmes and Doe," 18 *Vand. L. Rev.* 405, 433 (1965).

65. Wigmore to Holmes, Nov. 24, 1910; Dec. 23, 1910; Jan. 16, 1911; July 30, 1911; Nov. 19, 1911 (Wigmore Collection).

66. 29 *Harv. L. Rev.* 601 (1916)

67. Holmes to Wigmore, Apr. 13, 1916 (Harvard Law School Library).

68. Holmes to Frederick Pollock, Dec. 29, 1915. In Mark D. Howe, *Holmes — Pollock Letters* (1942), 1:229.

69. *Ibid.*, Nov. 24, 1919, 2:30.

70. For the titles of these writings see the forthcoming *Bibliography* by Kurt Schwerein referred to in the explanatory statement at the beginning of these notes.

71. *Recollections*, Charles H. Watson, p. 6 (Wigmore Collection).

72. Leon Green, "Fifty Years of Tort Law Teaching," 4 (1966) (Wigmore Collection).

73. Felix Frankfurter, "Foreword" in "John Henry Wigmore: A Centennial Tribute," 58 *Nw. U. L. Rev.* 443 (1963).

74. Leon Green to the author, May 4, 1964.

75. Roscoe Pound to Henry M. Bates, Mar. 24, 1921 (Harvard Law School Library).

76. See p. 41.

77. For the titles of these writings see the forthcoming *Bibliography* by Kurt Schwerin referred to in the explanatory statement at the beginning of these notes.

78. The *Bibliography* was an expansion of an order list prepared by Wigmore for the acquisition of materials for the Elbert H. Gary Library of the Law School.

79. See pp. 60–61.

80. Wigmore's files indicate both his leadership and how fully he participated in carrying the project through to a successful conclusion.

81. C. B. De Quiros, *Modern Theories of Criminality* x (1911).

82. *Id.* at vii.

83. Robert W. Millar, "John Henry Wigmore (1863–1943)," 46 *J. Crim.L. & C.* 4, 8 (1946).

84. *Id.*

85. Wigmore to Robert W. Millar, Feb. 8, 1914 (Wigmore Collection).

86. Wigmore, "The Limits of Counsel's Legitimate Defense," 2 *J. Crim.L. &C.* 663, 664 (1912).

87. *Id.*

88. Wigmore, "Trial by Publication," 2 *J. Crim. L. & C.* 668, 669 (1912).

89. People v. Schmitz, 7 Cal. App. 330, 94 Pac. 407 (1908).

90. Lateley Thomas, *A Debonair Scoundrel* (1962), p. 319.

91. *The Bulletin* (San Francisco), Jan. 25, 1909. Copy in *Opera Minora*, 11:5 (Wigmore Collection).

92. 3:474–537.

93. Because of the death of Paul Huvelin, the projected volume on the *History of Continental Commercial Law* was never published. See the Committee Report, Ass'n. Am. L. Schools, *1927 Handbook*, p. 119.

94. Holmes to Wigmore, Nov. 24, 1911, (Harvard Law School Library).

95. Wigmore to Holmes, Dec. 1, 1911 (Wigmore Collection).

96. Holmes to Frederick Pollock, Dec. 15, 1912. In Mark D. Howe, *Holmes — Pollock Letters* (1942), 1:205.

97. Holmes to Wigmore, Nov. 25, 1912 (Harvard Law School Library).

98. Holmes to Frederick Pollock, Dec. 15, 1912. In Howe, *Holmes — Pollock Letters*, 1:205.

99. Wigmore to Holmes, Nov. 27, 1912 (Wigmore Collection).

100. A translator of *A History of Germanic Private Law* (1918) by Rudolf Huebner.

101. *Recollections*, Francis S. Philbrick, p. 1 (Wigmore Collection).

102. *Ibid.*, p. 4.

103. *Ibid.*, p. 1. Wigmore to Holmes, Nov. 19, 1911 (Wigmore Collection).

104. 22 *Am. L. Rev.* 890 (1888). In a slightly revised form it later appeared in 1 *So. L. Q.* 1 (1916).

105. For further discussion see p. 43.

106. *N. U. School of Law Bull.*, ser. 3, no. 3, Nov.–Jan., 1904–5, pp. 13–28.

107. Edgar N. Durfee and Edwin D. Dickinson, "Book Review," 20 *Mich. L. Rev.* 566 (1922). For other reviews see Isaac Husik, 69 *U. Pa. L. Rev.* 399 (1921), and Harlan F. Stone, 30 *Yale L. J.* 536 (1921).

108. Benjamin N. Cardozo, *Selected Writings* (1947), p. 35.

109. William S. Holdsworth, "Wigmore as a Legal Historian," 29 *Ill. L. Rev.* 448, 453 (1934).

110. *Id.* at 448.

111. "The Path of the Law," in Oliver W. Holmes, *Collected Legal Papers* 167, 186 (1920).

112. Wigmore to Holmes, Apr. 1, 1921 (Wigmore Collection).

113. Holmes to Wigmore, Dec. 25, 1922 (Harvard Law School Library).

114. Holmes refers here to his introduction to *A General Survey of Events, Sources, Persons and Movements in Continental Legal History* (1912). Vol. 1 of Continental Legal History Series. Reprinted in Oliver W. Holmes *Collected Legal Papers* (1920).

115. Wigmore to Lewis Einstein, Feb. 5, 1923. In James B. Peabody, *Holmes — Einstein Letters* (1964), p. 209.

116. Holmes to Frederick Pollock, Oct. 12, 1923. In Howe, *Holmes-Pollock Letters* (1944), 2:121.

117. Holmes to Harold J. Laski, Feb. 5, 1923. In Howe, *Holmes-Laski Letters* (1953), 1:477.

118. Holmes to Harold J. Laski, May 31, 1923, *ibid.*, p. 503.

119. Wigmore to Holmes, Feb. 12, 1923 (Wigmore Collection).

120. The original plan called for thirteen volumes, but vol. 6, *The Positive Philosophy of Law*, by Icilio Vanni, was eliminated from the series. See "Committee Report," Ass'n Am. L. Schools, *1928 Handbook*, p. 154.

121. Ass'n Am. L. Schools, *1928 Proceedings* (1929), pp. 117, 154.

122. William S. Holdsworth, "Wigmore as a Legal Historian," 29 *Ill. L. Rev.* 448–49 (1934).

123. *Science of Legal Method, Select Essays by Various Authors* (vol. 9 of Modern Legal Philosophy Series) xxxviii (1917).

124. 28 *Harv. L. Rev.* 1 (1914).

125. Wigmore's introduction to Albert Kocourek, *Jural Relations* xxi (1927).

126. Wigmore to Holmes, Nov. 27, 1912 (Wigmore Collection).

127. Holmes to Wigmore, Dec. 2, 1912 (Harvard Law School Library).

128. Wigmore to Holmes, Feb. 18, 1911 (Wigmore Collection).

129. Luigi Miraglia, *Comparative Legal Philosophy Applied to Legal Institutions* (1912).

130. 7 *Am. Pol. Sci. Rev.* 145, 147 (1913).

131. W. W. Willoughby to Wigmore, Apr. 1, 1913 (Wigmore Collection).

132. Wigmore, "To Members of the American Political Science Association," Mar. 3, 1913 (Wigmore Collection).

133. *Ibid.*, pp. 2, 4.

134. The full title is *Evolution of Law: Select Readings on the Origin and Development of Legal Institutions*.

135. *Id.* at vol. 2, p. 456.

136. Holmes to Wigmore, Aug. 15, 1915 (Harvard Law School Library).

137. Edwin M. Borchard, "Book Review," 6 *Am. Pol. Sci. Rev.* 645, 648 (1912).

138. Roscoe Pound, "John Henry Wigmore," 56 *Harv. L. Rev.* 988, 989 (1943).

139. Wigmore to Holmes, Dec. 1, 1911 (Wigmore Collection). See also letter from Holmes to Wigmore, Dec. 4, 1911 (Harvard Law School Library).

140. Pp. 1–8 (Mar. 4, 1916) (Wigmore Collection).

141. *Ibid.*, p. 5.

142. *Ibid.*, p. 1.

143. The full title is *Science and Learning in France With a Survey of Opportunities for American Students in French Universities: An Appreciation by American Scholars* (1917).

144. See p. 87.

145. Wigmore to Holmes, Mar. 25, 1915 (Wigmore Collection). The Waterman case is reported in 235 U. S. 88 (1914).

146. Holmes to Wigmore, Apr. 22, 1915 (Harvard Law School Library).

147. Wigmore had commented on an Illinois case in 1911. See his "Trade-Name in a Cemetery," 5 *Ill. L. Rev.* 499 (1911).

148. Wigmore to Holmes, May 23, 1915 (Wigmore Collection).

149. 10 *Ill. L. Rev.* 178 (1915).

150. L. E. Waterman Co. v. Modern Pen Co., 235 U.S. 88, 93; 35 S.Ct. 91, 92; 59 L. Ed. 142, 145 (1914).

151. L. E. Waterman Co. v. Modern Pen Co., 193 Fed. 242, 248 (1912).

152. 10 *Ill. L. Rev.* 178, 180–81 (1915).

153. 235 U. S. 88, 98; 35 S.Ct. 91, 94; 59 L. Ed. 142, 147 (1914).

154. 10 *Ill. L. Rev.* 178, 181 (1915).

155. *Id.* at 182.

156. *Id.* at 184.

157. *Id.* at 189.

158. The cases are collected in an annotation in 44 *A. L. R.* 2d 1156, 1163 (1955).

159. Holmes to Wigmore, Mar. 16, 1917 (Harvard Law School Library).

160. The full title is *On the Witness Stand, Essays in Psychology and Crime* (1908).

161. *Recollections*, Robert H. Gault, p. 3 (Wigmore Collection).

162. 3 *Ill. L. Rev.* 399 (1909).

163. *Id.* at 433.

164. *Recollections*, Robert H. Gault, p. 4 (Wigmore Collection).

165. Wigmore to Sumner Curtis, Jan. 24, 1914 (Wigmore Collection).

166. Manton M. Wyvett [Dept. of State] to Wigmore, Jan. 31, 1914 (Wigmore Collection).

167. "American Naturalization and the Japanese," 28 *Am. L. Rev.* 818 (1894).

168. *Id.* at 827.

169. 9 *Ill. L. Rev.* 221 (1914). The full title is *A Treatise on the Law of Estoppel, or on Incontestable Rights.* According to Pound, Wigmore's work "Pointed the way for much that has been done in the present day development" of restitution. See Recollections, Roscoe Pound, p. 1 (Wigmore Collection).

170. Felix Frankfurter to Wigmore, Jan. 1, 1915 (Wigmore Collection).

171. *Ibid.*

172. "Book Review," 6 *Ill. L. Rev.* 285 (1911).

173. *Id.*

174. *Id.* at 288.

175. Virgil M. Harris to Wigmore, Jan. 6, 1912 (Wigmore Collection).

176. "Book Review," 11 *Ill. L. Rev.* 133 (1916).

177. *Id.*

178. *Id.* at 136.

179. William C. Jones to Wigmore, July 9, 1916 (Wigmore Collection).

180. "Book Review," 18 *A.B.A.J.* 399 (1932).

181. Wigmore to Holmes [Dec. 1931] (Wigmore Collection).

182. Holmes to Wigmore, Mar. 14, 1932 (Harvard Law School Library).

183. Wigmore to Holmes, June 30, 1916 (Wigmore Collection).

184. The book review in question was that of T.B., 14 *J. Soc'y Comp. Leg.* (N.S.) 276 (1914). The full title of the book is *The Great Jurists of the World.* It was edited by John Macdonald and Edward Manson (1914), and Zane contributed the essay on Jeremy Bentham.

185. Wigmore to John M. Zane, July 30, 1914 (Wigmore Collection).

186. *Recollections*, Francis S. Philbrick, p. 4 (Wigmore Collection).

187. Roscoe Pound, "Editorial," 56 *Harv. L. Rev.* 988, 989 (1943).

188. *Recollections*, Preface [Albert Kocourek], p. 6 (Wigmore Collection).

189. *Ibid.*, p. 7.

190. *Ibid.*

191. *Ibid.*, p. 8.

192. The lists are in the Wigmore Collection.

193. *Recollections*, Sarah B. Morgan, p. 24 (Wigmore Collection).

194. Wigmore to Arthur M. Harris, Sept. 20, 1913 (Wigmore Collection).

195. Ass'n Am. L. Schools, "John Henry Wigmore" [Memorial], *1943 Handbook* (1944), pp. 238, 243.

196. Ida F. Wright to the author, Aug. 20, 1960.

197. Ass'n Am. L. Schools, "John Henry Wigmore," pp. 238, 243.

198. The list appeared originally in *The Brief* (Phi Delta Phi) (1900), 2:124. Later expanded versions appear in 2 *Ill L. Rev.* 574 (1908), 17 *Ill. L. Rev.* 26 (1922), 52 *Lib. J.* 189 (1927).

199. *Recollections*, Nathan W. MacChesney, p. 5 (Wigmore Collection).

200. Wigmore, "A List of One Hundred Legal Novels," 17 *Ill. L. Rev.* 26 (1922).

201. Wigmore Collection.

202. Wigmore to John T. Richards, Mar. 19, 1917 (Wigmore Collection).

203. *Recollections*, Sarah B. Morgan, p. 25 (Wigmore Collection).

204. Arthur Train to Wigmore, June 7, 1920 (Wigmore Collection).

205. *Ibid.*, Apr. 22, 1921.

206. *Ibid.*

207. *Ibid.*, June 29, 1922.

208. *Ibid.*, Oct. 17, 1926.

209. *Ibid.*, Oct. 30, 1938.

210. *Ibid.*, Oct. 17, 1926.

211. *Ibid.*, Dec. 28, 1926.

212. *Ibid.*, Dec. 30, 1940.

213. *Ibid.*, June 15, 1941.

214. From Wigmore's Introduction to Arthur Train's *Mr. Tutt's Case Book* vii (1939).

215. Holmes to Wigmore, Nov. 8, 1905 (Harvard Law School Library).

216. Holmes to Frederick Pollock, Dec. 31, 1911. In Howe, *Holmes-Pollock Letters*, 1:187.

217. *Ibid.*, Dec. 29, 1915, p. 229.

218. Felix Frankfurter to Wigmore, March 9, 1912 (Wigmore Collection).

219. Henry M. Bates to Wigmore, Jan. 10, 1914. In *Celebration of the Twentieth Year of Service of Dean John Henry Wigmore to Northwestern University Law School* (1914).

220. *Celebration Legal Essays* 2 (1918).

CHAPTER 8. LEADER

1. "What is one of the most interesting facets of Dean Wigmore's career is that the course of it was carefully reasoned and planned even in detail. We have no information as to what this plan was, but there are many evidences that such a plan did in fact exist. If it could be reproduced it would resemble the discourses of an

Epictetus or the meditations of Marcus Aurelius.'' *Recollections*, Preface [Albert Kocourek], p. 10 (Wigmore Collection).

2. Albert Kocourek, ''John Henry Wigmore,'' 27 *J. Am. Jud Soc'y* 122, 124 (1943).

3. *Recollections*, Hugh Green, p. 1 (Wigmore Collection).

4. Edson R. Sunderland, *History of the American Bar Association and Its Work* (1953), p. 30.

5. *Ibid.*

6. 17 *A.B.A. Rep.* 453 (1894).

7. *Id.*

8. *Id.*

9. See the following *A.B.A. Reps.* — 25:704 (1902), 30 (Pt. 2) 111, 147, 187, 190 (1906), 31:1045 (1907), 34:865 (1909), 35:961 (1910), Ass'n Am. L. Schools, *1912 Handbook and Proceedings*, p. 49; Ass'n Am. L. Schools, *1920 Handbook and Proceedings*, pp. 5, 6, 7.

10. 36 *A.B.A. Rep.* 745, 750 (1911); Ass'n Am. L. Schools, *1920 Handbook and Proceedings*, p. 130. But Wigmore was opposed to the expulsion of a school without its name being given.

11. 34 *A.B.A. Rep.* 838, 941 (1909); also in Ass'n Am. L. Schools, *1909 Handbook and Proceedings*, p. 112.

12. 25 *A.B.A. Rep.* 715 (1902).

13. Wigmore, ''Nova Methodus Discendae Docendaeque Jurisprudentiae,'' 30 *Harv. L. Rev.* 812 (1917).

14. *Id.* 828.

15. 22 *A.B.A. Rep.* 451–52 (1900).

16. 30 *A.B.A. Rep.* (Pt. 2) 18 (1906).

17. 31 *A.B.A. Rep.* 513–600 (1907). However, Wigmore opposed a requirement that would be hard on aliens while acquiring citizenship, pointing out by way of example that in Chicago aliens went to shysters in the absence of lawyers of their own race. See 34 *A.B.A. Rep.* 743 (1909) and 37 *A.B.A. Rep.* 819 (1912). Wigmore also opposed the specification of required subjects, ''because it cramps the development of the school curriculum and misleads the students to give artificial weight to some subjects.'' See 40 *A.B.A. Rep.* 754 (1915) and 2 *A.B.A.J.* 56–57 (1916).

18. Wigmore, ''Should the Standards of Admission to the Bar be Based on Two Years or More of College Grade Education,'' 40 *A.B.A. Rep.* 735 (1915).

19. 2 *A.B.A.J.* 56–57 (1916).

20. 3 *A.B.A.J.* 14–15 (1917).

21. 30 *A.B.A. Rep.* (Pt. 2) 147 (1906).

22. 42 *A.B.A. Rep.* 187 (1917).

23. 29 *A.B.A. Rep.* 166 (1906); 42 *A.B.A. Rep.* 187 (1917); 43 *A.B.A. Rep.* 76, 198 (1918); 44 *A.B.A. Rep.* 264, 270 (1919): See also 4 *A.B.A.J.* 413 (1918); 5 *A.B.A.J.* 6 (1919).

24. *A.B.A. Rep.* 112 (1901); 25 *A.B.A. Rep.* 109 (1902); 37 *A.B.A. Rep.* 137 (1912).

25. 37 *A.B.A. Rep.* 136 (1912); 38 *A.B.A. Rep.* 468–70 (1913).

26. See the following *A.B.A. Reps.* — 25:101 (1902); 26:158 (1903); 27:121 (1904); 29 (Pt. 1):159 (1906); 33:162 (1908); 34:162 (1909).

27. 40 *A.B.A. Rep.* 735 (1915).

28. *Id.* at 736.

29. 30 *A.B.A. Rep.* (Pt. 2) 18, 136 (1906), 31 *A.B.A. Rep.* 1045 (1907).

30. 30 *A.B.A. Rep.* 146 (1906).

31. Ass'n Am. L. Schools, *Handbook and Proceedings* — 1902:14; 1915:33–35; 1919:5–6; 1920: 96, 100, 124, 155, 213–15. See also 11 *Ill. L. Rev.* 362 (1916); 3 *A.B.A.J.* 14 (1917).

32. See the following *A.B.A. Reps.* — 28:679 (1905); 30 (Pt. 2) 144–45, 187 (1906); 34:838, 941 (1909); 35:956 (1910); 36:746 (1911); 37:970 (1912).

33. 35 *A.B.A. Rep.* 962–63 (1910); 36 *A.B.A. Rep.* 747 (1911).

34. See p. 87.

35. *Recollections*, Manley O. Hudson, pp. 1–2 (Wigmore Collection).

36. 27 *A.B.A. Rep.* 464, 498 (1904).

37. Albion W. Small (Universal Exposition) to Wigmore, Mar. 29, 1904 (Wigmore Collection).

38. *N.U. Bull.*, Nov.–Jan., 1904–5, pp. 13–28. Copy in *Opera Minora*, vol. 6 (Wigmore Collection).

39. 33 *A.B.A. Rep.* 173 (1908); 34 *A.B.A. Rep.* 817, 820 (1909). See also the following *A.B.A. Reps.* 36:711–12 (1911); 37:909–10 (1912); 38:842 (1913); 39:1007 (1914); 40:883 (1915); 41:770 (1916); 43:501 (1918); 44:397 (1919).

40. Wigmore was elected a member of the council. 45 *A.B.A. Rep.* 338 (1920).

41. Edson R. Sunderland, *History of the American Bar Association and Its Work* (1953), p. 84.

42. Robert M. Hughes to Wigmore, Jan. 6, 1916 (Wigmore Collection).

43. Wigmore's proposal was adopted in 1933. See 58 *A.B.A. Rep.* 682 (1933).

44. James B. Scott to Wigmore, July 19, 1915 (Wigmore Collection).

45. Published in 10 *Ill. L. R.* 385 (1916).

46. (1920), 15:345.

47. Wigmore to Frank B. Kellogg, Mar. 31, 1913 (Wigmore Collection).

48. Sunderland, *History of American Bar Association and Its Work*, p. 85.

49. S. S. Gregory to Wigmore, Oct. 6, 1911 (Wigmore Collection).

50. *Ibid.*

51. Francis Rawle to Wigmore, Dec. 31, 1912; Frank B. Kellogg to Wigmore May 8, 1913 (Wigmore Collection).

52. 1 *A.B.A.J.* 1 (1915).

53. Wigmore to Francis Rawle, Dec. 31, 1912 (Wigmore Collection).

54. Wigmore to Carrol T. Bond, May 8, 1916 (Wigmore Collection).

55. *Ibid.*, Dec. 31, 1916 (Wigmore Collection).

56. Wigmore to Frank B. Kellogg, Mar. 31, 1913 (Wigmore Collection).

57. 38 *A.B.A. Rep.* 20 (1913).

58. 38 *A.B.A. Rep.* 69, 172 (1913).

59. Wigmore to George Whitelock, Aug. 12, 1915 (Wigmore Collection).

60. George Whitelock to Wigmore, Aug. 18, 1915 (Wigmore Collection.) For the 1914 report of the committee see 39 *A.B.A. Rep.* 685 (1914).

61. "The Long Hard Pull for Coordination," 20 *J. Am. Jud Soc'y* 153, 154 (1936).

62. Sunderland, *History of the American Bar Association*, p. 86. For a selection of the answers see "The Movement to Amend the Organization and Procedure of the Association," 1 *A.B.A.J.* 564 (1915). For the Report of the Committee in 1915 see 1 *A.B.A.J.* 383 (1915); 40 *A.B.A. Rep.* 39, 615 (1915).

63. Sunderland, *History of the American Bar Association and Its Work*, p. 86; 40 *A.B.A. Rep.* 40, 616 (1915).

64. Sunderland, *History of the American Bar Association*, p. 87.

65. *Ibid.*, p. 86.

66. Walter G. Smith to Wigmore, Jan. 14, 1916; Wigmore to Elihu Root, July 14, 1916; Elihu Root to Wigmore, July 16, 1916 (Wigmore Collection). For a

summary of the reorganization activities see "The Movement to Amend the Organization and Procedure of the Association," 1 *A.B.A.J.* 564 (1915).

67. "The Long Hard Pull for Coordination," 20 *J. Am. Jud. Soc'y* 153 (1936).

68. Wigmore, "Shall the Legal Profession be Reorganized," 4 *J. Crim. L. & C.* 641 (1914).

69. "Roscoe Pound's St. Paul Address of 1906," 20 *J. Am. Jud. Soc'y* 176 (1937). For the text of Roscoe Pound's address see 39 *A.B.A. Rep.* 615 (1915).

70. "The Long Hard Pull for Coordination," 20 *J. Am. Jud Soc'y* 153, 154 (1936).

71. Copy in *Opera Minora*, vol. 5 (Wigmore Collection).

72. *Id.*

73. See remarks of Joseph H. Merrill, 41 *A.B.A. Rep.* 640 (1916).

74. Wigmore to Elihu Root, July 14, 1916, and Root to Wigmore, July 16, 1916 (Wigmore Collection).

75. 41 *A.B.A. Rep.* 7, 8, 94, 588 (1916).

76. 3 *A.B.A.J.* 93, 580 (1917).

77. 42 *A.B.A. Rep.* 438 (1917).

78. 45 *A.B.A. Rep.* 396 (1920). For further details see M. Louise Rutherford, *The Influence of the American Bar Association on Public Opinion and Legislation* (1937).

79. Wigmore, "Topics of Mutual Interest to Our Two Professions," pp. 1–2. Address at Harvard Medical School, Feb. 28, 1935 (Wigmore Collection).

80. Wigmore, "Organizing the Power of the American Bar," 17 *A.B.A.J.* 387, 391 (1931).

81. See p. 166.

82. Wigmore was admitted to the Illinois bar in 1898.

83. See Wigmore, "The Recent Cases Department," 50 *Harv. L. Rev.* 862, 867 (1937).

84. Charles Small to Wigmore, May 9, 1908 (Wigmore Collection).

85. For a summary of Wigmore's activities as a member of the commission see "John Henry Wigmore," Nat'l Conf. of Commissioners on Uniform State Laws, *Handbook and Proceedings*, 53rd Annual Conf. (1943), p. 256.

86. See p. 209.

87. Herbert Harley to Wigmore, March 18, 1913 (Wigmore Collection).

88. Herbert Harley to Wigmore, June 1, 1936 (Wigmore Collection). See also Harley, "Concerning the American Judicature Society," 20 *J. Am. Jud. Soc'y* 9, 10, 15 (1936).

89. Roscoe Pound, "John Henry Wigmore," 56 *Harv. L. Rev.* 988, 989 (1943).

90. Franklin K. Lane to Wigmore, Jan. 8, 1913; Franklin K. Lane to Edward M. House, Dec. 13, 1912 (Wigmore Collection).

91. See Chap. 2, p. 9.

92. See Chap. 3, p. 16.

93. Anne Lane and Louise H. Wall, eds., *Letters of Franklin K. Lane Political and Personal* (1922).

94. Wigmore to President Woodrow Wilson, July 18, 1914 (Wigmore Collection).

95. Wigmore to Woodrow Wilson, Mar. 27, 1913 (Wigmore Collection).

96. Hyde's principal work was *International Law Chiefly as Interpreted and Applied by the United States*, 2 vols. (1922); 3 vols. (1945).

97. "The Fallacy of Intervention," *Nation*, April 7, 1898. Copy in *Opera Minora*, 9:204 (Wigmore Collection).

98. Wigmore to Woodrow Wilson, Mar. 7, 1914 (Wigmore Collection).

99. Wigmore, "Talk to Alumni," May 1914 (Wigmore Collection).

100. Louis Joughin to the author, Mar. 23, 1960.

101. Wigmore, "Address before American Association of University Professors," Jan. 18, 1936 (Wigmore Collection).

102. *Ibid.*

103. "Origins of the Association: Anniversary Address," 51 *Bulletin* 229, 233 (1965), Am. Ass'n Univ. Professors.

104. Henry Lerew to Wigmore [1915] (Wigmore Collection).

105. Wigmore, "Address before Meeting of American Association of University Professors," Jan. 18, 1936 (Wigmore Collection).

106. *Ibid.*

107. *Ibid.*, p. 2.

108. "President's Report," 2 *Bulletin*, No. 4, pp. 9, 52, Oct. 1916, Am. Ass'n Univ. Professors.

109. "Editorial." (Wigmore Collection).

110. Louis C. Brosseau to Wigmore, Oct. 15, 1914 (Wigmore Collection). Wigmore had been a vice-president in 1901–2.

111. Wigmore's file shows that he did a great deal of work, including careful planning.

112. Wigmore to George W. Goethals, Oct. 28, 1914 (Wigmore Collection).

113. *Ibid.*

114. Invitation to the dinner (Wigmore Collection).

115. Joseph Sargent to Wigmore, June 22, 1916 (Wigmore Collection).

116. Notice of appointment from Winthrop H. Wade to Wigmore, Oct. 9, 1916 (Wigmore Collection).

117. These included many distinguished visitors from abroad.

118. Wigmore's files show wide support through membership often supplemented by active participation.

119. *Ibid.*

120. Wigmore to Ignacio Villamon, Sept. 23, 1913 (Wigmore Collection).

121. "A Model Report on Crime From an Attorney General's Office," 4 *J. Crim. L. & C.* 479 (1913).

122. The full title is *The Individual Delinquent; a Text-Book of Diagnosis and Prognosis for All Concerned in Understanding Offenders* (1915).

123. William Healy to Wigmore, June 8, 1915 (Wigmore Collection).

124. Wigmore to Robert Lansing, July 20, 1915 (Wigmore Collection).

125. Wigmore to C. E. Humiston, Feb. 11, 1914 (Wigmore Collection).

126. Wigmore to Samuel Drury, May 31, 1917 (Wigmore Collection).

127. Fred G. Shaffer to Wigmore, May 6, 1907 (Wigmore Collection).

128. R. H. Aishton to Wigmore, Dec. 12, 1916 (Wigmore Collection).

129. Wigmore to the Mayor [Evanston], April 23, 1928 (Wigmore Collection).

130. To Wigmore from Fred S. James, Sept. 10, 1914; James R. Smart, Sept. 14, 1914; and Samuel Topliff, Sept. 10, 1915 (Wigmore Collection).

131. Wigmore to General Superintendent (Northwestern Elevated Railway Co.), May 11, 1914 (Wigmore Collection).

132. Wigmore to the *Boston Transcript*, Apr. 14, 1914 (Wigmore Collection).

133. John F. Hayford to Wigmore, June 6, 1911; copy of *Memorial* in Wigmore Collection.

134. Franklin K. Lane to Wigmore, Feb. 19, 1912. In Anne Lane and Louise H. Wall, eds., *Letters of Franklin K. Lane Political and Personal* (1922).

135. Franklin K. Lane to Edward M. House, Dec. 13, 1912. In Lane and Wall, *Letters of Lane*.

136. "John Henry Wigmore: A Personal Portrait," 13 *Ill. L. Rev.* 340 (1918).

137. *Id.* at 344.

138. Herbert Harley to Newman F. Baker, Feb. 28, 1941 (author's collection).

CHAPTER 9. COLONEL

1. Wigmore from W. A. Bethel, Sept. 30, 1916, and E. H. Crowder, Nov. 19, 1916. See also Recollections, Nathan W. MacChesney, p. 15 (Wigmore Collection).

2. Wigmore, "General Crowder, General Ansell and the Administration of Military Justice," n.d., p. 2 (Wigmore Collection).

3. Wigmore to E. H. Crowder, Nov. 20, 1916 (Wigmore Collection).

4. Wigmore to Thomas F. Holgate, July 14, 1917 (Wigmore Collection). For an account of the Law School during the war period see reprint of Wigmore's report as dean for 1917–18 and 1918–19 in *Northwestern Univ. Bull.*, 23 no. 8 (Aug. 26, 1922).

5. Thomas F. Holgale to Wigmore, Sept. 12 and 18, 1917 (Wigmore Collection).

6. *Recollections*, Sarah B. Morgan, p. 2 (Wigmore Collection).

7. William L. Howard to Wigmore, Oct. 19, 1917 (Wigmore Collection).

8. Lawrence E. Johnson to Wigmore, Dec. 25, 1917 (Wigmore Collection).

9. Wigmore, "General Crowder, General Ansell and the Administration of Military Justice," p. 2; and Wigmore to E. H. Crowder, June 13, 1916 (Wigmore Collection).

10. See "Letter to the Editor" in *Nation*, Sept. 17, 1914, p. 347.

11. Reproduced in "John Henry Wigmore," 27 *J. Am. Jud. Soc'y* 6 (1943).

12. The full title is "Memorandum Submitted to the President of the United States Proposing a Neutral International Conference and a Peaceful War" (Nov. 1914). Privately printed. Copy in *Opera Minora*, vol. 14 (Wigmore Collection).

13. Wigmore to William J. Bryan, Sept. 10, 1914 (Wigmore Collection).

14. *Chicago Tribune*, Dec. 22, 1916.

15. Wigmore to Franklin K. Lane July 20, 1915 (Wigmore Collection).

16. Franklin K. Lane to Wigmore, Dec. 8, 1915 (Wigmore Collection).

17. Wigmore to Lawrence A. Lowell and S. H. Dent, Feb. 17, 1917 (Wigmore Collection).

18. Wigmore, "The League of Nations from the Lawyer's Point of View," 34 *Int. J. of Ethics* 112, 119 (1924).

19. Wigmore, "The Lawyer's Honor in War-Time," 12 *Ill. L. Rev.* 117 (1917).

20. Wigmore, "Suggested Memorandum on War Service," 3 *A.B.A.J.* 341, 342 (1917).

21. Copy in Wigmore Collection.

22. See letters to Wigmore from A. E. Garton, Sept. 8, 1917; Chancellor L. Jenks, Nov. 19, 1917; Kenneth S. Clark, Feb. 28, 1918 (Wigmore Collection).

23. Originally Wigmore had an ill-fitting uniform, as one existing photograph dramatically reveals. However, the photograph reproduced in this volume is the one recalled by most of his contemporaries.

24. *Recollections*, Manley O. Hudson, p. 2 (Wigmore Collection).

25. *Recollections*, Sarah B. Morgan, pp. 9–10 (Wigmore Collection).

26. Communication from Judge Advocate General to Chief of Staff, "Conditions of Manpower as Revealed by Draft Statistics" (Wigmore Collection). See also *Recollections*, Sarah B. Morgan, p. 2 (Wigmore Collection).

27. *Recollections*, Louis B. Wehle, p. 2 (Wigmore Collection).

28. *Recollections*, Sarah B. Morgan, p. 2 (Wigmore Collection).

29. Wigmore, "The Conduct of the War in Washington, A Critique of Men and Methods" n.d., p. 75 (Wigmore Collection).

30. Carl Byoir to E. H. Crowder, Sept. 26, 1918 (Wigmore Collection).

31. Wigmore, "Speech at Mass-Meeting," Apr. 7, 1924, p. 5 (Wigmore Collection).

32. *Ibid.*, p. 4.

33. Editorial Comment, "John Henry Wigmore," 30 *Military L. Rev.* iv. (1965).

34. Sarah B. Morgan to the author, Apr. 23, 1965.

35. *Ibid.*, Mar. 14, 1967.

36. Wigmore, "General Crowder, General Ansell and the Administration of Military Justice," p. 2.

37. Wigmore, "Soldier's and Sailor's Civil Relief Act," 27 *A.B.A.J.* 67 (1941).

38. *Recollections*, Sarah B. Morgan, p. 2 (Wigmore Collection).

39. Wigmore to E. H. Crowder, Jan. 20, 1918 (Wigmore Collection).

40. Mansfield Ferry, Samuel Rosenbaum, and Wigmore, "The Soldier's and Sailor's Civil Relief Bill," 12 *Ill. L. Rev.* 449 (1918).

41. Wigmore, "General Crowder, General Ansell and the Administration of Military Justice," p. 3.

42. "Modern Penal Methods in Our Army," 9 *J. Crim. L. & Crim.* 163 (1918).

43. Wigmore, "General Crowder, General Ansell and the Administration of Military Justice," p. 3.

44. Wigmore to Newton D. Baker, Apr. 30, 1919 (Wigmore Collection).

45. Wigmore, "General Crowder, General Ansell and the Administration of Military Justice," p. 3.

46. Wigmore to Albert Kocourek, Feb. 1, 1918 (Wigmore Collection).

47. For a general discussion see Wigmore, "The Student Army Training Corps," *Educational Record* (1922), 3:258. Copy in *Opera Minora*, vol. 11 (Wigmore Collection).

48. Wigmore, "Memorandum for the Committee on Education and Special Training," Sept. 4, 1918 (Wigmore Collection).

49. *Ibid.*, p. 1

50. *Ibid.*

51. *Ibid.*, p. 3.

52. *Ibid.*, p. 5.

53. *Ibid.*

54. *Ibid.*, p. 6.

55. Wigmore, "Memorandum for the Committee on Education and Special Training to the Judge Advocate General," Sept. 9, 1918 (Wigmore Collection). The memorandum was approved in his own handwriting by General Crowder. See p. 6.

56. *Ibid.*, p. 2.

57. Wigmore, "The Student Army Training Corps." Copy in *Opera Minora*, vol. ix. For a fuller statement see *Northwestern Univ. Bull.* Aug. 26, 1922), 23, no. 8:4.

58. Wigmore, "The Student Army Training Corps," p. 258.

59. *Ibid.*, p. 259.

60. Wigmore, "The Conduct of the War in Washington, A Critique of Men and Methods," n.d., p. 30 (Wigmore Collection).

61. "Memorandum for General Crowder from Colonel Wigmore," Nov. 8, 1918, p. 6 (Wigmore Collection).

62. Samuel Gompers to Newton D. Baker, Nov. 29, 1918 (Wigmore Collection).

63. Newton D. Baker to Samuel Gompers, Nov. 30, 1918 (Wigmore Collection).

64. Wigmore, "General Crowder, General Ansell and the Administration of Military Justice," p. 3.

65. David A. Lockmiller, *Enoch H. Crowder Lawyer and Statesman* (1955), p. 181.

66. Judge Advocate General to Chief of Staff, Aug. 18, 1919 (Wigmore Collection).

67. Newton D. Baker to Wigmore, Jan. 1, 1919 (Wigmore Collection).

68. Chalmers Martin to Wigmore, Jan. 11, 1919 (Wigmore Collection).

69. Newton D. Baker to Wigmore, Oct. 25, 1918 (Wigmore Collection).

70. "Memorandum for the Secretary of War from Colonel John H. Wigmore," Jan. 28, 1919 (Wigmore Collection).

71. "Memorandum for the Secretary of War from Colonel John H. Wigmore, Subject: Army Social System," May 17, 1919 (Wigmore Collection).

72. *Recollections*, Louis B. Wehle, p. 3 (Wigmore Collection).

73. *Recollections*, Mary E. Goodhue, p. 3. See also *Recollections*, Sarah B. Morgan, p. 2 (Wigmore Collection).

74. *Recollections*, Mary E. Goodhue, p. 3 (Wigmore Collection).

75. Burton C. Bovard to Wigmore, Aug. 22, 1917 (Wigmore Collection).

76. *Recollections*, Sarah B. Morgan, p. 4 (Wigmore Collection).

77. Wigmore to E. H. Crowder, Feb. 13, 1918 (Wigmore Collection).

78. *Ibid.*

79. Wigmore to E. H. Crowder, Feb. 25, 1918 (Wigmore Collection).

80. *Ibid.*

81. *Ibid.*

82. *Cong. Rec.*, Jan. 3, 1919.

83. Wigmore, "General Crowder, General Ansell and the Administration of Military Justice," p. 7.

84. Wigmore to E. H. Crowder, Feb. 21, 1919 (Wigmore Collection).

85. "General Crowder, General Ansell and the Administration of Military Justice," p. 7.

86. *Ibid.*

87. *Ibid.*, p. 88.

88. *Ibid.*

89. Lockmiller, *Enoch H. Crowder Lawyer and Statesman*, pp. 200–201.

90. Wigmore, "General Crowder, General Ansell and the Administration of Military Justice," p. 27.

91. *Ibid.*, p. 24.

92. *Military Justice During the War, A Letter from the Judge Advocate General of the Army to the Secretary of War in Reply to a Request for Information* (1919), p. 4.

93. *Ibid.*, p. 62.

94. *Ibid.*, p. 9.

95. *Ibid.*, p. 10.
96. *Ibid.* See also 57 Cong. Rec. 1988 (Jan. 23, 1918).
97. *Military Justice During the War*, p. 4.
98. *Ibid.*
99. *Ibid.*, p. 11.
100. *Ibid.*
101. Wigmore to George T. Page, Feb. 24, 1919 (Wigmore Collection).
102. *Military Justice During the War*, pp. 11–12.
103. The Appendix was printed separately.
104. *Military Justice During the War*, p. 8.
105. Newton D. Baker to Wigmore, Mar. 21, 1919 (Wigmore Collection).
106. E. H. Crowder to Wigmore, Apr. 24, 1919 (Wigmore Collection).
107. Newton D. Baker to Wigmore, Mar. 26, 1919 (Wigmore Collection).
108. Wigmore to Captain Wilrath, Mar. 21, 1919 (Wigmore Collection).
109. George W. Chamberlain to Attorney General, Apr. 9, 1919 (Wigmore Collection).
110. A. Mitchell Palmer to George W. Chamberlain, Apr. 26, 1919 (Wigmore Collection).
111. Wigmore to Newton D. Baker, Apr. 30, 1919 (Wigmore Collection).
112. Maryland State Bar Ass'n, *Proceedings of the Twenty-Fourth Annual Meeting* 183, 188 (1919).
113. 4 *J. Am. Jud. Soc'y* 151 (1921), 10 *J. Crim. L. & Crim.* 170 (1919), 52 *Chicago Legal News* 135 (1919).
114. New York County Lawyer's Ass'n, *Year Book* 212–17 (1919).
115. Wigmore to Arthur Train, Feb. 20, 1919 (Wigmore Collection).
116. Arthur Train to Wigmore, Mar. 4, 1919 (Wigmore Collection).
117. George H. Lorimer to Arthur Train, Feb. 24, 1919 (Wigmore Collection).
118. *Collier's, The National Weekly*, Apr. 19, 1919, p. 5.
119. Wigmore to Arthur Train, Apr. 21, 1919 (Wigmore Collection).
120. 88 *Cent. L. J.* 338 (1919).
121. 57 *Cong. Rec.*, Pt. 1, p. 869 (1918–19).
122. Private Clark E. Turner, File 122–560.
123. Wigmore to George T. Page, Feb. 18, 1919 (Wigmore Collection).
124. George T. Page to Wigmore, Feb. 20, 1919 (Wigmore Collection).
125. Wigmore to George T. Page, Feb. 24, 1919 (Wigmore Collection).
126. Wigmore to George T. Page, Feb. 26, 1919 (Wigmore Collection).
127. Lockmiller, *Enoch H. Crowder, Lawyer and Statesman*, p. 211.
128. *Ibid.*, p. 212.
129. *Ibid.*
130. *Ibid.*, p. 225.
131. *Ibid.*, p. 213.
132. Judge Advocate to Chief of Staff, Aug. 18, 1919 (Wigmore Collection).
133. In Wigmore Collection.
134. Wigmore to Edwin Wildman, Mar. 5, 1919 (Wigmore Collection).
135. Sarah B. Morgan to Edwin Wildman, Apr. 7, 1919 (Wigmore Collection). The correspondence shows that *The Atlantic, Scribners* and the *World's Work* were also approached.
136. Wigmore, "The Conduct of the War in Washington, A Critique of Men and Methods," p. 13.
137. *Ibid.*, pp. 86–87.
138. *Ibid.*, p. 22.
139. *Ibid.*, p. 24.

140. *Ibid.*, p. 28.
141. *Ibid.*, p. 29.
142. *Ibid.*, p. 30.
143. *Ibid.*, pp. 80, 83–84.
144. *Ibid.*, pp. 82–83.
145. *Ibid.*, p. 85.
146. *Ibid.*, pp. 3–4.
147. *Ibid.*, p. 21.
148. In Wigmore Collection.
149. Wigmore to J. A. Hull, May 28, 1925 (Wigmore Collection).

CHAPTER 10. PATRIOT

1. *Recollections*, Sarah B. Morgan, p. 38 (Wigmore Collection).
2. Wigmore to Chicago Military Stores, May 21, 1928 (Wigmore Collection).
3. Wigmore to Walter D. Scott, May 3, 1921 (Wigmore Collection).
4. Ferre C. Watkins to Wigmore, Jan. 15, 1927, Feb. 9, 1927 (Wigmore Collection).
5. *Recollections*, Sarah B. Morgan, p. 35 (Wigmore Collection); Sarah B. Morgan to author, May 30, 1963.
6. Copy of resolution attached to letter, Wigmore to L. S. Hellstrom, Mar. 12, 1938 (Wigmore Collection).
7. Marcel Sevel to Wigmore, Nov. 1, 1939 (Wigmore Collection).
8. W. A. Graham to Wigmore, Dec. 16, 1925, Jan. 15, 1926 (Wigmore Collection).
9. "Judge Advocates Organize Association," 14 *A.B.A.J.* 243 (1928).
10. W. J. Patterson to Wigmore, Oct. 31, 1926, Nov. 8, 1926 (Wigmore Collection).
11. Wigmore to James G. Harbord, June 23, 1936 (Wigmore Collection).
12. Wigmore to *Adventure*, July 6, 1925 (Wigmore Collection).
13. Wigmore to editor of *Evanston News-Index*, Apr. 9, 1924.
14. *Evanston News-Index*, Apr. 17, 1924.
15. Memorandum from Wigmore to Walter D. Scott, Apr. 15, 1924 (Wigmore Collection).
16. Letter from Wigmore to Walter D. Scott, Apr. 15, 1924 (Wigmore Collection). See 30 *Stats. at Large* 361 (1898).
17. Wigmore, "Speech at Mass-Meeting" Apr. 7, 1924 (Wigmore Collection).
18. Wigmore to Walter D. Scott, Apr. 15, 1924 (Wigmore Collection).
19. Walter D. Scott to Wigmore, Apr. 8, 1924 (Wigmore Collection).
20. Memorandum from Walter D. Scott, Apr. 15, 1924; and Wigmore, "Speech at Mass-Meeting," Apr. 7, 1924 (Wigmore Collection).
21. Letter and attached list, Wigmore to Walter D. Scott, Oct. 25, 1927 (Wigmore Collection).
22. *Recollections*, Nathan W. MacChesney, pp. 24–25 (Wigmore Collection).
23. James F. Oates, "Wigmore the Lawyer and Business," pp. 6–7 (Wigmore Collection).
24. Abrams et al. v. United States, 250 U.S. 616 (1919).
25. *Id.* at 626.
26. *Id.* at 628.
27. Wigmore, "Abrams v. U.S.: Freedom of Speech and Freedom of Thuggery in War-Time and Peace-Time," 14 *Ill. L. Rev.* 539, 549–50 (1920).
28. *Id.* at 545.

29. Oliver W. Holmes to Frederick Pollock, Apr. 25, 1920, in Mark D. Howe, *Holmes-Pollock Letters* (1942), 2:42.

30. In his letter to Holmes of Dec. 1, 1919 Pollock said, "I don't see why there was not enough evidence to go to the jury on the fourth count." *Ibid.*, p. 31.

31. *Ibid.*, pp. 44–45.

32. *Ibid.*, p. 48.

33. Harold J. Laski to Oliver W. Holmes, Nov. 12, 1919, in Mark D. Howe, *Holmes-Laski Letters* (1953), 1:220.

34. Letter of Nov. 27, 1919. *Ibid.*, pp. 222–23.

35. L.G.G., "Constitutional Law-Espionage Act — Abrams v. United States," 14 *Ill. L. Rev.* 601 (1920).

36. Zechariah Chafee, "A Contemporary State Trial — The United States Versus Jacob Abrams et. al.," 33 *Harv. L. Rev.* 747, 774 (1920).

37. Newton D. Baker to Wigmore, May 3, 1920 (Wigmore Collection).

38. *Recollections*, Preface [Albert Kocourek], p. 9 (Wigmore Collection).

39. 19 *Ill. L. Rev.* 496, 497 (1925).

40. See *The Sacco-Vanzetti Case, Transcript of the Record of the Trial of Nichola Sacco and Bartolomeo Vanzetti in the Courts of Massachusetts and Subsequent Proceedings, 1920–27*, 5 vols. (1928–29).

41. Felix Frankfurter, "The Case of Sacco and Vanzetti," *Atlantic Monthly* (1927), 139:409.

42. Felix Frankfurter, *The Case of Sacco and Vanzetti, A Critical Analysis for Lawyers and Laymen* (1927). Reprinted with a new introduction by Edmund M. Morgan in 1954.

43. Apr. 25, 1927, p. 1, col. 5, and May 10, 1927, p. 15, col. 3. Frankfurter's replies appeared in the *Boston Transcript* of Apr. 26, 1927, p. 15, col. 3, and in the *Boston Herald* of May 11, 1927, p. 3, col. 1 (photocopies in Wigmore Collection).

44. Walter D. Scott to Wigmore, May 25, 1927 (Wigmore Collection).

45. *Boston Evening Transcript*, Apr. 25, 1927, p. 1, col. 5 (photocopy in Wigmore Collection).

46. *Ibid.*

47. *Ibid.*, May 10, 1927, p. 15, col. 3 (photocopy in Wigmore Collection).

48. Because someone might conclude that anti-Semitism colored his approach, it should be stated that in all the mass of materials examined by the author, not one word has been found to support this thesis. As this book makes perfectly evident, Wigmore was exceptionally free from racial and religious bias. George L. Joughin summarized his explanation of Wigmore's behavior as follows, "The only reasonable conclusion is that he, like so many men infinitely less wise, temporarily lost his capacity to function as a social creature." George L. Joughin and Edmund M. Morgan, *The Legacy of Sacco and Vanzetti* (1948), p. 262.

49. Morris L. Forer to the author, Aug. 23, 1968.

50. "John Henry Wigmore: A Centennial Tribute," 58 *Nw. U.L. Rev.* 443 (1963). Reprinted in Philip B. Kurland, *Of Law and Life and Other Things that Matter* (1965), p. 256.

51. Fred A. Moore to Wigmore, Dec. 15, 1930, and Dec. 27, 1930, and Hamilton Fish to Wigmore, Dec. 29, 1930 (Wigmore Collection).

52. Dec. 20, 1930.

53. Wigmore to Fred A. Moore, Dec. 30, 1930 (Wigmore Collection).

54. 283 *U. S.* 605 (1931).

55. *Id.* at 627.

56. "United States v. Macintosh," 26 *Ill. L. Rev.* 371 (1931).

57. "The Mitchell Court-Martial," 20 *Ill. L. Rev.* 489 (1926).

58. *Id.* at 490.

59. *Id.* at 491.

60. *Id.* at 490.

61. *Id.* at 487, 488.

62. "Demagogic Abuse of Courts-Martial: The Mitchell Trial," 20 *Ill. L. Rev.* 742 (1926).

63. Edward J. Edwards to Wigmore, Nov. 28 and Dec. 5, 1898 (Wigmore Collection).

CHAPTER 11. NEW LAW SCHOOL ON LAKE MICHIGAN

1. Wigmore to E. H. Crowder, May 1, 1919; Wigmore to E. H. Crowder, Nov. 6, 1922; E. H. Crowder to Wigmore, May 26, 1919, May 13, 1923 (Wigmore Collection).

2. Wigmore to E. H. Crowder, Nov. 6, 1922 (Wigmore Collection).

3. Nathan W. MacChesney, "Alumni President's Page," *Northwestern Univ. Alumni News* (May 1924), 3, no. 7:3.

4. Wigmore to Walter D. Scott, Dec. 4, 1936 (Wigmore Collection).

5. Law Faculty Minutes, June 5, 1919.

6. "Memorandum on the Suggestions that the Law School be Removed to Evanston," n. d. (Law Faculty Records).

7. Wigmore to Lynn H. Hough, June 24, 1919 (Wigmore Collection).

8. *Ibid.*, p. 2.

9. *Ibid.*, p. 3.

10. MacChesney, "Alumni President's Page," *Northwestern Univ. Alumni News* (May 1924), 3, no. 7:3.

11. "Seven Points of Chicago's Need for an Endowment for Legal Research and Service to the Community" (n.d.) and "Book of Information" (n.d.) (Wigmore Collection).

12. Wigmore, "My Creed for America," p. xix (Wigmore Collection).

13. "Book of Information" (n.d.), p. 28 (Wigmore Collection).

14. Copy in Wigmore Collection.

15. "'Book of Information," p. 28.

16. "Seven Points of Chicago's Need for an Endowment for Legal Research and Service to the Community" (n.d.) (Wigmore Collection).

17. James A. Rahl and Kurt Schwerin, *Northwestern University School of Law — A Short History* (1960), pp. 36–37.

18. *Northwestern Univ. Alumni News* (May 1923), 2, no. 7:11.

19. Wigmore to Walter D. Scott, Dec. 16, 1920 (Wigmore Collection).

20. *Northwestern Univ. Alumni News* (May 1923), 2, no. 7:11.

21. Sarah B. Morgan to the author, Sept. 12, 1965.

22. Wigmore to Walter D. Scott, Sept. 30, 1925 (Deering Library, Northwestern Univ); and Wigmore to Walter D. Scott, Nov. 21, 1922 (Wigmore Collection).

23. Rahl and Schwerin, *Northwestern University School of Law — A Short History*, p. 40.

24. *Ibid.*, p. 41.

25. *Recollections*, Nathan W. MacChesney, p. 33 (Wigmore Collection).

26. Wigmore to Walter D. Scott, May 5, 1925 (Deering Library, Northwestern Univ.)

27. *Recollections*, Nathan W. MacChesney, p. 34 (Wigmore Collection).

28. *Ibid.*, p. 35.

29. Sarah B. Morgan to the author, Mar. 10, 1965.

30. Wigmore to Walter D. Scott, Oct. 4, 1923 (Wigmore Collection).

31. *Ibid.*, Aug. 17, 1922.

32. Wigmore, "Remarks on September 8, 1922," p. 20 (Wigmore Collection).

33. *Recollections*, Nathan W. MacChesney, p. 26 (Wigmore Collection).

34. *Ibid.*, p. 27.

35. Wigmore to Walter D. Scott, Oct. 8, 1923 (Wigmore Collection).

36. *Ibid.*, Mar. 5, 1924.

37. Letter reproduced at the beginning of *Report of the Dean of the Faculty of Law on an Educational Survey 1925* (1927).

38. Leon Green to Wigmore, Nov. 25, 1927 (Wigmore Collection).

39. Wigmore to Walter D. Scott, May 8, 1929 (Wigmore Collection).

40. *Ibid.*, Feb. 3, 1921.

41. Wigmore, *Report of the Dean of the Faculty of Law on an Educational Survey 1925* (1927), p. 38.

42. Rahl and Schwerin, *Northwestern University School of Law — A Short History*, p. 34.

43. Copy in Wigmore Collection.

44. Copy in Wigmore Collection.

45. *Recollections*, Sarah B. Morgan, p. 10 (Wigmore Collection).

46. *Recollections*, Mary E. Goodhue, p. 6 (Wigmore Collection).

47. *Recollections*, Sarah B. Morgan, p. 31 (Wigmore Collection).

48. Wigmore, "A Course on Profession of the Bar," 7 *Am. Law School Rev.* 273 (1931).

49. Lowell Hastings to the author, Sept. 17, 1965.

50. Based on "Statement Prepared for the Author" by R. G. Howlett, May 20, 1964.

51. *Recollections*, Nelson G. Wettling, p. 1 (Wigmore Collection).

52. *Recollections*, Sarah B. Morgan, p. 14 (Wigmore Collection).

53. Lowell Hastings to the author, Sept. 17, 1965.

54. *Recollections*, James F. Oates, p. 3 (Wigmore Collection).

55. *Recollections*, Sarah B. Morgan, p. 21 (Wigmore Collection).

56. *Ibid.*, p. 22.

57. Wigmore to H. C. Jones, Oct. 30, 1914 (Wigmore Collection).

58. See "Coefficient of Grading Student's Work-Memo to Faculty," July 30, 1929. During the years 1924–25 through 1928–29 Wigmore was almost at the bottom among ten faculty members in the number of As and Bs granted.

59. *Recollections*, Stuart S. Ball, p. 7 (Wigmore Collection).

60. Law Faculty Minutes, Oct. 9, 1916, Sept. 22, 1919.

61. Rahl and Schwerin, *Northwestern University School of Law — A Short History*, p. 31.

62. Wigmore, "Minority Report of Committee on Four-Year Curriculum," Assn. Am. L. Schools, *1920 Handbook* 215, 219.

63. For Wigmore's minority report see *ibid*.

64. Rahl and Schwerin, *Northwestern University School of Law — A Short History*, p. 33.

65. *Recollections*, Mary E. Goodhue, p. 3 (Wigmore Collection).

66. Nelson G. Wettling to Wigmore, Jan. 12, 1926 (Wigmore Collection).

67. Dated Jan. 26, 1923 (Wigmore Collection).

68. Wigmore to Lymas, July 18, 1924 (Wigmore Collection).

69. Arthur Goldberg, "Wigmore — Teacher and Humanitarian," 58 *Nw. U. L. Rev.* 453, 454 (1963).

70. Copy in Wigmore Collection.

71. Quoted in Sarah B. Morgan, "Wigmore — The Man," 58 *Nw. U. L. Rev.* 461, 463 (1963).

72. Copy in Wigmore Collection.

73. Wigmore to A. G. Sheasby, Sept. 9, 1929 (Wigmore Collection).

74. *Recollections*, Stuart S. Ball, p. 10 (Wigmore Collection).

75. Wigmore to the Songfest Committee of the Junior Bar Association, Apr. 25, 1941 (Wigmore Collection).

76. *Recollections*, Stuart S. Ball, p. 10. (Wigmore Collection). In a letter dated Oct. 31, 1929, Cranston Spray of the Chicago Bar told Wigmore that he liked his song so much that he thought he would sing it himself.

77. *Recollections*, Francis M. Wigmore, p. 4. The arthritis probably provides the explanation for the conflicting reports of Wigmore's capacity as a piano player. Mrs. Margaret G. Belknap said he played "gloriously" (*Recollections*, p. 5) and Robert H. Gault said he handled the key board "creditably" (*Recollections*, p. 9). The record contains numerous references to Wigmore's piano playing which are entirely favorable.

78. *Recollections*, Sarah B. Morgan, p. 12 (Wigmore Collection).

79. Sarah B. Morgan to the author, Aug. 30, 1970.

80. Sarah B. Morgan to the author, May 25, 1966.

81. Sarah B. Morgan to the author, Jan. 18, 1967.

82. *Recollections*, Beatrice W. Hunter, p. 4 (Wigmore Collection).

83. *Recollections*, Sarah B. Morgan, p. 29 (Wigmore Collection).

84. Copy in Wigmore Collection.

85. Stuart S. Ball. According to Lowell Hastings, Ball also served as a marshal, although he is not mentioned in Wigmore's memorandum of instructions.

86. Lowell Hastings to the author, Aug. 24, 1965.

87. *Recollections*, Stuart S. Ball, p. 13 (Wigmore Collection).

88. William Holdsworth, *A History of English Law*. Edited by A. L. Goodhart and H. G. Hanbury, 16 vols. (1922–).

89. William S. Holdsworth to Wigmore, Feb. 29, 1924 (Wigmore Collection).

90. Arthur Goodhart to Wigmore, Oct. 11, 1926 (Wigmore Collection).

91. See book reviews by Robert H. Wettach, 6 *N.C. L. Rev.* 509, 511 (1928) and Charles Morse, 6 *Can. Bar Rev.* 375, 377 (1928).

92. "Bar Welcomes Historian of English Law," 13 *A.B.A.J.* 183 (1927).

93. *Id.*

94. For further details see *A Description of the New Buildings: Levy Mayer Hall and Elbert H. Gary Law Library Building* (n.d.).

95. *Recollections*, Mary E. Goodhue, p. 4 (Wigmore Collection).

CHAPTER 12. RETIREMENT AS DEAN

1. Wigmore to Walter D. Scott, Apr. 16, and May 21, 1928 (Wigmore Collection).

2. *Ibid.*, May 18, 1928.

3. University Trustee Minutes, Exec. Comm., July 8, 1929.

4. Wigmore to Walter D. Scott, Apr. 16, 1928 (Wigmore Collection).

5. *Ibid.*, May 2, 1928.

6. *Ibid.*, May 18, 1928.

7. *Ibid.*, Aug. 30, 1929.

8. *Ibid.*, Sept. 5, 1929.

9. *Ibid.*, Sept. 9, 1929.

10. Edmund James, former president, and Robert Sheppard, former treasurer, of Northwestern University.

11. Wigmore to George A. Mason, Sept. 3, 1929 (Wigmore Collection).

12. Walter D. Scott to Wigmore, Sept. 5, 1929, and Wigmore to Walter D. Scott, Sept. 9, 1929 (Wigmore Collection).

13. Wigmore to George A. Mason, Aug. 8, 1929 (Wigmore Collection).

14. Copies of letters in Wigmore Collection.

15. William A. Dyche, business manager, and Nathan William MacChesney, member of the Board of Trustees, Northwestern University.

16. Wigmore to George A. Mason, Sept. 3, 1929 (Wigmore Collection).

17. University Trustee Minutes, Exec. Comm., Sept. 24, 1929.

18. Lewis B. Wehle to Wigmore, Sept. 30, 1929 (Wigmore Collection).

19. Wigmore to Frederic B. Crossley, July 10, 1929, and Edward F. Albertsworth to Wigmore, Dec. 3, 1938 (Wigmore Collection). Miss Sarah B. Morgan, Wigmore's secretary, confirms Wigmore's preference for Miller; she believes that Crossley played a decisive role in the selection. Sarah B. Morgan to Roalfe, Sept. 12, 1965.

20. James A. Rahl and Kurt Schwerin, *Northwestern University School of Law — A Short History* (1960), p. 42.

21. Leon Green, "Relations Between Dean Wigmore and His Successor" (1963) p. 3 (Wigmore Collection).

22. Leon Green to Wigmore, July 12, 1927 (Wigmore Collection).

23. Green, "Relations Between Dean Wigmore and His Successor," p. 5.

24. *Ibid.*, p. 6.

25. *Ibid.*, p. 7.

26. Northwestern University School of Law, "Chronicles of the School" (Aug. 29, 1929), p. 4.

27. Leon Green, "Relations Between Dean Wigmore and His Successor," p. 9.

28. *Ibid.*

29. Extract from a letter of a graduate of the Class of 1929 to his father in Chicago in February 1932, source unknown (Wigmore Collection).

30. In Wigmore Collection.

31. Copy in Wigmore Collection.

32. *Recollections*, Lawrence D. Egbert, p. 2 (Wigmore Collection).

33. Wigmore, "Memorandum to Some of My Trustee Friends" (n.d.) (Wigmore Collection).

34. Wigmore to Walter D. Scott, Aug. 16, 1929 (Wigmore Collection).

CHAPTER 13. DEAN EMERITUS

1. John Knox, "Recollections of John H. Wigmore" (Sept. 10, 1963), p. 3, a statement prepared for the author.

2. Leon Green, "Relations Between Dean Wigmore and His Successor" (n.d.), p. 12 (Wigmore Collection).

3. *Ibid.*, p. 13.

4. *Ibid.*, p. 14.

5. Wigmore to Eijchi Kiyooka, Sept. 9, 1935 (Wigmore Collection).

6. Ass'n. Am. L. Schools, *Handbook and Proceedings*, 1940:7; 1941:6–7; 1942:135, 152.

7. Statement made by Leon Green to the author.

8. Wigmore to Graham, May 14, 1936 (Wigmore Collection).

9. Wigmore to Margaret G. Belknap, Nov. 1, 1931 (Wigmore Collection).

10. "Education for the Law," 63 A.B.A.R. 722 (1938).

11. Lord Macmillan to Wigmore, Aug. 25, 1942 (Wigmore Collection).

12. Wigmore to Walter D. Scott, Oct. 25, 1929 (Wigmore Collection).

13. Green, "Relations of Dean Wigmore to His Successor," p. 10.

14. *Ibid.*

15. Petition dated May 28, 1934 (Wigmore Collection). There were 290 students enrolled at that time.

16. See *Chicago Herald-Examiner*, June 13, 1934.

17. Sarah B. Morgan to author, June 1, 1966.

18. "An Appreciation of John Henry Wigmore Adopted by the Board of Trustees of Northwestern University, June 16, 1934" (Wigmore Collection).

19. Wigmore to Margaret G. Belknap, Nov. 1, 1931 (Wigmore Collection).

20. Herbert S. Harley to Newman F. Baker, Feb. 28, 1941 (Roalfe Collection).

21. Wigmore to Mayor of Evanston, June 6, 1931; Wigmore to Park District Board, June 19, 1936 (Wigmore Collection).

22. "Dean Wigmore Attacks City's Beach Fee Plan," *Evanston News Index*, July 3, 1931.

23. Wigmore to Edward F. Albertsworth, Apr. 26, 1939 (Wigmore Collection).

24. *Recollections*, Margaret G. Belknap, p. 6 (Wigmore Collection).

25. *Recollections*, Sarah B. Morgan, p. 18 (Wigmore Collection).

26. *Recollections*, Margaret G. Belknap, p. 9 (Wigmore Collection).

27. Copy in Wigmore Collection.

28. *Recollections*, Mary E. Goodhue, p. 6 (Wigmore Collection).

29. Wigmore to George A. Mason, Mar. 26, 1934 (Wigmore Collection).

30. *Ibid.*

31. *Ibid.* See note added by Mason.

32. R. Allan Stephens to Wigmore, Oct. 3, 1934 (Wigmore Collection).

33. "To Deans of Law Schools," Dec. 1, 1933 (Wigmore Collection).

34. Roscoe Pound to Wigmore, Oct. 5, 1934 (Wigmore Collection).

35. Wigmore to Roscoe Pound, Oct. 18, 1934 and Nov. 5, 1934; Roscoe Pound to Wigmore, Oct. 22, 1934 (Wigmore Collection).

36. Wigmore to Roscoe Pound, Oct. 18, 1934, Jan. 3, 1935 (Wigmore Collection).

37. Typed copy in Wigmore Collection.

38. Wigmore to Roscoe Pound, Jan. 3, 1935 (Wigmore Collection).

39. Typed copy in Wigmore Collection.

40. "Pragmatic Postulates in Nomologic Pedagogy" p. 3 (typed copy in Wigmore Collection).

41. Wigmore was, of course, greatly interested in the kind and quality of education that was provided at the college level, and in preparation for legal training, and he believed that there was a great deal of room for improvement. See *The Aims and Defects of College Education, Comments and Suggestions by Prominent Americans, an Original Investigation* (1915), pp. 21–22; "Honor to Brains," Oct. 21, 1931 (Wigmore Collection). The emergence of the field of aptitude testing, new at least in its application to law school admissions, was just what was needed to trigger his propensity for coined words, and he started his comment as follows, "Juristic Psychopoyemetrology, Or, How to Find Out Whether a Boy Has the Makings of a Lawyer," 24 *Ill. L. Rev.* 454,455 (1929). See also "Tests of Legal Aptitude," 24 *Ill. L. Rev.* 680 (1930).

42. "Pragmatic Postulates in Homologic Pedagogy," p. 11 (Wigmore Collection).

43. *Ibid.*, p. 13.

44. *Ibid.*, p. 15.

45. *Ibid.*, p. 17.

46. *Ibid.*, p. 19. Presumably this quotation is from Holmes's address, "Memorial Day," published in *Speeches by Oliver Wendell Holmes* (1934), but there is some variation between Holmes's statement and that of Wigmore. See p. 11 of *Holmes Speeches*.

47. Typed copy in Wigmore Collection.

48. Wigmore, "Advice of a Veteran to Young Lawyers," p. 2. Typed copy in Wigmore Collection.

49. *Ibid.*, p. 3.

50. *Ibid.*, pp. 4–12.

51. *Ibid.*, p. 5.

52. *Ibid.*, p. 17.

53. Typed copy in Wigmore Coll.

54. Wigmore, "Topics of Mutual Interest to Our Two Professions," p. 13 (typed copy in Wigmore Collection).

55. *Recollections*, Roscoe Pound, p. 4 (Wigmore Collection).

56. Wigmore to Roscoe Pound, June 12, 1936 (Wigmore Collection).

57. Roscoe Pound to Wigmore, June 8, 1936 (Wigmore Collection).

58. Wigmore to Holmes, Aug. 21, 1933 (Harvard Law School Library).

59. *Recollections*, Sarah B. Morgan, p. 19 (Wigmore Collection).

60. Wigmore to the Attorney General, Nov. 29, 1935 (Wigmore Collection).

61. "Unpacking the Court," *New Republic* (1937), 90:67.

62. *Chicago Daily News*, Mar. 24, 1937, p. 6.

63. "Case for the Sit-Down Strike," *New Republic* (1937), 90:199.

64. Frederick D. Fagg, Jr., to Wigmore, July 10, 1939 (Wigmore Collection).

65. For further information concerning the relationship between Wigmore and Green, see correspondence between Wigmore and Albertsworth (Wigmore Collection).

66. *Recollections*, Sarah B. Morgan, p. 24 (Wigmore Collection).

67. "Wigmore Celebrates Eightieth Birthday," *Northwestern University News*, Apr. 2, 1943, vol. 1, no. 2.

68. *Recollections*, Charles H. Watson, p. 7 (Wigmore Collection).

69. "Wigmore Celebrates Eightieth Birthday."

70. *Recollections*, Margaret G. Belknap, p. 10 (Wigmore Collection).

71. *Recollections*, Helen K. McNamara, p. 8 (Wigmore Collection).

CHAPTER 14. ADMINISTRATION OF JUSTICE

1. The 1915 *Supplement* was cumulative and covered the years 1904–14.

2. Work on a sustained basis began in 1919. See Wigmore to Little, Brown and Company, Apr. 25, 1919 (Wigmore Collection).

3. *Recollections*, Sarah B. Morgan, p. 15 (Wigmore Collection).

4. *Ibid.*, p. 27.

5. William L. Burdick, "The Revision of the Federal Statutes," 11 *A.B.A.J.* 178, 182 (1925).

6. *Ibid.*

7. So as to reflect the inclusion of Anglo-American law as well as that of the United States, the second edition was entitled *A Treatise on the Anglo-American System of Evidence in Trials at Common Law, Including the Statutes and Decisions of all Jurisdictions of the United States and Canada*. The possibility of

authorizing an English edition published by an English publisher was considered, but the project never materialized.

8. "Book Review," 37 *Harv. L. Rev.* 513, 521 (1924).

9. Anon., "Book Review," 73 *U.S. Law Rev.* 479 (1939).

10. *Recollections*, Sarah B. Morgan, p. 20 (Wigmore Collection).

11. For further details see p. 252.

12. For the titles of these writings see the forthcoming *Bibliography* by Kurt Schwerin referred to in the explanatory statement at the beginning of these notes.

13. "Dean Wigmore's Credo," *Alumni Journal* [Northwestern Univ.], July 9, 1921, p. 28. Also privately printed as "My Creed for the Nation" (Wigmore Collection).

14. "No Jealousies Between Administration and Judicial Tribunals," 15 *Ill. L. Rev.* 223, 224 (1920).

15. Wigmore, "A New Field for Systematic Justice," 10 *Ill. L. Rev.* 592 (1916).

16. Wigmore, "At Last — The Industrial Court," 14 *Ill. L. Rev.* 585 (1920).

17. The full title is *The Principles of Judicial Proof or the Process of Proof As Given by Logic, Psychology and General Experience and Illustrated in Judicial Trials.*

18. Zachariah Chafee, Jr., "Book Review," 80 *U. of Pa. L. Rev.* 319, 322 (1931).

19. Edmund M. Morgan, "Book Review," 31 *Colum. L. Rev.* 1229 (1931).

20. *Third Edition* ix (1937).

21. See William H. Wicker, "Book Review," 15 *Tenn. L. Rev.* 404 (1938), and Mason Ladd, "Book Review," 23 *Iowa L. Rev.* 440 (1938).

22. Robert H. Gault, "The Psychologic Interest," 32 *J. Crim. L. & Crim.* 264 (1941).

23. Robert W. Wilson, "Wigmore's Method of Analyzing Evidence," 50 *A.B.A.J.* 510 (1964).

24. *Third Edition* viii (1932).

25. Mrs. Wigmore to Margaret G. Belknap, Mar. 9, 1932 (Wigmore Collection).

26. Robert T. Donley, "Book Review," 40 *West Va. L. Qt.* 300 (1934).

27. Charles B. Whittier, "Book Review," 27 *Ill. L. Rev.* 586 (1933); Leslie J. Tompkins, "Book Review," 10 *N.Y.U. L. Qt.* 259 (1932).

28. Paul L. Sayre, "Book Review," 18 *Iowa L. Rev.* 420 (1933).

29. "Preface" viii.

30. Wilbur H. Cherry, "Book Review," 20 *Minn. L. Rev.* 842 (1936).

31. Charles T. McCormick, "Book Review," 30 *Ill. L. Rev.* 686 (1936).

32. Ralph T. Catterall, "Book Review," 22 *Va. L. Rev.* 491, 492 (1936).

33. The full title is *Wigmore's Code of the Rules of Evidence in Trials at Law.*

34. It was reprinted in 1938.

35. "Book Review," 21 *Cornell L. Qt.* 386, 387 (1936).

36. 30 *Ill. L. Rev.* 686, 688 (1936).

37. For book reviews see Robert McWilliam, 17 *State Bar Jr. of Calif.* 313 (1942) and John A. Metz, Jr., 14 *Penn. B. A. Qt.* 94 (1942).

38. Quoted by Wigmore in "First Aid for Trial by Jury," 20 *Ill. L. Rev.* 106 (1925).

39. *Id.* at 107.

40. 12 *J. Am. Jud. Soc'y* 166 (1929).

41. For responses from readers see "Side Lights on Trial by Jury," 13 *J. Am. Jud. Soc'y.* 82 (1929).

42. "Jury-Trial Rules of Evidence in the Next Century," 1 *Law: A Century of Progress 1835–1935* (1937), 1:347.

43. *Ibid.*, p. 348.

44. *Ibid.*, p. 350.

45. Wigmore, "Senate Bill no. 624: To Ruin Jury Trial in the Federal Courts," 19 *Ill. L. Rev.* 97 (1924).

46. *Id.* at 98.

47. "Wanted — A Chief Judicial Superintendent," 11 *Ill. L. Rev.* 45 (1916).

48. *Id.* at 47.

49. *Id.* at 46.

50. "Judicial Superintendence in Ohio," 7 *J. Am. Jud. Soc'y* 3 (1923).

51. "Judges and Politics," 4 *Ill. L. Rev.* 417 (1910).

52. "Giving Political Orders to the Judiciary," 11 *Ill. L. Rev.* 108 (1916).

53. "Oh, There Be Players!," 27 *Ill. L. Rev.* 178 (1932).

54. "And Pilate Answered and Said Again Unto the Multitude 'What Will Ye Then That I Should Do?'," 19 *Ill. L. Rev.* 93 (1924).

55. *Id.* at 95.

56. Wigmore, "A New Way to Nominate Supreme Court Judges," 22 *J. Am. Jud. Soc'y* 207 (1939).

57. *Id.* at 208.

58. "The Federal Senate and the Federal Judges," 7 *Ill. L. Rev.* 443 (1913).

59. 22 *A.B.A.J.* 227 (1936).

60. For another attempt using the field of taxation see Albert S. Faught, "Grading the Federal Courts in Taxation Cases," 22 *A.B.A.J.* 396 (1936).

61. 22 *A.B.A.J.* 227,228 (1936).

62. Wigmore, "All Legislative Rules for Judiciary Procedure are Void Constitutionally," 23 *Ill. L. Rev.* 276 (1928).

63. 61 *A.B.A. Rep.* 453 (1936).

64. "A Critique of the Federal Court Rules Draft," 61 *A.B.A. Rep.* 453 (1936). Also printed in 22 *A.B.A.J.* 811 (1936).

65. *Id.* at 459.

66. See William D. Mitchell, "Some of the Problems Confronting the Advisory Committee," 23 *A.B.A.J.* 966, 968–69 (1937).

67. Wigmore to Everett P. Wheeler, Dec. 31, 1921 (Wigmore Collection).

68. 23 *Ill. L. Rev.* 276 (1928). For comments on Wigmore's statement see 24 *J. Am. Jud. Soc'y* 41, 101, 115 (1940–41).

69. "Dean Wigmore's Credo," p. 28 [also "My Creed for the Nation"].

70. "The Cumulative Burden of Reports," 25 *J.Am. Jud. Soc'y* 174 (1942).

71. 228 *N. Y.* 475, 127 *N. E.* 584 (1920).

72. Wigmore, "Are the Yellow Cabs Common Carriers?," 15 *Ill. L. Rev.* 474 (1921).

73. "John H. Wigmore Offers a Suggestion," 22 *J. Am. Jud. Soc'y* 166 (1938). For comments on Wigmore's proposal see *id.* at 223, 269.

74. Wigmore, "Federal Administrative Agencies: How to Locate Their Rules of Practice and Their Rulings With Special Reference to Their Rules of Evidence," 25 *A.B.A.J.* 25 (1939).

75. *Id.* at 166.

76. "The Federal Register and Code of Federal Regulations," 29 *A.B.A.J.* 10 (1943).

77. *Id.* at 149.

78. G. B. Rose to Wigmore, Feb. 27, 1939 (Wigmore Collection).

79. See p. 15.

80. Wigmore, "The Criminal Law Section of the American Bar Association," 12 *J. Crim. L. & C.* 314 (1921); "The Criminal Law Section," 16 *Ill. L. Rev.* 226 (1921).

81. "Proceedings of the Criminal Law Section," 45 *A.B.A. Rep.* 423 (1920).

82. Wigmore, "The Criminal Law Section of the American Bar Association," pp. 314, 315.

83. Edson R. Sunderland, *History of the American Bar Association* (1953), p. 121.

84. Leon Green, "Relations Between Dean Wigmore and His Successor," (1963), p. 12 (Wigmore Collection).

85. Published in 1929 by the Illinois Association of Criminal Justice. For a book review see Herbert B. Ehrmann, 43 *Harv. L. Rev.* 341 (1929). For a discussion of the *Report* see Ass'n Am. L. Schools, *1928 Handbook and Proceedings*, p. 68.

86. Illinois Association of Criminal Justice, *The Illinois Crime Survey* (1929), p. 5

87. *Id.* at 6.

88. See the association's *Handbook and Proceedings* for the years 1926–30.

89. *Northwestern Univ. Alumni News* (Jan. 1930), 9, no. 3:20. An earlier attempt was made in 1921 but apparently did not get under way. See "The Bureau of Criminal Analysis," 12 *J. Crim. L. & C.* 11 (1921).

90. Wigmore, "Topics of Mutual Interest to Our Two Professions," p. 12. Address at the Harvard Medical School, Feb. 28, 1935 (Wigmore Collection).

91. August Vollmer, "John Henry Wigmore and the Modern Police," 32 *J. Crim. L. & C.* 293, 295 (1941).

92. "A Tribute to John Henry Wigmore," 32 *J. Crim. L. & C.* 291 (1941).

93. *Id.* at 495.

94. For a fuller discussion see "The Loeb-Leopold Murder of Franks in Chicago, May 21, 1924," 15 *J. Crim. L. & C.* 347 (1924). See also the comment of H. I. Gosline and Wigmore's reply in "The Loeb-Leopold Case Again," 15 *J. Crim. L. & C.* 501 (1925).

95. Wigmore, "Legitimate Bounds in the Defense of Accused Persons," 19 *Ill. L. Rev.* 95 (1924).

96. Wigmore, "To Abolish Partisanship of Expert Witnesses, As Illustrated in the Loeb-Leopold Case," 15 *J. Crim. L. & C.* 341 (1934).

97. *Id.* at 342.

98. Wigmore, "The Judge's Sentence in the Loeb-Leopold Murder," 19 *Ill. L. Rev.* 167, 168 (1924). See also "The Judge's Sentence and the Psychiatrists in the Loeb-Leopold Case," 15 *J. Crim. L. & C.* 400 (1924).

99. Wigmore, "The Judge's Sentence in the Loeb-Leopold Murder," at 169.

100. Wigmore, "The Judge's Sentence and the Psychiatrists in the Loeb-Leopold Case," at 400. However, Leopold did reform and, after a long term of useful service behind prison walls, he was released on parole on Mar. 13, 1958.

101. *Id.* at 405.

102. Wigmore, 1 *Treatise on Evidence* 210 (2d ed., 1923).

103. "Better Not Park There! You're Liable to Get Pinched," 22 *J. Crim. L. & C.* 5 (1931).

104. *Id.* at 7.

105. Wigmore to Louis N. Robinson, Jan. 21, 1914 (Wigmore Collection).

106. "Book Review," 7 *Ill. L. Rev.* 395, 396 (1913).

107. Wigmore, "The Bill to Make Compensation to Persons Erroneously Convicted of Crime," 3 *J. Crim. L. & C.* 665 (1913).

108. "Book Review," 23 *J. Crim. L. & C.* 320, 321 (1932).

109. Wigmore, "The Public Defender in Our Cities," 25 *Ill. L. Rev.* 687 (1931).

110. "Dean Wigmore's Credo," p. 32 [also "My Creed for the Nation"].

111. "On Behalf of the Law Faculty," 34 *J. Crim. L. & C.* 85, 86 (1943).

112. "Report of the Standing Committee on Legal Aid Work," 65 *A.B.A. Rep.* 187,191 (1940).

113. See *Reports* of the Legal Aid Society (Wigmore Collection).

114. 21 *Legal Aid Brief Case* 205 (1963).

115. Emery A. Brownell, *Legal Aid in the United States* 148 (1951).

116. *Id.* See also *A.B.A. Reps.* 47:408 (1922), 48:377, 569 (1923).

117. James J. Forrestal to Wigmore, Oct. 22, 1923 (Wigmore Collection).

118. 21 *Legal Aid Brief Case* 205 (1963).

119. *Id.*

120. Sarah B. Morgan to the author, May 25, 1961.

121. *Recollections*, Sarah B. Morgan, p. 19 (Wigmore Collection).

122. The full title is *A Treatise on the Anglo-American System of Evidence in Trials at Common Law, Including the Statutes and Judicial Decisions of All Jurisdictions of the United States and Canada.* Wigmore collaborated with Richmond Rucker in the preparation of the 1943 pocket supplements.

123. Edmund M. Morgan, "Book Review," 29 *Ill. L. Rev.* 550, 552 (1934).

124. 1 *Third Edition* xi (1940).

125. Robert T. Donley, "Book Review," 40 *West Va. L. Qt.* 300, 301 (1934).

126. 7 *Third Edition*, 169 (1940).

127. 1934 Supplement p. 90.

128. 1 *Third Edition* vii (1940).

129. *Id.* at viii.

130. Wigmore, *Code of the Rules of Evidence in Trials at Law* xiii, 3d ed. (1942).

131. Charles T. McCormick, "Book Review," 35 *Ill. L. Rec.* 540, 544 (1941).

132. *Id.* at 545.

133. 5 *Third Edition*, 362, § 1520 (1940).

134. 6 *Third Edition*, 100, § 1732, note 6 (1940).

135. 7 *Third Edition*, 113, § 1971, note 5 (1940).

136. 9 *Third Edition*, p. 326, § 2498 (1940).

137. 265 *Fed.* 504 (1920).

138. "Criminal Pleading — Assault With Intent — Fatuous Technicalities," 15 *Ill. L.* Rev. 411, 412 (1921).

139. Albert S. Osborn, *Questioned Document Problems, The Discovery and Truth of the Facts* (1944), p. 358. Wigmore died before the publication of this book and Osborn dedicated it to him.

140. Edmund M. Morgan, "Book Review," 20 *Boston U. L. Rev.* 776, 778 (1940).

141. He was seventy-seven when the *Treatise* was published in 1940.

142. 1 *Treatise on Evidence* viii (1st ed., 1904).

143. 1 *Third Edition*, xii (1940).

144. 20 *Boston U. L. Rev.* 776,793 (1940).

145. 58 *Nw. U.L. Rev.*, 443 (1963).

CHAPTER 15. A CONTINUING LEADERSHIP: LAW, PUBLIC SERVICE, RELIGION

1. For the activities referred to in this paragraph see Ass'n Am. L. Schools,. *Handbook and Proceedings*, Criminal Law, 1930:117; 1931:118, 146–57;

1932:141–43. Curriculum, 1920:5, 76. Evidence, 1920:64, 73–74; 1921:29; 1926:92. Jurisprudence, 1931:121; 1932:127. Juristic Center, 1920:6. Legal history, 1931:121; 1932:116, 127; 1933:169–70. Legal aid, 1936:207; 1937:209, 221; 1938:259. Legal procedure, 1920:123–24, 226; 1921:32; 1922:6, 149, 150; 1923:6, 29, 36, 112; 1924:29, 37, 97–98. Library problems, 1943:218 (see also 30 *Law Lib. J.* 2, 1937). Memorials, 1929:121; 1931:118, 162; 1932:115, 145. Professional doctorates, 1921:6. Torts, 1921:29. Reviewing law books, 1933:32.

2. 16 *Ill. L. Rev.* 499 (1922).

3. *Id.* at 501.

4. Ass'n Am. L. Schools, *1944 Handbook and Proceedings*, p. 173.

5. Ass'n Am. L. Schools, *1924 Handbook and Proceedings*, pp. 56, 62.

6. *Ibid.*, p. 51.

7. Ass'n Am. L. Schools *1933 Handbook and Proceedings*, p. 93.

8. See Ass'n Am. L. Schools, *Song Annals 1926–1936*, in *Opera Minora*, vol. 13 (Wigmore Collection).

9. *Recollections*, Manley O. Hudson, p. 2 (Wigmore Collection).

10. *Recollections*, Nathan W. MacChesney, p. 6 (Wigmore Collection).

11. *Recollections*, John W. Curran, p. 1 (Wigmore Collection).

12. 56 *A.B.A. Rep.* 513 (1931).

13. *Id.* at 716, 718.

14. 64 *A.B.A. Rep.* 44 (1939).

15. 63 *A.B.A. Rep.* 570 (1938).

16. Charles T. McCormick, "Book Review," 35 *Ill. L. Rev.* 540, 544 (1941).

17. See "Plan to Rid Evidence Rules of their Flees," 22 *J. Am. Jud. Soc'y* 136 (1938).

18. "Wigmore Collection of Jurisprudence in Cleveland Public Library," 24 *A.B.A.J.* 823 (1938).

19. Published under the same title as *Law Series I, Lecture No. 6.*

20. See "Note," 20 *A.B.A.J.* 744 (1934).

21. *Id.*

22. Sarah B. Morgan to the author, Apr. 20, 1967.

23. 48 *A.B.A. Rep.* 77, 135, 473 (1923).

24. *Id.* at 87.

25. 16 *A.B.A.J.* 62 (1930).

26. "Organizing the Powers of the American Bar," 17 *A.B.A.J.* 387 (1931).

27. *Id.* at 391.

28. 61 *A.B.A. Rep.* 919–20 (1936).

29. 67 *A.B.A. Rep.* 36 (1942), 68 *A.B.A. Rep.* 436 (1943).

30. "Soldier's and Sailor's Civil Relief Act," 27 *A.B.A.J.* 67 (1941).

31. "Legislative Preparedness," 21 *Ill. L. Rev.* 488 (1927).

32. *Recollections*, Nathan W. MacChesney, p. 21 (Wigmore Collection).

33. Based on statement made by George Anderson to the author, Mar. 27, 1951.

34. *Recollections*, Stuart S. Ball, p. 10 (Wigmore Collection).

35. Typed copy in Wigmore Collection.

36. 22 *A.B.A.J.* 506 (1936).

37. Wigmore, "Illinois Takes Lead in Bar Admission Standards," 18 *Ill. L. Rev.* 199 (1923).

38. "The Right to Be an Incompetent Lawyer," 22 *Ill. L. Rev.* 428 (1927).

39. *Id.* at 429.

40. See note, "Information at the Source" in 14 *A.B.A.J.* 143 (1928). No copy of his remarks has been located.

41. Quoted by I. Maurice Wormser in "Fewer Lawyers and Better Ones," 15 *A.B.A.J.* 206 (1929).

42. "Dean Wigmore's Credo," *Alumni Journal* [Northwestern Univ.], July 9, 1921, p. 28. Also printed privately as "My Creed for the Nation" (Wigmore Collection).

43. "Unprogressive Bar, Unprogressive Legislature, Unprogressive Justice," 20 *Ill. L. Rev.* 271 (1925).

44. Ass'n Am. Law Schools, *1933 Handbook and Proceedings*, p. 56.

45. For an account of the presentation see, "American Bar Association Medal Presented," 18 *A.B.A.J.* 741 (1932). See also 57 *A.B.A.Rep.* 178 (1932). See also Charles B. Stephens "A Door Closes," 31 *Ill. Bar. J.* 300 (1943).

46. Roscoe Pound to Wigmore, Oct. 25, 1932 (Wigmore Collection). Wigmore to William H. Taft (n.d.) (Wigmore Collection).

47. "The American Corpus Juris Criticized," *Green Bag* (1910), 22:428. For the original proposal see p. 59. For comments see pp. 420, 457.

48. Wigmore to William H. Taft (n.d.) (Wigmore Collection).

49. American Law Institute, *Restatement in the Courts, Permanent Edition, Glossary . . . History of the American Law Institute and the First Restatement of the Law* (1945), p. 26.

50. "American Law Institute Undertakes Code of Evidence," 25 *A.B.A.J.* 380, 471 (1939).

51. In this connection see "Jury Trial Rules of Evidence in the Next Century," in *Law: A Century of Progress 1835–1935* (1937), 1:347.

52. For the postulates set out in full see "The American Law Institute Code of Evidence: A Dissent," 28 *A.B.A.J.* 23 (1942).

53. "Dean Wigmore States His Position," 26 *A.B.A.J.* 476–77 (1940).

54. *Id.* at 476.

55. 28 *A.B.A.J.* 23 (1942).

56. *Id.* at 27–28.

57. Robert A. Leflar, "Book Review," 6 *Mo. L. Rev.* 41, 49 (1941).

58. Leon Green to the author, May 14, 1971.

59. Based on statement of Jerome Hall made to the author on Apr. 22, 1962.

60. Nat'l Conf. of Commissioners on Uniform State Laws, *Handbook and Proceedings*, 43rd Ann. Conf. (1933), pp. 20, 35, 139.

61. Nat'l Conf. of Commissioners on Uniform State Laws, *Handbook and Proceedings*, 30th Ann. Conf. (1920), p. 6.

62. See Wigmore, "Uniformity of Laws — Compacts Between States," 19 *Ill. L. Rev.* 479 (1925); "Dam Legislation, Federal and State," 23 *Ill. L. Rev.* 482 (1929); "Interstate Compacts As Solution for Lack of State Power," 26 *Ill. L. Rev.* 318 (1931).

63. Nat'l Conf. of Commissioners on Uniform State Laws, *Handbook and Proceedings*, 31st Ann. Conf. (1921), p. 297. Freund, in a concurring memorandum, stated that he believed the majority report overestimated the value of the compact method. See p. 357.

64. *Ibid.*, p. 299.

65. For favorable comments on the report see the following *Handbooks* of the commission, 36th Ann. Conf. (1926), p. 26; 37th Ann. Conf. (1927), p. 775; 38th Ann. Conf. (1928) p. 45; 41st Ann. Conf. (1931) pp. 357, 358, 360; 42nd Ann. Conf. (1932), p. 280; 44th Ann. Conf. (1934), p. 51; 45th Ann. Conf. (1935), pp. 87–88.

66. Nat'l Conf. of Commissioners on Uniform State Laws, *Handbook and Proceedings*, 37th Ann. Conf. (1927), p. 775; 38th Ann. Conf. (1928), p. 45.

67. For a summary of Wigmore's work as a member of the Commission on Uniform State Laws see Nat'l. Conf. of Commissioners on Uniform State Laws, *Handbook and Proceedings*, 53rd Ann. Conf. (1943), pp. 89, 256.

68. 51 *A.B.A. Rep.* 648 (1926), 52 *A.B.A. Rep.* 24 (1927).

69. Nat'l Conf. of Commissioners on Uniform State Laws, *Handbook and Proceedings*, 35th Ann. Conf. (1925), pp. 343–44.

70. *Ibid.*, 48th Ann. Conf. (1938), p. 33.

71. *Ibid.*, p. 34.

72. *Ibid.*, pp. 95–96, 125–26. Wigmore's physician described the illness as auricular fibrillation.

73. *Ibid.*, p. 125.

74. *Ibid.*, p. 214.

75. *Ibid.*

76. Nat'l Conf. of Commissioners on Uniform State Laws, *Handbook and Proceedings*, 53rd Ann. Conf. (1943), pp. 91–92.

77. (Wigmore Collection).

78. *Cincinnati Times*, Aug. 30, 1921 (Wigmore Collection).

79. Copies in Wigmore Collection.

80. Rowe to Wigmore, Mar. 30, 1920, Wigmore to Rowe, Apr. 1, 1920 (Wigmore Collection).

81. Wigmore to Newton D. Baker, Feb. 15, 1935 (Wigmore Collection).

82. "Dean Wigmore's Credo," p. 29 [also "My Creed for the Nation"].

83. Ralph E. Church to Wigmore, Apr. 25, 1940 (Wigmore Collection).

84. Wigmore to Lord MacMillan, July 28, 1938 (Wigmore Collection).

85. *Republican Times*, Ottawa, Illinois, Dec. 16, 1937 (Wigmore Collection).

86. Quoted by Wigmore in his "Bureaucracy and Dictatorship; What Are They? And Why?" (1937), p. 1 (Wigmore Collection).

87. Wigmore to Floyd E. Thompson, Feb. 21, 1928 (Wigmore Collection).

88. Preserved in typed draft but not included in "My Creed for the Nation" (Wigmore Collection).

89. *Ibid.*

90. "Dean Wigmore's Credo," p. 30 [also "My Creed for the Nation"].

91. Preserved in typed draft but not included in "My Creed for the Nation" (Wigmore Collection).

92. Wigmore, "A Constitutional Way to Reach the Housing Profiteer," 15 *Ill. L. Rev.* 359 (1921).

93. In typed draft of statements not included in "My Creed for the Nation" (Wigmore Collection).

94. Copy in Wigmore Collection.

95. *Ibid.*, p. 3.

96. *Ibid.*, p. 4.

97. *Ibid.*, pp. 4–5.

98. *Ibid.*, pp. 6–8.

99. *Ibid.*

100. *Ibid.*, pp. 10–11.

101. *Ibid.*, pp. 13–14.

102. *Northwestern Univ. Bull.* (Aug. 18, 1923), 24:3, 19.

103. "Dean Wigmore's Credo" p. 30 [also "My Creed for the Nation"].

104. 19 *Ill. L. Rev.* 659 (1925). See also "How the U.S. Senate Has Blocked a Good Measure," 11 *A.B.A.J.* 339 (1925), and reply to Wigmore, p. 404.

105. *Id.* at 663.

106. "The Unconstitutional Senate," 20 *Ill. L. Rev.* 61 (1925). See also "Did the United States Constitution Create 97 Veto Powers?," 20 *Ill. L. Rev.* 589 (1926) and "Legal Fiction as a Mode of Legislation," 20 *Ill. L. Rev.* 687 (1926).

107. "Scopotropismic Senators Stalled by a Sturdy Scott," 22 *Ill. L. Rev.* 883, 886 (1928).

108. *Ada, Oklahoma News*, Apr. 24, 1934 (Wigmore Collection).

109. "A Program for Legislative Efficiency by Constitutional Amendment," 24 *Ill. L. Rev.* 315, 316 (1929).

110. *Id.* at 315.

111. "Dean Wigmore's Credo," p. 29 [also "My Creed for the Nation"].

112. "The Draft Constitution, Fifty Years of Progress," 17 *Ill. L. Rev.* 293, 294 (1922).

113. "Dean Wigmore's Credo," p. 32 [also "My Creed for the Nation"].

114. *Ibid.*, p. 33.

115. Wigmore to Golton, Feb. 12, 1915 (Wigmore Collection).

116. "Dean Wigmore's Credo," p. 32 [also "My Creed for the Nation"].

117. "Drafting the Repeal of the Eighteenth Amendment," 27 *Ill. L. Rev.* 527, 528 (1933).

118. Wigmore, "Book Review," 28 *Ill. L. Rev.* 441 (1933). The National Industrial Recovery Act was declared unconstitutional by the Supreme Court in 1935. See A.L.A. Schechter Poultry Corp. et al. v. U.S., 295 U.S. 495 (1935).

119. Wigmore to Richard Aldworth, Dec. 23, 1937 (Wigmore Collection).

120. Nat'l Conf. of Commissioners on Uniform State Laws, *Handbook and Proceedings*, 46th Ann. Conf. (1936), p. 126.

121. A statement entitled "Observations Re JHW Contributions to Air Law for the Consideration of WRR" prepared by Frederick D. Fagg, Jr., expressly for the use of the author has been of substantial assistance in dealing with Wigmore's activities in the field of air law. Hereafter, it will be referred to only when a direct quotation is involved.

122. Wigmore, "Fred Dow Fagg, Jr., Director of Air Commerce," 8 *J. Air L.* 214 (1937).

123. *Id.* at 215.

124. "Air Law Institute Planned at Northwestern University," 15 *A.B.A.J.* 458 (1929).

125. In 1939 the title was changed to *Journal of Air Law and Commerce.*

126. *Recollections*, Nathan W. MacChesney, p. 23 (Wigmore Collection).

127. Frederick D. Fagg, Jr., "Observations Re JHW Contributions to Air Law for the Consideration of WRR," p. 4 (author's collection).

128. *Recollections*, Frederick D. Fagg, Jr., p. 2 (Wigmore Collection).

129. Frederick D. Fagg, Jr., to Sarah B. Morgan, Apr. 3, 1963 (Wigmore Collection).

130. Fagg, "Observations Re JHW Contributions to Air Law for the Consideration of WRR," p. 5.

131. *Ibid.*

132. *Ibid.*

133. Mrs. Wigmore to Wigmore, Dec. 2, 1934 (Wigmore Collection).

134. *Ibid.*, Dec. 12, 1934 (Wigmore Collection).

135. *Ibid.*, Dec. 2, 1934.

136. Fagg, "Observations Re JHW Contributions to Air Law for Consideration of WRR," p. 5.

137. *Ibid.*, p. 6.

138. *Ibid.*, p. 7.

139. *Ibid.*, p. 10.

140. *Recollections*, Frederick D. Fagg, Jr., p. 5 (Wigmore Collection).

141. Fagg, "Observations Re JHW Contributions to Air Law for Consideration of WRR," p. 10.

142. *Ibid.*, p. 11.

143. "Dean Wigmore's Credo," p. 31 [also "My Creed for the Nation"].

144. Wigmore to Oliver W. Holmes, July 30, 1911 (Wigmore Collection).

145. Preserved in typed draft but not included in "My Creed for the Nation" (Wigmore Collection).

146. Wigmore to Foster D. Boswell, Apr. 8, 1914 (Wigmore Collection).

147. William F. McDowell to Wigmore, Aug. 10, 1916 (Wigmore Collection).

148. Charles B. Megan, "On Behalf of the Bar," 38 *Ill. L. Rev.* 12, 14 (1943).

149. *Recollections*, Nathan W. MacChesney, p. 45 (Wigmore Collection).

150. *Recollections*, Edward A. Harriman, p. 2 (Wigmore Collection).

151. *Recollections*, Albert Kocourek (Preface), pp. 4, 11 (Wigmore Collection).

152. *Recollections*, Edward A. Harriman, p. 2 (Wigmore Collection).

CHAPTER 16. THE WORLD COMMUNITY

1. In 1919 the French government conferred upon Wigmore the title of Chevalier de la Légion d'honneur.

2. *Recollections*, Stuart S. Ball, p. 9 (Wigmore Collection).

3. *Recollections*, Francis M. Wigmore, p. 5 (Wigmore Collection).

4. *Recollections*, Sarah B. Morgan, p. 12 (Wigmore Collection).

5. *Ibid.*, p. 11.

6. Sarah B. Morgan to the author, Feb. 22, 1960.

7. Based upon a statement made by Sarah B. Morgan to the author, May 25, 1966.

8. It seems likely that the priest, at least sometimes, had other business in Chicago and that Wigmore did not assume the entire expense of the trip to Chicago and return.

9. Sarah B. Morgan to the author, Feb. 22, 1960.

10. Based upon a statement by Sarah B. Morgan to the author, May 25, 1966.

11. Wigmore quickly came to recognize the menace of Italian fascism.

12. Wigmore, "The Case of Italy v. Greece Under International Law and the Pact of Nations," 18 *Ill. L. Rev.* 131, 135 (1923).

13. Wigmore to Henry S. Bacon, Dec. 10, 1938 (Wigmore Collection).

14. Wigmore, "Elihu Root and Our Mexican Backsliding," 21 *Ill. L. Rev.* 610 (1927). See also "Does Might Make Right With Latin America," 22 *Ill. L. Rev.* 648 (1928).

15. Wigmore, "The United States and Trial by Battle," 19 *Ill. L. Rev.* 257 (1924).

16. Wigmore, "Should the United States Yield Up Its Extra Territorial Jurisdiction in China," 20 *Ill. L. Rev.* 365 (1925).

17. *Id.* at 367.

18. "Domicile, Double Allegiance, and World Citizenship," 21 *Ill. L. Rev.* 761, 770 (1927). See also "Domicile and Double Allegiance, Again," 23 *Ill. L. Rev.* 153 (1928).

19. "Dean Wigmore's Credo," *Alumni Journal* [Northwestern Univ.] July 9,

1921, p. 31. Also privately printed as "My Creed for the Nation" (1921) (Wigmore Collection).

20. *Ibid.*, p. 30.

21. Preserved in typed draft but not included in "My Creed for the Nation."

22. *Recollections*, Charles C. Hyde, p. 2 (Wigmore Collection).

23. "Dean Wigmore's Credo" [also "My Creed for the Nation"].

24. Wigmore to George E. Mills, Mar. 7, 1924 (Wigmore Collection).

25. *Recollections*, Manley O. Hudson, p. 2 (Wigmore Collection).

26. *Evanston News* [Ill.], Sept. 27, 1923.

27. "The League from a Lawyer's Point of View," 34 *Int. Jr. of Ethics* 112 (1923).

28. Unidentified newspaper clipping.

29. "Wigmore to Margaret G. Belknap, July —, 1932 (Wigmore Collection).

30. Hugh R. Wilson to Wigmore, Sept. 8, 1938 (Wigmore Collection).

31. Based on a statement in typed draft but not included in "My Creed for the Nation."

32. "The World Court of Justice," 16 *Ill. L. Rev.* 207 (1921).

33. The fifth reservation read: "The Court shall not render any advisory opinion, except publicly after due notice to all States adhering to the Court and to all interested States, and after public hearing given to any State concerned; nor shall it without the consent of the United States *entertain any request* for an advisory opinion touching any dispute or question in which the United States has or claims an interest."

34. "The Fifth Reservation and the Senate Stronghold," 21 *Ill. L. Rev.* 36–37 (1926).

35. "Congratulations to the World Court Upon This Accession to Its Membership." 15 *A.B.A.J.* 264 (1929).

36. Wigmore, "Shall the World Court be Open to the Public," 10 *A.B.A.J.* 471 (1924).

37. *Recollections*, Manley O. Hudson, p. 3 (Wigmore Collection).

38. Wigmore, "Shall the World Court be Open to the Public," 10 *A.B.A.J.* 471, 475 (1924).

39. "Dean Wigmore's Reply," 10 *A.B.A.J.* 712 (1924).

40. Manley O. Hudson, "Is the World Court Open to the Public," 10 *A.B.A.J.* 711 (1924).

41. Wigmore, "Shall the World Court be Open to the Public," 10 *A.B.A.J.* 471, 473 (1924).

42. "Dean Wigmore's Reply," p. 712.

43. Wigmore to Manley O. Hudson, June 24, 1931 (Wigmore Collection).

44. "Book Review," 30 *Ill. L. Rev.* 550 (1935).

45. "Memorial Proposing Dean John H. Wigmore of Northwestern University (Chicago) for the Permanent Court of International Justice" (Wigmore Collection).

46. S.B.M. [Sarah B. Morgan] to Walter B. Wolf, Mar. 18, 1930 (Wigmore Collection).

47. Law Faculty Minutes, Apr. 14, 1930.

48. Manley O. Hudson to Wigmore, July 29, 1930 (Wigmore Collection).

49. *Nation* (1930), 130:504.

50. Albert Kocourek to Wigmore, Apr. 22, 1930 (Wigmore Collection).

51. Wigmore to Secretary General, Aug. 2, 1930 (Wigmore Collection).

52. Albert Kocourek to Wigmore, Apr. 22, 1930. In his letter Kocourek refers to Wigmore's justification, but Wigmore's letter has not been located.

53. Wigmore to Manley O. Hudson, Sept. 5, 1930 (Wigmore Collection).

54. Wigmore to Newton D. Baker, Feb. 15, 1935 (Wigmore Collection).

55. See p. 142.

56. "The Treaty Veto of the American Senate," 16 *Iowa L. Rev.* 150 (1930).

57. "The Senate's Neglect of the Nation's International Interests," 26 *Ill. L. Rev.* 794 (1932).

58. *Id.* at 795.

59. *Id.* at 796.

60. Wigmore, "The Importance of American International Law Today for American Practitioners," 9 *J.B.A. Dist. Col.* 255 (1942).

61. *Id.* at 256.

62. The general title is *To Popularize for Lawyers the Study of American International Law, A Syllabus of American International Law for American Practitioners.* Part I was published in 1941 and Part II in 1942.

63. The full title is *A Guide to American International Law and Practice, as Found in the United States Constitution, Treaties, Statutes, Decisions, Executive Orders, Administrative Regulations, Diplomatic Correspondence and Army and Navy Instructions, Including War-Time Law* (1943). Franklin B. Snyder, "On Behalf of the University," 34 *J. Crim. L. & Crim.* 90 (1943).

64. *Recollections*, Manley O. Hudson, p. 3 (Wigmore Collection).

65. 53 *A.B.A. Rep.* 514 (1928).

66. 57 *A.B.A. Rep.* 19 (1932).

67. James O. Murdock "The Founding of the Section and Dean John Henry Wigmore," 7 *Int'l and Comp. L. Bull.* (A.B.A.) 4, 6 (1963). For the proceedings of the first meeting see 59 *A.B.A. Rep.* 196, 653 (1934).

68. The full title is "Should the World's Legal Profession Organize? — Reasons for Taking This Step — Outline of Plan for Consideration," 18 *A.B.A.J.* 552 (1932).

69. 59 *A.B.A. Rep* 217 (1934). For report see pp. 620, 627, 629.

70. *Id.* at 27. See also 60 *A.B.A. Rep.* 27 (1935).

71. 61 *A.B.A. Rep.* 277 (1936).

72. "Affiliation of American Bar Association Announced at Recent Meeting of International Union of Lawyers in Vienna," 22 *A.B.A.J.* 751 (1936). Wigmore reviews the proceedings of the Ninth Congress of the Union in 25 *A.B.A.J.* 433 (1939).

73. Wigmore, "A World Congress of Bar Assoications," 23 *A.B.A.J.* 568 (1937).

74. "International Law Section Holds Spring Meeting," 26 *A.B.A.J.* 338, 741 (1940). Wigmore also served on the American Association of Law Schools Committee on Inter-American Cooperation. Ass'n Am. L. Schools, *1942 Handbook and Proceedings*, pp. 113, 150.

75. Wigmore, "Lawyers of the Americas, Wake Up," 46 *Law Notes* [U.S.] no. 3, p. 17 (Oct. 1942).

76. Wigmore to Holmes, Mar. 24 and June 7, 1924 (Wigmore Collection).

77. For the titles of these writings see the forthcoming *Bibliography* by Kurt Schwerin referred to in the explanatory statement at the beginning of these notes.

78. See also "Some Legal Systems that Have Disappeared," 2 *La. L. Rev.* 1 (1939).

79. Wigmore to Walter D. Scott, May 5, 1925 (Deering Library, Northwestern Univ.).

80. Wigmore, "A New Way of Teaching Comparative Law," *J. Soc'y Pub. Teachers of Law*, 1926, p. 6.

81. "Announcement" (Wigmore Collection).

82. Wigmore to Holmes, Apr. 5, 1926 (Wigmore Collection).

83. JHW Diary, Aug. 12, 1926 (Wigmore Collection).

84. *Recollections*, Nelson G. Wettling, p. 2 (Wigmore Collection).

85. Based on a statement made to the author by Sarah B. Morgan, Feb. 12, 1962.

86. Henry B. Witham, "Book Review," 15 *Tenn. L. Rev.* 834 (1939).

87. Frederick C. Hicks, "Book Review," 15 *A.B.A.J.* 576 (1929).

88. H. G., "Book Review," 85 *U. Pa. L. Rev.* 656 (1937).

89. Harold D. Hazeltine to Wigmore, Mar. 23, 1929 (Wigmore Collection).

90. *Recollections*, Roscoe Pound, p. 2 (Wigmore Collection).

91. Theodore F. T. Plucknett, "Book Review," 42 *Harv. L. Rev.* 587, 588 (1929).

92. John Hanna, "Book Review," 45 *Pol. Sc. Rev.* 137, 138 (1930).

93. A. L. Goodhart, "Book Review," 38 *Yale L. J.* 554 (1929). For Frederick Pollock's critical comment see letter from Pollock to Holmes, Jan. 21 (1929), in Mark D. Howe, *Holmes-Pollock Letters* (1942), 2:237.

94. Theodore F. T. Plucknett, "Book Review," 42 *Harv. L. Rev.* 587,588 (1929).

95. Wigmore, *A Panorama of the World's Legal Systems* (1928), 3:1129.

96. William S. Holdsworth to Wigmore, July 16, 1929 (Wigmore Collection).

97. Institut Japanais de Droit Comparé, Problèmes Contemporains de Droit Comparé, Tome Deuxième, *Problèmes Divers de Droit Comparé* (1962), p. 541.

98. *Panorama of the World's Legal Systems*, 1:3, n. 22.

99. *Ibid.*, p. xiv.

100. The one-volume edition attracted wide attention in the press. The *American Weekly*, the magazine of the Hearst papers, with an estimated circulation of 6,000,000, carried a full-page spread on Aug. 2, 1936.

101. The full title is *A Kaleidoscope of Justice: Containing Authentic Accounts of Trial Scenes from All Times and Climes* (1941).

102. Arthur Train, "Book Review," 27 *A.B.A.J.* 607 (1941).

103. 6 *Tulane L. Rev.* 48 (1931).

104. 36 *Ill. L. Rev.* 371 (1941).

105. 10 *Harv. L. Rev.* 321, 389 (1897).

106. Elmer Balogh to Wigmore, Aug. 6, 1930 (Wigmore Collection).

107. 18 *A.B.A.J.* 88 (1932). Wigmore was also appointed chairman of a committee on International Bar Relations. 19 *A.B.A.J.* 2 (1933).

108. 18 *A.B.A.J.* 273 (1932). See also 16 *A.B.A.J.* 677, 745 (1930) and 17 *A.B.A.J.* 828 (1931).

109. Wigmore to Elmer Balogh, Jan. 2, 1932 (Wigmore Collection).

110. 18 *A.B.A.J.* 88 (1932).

111. Wigmore to Margaret G. Belknap, May 12, 1932 (Wigmore Collection).

112. Ass'n Am. L. Schools, *Handbook and Proceedings*, 1930:118, 159–60; 1931:102–3, 119, 172–73; 1932:155–57; 18 *A.B.A.J.* 359, 673–75 (1932).

113. "Speech of Wigmore at the Congress of Comparative Law, Aug. 21, 1932" (Wigmore Collection).

114. Charles C. Linthicum Foundation, Northwestern University School of Law (Chicago, May 1932).

115. Donald Harper to Wigmore, Oct. 14, 1932 (Wigmore Collection).

116. Article I, Constitution of the International Bar Association.

117. Report of Committee of Conference of State Bar Delegates on 1932 International Congress of Comparative Law, 18 *A.B.A. J.* 673 (1932).

118. *Id.* at 674.

119. Wigmore, "St. Ives, Patron Saint of Lawyers," 18 *A.B.A.J.* 157 (1932). Also in 5 *Fordham L. Rev.* 401 (1936). As to other lawyer-saints see, Wigmore, "How Many Lawyers Were Ever Made Saints?," 23 *Ill. L. Rev.* 199 (1928).

120. Wigmore, "A Visit to the Shrine of St. Ives, Patron of Our Profession," 18 *A.B.A.J.* 794 (1932).

121. *Id.* at 795.

122. See 21 *A.B.A.J.* 328, 558, 810 (1935).

123. Wigmore to Louis B. Wehle, Nov. 14, 1939 (Wigmore Collection).

124. For an account of the ceremony see "Presentation of St. Ives Memorial Window by American Lawyers," 22 *A.B.A.J.* 459 (1936). See also "The Memorial to St. Ives: Its Meaning," 22 *A.B.A.J.* 255 (1936).

125. Wigmore to Henry S. Bacon, Dec. 10, 1938 (Wigmore Collection).

126. Wigmore's activities during this visit to Japan are summarized in an interview entitled "John H. Wigmore Revisits Japan" (n.d.) to which no further reference will be made unless it is quoted directly (Wigmore Collection).

127. Akira Yomada to the author, Feb. 21, 1964.

128. Shinzo Koizumi, "A Japanese Appreciation of Dr. Wigmore's Personality and Work" (a manuscript copy of a partial translation from the Japanese), p. 3 (n.d.) (Wigmore Collection).

129. Kenzo Takayanagi, "World of Law — East and West," *Northwestern Review*, Vol. 1, no. 3, Spring 1966, p. 15.

130. To date a number of parts have been published under the title *Law and Justice in Tokugawa, Japan*, but publication is not yet complete.

131. Kenzo Yakayanagi, "Jurisprudence: East and West — Wigmore's Remarkable Contributions," an address at the annual dinner of the John Henry Wigmore Club, Feb. 3, 1966 (Wigmore Collection).

132. Wigmore to Shinzo Koizumi, Sept. 11, 1940 (Wigmore Collection).

133. Kenzo Takayanagi to the author, Dec. 20, 1965.

134. "John H. Wigmore Revisits Japan," p. 13. Wigmore left Yokohama for Seattle on June 6, 1935.

135. *Chicago Daily News*, Sept. 11, 1935.

136. "Dean Wigmore Decorated for Legal Work in Japan," 21 *A.B.A.J.* 697, (1935).

137. Wigmore to the Secretary of State, Feb. 19, 1940 (Wigmore Collection).

138. Wigmore to S. K. Richtmyer, Nov. 29, 1939 (Wigmore Collection).

139. Warren E. Seavey to Wigmore, May 13, 1940; Wigmore to Seavey, May 25, 1940 (Wigmore Collection).

140. *Asia* (1942), 42:623.

141. Wigmore to Hallett Abend, Nov. 4, 1942 (Wigmore Collection).

142. Arthur Krock, "Infamous Prelude to Pearl Harbor," *New York Times Magazine*, Nov. 8, 1942, p. 3.

143. Wigmore to Arthur Krock, Nov. 13, 1942; Arthur Krock to Wigmore, Nov. 17, 1942 (Wigmore Collection).

144. Roscoe Pound to Wigmore, Nov. 27, 1935 (Wigmore Collection).

145. *Recollections*, Louis B. Wehle, p. 4 (Wigmore Collection).

146. Wigmore to Nicholas M. Butler, Mar. 20, 1936 (Wigmore Collection).

147. "Second International Congress of Comparative Law to be Held at The Hague, July 26–August 1, 1937," 22 *A.B.A.J.* 428 (1936), "Important Meeting of Comparative Law Congress," 23 *A.B.A.J.* 311 (1937).

148. Wigmore from Olive C. Ricker, May 22, 1937; Wigmore from James O. Murdock, July 16, 1937 (Wigmore Collection).

149. "The Congress of Comparative Law," 23 *A.B.A.J.* 783 (783 (1937). For another account see Murry Seasongood, "The Second International Congress of Comparative Law," 31 *Law Lib. J.* 47 (1938).

150. *Id.* at 784.

151. 62 *A.B.A. Rep.* 395 (1937).

152. *Recollections*, Jerome Hall, p. 2 (Wigmore Collection).

153. Wigmore to Elihu Root, Dec. 1, 1936; Wigmore to Nicholas M. Butler, May 12, 1937 (Wigmore Collection).

154. Wigmore, "The Congress of Comparative Law," 23 *A B.A.J.* 783, 784 (1937).

155. *Recollections*, Jerome Hall, p. 2 (Wigmore Collection).

156. *Ibid.*, p. 3.

157. *Ibid.*, p. 5.

158. "Bullets or Boycotts, Which Shall be the Measure to Enforce World Peace," 29 *A.B.A.J.* 491 (1943).

159. *Id.* at 492.

160. *Id.* at 492–93.

161. *Id.* at 493.

162. 28 *A.B.A.J.* 526 (1942).

163. *Id.* at 526–27.

164. Wigmore, "Book Review," 29 *Geo. L. J.* 263, 264 (1940).

165. *Id.* at 265.

CHAPTER 17. EPILOGUE

1. Rodney Robertson to the author, May 2, 1963, in which he quotes from a letter from Mrs. Wigmore to Alfred McIntyre (Little, Brown and Company), Aug. 16, 1943.

2. John W. Curran, "Dean Wigmore at His Last Meeting of the Editorial Board," 34 *J. Crim. L. & Crim.* 93 (1943). For further details see the foregoing article and "John Henry Wigmore" [Editorial] at p. 3.

3. *Id.* at 94.

4. Rodney Robertson to the author, May 2, 1963, in which he quotes from Mrs. Wigmore's Aug. 16, 1943, letter to Alfred McIntyre.

5. Albert Kocourek, "John Henry Wigmore," 27 *J. Am. Jud. Soc'y* 122, 124 (1943).

6. Sarah B. Morgan to the author, Sept. 12, 1965.

7. As to the funeral and burial arrangements see *ibid.*, and letter of Joel Hunter to the author, Nov. 5, 1965. Bishop Stewart died in 1940 and before the death of Wigmore.

8. *Recollections*, Helen K. McNamara, p. 9 (Wigmore Collection).

9. *Recollections*, Nathan W. MacChesney, p. 16 (Wigmore Collection).

10. For a statement by the University Board of Trustees see Trustee Minutes, Apr. 27, 1943.

11. For a record of the service see "John Henry Wigmore," 34 *J. Crim. L. & Crim.* 75 (1943).

12. Robert W. Millar, "On Behalf of the Law Faculty," 34 *J. Crim. L. & Crim.* 85 (1943). See also Law Faculty Minutes, Oct. 18, 1943.

13. Nat'l Conf. of Commissioners on Uniform State Laws, *Handbook and Proceedings*, 53rd Ann. Conf. (1943), pp. 255, 256.

14. *Recollections*, Jerome Hall, p. 4 (Wigmore Collection).

15. *Recollections*, Margaret G. Belknap, p. 11 (Wigmore Collection). The

Margaret to whom the note is addressed is Margaret G. Belknap, a lifelong friend of the Wigmores but not in fact a relative.

16. "The Orange Deed Corrected," 31 *Ill. Bar J.* 315 (1943).

17. "Our Naturalization Law, a Post-War International Problem," 29 *A.B.A.J.* 313 (1943). See also comment by the editor, p. 273.

18. 29 *A.B.A.J.* 491 (1943).

19. Wigmore to Charles Lobingier, Apr. 19, 1943 (Wigmore Collection).

20. Wigmore wanted living quarters for law students as an integral part of the quadrangle.

21. Ass'n Am. L. Schools, *1943 Handbook and Proceedings*, pp. 238, 239.

22. The forthcoming *Bibliography* by Karl Schwerin has 903 entries. However, as they are grouped by types of publications, i.e., books, articles, addresses, etc., there is some duplication.

23. "John Henry Wigmore" (Memorial), Ass'n. Am. L. Schools, *1943 Handbook and Proceedings*, pp. 238, 241.

24. *Recollections*, Preface [Albert Kocourek], p. 10 (Wigmore Collection).

25. Albert Kocourek, "John Henry Wigmore," 27 *J. Am. Jud. Soc'y* 122, 124 (1943).

26. "John Henry Wigmore" (Memorial), Ass'n Am. L. Schools, *1943 Handbook and Proceedings*, pp. 238, 245.

27. Sheldon Glueck, "John Henry Wigmore — Pioneer," 32 *J. Crim. L. & Crim.* 267, 268 (1942).

28. Holmes to Student Committee [Northwestern Univ. L. School], Nov. 8, 1929 (Wigmore Collection).

29. *Recollections*, Manley O. Hudson, p. 5 (Wigmore Collection).

Index

IIIIIIIII(،JIIIIIIIIIIC3IIIIIIIIIC3IIIIIIIIIIC3IIIIIIIIIC3IIIIIIIIIIC3IIIIIIIIIIC3IIIIIIIIIC3IIIIIIIIIIC3IIIIIIIIIC3IIIIIIIIIIC3IIIIIIIIIIC3IIIIIIIII